SAGES, SAINTS & KINGS OF ANCIENT INDIA

An English Edition of the Pauranik Caritavali

SAGES, SAINTS & KINGS OF ANCIENT INDIA

An English Edition of the Pauranik Caritavali

Swami B. B. Tirtha

MANDALA
SAN RAFAEL | LOS ANGELES | LONDON

MANDALA
Mandala Publishing
P.O. Box 3088
San Rafael, CA 94912
www.MandalaEarth.com

Find us on Facebook: www.facebook.com/mandalaearth
Follow us on Twitter: @mandalaearth

Other books by Swami B. B. Tirtha

Sri Chaitanya & His Associates
A Taste of Transcendence
Suddha Bhakti: The Path of Pure Devotion
Dasavatara: The Ten Manifestations of Godhead
Hari Katha and Vaishnava Aparadha
The Holy Life of Srila B. D. Madhava Gosvami Maharaja
Sri Arcana Paddhati: The Puja Book
Affectionately Yours
Sri Guru-Tattva
The Philosophy of Love

We wish to thank and acknowledge that certain verses from the *Srimad-Bhagavatam* and *Sri Caitanya-Caritamrta* are used with permission. Copyright Bhaktivedanta Book Trust International www.krishna.com.

Published by Mandala Publishing.

Library of Congress Cataloging-in-Publication Data available.
ISBN: 978-1-64722-674-9 (Hardcover)
ISBN: 978-1-64722-675-6 (Softcover)

Readers interested in this subject matter should visit these websites:
www.bbtirtha.org, www.sreecgmath.org

Printed in India

All Glories to Śrī Śrī Guru and Gaurāṅga!

Śrīla Bhakti Ballabh Tīrtha Gosvāmī Mahārāja

Śrīla Bhakti Dayita Mādhava Gosvāmī Mahārāja

Śrīla Bhakti Siddhānta Sarasvatī Ṭhākura Prabhupāda

Contents

Preface

Sages, Saints and Kings of Ancient India describes many great personalities whose activities demonstrate the characteristics and conduct conducive to devotion to the Supreme Lord Śrī Kṛṣṇa. The primary sources for the narratives in this publication are the paurāṇik literatures, which, as stated in the *Chāndogya Upaniṣad* (7.1.2), are considered to be the fifth Veda: *itihāsapurāṇaṁ pañcamaṁ vedānāṁ*.

The Purāṇas reveal the esoteric truths of the Vedas in the form of histories, accessible to all. Essentially, history may be considered a record of the activities of outstanding and influential persons, and one repeatedly encounters a number of important sages, saints and saintly kings throughout the entire Vedic corpus who may be familiar to a reader with a background in Indian theology or philosophy. However, to some, these personalities and their pastimes may be less familiar or entirely unknown. Therefore, His Divine Grace Śrīla Bhakti Ballabh Tīrtha Gosvāmī Mahārāja has prepared the present volume in the context of his own sagacious realizations to better acquaint the reader with some of these notable persons, and to provide spiritual inspiration and sustenance for enthusiastic votaries of the devotional path.

There are those who may be inclined to dismiss these transcendental histories as mere myths or metaphors. However, to a sincere aspirant of the *bhakti* (devotional) tradition, the practical and positive transformative potency of these narratives is an undeniable fact, especially when narrated by a contemporary sage strictly adhering to the Vedic standard, faithfully maintained by an authentic *sampradāya*, or lineage of saintly predecessors.

We humbly pray that His Divine Grace Śrīla Bhakti Ballabh Tīrtha Gosvāmī Mahārāja and the Divine Couple, Śrī Śrī Rādhā-Kṛṣṇa, will be pleased by this publication, and that the sincere reader may be blessed by Them to appreciate and act upon the eternal truths contained herein. We also humbly beg the readers' forgiveness for any inadvertent errors or omissions.

—The Publishers

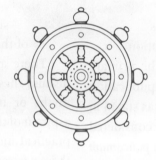

Introduction

In a lecture delivered at Śrī Saccidānanda Maṭha in Cuttack, Odisha, on July 9th, 1929, His Divine Grace Oṁ Viṣṇupāda 108 Śrī Śrīmad Bhakti Siddhānta Sarasvatī Gosvāmī Ṭhākura, founder of the worldwide Śrī Caitanya Maṭha and Śrī Gauḍīya Maṭha, spoke the following words: *adhokṣaja tattva śravaṇaik vedya.*

By these words, he preached that *śravaṇa* (hearing) is the only perfect path for devotional practitioners. Vedānta-sūtras like *śāstra-yonitvāt* (*Vedānta-sūtra* 1.1.3), and *śrutes tu śabda-mūlatvāt* (*Vedānta-sūtra* 2.1.27) confirm the authenticity of the words of *śruti* regarding the subject matter of spiritual knowledge.

In Chapter 16, Verse 24 of *Śrīmad Bhagavad-gītā*, Lord Kṛṣṇa instructs Arjuna as follows:

tasmāc chāstraṁ pramāṇaṁ te
kāryākārya-vyavasthitau
jñātvā śāstra-vidhānoktaṁ
karma kartum ihārhasi

"One should therefore understand what is duty and what is not duty by the regulations of the scriptures. Knowing such rules and regulations, one should act accordingly, so that one may gradually be elevated."

Thus, knowledge about Brahman can only be obtained via the words of Vedānta. Furthermore, one can only come to know about Adhokṣaja Lord Śrī Hari by hearing the pastimes of the Supreme Lord from unalloyed pure devotees. The pure devotees speak *śabda-brahma* (transcendental sound), which is understood to be self-evident, and the hearing of which is the only authentic means to learn about the absolute meaning. The *Skanda Purāṇa* declares that the four Vedas, *Mahābhārata*, *Mūla-Rāmāyaṇa* and *Pañcarātra* are counted as authentic scriptures:

ṛg-yajuḥ-sāmātharvāś ca bhārataṁ pañcarātrakam
mūlarāmāyaṇaṁ caiva śāstram ity abhidhīyate
yacchanukulametasya taccha śāstram prakīrtitām
ato nyagrantha vistaro naiva
śāstram kuvatarm tataḥ

"The *Ṛg Veda*, *Yajur Veda*, *Sāma Veda*, *Atharva Veda*, *Mahābhārata*, *Pañcarātra* and original *Rāmāyaṇa* are all considered Vedic literature. The Purāṇas (such as the *Brahma-vaivarta Purāṇa*, *Nāradīya Purāṇa*, *Viṣṇu Purāṇa* and *Bhāgavata Purāṇa*) are especially meant for Vaiṣṇavas and are also Vedic literature. As such, whatever is stated within the Purāṇas, *Mahābhārata* and *Rāmāyaṇa* is self-evident. There is no need for interpretation."

Although we need to understand and refer to the scriptures mentioned in the preceding quoted verse, above all we are to take shelter of the most authentic of all scriptures, namely *Śrīmad Bhāgavatam*, written by the literary *avatāra* (descended personal manifestation of Kṛṣṇa) named Śrīla Kṛṣṇa-dvaipāyana Vedavyāsa Muni. Hence, as per the *Garuḍa Purāṇa*, it is stated:

artho 'yaṁ brahma-sūtrāṇāṁ
bhāratārtha-vinirṇayaḥ
gāyatrī-bhāṣya-rūpo 'sau
vedārtha-paribṛṁhitaḥ

"The *Śrīmad Bhāgavatam* is the authorized explanation of *Brahma-sūtra*, and it is a further explanation of *Mahābhārata*. It is the commentary of the Gāyatrī Mantra and the essence of all Vedic knowledge."

Śrīla Vrindāvana Dasa Ṭhākura, who is non-different from Śrīla Vyāsadeva, has glorified the superiority of the *Śrīmad Bhāgavatam* as follows in the simplest language:

cāri veda dadhi bhāgavata navanīta
mathilena śuka khāilena parīkṣita

The understanding of this verse is that the four Vedas are like curd (yogurt), whereas the *Śrīmad Bhāgavatam* is like the butter resulting from the churning of the four Vedas. Śrīla Śukadeva Goswāmī churned the curd in order to get butter and Parīkṣit Mahārāja tasted the butter.

The four Vedas (*Ṛk*, *Yajur*, *Sāma* and *Atharva*), *Mahābhārata*, *Mūla-Rāmāyaṇa* and *Pañcarātra* are called *sad-śāstra*, eternal scriptures. Concomitantly, the scriptures that confirm the teachings of these eternal scriptures also fall into the category of *sad-śāstra*. However, all scriptures not subscribing to the above-mentioned standard fall into the category of *asad-śāstra*, non-eternal scriptures.

Śrīmad Bhāgavatam is the explanation of the Brahma-sūtras and purport of the *Mahābhārata*. Above all, *Śrīmad Bhāgavatam* is the commentary on Gāyatrī and the true purport of all the Vedas.

Śrī Caitanya Mahāprabhu accepted *Śrīmad Bhāgavatam* as the best among all authentic scriptures, and instructed us to hear it regularly. In his commentary on the *Bhāgavatam* called *Krama-sandarbha*, Śrīla Jīva Goswāmī (one of the famous six *gosvāmī* followers of Śrī Caitanya Mahāprabhu) wrote the following on *Śrīmad Bhāgavatam* 7.5.18: *tatrāpi śravaṇe śrīmad bhāgavatam śravaṇastu param śreṣṭhaṁ.*

While studying *Śrīmad Bhāgavatam*, *Mahābhārata*, *Rāmāyaṇa* and other scriptures we come across many famous sages, saints, and saintly kings. By learning about the pastimes of these legendary personalities, we can more easily understand the actual purport of all Vedic scriptures. Thus, an attempt is hereby made to compose this *purāṇic caritāvalī* (narrative of great *purāṇic* personalities).

— Bhakti Ballabh Tīrtha

King Hariścandra

Ikṣvāku was one of the ten sons of Vaivasvata Manu. He was the father of Vikukṣi, who was also known as Saśāda. Dhundhumāra, Dṛḍhāśva, Haryaśva, Nikumbha, Kṛśāśva, Senajit, Yauvanāśva, Māndhātā, Pūrukutsa, Trasaddasyu, Amaranya, Haryaśva, Aruṇa, Tribandhana and Satyavrata were born successively in the Purañjaya Dynasty. This Satyavrata later became famous as Triśaṅku. Satyaramā of the Kaikeya Dynasty, the wife of King Triśanku of the Solar Dynasty (Sūrya-vaṁśa), gave birth to King Hariścandra. Hariścandra was also known as Traiśankava. (*Harivaṁśa Purāṇa* 12-13)

King Hariścandra possessed all the virtues delineated in the *śāstras*. Desiring to enjoy all the pleasures of heaven in his mortal human body, King Triśaṅku stepped down from his position as king and conferred the royal crown to his son Hariścandra. In order to fulfill his desire, he initially approached the sage named Vaśiṣṭha, but he declined his request. Later on, he requested the hundred sons of Sage Vaśiṣṭha to perform the required *yajña*, but they also refused his proposal. On the contrary, due to the curse of Vaśiṣṭha's son, Triśaṅku became a *caṇḍāla* (person of low-caste who earns a living by cremating the dead). In order to achieve liberation from the curse and to go to heaven, Triśaṅku then took shelter of the great sage Viśvāmitra, the son of Gādhi. Viśvāmitra became compassionate toward Triśaṅku and asked the sages to perform a *yajña* in order to send Triśaṅku to heaven in his human body. Out of fear of Viśvāmitra, the sages performed the *yajña* but the demigods did not accept the offerings and, becoming angry, Viśvāmitra then sent Triśaṅku to heaven by the power of his severe penance. When Indra saw Triśaṅku coming toward heaven he criticized Triśaṅku as follows: "You are a *caṇḍāla*, a low-caste person, and are unqualified to receive the same respect as the inhabitants of heaven, therefore you must fall back to earth." As the disappointed Triśaṅku began his descent back to earth, he prayed to Viśvāmitra, who suspended him in mid-air by exclaiming the word "*Tiśtha!*" and reassured him by saying, "Please do not worry if Indra will not allow you to stay in heaven. I shall create a new universe with a new heaven in it." Having said so, Viśvāmitra began preparations for a *yajña* with the aim of creating a new universe. However, at the same time, Indra (husband of Śacī and king of the demigods) rushed to stop him and pleaded with Viśvāmitra not to create another world. Thus, to please Viśvāmitra, Indra transformed Triśaṅku's human body into a heavenly body and took him to heaven in his heavenly airplane.

King Hariścandra of Ayodhyā was happy to learn about his father's ascent to heaven by the grace of Viśvāmitra, and thus he ruled his empire with great pleasure. However, the one thing lacking in his life was that, after many years had passed, still he did not have a son, so he went to Sage Vaśiṣṭha and expressed his grief by saying, "A person without a son does not attain liberation and such a person becomes grief stricken and most unfortunate." Upon hearing his lament, Vaśiṣṭha felt compassion for the king and asked him to worship the demigod Varuṇa (demigod of water), as there is no other demigod who can bestow a child upon his devotee. As per the instructions of his spiritual master, Hariścandra sat on the bank of River Gaṅgā performing penance while meditating upon Varuṇa, whereupon, being very much satisfied with the penance of the king, Varuṇa appeared and addressed him, "O King, what kind of boon do you want?" King Hariścandra earnestly requested Varuṇa to bless him with a son. Varuṇa then smiled and said, "As per your desire you will get a brilliant son, but whenever I ask, you should offer me your son as a sacrifice in *yajña* without any hesitation. If you agree, I shall grant your wish."

The king agreed, if only to cease being known as son-less. King Hariścandra had one hundred beautiful queens, including the virtuous Śaibya, the daughter of King Śibi, who was his principal queen. By the blessings of Varuṇa she became pregnant and, at an auspicious time on an auspicious day, she gave birth to a very sweet child bearing all the auspicious symptoms. The king was very happy with the birth of his son, so he donated many items in charity and began organizing daily festivals in his palace. Many joyful days passed in this way until one day Varuṇa came to him, disguised as a *brāhmaṇa*. Varuṇa first blessed the king and, after introducing himself, reminded the king of his promise to surrender his son for a fire sacrifice. The king was stunned and did not know what to do, as he was perplexed by his promise to Varuṇa on the one side and his boundless love for his son on the other.

After properly worshiping Varuṇa the king implored him, "You are all-knowing and aware of all the rituals and practices of *sanātana-dharma*; therefore you know that in a sacrificial *yajña*, ten days after the birth of a child, the father is supposed to perform certain rites and the mother is considered pure after one month. Therefore, please grant me a month so I may perform those rites." On hearing this, Varuṇa said, "All right, for now I am going, but I shall return after one month, at which time you can conduct the naming ceremony of your child and give him to me for sacrifice."

The king was most relieved and made donations of millions of cows and heaps of sesame seeds. He performed the name-giving ceremony and called his son Rohita. After a month had passed, Varuṇa again came in the guise of a *brāhmaṇa* and repeatedly asked the king to perform the fire sacrifice, but the king was thoroughly illusioned by the love he had for his son. Looking to save his son, he said to Varuṇa, "It is my good fortune that you have bestowed your grace upon me and have paid an auspicious visit to my home. You are kind to the poor and I shall definitely fulfill your wish, but the wise say it is improper to perform a fire sacrifice until the one to be sacrificed has his own teeth. Thus, it would be better if we were to wait until then."

As before, Varuṇa reluctantly agreed and left. However, upon his return, Varuṇa was sent away once more by the king who then said, "Wise men say that it will be improper to have a sacrificial fire until the *cūḍākāraṇa* rites (shaving of the head) are performed." Unhappy and disappointed, Varuṇa said, "Captivated by the love of your son, you are postponing the sacrificial fire again and again, though all the essential items for the performance of the *yajña* are readily available. I will curse you if you do not give me your son after completing the *cūḍākāraṇa* rites. You have taken birth in the Ikṣvāku Dynasty, so surely you must keep your promise." Varuṇa then returned to his abode again and the king continued to rule his kingdom happily. He organized a grand ceremonial festival on the occasion of the *cūḍākāraṇa* rites of his son Rohita, and the queen was sitting with her son on her lap when the effulgent Varuṇa appeared before them. The king, becoming frightened, bowed down before Varuṇa with folded hands and prayed, "I am always ready to obey your order; nevertheless, I request you to hear my point and, if you find it to be rational, then please accept it. According to the *Vedas*, the three higher classes (*brāhmaṇas*, *kṣatriyas* and *vaiśyās*) are considered to be *śudras* (lowest class) until the *upanāyana-saṁskāra* or sacred thread rite is performed. Only after accepting the sacred thread are they known as *dvīja* (twice-born). They are unworthy of becoming the sacrificial offering until this rite is performed, and the scriptures direct that the sacred thread ceremony for *brāhmaṇas* should be performed at eight years of age, for *kṣatriyas* at eleven years of age and for *vaiśyās* at twelve years of age. Thus, considering me to be your unworthy servant, please permit me to perform the sacred thread ceremony of my son. You are all-learned, expert in all scriptures and the custodian of the people." Varuṇa was pleased to hear the humble words of the king and agreed, whereupon he left. The king and queen heaved a sigh of relief. When the prince turned ten, the king began preparations for the sacred thread ceremony, and when his son turned eleven, the king organized the ceremony as prescribed. At that time, Varuṇa once again appeared in the garb of a *brāhmaṇa*. The king, recognizing him, stood with folded hands and said, "My lord! My son has accepted the sacred thread and now he is eligible to be a sacrificial offering for the sacrificial fire. By your grace the curse of infertility is no more upon us. Please believe me when I say that I will give large amounts of money in charity for your satisfaction in this sacrificial fire, but I wish to perform the sacrifice after my son returns from his teacher's *āśrama*. So I beg you to please be merciful upon me and grant me some more time." Varuṇa replied, "O King! You are deluded by the love of your son. You have been concocting various excuses and are trying to cheat me in a bid to save your beloved son. I am leaving, but rest assured, I will return!" The king was relieved as Varuṇa left and he realized that, yet again, his son had been protected.

By now, Prince Rohita had matured and had overheard the latest discussion between Varuṇa and his father. Upon further inquiry, he learned the reason for his father's anxiety. So, in order to protect himself and relieve his father, he consulted his ministers. They suggested that he should leave the palace, so he left for the forest without informing his father. The king became very morose upon hearing the news of Rohita's sudden departure, and so he sent his men to search for the prince in the forest. After some time, Varuṇa once again came to the grieving king and asked him to perform the rite of the sacrificial fire. The king offered his obeisances and said, "O Varuṇa! My son was scared and ran away. I am unaware of his present whereabouts. I have already sent many soldiers out to search for him, but they have been unable to locate him. My son has absconded, so please instruct me as to what I should do? You are omniscient and know everything. I am not at fault and am most unfortunate." When Varuṇa heard that the king was once again unable to fulfill his promise to him, he became furious and cursed the king by saying, "May you suffer from severe *jalodara*!"[1]

The king immediately fell ill and suffered from severe unbearable pain in his stomach. Rohita became very anxious after learning that his father had suddenly fallen ill, so he became desperate to see him. Indra, the king of the demigods, then came in the guise of a *brāhmaṇa* and stopped Rohita from going to his father by saying, "If you go to your father now, he will definitely sacrifice you in the sacrificial fire, so that he might be rescued from his suffering condition. You know this is true, so why are you still trying to go there to embrace death? You should understand that people love their own self the most. All material and family relations are formed for the comfort of the self. On the other hand, if your father dies, then you

---

1 ascites; an abnormal buildup of fluid in the abdomen

will become king." The persuasive words of Indra convinced Rohita to stay in the forest for another year, but the knowledge of his father's persistent ailment continued to haunt his mind. He once again became desperate to meet his father even if it would mean his own death, but Indra returned in the guise of a *brāhmaṇa* and tried to dissuade Rohita by various means. Meanwhile, being unable to tolerate the pain any longer, Hariścandra asked Sage Vaśiṣṭha for some means of amelioration. Vaśiṣṭha told him, "You should purchase a son and give him up for the sacrificial fire; this will liberate you from your sins. The learned *brāhmaṇas* state that there are ten types of sons, one of which is the son that is purchased. Such a son is known as a *krīta-putra*. A sacrificial fire with such a son as an offering will definitely please Varuṇa. Some poor, greedy *brāhmaṇa* in your kingdom might give his son to you in exchange for some wealth." After hearing from Vaśiṣṭha the means of his cure, the king immediately ordered his ministers to search for a boy who could be purchased, so after searching for some time, the ministers approached a *brāhmaṇa* named Ajigarta. He had three sons: Śunaḥśepuccha, Śunaḥśepha and Śunaḥśelangula. The ministers offered Ajigarta one hundred cows in exchange for one of his sons, who would be used for the sacrificial fire. Ajigarta only agreed to give up his son because he was suffering from hunger and poverty. The *brāhmaṇa* thought that since his eldest son had the right to perform all religious rites, he should stay, but his wife refused to give up their youngest son out of affection. So, after some deliberation, he decided to surrender his middle son, Śunaḥśepha, in exchange for the promised one hundred cows. The ministers then brought Śunaḥśepha to the king, who announced the boy to be the sacrificial offering for the sacrificial fire. When the time for the sacrificial aspect of the *yajña* ceremony drew near, Śunaḥśepha became very frightened when he was tied to a wooden sacrificial altar, and began to cry. The sages observed the distressful situation and were unable to perform the sacrifice. Therefore, a mercenary was handed the sword meant for performing the sacrifice, but when he heard Śunaḥśepha's screams, he also refused to kill him, even when he was offered extra money. The king then asked the *brāhmaṇas*, "What should be done?" As Śunaḥśepha's screams grew louder, the voices of protestation and resentment also grew louder. Suddenly Ajigarta, the father of Śunaḥśepha, who was sitting among the crowd, stood up and said, "O King! Please calm yourself! I could be the solution to your problem, but in that case, you would need to pay me double the amount paid earlier. You will learn that an extremely greedy man can develop animosity even toward his own son." The king was pleased to hear this and agreed to give an additional one hundred good quality cows to Ajigarta. However, all the assembled learned persons shouted, "This cruel and sinful *brāhmaṇa* is definitely a demon. The scriptures say: '*ātmā vaijayte putra*', which means you destroy your own self by killing your son. You are a self-destroyer, a sinner and a low-caste person. Shame on you!"

Observing the commotion, Sage Viśvāmitra, the son of Kauśika, out of compassion, approached the king and asked him to spare Śunaḥśepha. He said to the king, "By such an act of mercy your sacrifice will be considered complete and your suffering will end. Benevolence is the holiest act and violence is the most heinous sin, so the sacrificial rites have not been prescribed in the scriptures to advocate the spread of violence and cruelty. The *Tantra-śāstra* (branch of the Vedic scriptures) has only prescribed such sacrifice based upon one's eligibility, so that those who constantly chase after material desires may gradually realize the truth and become kind-hearted. The sacrifice mentioned in those scriptures is not meant to promote violence. O King! How can one justify the killing of another's body in order to save one's own body? Mercy toward all beings, control of the senses and satisfaction with whatever one obtains by honest means pleases the Almighty. Every animate being desires to live, and one must consider all beings to be on the same platform as oneself when judging their merits. Since you are now trying to become happy by killing this *brāhmaṇa* boy, why should he not also desire to become happy by protecting his body? If anyone should kill another person simply for one's own comfort, when there is no cause for hostility, it is certain that the slayer will be killed by the slain person in his next birth. Śunaḥśepha's father is a very cruel and ill-intentioned person, who is ready to kill even his own son for a small amount of money. You well know that the king shares one-sixth of the fruit of any sin committed in his kingdom, so the king must forbid any sin in his kingdom, including Ajigarta selling his son. You were born in the Solar Dynasty and you are the son of the pious Triśaṅku. Being *ārya* (noble), why are you now behaving like someone who is non-*ārya*? Please take to heart what I am saying and liberate this poor boy, as this will bring you happiness in all respects. Due to the curse of Vaśiṣṭha's sons, your father became a *caṇḍāla* and, by the influence of my penance, I transferred him to heaven in his human body." Despite the honest preaching efforts and explanations given by Sage Viśvāmitra, they were still insufficient to motivate the king to revoke his decision. Viśvāmitra then became enraged and went to Śunaḥśepha and gave the Varuṇa *mantra* to him. The sage then asked the boy to continuously recite this *mantra* while meditating on Varuṇa. Śunaḥśepha did as he was told and, by the power of the *mantra*, Varuṇa appeared. King Hariścandra, who was suffering from ascites, also bowed down to Varuṇa and prayed thus: "O ocean of kindness! Being unwise, I have committed an offense toward you but, being kind-hearted, still you have purified me by your audience. Please forgive my sins. My son became frightened and ran away. To satisfy you, I bought a *brāhmaṇa* boy instead. If you are pleased with me, then my suffering will disappear."

Pleased by the king's compassionate prayers, Varuṇa requested him to release Śunaḥśepha. He told the king that, by his doing so, his vow would be considered fulfilled and he would become free of his illness. Thus, by the king's order, Śunaḥśepha was set free and the king regained his health. A loud applause filled the sacrificial arena and the king performed the completion rites of the *yajña*.

Devī Bhāgavatam narrates the story of King Hariścandra in detail. *Śrīmad Bhāgavatam*, composed by Śrī Kṛṣṇa-dvaipāyana Vedavyāsa, mentions the story of King Hariścandra only in brief and the two narrations differ slightly. Regardless of which version one reads, the king's prayers to the demigods, and their subsequent mercy, rescued Śunaḥśepha, who was to become the sacrificial animal offered in a sacrificial fire. This same boy later became famous as Devarāta.

In the 7th Chapter of the 9th Canto of *Śrīmad Bhāgavatam*, this narration is given succinctly: Following the advice of Sage Nārada, King Hariścandra meditated upon Varuṇa and was blessed with a son. Varuṇa blessed him with the son on the condition that the king would offer his son at a later date in a sacrificial fire to please Varuṇa. When Varuṇa approached Hariścandra to perform the *yajña*, Hariścandra asked him to come back after ten days; the second time he asked him to come back when his son's teeth had grown in; the third time he asked him to come back when his son had lost his teeth; the fourth time, after getting new teeth again and the fifth time he said that the sacrificial animal is eligible for sacrifice only after he is fit to fight in battle wearing armour. In this way, he kept on postponing the sacrifice, but when Rohita learned that he was to be sacrificed like an animal in a *yajña*, he took a bow and a quiver of arrows and ran away to the forest. He tried to return after learning about his father's ailment, but Indra, the king of the demigods, managed to stop him. On Indra's advice, Rohita remained in the forest for another year and then spent five more years going on pilgrimage. After that, he again thought of returning to his father's kingdom, when Indra, in the guise of a *brāhmaṇa*, appeared and again stopped him from returning. After yet another year, Rohita finally went back to his father's kingdom and bought Ajīgarta's middle son, whom he presented to his father as the sacrificial animal for the *yajña*. The king then offered Ajīgarta's son as a sacrifice to Varuṇa and was cured of his curse. For the *yajña*, Viśvāmitra acted as *hota*, Jamadagni took the role of *adhvaryu*, Vaśiṣṭha took the role of *brahma* and Ayāsya acted as *udgata* (four types of priests necessary for the correct performance of a *yajña*). Indra was also pleased by the *yajña* and presented a golden chariot to the king.

In the *Śrīmad Bhāgavatam*, 9th Canto, 16th Chapter, this incident has been described as follows:

Śunaḥśepha's father Ajīgarta sold his son to Hariścandra for sacrifice in a *yajña*. When he was brought to the sacrificial fire, Śunaḥśepha prayed to the demigods and was rescued. Śunaḥśepha was born in the Bhṛgu Dynasty, but since the demigods had protected him he became famous as "Devarāta" of the Gādhi Dynasty. Sage Viśvāmitra adopted him as his son and asked his other sons to treat him as their elder brother. Once the *yajña* was completed, Śunaḥśepha, with folded hands, asked the wise men present in the assembly to consult the scriptures to enable him to understand exactly whose son he was. After consultation, the wise men concluded that since he was born of Ajīgarta's potency, he was actually the son of Ajīgarta.

Sage Vāmadeva objected by saying, "Since Ajīgarta sold him to the king for a sum of money, the king is legitimately the father of Śunaḥśepha. Otherwise, Varuṇa is his lawful father, as he is the one who rescued him. As per the scriptures, one who fathers, one who feeds (gives grains to eat), one who protects (liberates from fear), one who educates or one who gives money to a child are all equally considered the real father." After this, a loud discussion began regarding the question of who should be designated as Śunaḥśepha's father. When Sage Vaśiṣṭha heard the commotion, he entered into the discussion and said, "Please hear what the scriptures have to say on this subject. When a heartless, emotionless father sells his son in exchange for money, he ceases to be his father. And the moment King Hariścandra offered his purchased son as a sacrificial offering for a yajña he also ceased to be his father. Furthermore, Varuṇa came to save him only after the boy had pleaded for his life a number of times; so he is not his lawful father either. Therefore, the conclusion is that none of them had selfless love for the boy but, out of compassion, Viśvāmitra guided the boy by instructing him to chant hymns in worship of Varuṇa as a means of saving himself. Due to this, he is the legitimate father." Everyone agreed with Sage Vaśiṣṭha. Viśvāmitra then called Śunaḥśepha, held his hand affectionately, and together they left in an ebullient mood. King Hariścandra became healthy again and happily ruled his kingdom.

When Prince Rohita heard the news, he was elated and, coming out of hiding, he quickly returned home from the forest. As soon as King Hariścandra learned this news from his messengers, he became extremely joyful and ran out to meet him. Upon seeing his father coming to him in haste, Rohita became filled with emotion and immediately fell at his feet, crying due to separation grief. The king quickly picked up his son, embraced him and started kissing him profusely out of parental love. He then affectionately made Rohita sit on his lap and both of them broke out in tears. Thereafter, the king ruled the kingdom happily along with his son. After some time, the king developed a desire to perform a *rājasūya-yajña* (royal sacrifice performed by the warrior class to prove their might across the planet), so he appointed Sage Vaśiṣṭha, the spiritual master of his dynasty, as the performer of the *yajña*. Once the *yajña* had been accomplished, the king offered his respectful prayers to Sage Vaśiṣṭha and gave him a large sum of money in charity. Vaśiṣṭha accepted this and went to Indra's palace, where he met Sage Viśvāmitra. When Viśvāmitra noticed the respect offered to Vaśiṣṭha, he was surprised and asked him for the reason for his being the recipient of so much respect and a significant offering. Vaśiṣṭha then proceeded to describe the glory, truthfulness, charity, generosity and other qualities of Hariścandra to Viśvāmitra, and informed him that Hariścandra gave him a large sum of money in charity for the completion of the *rājasūya-yajña*. He further stated that King Hariścandra was not only truthful and generous, but also equally brave and pious, and that there was no one like him in the past and no one likely to be so in the future.

Hearing all this from Vaśiṣṭha, Viśvāmitra became enraged and said, "Hariścandra cheated the demigod Varuṇa after failing to fulfill his promise of offering his son to him in sacrifice, yet you are praising that hypocrite and liar! I even dare say that you may cease calling me Viśvāmitra if I do not prove that man to be a miser and a liar. Should I be wrong, then may I stand to lose all the good fruits earned from my performing penance, but should I succeed in proving this, then you, Vaśiṣṭha, will stand to lose all the good fruits earned due to your penance." After this heated exchange, both sages went back to their respective homes.

One day Hariścandra went hunting in a forest and saw a beautiful young girl who was weeping. The king, feeling sympathy for the young girl, asked her, "Who are you? Why are you crying? What seems to be the problem?" Upon hearing Hariścandra's compassionate query, the beautiful girl told him, "I am the mystical Kāmiṇī, but penance performed by Sage Viśvāmitra is disturbing me considerably." The king then consoled her and went to the place where Viśvāmitra was performing his penance. Hariścandra offered his respects and requested the sage to stop his penance because it was troubling others. Viśvāmitra was annoyed but did not say anything. When Hariścandra left, the sage sent forth a demon in the form of a boar to punish the king for disturbing his penance. The immense boar-demon, generating great fear by grunting loudly, first embarked on a rampage among the general populace and then ran into the king's garden, where he began uprooting the trees. The guards' arrows were unable to deter the boar and, in a state of terror, they ran to inform the king. The king asked them, "Why are you in so much anxiety?" They replied, "O great king, we are not troubled by any hitherto recognizable powerful entity, but by an extraordinarily large boar. We are unable to defeat him, so now we beg you to please come to our aid." The king did not hesitate and took with him his cavalry, which, aside from soldiers riding on horseback, also included soldiers riding elephants and chariots, and other soldiers. In this way, the king approached the garden, where he saw the boar and, without hesitation, proceeded to attack it. However, all his efforts were in vain. The demonic boar then retreated into the forest and the king continued to chase after him, but eventually the king became tired of running after the demon, so he aborted the chase. By now he was not only separated from his army but was also hungry and thirsty, and he noticed he was now lost in the forest as well. As such, it was much to his relief when he happened upon a river of clear water. He first let his horse drink from it and then he drank to his full satisfaction. After satiating his thirst, he tried to rest, but could not find any peace on account of his anxiety regarding his being lost in the forest. He then repeatedly attempted to find his way back to the city, but without success. After some time, Sage Viśvāmitra came to him in the guise of a *brāhmaṇa*. As the king paid his obeisances, the *brāhmaṇa* asked the king, "What are you doing here in this dense forest?"

The king replied, "A huge boar uprooted all the trees of my garden. I tried to kill him with the help of my army, but the mystical boar disappeared. I chased after the creature and am now lost in this forest. However, by my extreme good fortune, I have somehow been granted your audience today. I am Hariścandra, the king of Ayodhyā, and I have performed a great *rājasūya-yajña*. Thus, I am under oath to fulfill the demands of anyone who asks something of me. If you require wealth, then please come to Ayodhyā and I shall give it to you." Viśvāmitra replied, "O King! You are presently at a great pilgrimage site. You must bathe in these waters, offer prayers to the ancestors and then give something in charity. Svāyambhuva Manu has said that one who does not bathe during holy pilgrimage, who does not offer prayers to the ancestors and who does not give a donation at a holy place is a killer of the self and a great sinner. Therefore, you must perform some pious activity here as per your preference. After that I will show you the way back home." The king was impressed and did everything as instructed by the sage. Then he desired to donate something to the *brāhmaṇa*. He said, "I have promised the sages at the *rājasūya-yajña* that I shall fulfill the demand of anyone who requests something of me, so it goes without saying that I shall definitely fulfill the demand of a *brāhmaṇa* asking me for something at a holy place."

Viśvāmitra, disguised as a *brāhmaṇa,* then praised the king and said, "O King, you are great among all the Sūrya-vaṁśa kings (kings of the Solar Dynasty); there is no other king like you." After his flattering words, the *brāhmaṇa* asked for some wealth to support the marriage of his son. The *brāhmaṇa* then exhibited his mystical powers and revealed a handsome prince along with a beautiful ten-year-old damsel, and asked the king for additional wealth to support their marriage as well. He told the king that he would receive a larger reward than the results of the *rājasūya-yajña* if he would sponsor their marriage. The king agreed immediately, after which, the *brāhmaṇa* pointed out the correct path back to his kingdom. Thus, via Viśvāmitra's directions, the king was able to find his way back home again. Later, when Hariścandra was performing another *yajña*, Viśvāmitra arrived and requested the promised wealth for the marriage. The king said, "O *brāhmaṇa*! Please let me know what you desire and I shall give you whatever you ask, even though it may be beyond my reach."

Viśvāmitra, disguised as a *brāhmaṇa*, said, "O great King, if you would indulge me, I would like to have your whole kingdom, including all the horses, elephants and all the diamonds, jewels and gold in your treasury." Enchanted by the sage's manner of speaking, and being compelled to uphold his vow, the king agreed to the *brāhmaṇa's* request. Sage Viśvāmitra then asked the king for some *dakṣiṇā* (token gift given to a *brāhmaṇa* in addition to a donation), as King Manu has stated that all donations are worthless if *dakṣiṇā* is not given along with them. When the king inquired about the amount, the *brāhmaṇa* demanded 225 *seras* (1 *sera* or 80 *tolas* = 0.93 kg) of gold. The king agreed to give the 225 *seras* to the *brāhmaṇa* as *dakṣiṇā*, but now he thought: *"What am I to do? Oh! This* brāhmaṇa *is a cheat and has come to steal and deprive me of all I have. I have given him my kingdom, elephants, horses and wealth. Now I am left with nothing, so how will I be able to give him the 225* seras *worth of gold that he is now demanding from me? This bandit in the guise of a* brāhmaṇa *has certainly looted me."* In this way he began to lament, and his soldiers, the commander of his army, his queens and principal queen Śaibyā became very worried. Aware of this, Viśvāmitra reminded the king about his promise.

The king told him, "You are right. Although I do not have anything at this time, I will give the agreed amount as soon as I can obtain it." The king sat on the platform of the *yajña-śala* (place where *yajñas* are performed) and immediately donated everything except his wife and son. As the king prepared to leave his kingdom to go to the forest along with his wife and son, the residents of Ayodhyā became morose and started cursing and abusing Viśvāmitra for his foul play. The cruel Viśvāmitra then met the king on the way to the forest and said, "If you cannot give me the gold as promised, just tell me straightforwardly. If you still harbor the desire for your kingdom, then you are at liberty to take it back."

With folded hands the king then humbly said, "My dear lord! Please have patience with me. I will neither eat nor drink until I have given you the gold as promised. Please bear with me until I have collected the money."

Viśvāmitra said, "You have donated everything and now that you no longer own anything, how will it be possible for you to give me anything in charity? Please, just admit that you will not be able to give me anything, so that I may abandon the hope of receiving the gold from you and then be free to leave this place." The king would not give up, however, so he thought that, maybe, in order to clear his debt, he could sell himself along with his wife and son, as they were all in good health. Thus, he said to Viśvāmitra, "O saint! If you please, you may sell my wife, son and me to anyone in Vārāṇasī for 225 *seras* of gold. May we then stay like slaves to the buyers, but we shall never back out of our promise. Thus, may you now be happy and please do not worry." The king then went to Kāśī-dhāma, where he was mesmerized by the beauty of the city and pondered: *"Since Kāśī is under the jurisdiction of Lord Mahādeva* (the great god Śiva, the holder of a trident)*, this area cannot be under the rule of any human and is beyond the limits of my kingdom. Therefore, staying here won't create any problems for me."* With this belief, he began to reside there but, after some time, Sage Viśvāmitra approached him and asked for his bounty (*dakṣiṇā*). The king told him, "I do not have anything but myself, my wife and son." However, Sage Viśvāmitra ruthlessly insisted that, as per the agreement, the time period of one month was about to pass.

Time was running out for the king, as only half a day remained before the one month time period would come to pass, so the king humbly requested Sage Viśvāmitra to wait. However, Viśvāmitra warned that if he were not to get his promised *dakṣiṇā*, then he would return and curse the king. The king was worried and wondered: *"What should I do? I belong to the warrior class; thus I cannot beg, as begging is not allowed for a kṣatriya. However, if I should die without giving the designated donation to the brāhmaṇa, I might become a ghost as the result of the sin of stealing a brāhmaṇa's wealth. Therefore, it will be better to sell myself."* When Queen Śaibyā saw her husband so pale and worried, she consoled him and encouraged him to follow the righteous path and code of conduct prescribed by the scriptures. She said, "Truth is the ultimate religion. King Yayāti went to heaven by performing a thousand *rājasūya-yajñas*, but was hurled back to the earthly plane because of a single lie." After listening to his wife, the king replied, "How can I protect the truth? I am left with nothing but you and our son. Our son is our only hope for the future of our dynasty. How can I sell him and how can I sell you, as one's wife should never be sold either?" Queen Śaibyā then humbly told the king, "O my husband, just please sell me and our son at an appropriate price, so that you may be enabled to uphold *dharma*." The king fell unconscious upon hearing these heart-breaking words from his queen. When he regained consciousness, his wife did not hesitate to repeat her words and, as a result, he fell unconscious yet again. The queen was petrified and began weeping as she said, "He who always slept on a bed of roses is now lying on the bare ground. Oh! Why is my husband, who is the king of the whole planet and who has donated millions of gold coins to *brāhmaṇas*, lying on the bare ground?" Having spoken thus, Śaibyā also fell on the ground unconscious, being unable to control her grief. Prince Rohita, upon observing the miserable condition of his parents, also fell at their feet. Furthermore, because he was in distress due to hunger, Rohita screamed and begged his parents, "O mother! O father! I am suffering from hunger and my mouth is dry, so please give me something to eat." At that time, Viśvāmitra, a former member of the *kṣatriya* class who had engaged in severe penance to become a *brāhmaṇa*, mercilessly entered the scene like a predator. When the king regained consciousness and opened his eyes, the first thing he saw was Viśvāmitra, which instantly resulted in him losing consciousness again. In order to wake him up, Viśvāmitra sprinkled water on the king's face and eyes, causing the king to regain his senses.

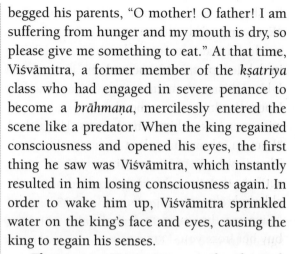

Thereupon, Viśvāmitra angrily shouted, "It is better that you keep your word than perform thousands of *aśvamedha-yajñas* (horse sacrifices). I will definitely curse you if you fail to give me the promised *dakṣiṇā* before sunset." When the sage left, the king became even more anxious and apprehensive. At that very moment, some learned *brāhmaṇas* came by and the queen was relieved to see them. She thought that there would be no harm in asking the *brāhmaṇas* for money, since they are to be seen as the fathers and teachers of the other three *varṇas* (castes). As such, she advised the king to ask them for money, but the king would not agree and replied, "My dear queen, protecting the surrendered, donating, and taking care of the public are the duties of the warrior class (*kṣatriyas*). Warriors never beg." Upon hearing this, the queen replied, "If it is your duty to give in charity, then you may sell your wife, as she is also your property and then, with the amount of gold received by selling me, you can give the promised *dakṣiṇā* to Viśvāmitra." Eventually, in order to uphold religion and because of the repeated requests of his queen, the king, who was overwhelmed with grief, succumbed to the proposal. Therefore, with a heavy heart, he decided to sell his wife. As he stood in a morose mood on the main avenue of the city, he shouted to the citizens with a grave voice: "Everyone, please listen to me. If anyone is in need of a maid, he may take this woman; I am in debt, so please pay me and take her, though I love this woman more than my own life." Upon hearing such unbecoming words, some wise men asked him who he was. He replied, "I am an inhuman, violent and merciless devil. That is why I am committing such a heinous act." At that time, Viśvāmitra, disguised as an elderly *brāhmaṇa*, approached the king, saying, "Give me this maid as I shall pay enough to buy her from you. I am a rich man and my wife is too young for household work, so you can sell her to me." Viśvāmitra inquired about the cost and said, "According to the scriptures, the price of a trustworthy woman who has thirty-two virtues and many other good qualities, is one *crore* (10 million) gold coins and for a man it is ten *crores* (100 hundred million) gold coins." Hearing this, the king kept quiet, and thus the elderly *brāhmaṇa* paid for the queen by placing 10 million gold coins on the bark of a tree on the ground and then he pulled her away by her hair, treating her as his slave. Realizing the finality of her situation, the queen became desperate to see her son once more before leaving, so she glanced at him and addressed him with these heart-rending words: "O my dear royal prince! I am a slave now, so please do not touch me, as I am unworthy of being your

mother." As the *brāhmaṇa* dragged the queen away by her hair, her son Rohita screamed out, "Mother! Mother!" and ran after her. He was unable to run properly and kept on falling, but still he managed to reach his mother and catch hold of her clothes. Upon seeing this, the *brāhmaṇa* became furious and hit him with his stick. The boy wept as he was being beaten but, nonetheless, he held onto his mother's cloth firmly. The queen didn't know what to do; thus she requested the *brāhmaṇa* to buy the prince. As per the scriptures, a man possessing thirty-two virtues is worth 100 million gold coins (ten *crores*). The *brāhmaṇa* agreed to the proposal and placed 100 million gold coins on a piece of cloth as a measure of payment for the young prince, and then he tied both of them and started to move forward feeling pleased. Before being pulled along, the queen circumambulated her husband and offered him her obeisances. She said, "If I succeed in satisfying the *brāhmaṇa*, then it might culminate in meeting you again." The king grieved tremendously, seeing how his queen and son were being pulled and beaten like animals by the *brāhmaṇa*. He felt utterly disgraced that he had stained the spotless name of his dynasty and said to himself, "All this is happening because of my sins." As the king was sitting there, grieving in separation from his family, the brutal and heartless Viśvāmitra, accompanied by his disciples, arrived at that place. Knowing very well that the king had acquired all the money for the promised *dakṣiṇā*, the sage tricked him in the hope that he would make him fall from his righteous path. He told Hariścandra, "O King! Need I remind you that you promised to give me unlimited wealth when I next came to Ayodhyā?" The king offered his respects to Viśvāmitra and replied, "O *brāhmaṇa*! As *dakṣiṇā* of the kingdom please accept 225 *seras* (210 kg) of gold, and the remaining gold as compensation for the *rājasūya-yajña*." The sage then asked the king, "By what means have you acquired this wealth? I shall take the money only if it has been raised by using proper means." The king replied, "O sage, I obtained one *crore* of gold coins by selling my wife and ten *crores* of gold coins by selling my son. Therefore, by these means, I received the sum total of eleven *crores* of gold coins." Having spoken thus, the king gave Viśvāmitra eleven *crores* (110 million) of gold coins.

After collecting the money, Viśvāmitra shouted angrily at the king and said, "O low-caste warrior! This amount of money could never be considered enough *dakṣiṇā* for performing a *rājasūya-yajña*! Immediately go and arrange for an adequate amount, because if you fail to do so, you had better be prepared to suffer the wrath of my destructive and celestial power!"

After the king had pleaded with him for some time, Viśvāmitra agreed to wait until the afternoon. The king wept profusely and saw that only one *prahara* (three hour period of the day) was left before sunset. He called to the people loudly and said, "If anyone wishes to buy my ghost-like body, that is, a body devoid of feelings, and in return is benefited, then please do so. What will you pay for this body?" No one came forward. Then, Dharmadeva (demigod of righteousness) appeared in the guise of a *caṇḍāla* whose looks were frightful, and whose body emitted a foul odor. His chest was oddly deformed, he was of black color, a moustache and beard covered his face, he had an elongated belly, and was wearing a garland of skulls. Just by seeing him one could not help but be repulsed by him. He was carrying a stick in his hand and said to King Hariścandra, "I need a servant and can accept you as my slave. Please tell me how much money I should pay for you?" The king asked, "Who are you?" The *caṇḍāla* then introduced himself: "I am Vīrabāhu, the chief *caṇḍāla* of the cremation grounds, and I require someone to collect the clothes of the dead." The king replied, "I will work only for someone of the warrior or priestly class; otherwise I will be degraded from *dharma* (righteous path)." The *caṇḍāla* replied, "To adhere to one's words is the greatest doctrine. You yourself vociferously proclaimed that anyone who needs a servant could come forward and buy you. Now it seems you are backing out. Tell me, is this the correct path to follow?" At that moment, Viśvāmitra appeared and angrily asked the king, "This *caṇḍāla* has come forward to buy you for any given price. Why do you not accept the money offered by him so you can pay me my share? You are deluded by the false ego of belonging to the kings of the Solar Dynasty. If you fail to pay me my money by not selling yourself to this *caṇḍāla*, I shall surely curse you." King Hariścandra was petrified, so he said, "O *brāhmaṇa*! Please accept me as your slave from now on and give me your orders, which I shall readily obey." Viśvāmitra then accepted the king as his slave and asked the chief *caṇḍāla* to purchase him by paying the right price, as he needed the money. The *caṇḍāla* was pleased to hear this and donated ten *yojanas* (one *yojana* = approx. eight miles) of land in Prayāga (an area rich with diamond mines) to Viśvāmitra, which the *brāhmaṇa* readily accepted. After all his debts with the *brāhmaṇa* were settled, the king felt very much relieved. Instantaneously, a celestial voice announced that the king was now freed of all his debts. Flowers were showered from heaven on Hariścandra, and Indra and all the other demigods praised him. As he had accepted Viśvāmitra as his master and had decided to follow his instructions, the king prepared to leave as a slave to the *caṇḍāla*, as ordered by Viśvāmitra. The *caṇḍāla* tied the king and repeatedly beat him as he dragged him along. The *caṇḍāla* then told the king, "You will have to speak many lies from now on." He brought the king home and slept comfortably after having bound him with chains. Meanwhile, in stark contrast, the king could not sleep by dint of his being separated from his near and dear ones, and because of the pain he suffered as a result of being beaten by a stick. Reflecting upon the sufferings of his son and wife, the king cried and thought: "How unfortunate am I? I have lost my kingdom, my wife and son—my kith and kin are gone from me and I have now become a *caṇḍāla*."

At first, the chief *caṇḍāla* made it a daily routine to ridicule Hariścandra again and again. Later, he released him from his chains and instructed him to stay in a large crematorium situated in the south of Kāśī-dhāma, where he was to safeguard the clothes collected from the dead bodies that were brought there. He then gave him his own old, worn-out stick. Having become a *caṇḍāla*, the unfortunate king went to the crematorium, which was filled with the foul smell of the dead. He saw many groups of vultures, dogs and jackals fighting with each other, barking, growling and eating the bodies of the dead. Stinking corpses were lying here and there and the bones of the deceased and their remains were scattered all around. They were so plentiful that it made walking across them difficult. Semi-burned heads, jaws and bodies of human beings were lying everywhere, as if ridiculing the false ego of mankind. It was a gruesome scene where the grieving relatives of the dead were all around, crying loudly in separation grief. The cremation flames of the burning dead bodies, mixed with the pitiful cries of the bereaved parties, created a scenario as if it were doomsday. The king cursed his destiny and began collecting the clothes of the dead bodies.

After a while, it became impossible to recognize the weakened king. He was now drenched in the dirty discharge of dead bodies and even started to behave like a *caṇḍāla*, arguing with the relatives of the dead who came for the cremation. The king was in a pathetic condition; his worn and torn dress was tied and knotted in various places and his feet, hands, face and body were covered by the ashes and burns from sparks that came flying out of the fire from the funeral pyre. He had wrapped a cloth torn from a shroud around his head and survived on *pindas* (balls made of flour or rice presented as an offering to the deceased) left by the relatives of the deceased. The king felt as if a whole century had passed, though in reality, only one year had passed in this condition without sleeping. Queen Śaibyā and Prince Rohita were also suffering intensely every day and night, as they were working like slaves in the house of the *brāhmaṇa* who had purchased them. One day, Rohita went out to play with some friends. He and his friends combined this activity with going into the forest to collect some ingredients for his master's sacrificial fire: dry wood, *kuśa* (sacred grass), twigs to ignite the fire and also some wood of a *palāśa* tree. However, due to carrying such a heavy load on his head he became tired, so he sat down. Carrying the load had made him thirsty, so he went to a nearby pond, lowered his head to place his load on the ground and drank some water. After taking some rest, he was about to pick up his load (which was resting over a hole) from the ground, when a black poisonous cobra snake (as per the instructions of Viśvāmitra) came out of the hole and bit him. Rohita died instantaneously and his friends were very frightened when they realized that he was dead. They ran to the *brāhmaṇa's* house and informed his mother about the unfortunate incident. The queen instantly lost her senses and fell to the ground. When the *brāhmaṇa* returned home he was annoyed to find his slave, the queen, lying on the ground, so he sprinkled some water on her face, which brought her back to her senses. Her callous master then started shouting and abusing her by saying, "What is this? Why are you sleeping in the evening? Are you aware that doing so is an omen of bad luck and poverty?" Still shocked by the loss of her son, the queen did not reply and kept on crying, which infuriated the *brāhmaṇa*. Then he castigated her by saying, "When I bought you, I bought a slave, so why are you avoiding work and why did your husband take my money if you cannot serve me adequately?"

The queen repeatedly requested the *brāhmaṇa* to allow her to have a glimpse of her dead son's body, but the cruel *brāhmaṇa* would not budge and ordered her to continue working instead. By the time she finished massaging her master's feet it was midnight. The *brāhmaṇa* then permitted her to go to her son, cautioning her to return immediately after his cremation, so that her morning activities would not be postponed. In the dead of night, outside of Vārāṇasī, the lonely queen finally saw her son lying dead on a pile of wood. Seeing her son like that, she was overcome with emotion and began weeping in desperation. Her painful cries were such that even a stonehearted person would be moved by them. Finally, she fell unconscious on the dead body of her son. When she regained her senses, she kissed his lifeless face and cried out, "O King! Where are you? Please come at once and see your beloved son Rohita. Why won't you come?" The continuous crying of the queen woke the watchmen from their sleep. At first, they were amazed to see a lone woman at midnight, crying with a dead boy on her lap, and repeatedly asked her to identify herself. However, being absorbed in grief, the queen did not reply. Then the watchmen considered the possibility of her being a child-killing witch, as that would explain why she was out of the city at that hour. They considered it quite likely that she would kill and devour children. The gatekeepers then surrounded her, with one of them catching her hands, another her hair and another holding her by her neck. In this way, they dragged her to the *caṇḍāla* Vīrabāhu. They told the *caṇḍāla*, "This woman is a child-killing witch, and she should be killed and thrown out of the city." Vīrabāhu praised them and said, "You have done a very good job. I have only ever heard about such a witch, but have never actually seen one. Perhaps she has killed and eaten many children. You will be praised for catching such a demon. Surely, it is considered a pious deed and not a sin if one kills someone who is the killer of a *brāhmaṇa*, cow, woman, child, one who steals gold, sets a house on fire, drinks alcohol, copulates with his spiritual master's wife or one who blasphemes pure devotees."

Then the *caṇḍāla* Vīrabāhu, after tying the queen with a piece of rope pulled from her hair, started beating her and dragged her to Hariścandra. Shouting in his harsh voice, he then ordered the former king to kill her. King Hariścandra replied, "To kill a woman is a great sin, as a woman is to be protected at all times. The sages have implored us not to kill women. They have also told us that if a man kills a woman, he has to suffer the agony of passing through the Raurava hell (one of twenty-eight hells) for an infinitely long period. I am under oath that I shall never kill any woman in my lifetime. Therefore I refuse to kill her, so you should have someone else do it."

The *caṇḍāla* again ordered Hariścandra by saying that there is no duty for a slave other than obeying his or her master. The king said, "O master! Please ask me for any other gruesome work and I shall do it. If you have an enemy I shall gladly kill him and hand over his kingdom to you. If Indra or any great heavenly person such as another demigod, a demon, mystic, Gandharva, celestial serpent and so on is your enemy, I shall kill him and thus fulfill your wish."

The *caṇḍāla* Vīrabāhu replied, "When a slave brings loss to his master, he cannot escape hell even after ten thousand *kalpas*.[2] Therefore, do not give me such lame excuses; take this sword and behead this witch!" In response to this, the king raised the sword to kill her, as the appearance of the queen and that of his own self had transformed so drastically that they were unable to recognize each other. By now, the queen actually wanted to die because her son had died. Though in profuse grief, still she prayed to the king, "O *caṇḍāla*! I want to make one final request. The dead body of my son is lying outside the city of Vārāṇasī, so I ask you to spare me some time until he is cremated." The king (looking like a *caṇḍāla)* agreed to her request. Then the queen, in dirty attire and with dust-laden hair, carried the dead body of her son to the cremation ground while crying loudly. She then placed his body on the ground and, upon seeing her dead son like that, lost all control and cried out, without realization of her husband's immediate presence, "O King! Please come and have a glimpse of your child. He is lying here on the ground. He died from a snake bite while playing with his friends."

The lament of the woman made Hariścandra curious, and thus he removed the cloth from the head of the dead boy to identify him. Although they were almost face-to-face, the king failed to recognize his wife due to the length of time that had passed since they had become separated. This was exacerbated by the daily crises and miseries they had endured, giving their faces a totally different appearance. The queen also was unable to recognize the king because of his now long tangled hair and body as thin as the bark of a tree. Gazing at the dead body, King Hariścandra was astonished to see a charming face and princely virtues on the body of the dead child. The child had large lotus-eyes, red lips, a wide chest, long arms reaching to the knees and very fine, beautiful fingers. He understood this child to be of royal descent and, upon observing the child's face, remembered his own past while weeping at the thought of this being his son Rohita. Tears began to flow from his eyes as he considered whether or not this could be his son. The queen was surprised to see the changed expression on the face of the *caṇḍāla*. Overwhelmed with grief she said, "I do not know what sinful acts have brought these dreadful events upon me. O my lord! O my husband! O my king! Where are you staying peacefully now, after you left me? I am drowning in an ocean of grief. O God! What have you done? You have made King Hariścandra lose his kingdom, leave his relatives and sell his wife and son."

Upon hearing his own name and past history, the king recalled everything and exclaimed, "Oh! She is my wife Śaibyā and he is my dear son Rohita!" Grief stricken, he fell down and lost his senses, and the queen also fell unconscious, as the words of the king triggered strong emotions of remembrance of her husband. She became overwhelmed due to being separated from him for such a long time. Both were weeping when they regained their senses. The king cried, "I lost my kingdom, my relatives, my wealth—everything—due to ill-fortune. I do not grieve for this at all but, O cruel gods, you have also taken away my only son! Now I am torn asunder by this heart-breaking sorrow." Upon hearing this,

2 One kalpa = one day of Brahmā, which is equivalent to 71 catur-yugas.

Queen Śaibyā slowly recognized the voice of her husband as she wondered at his words: *"He lost his kingdom? How is it that a king is staying in a crematorium?"* Then, after staring at the king for some time, she finally concluded that the *caṇḍāla* was actually her husband! She was simultaneously surprised and pleased, which eventually made her lose consciousness again. After coming to consciousness, she began to cry, "O cruel Almighty! Disgrace to You! You made the king lose his kingdom, leave his relatives and sell his wife and son. As if this were not enough, You made him a *caṇḍāla* as well! It is very pathetic to learn that You forced the king to live in this horrible place that is strewn all over with ashes; burning pyres filled with half-burned corpses; bones and flesh spread throughout; full of jackals, vultures and other creatures that howl, bark, growl and so on. They jump on the burning pyres to eat the corpses." After listening to Śaibyā's narration of the whole sequence of events leading up to their son's death, the king lifted his son's body and began kissing it profusely. Then he fell unconscious. After the king regained his senses, Śaibyā requested him, "O dear husband! As ordered by your master, please behead me using the sword and thus kill me. You must not be known as a liar. Do not hesitate to follow the instructions of your master."

Upon hearing the words uttered by the queen, the king fell unconscious yet again. Upon regaining his senses, he decided that, as he had lost his only son, he had no reason to continue his life. Thus, he planned to burn himself to death by sitting on the burning funeral pyre of his son. The king then told his queen, "O my dear queen, go and serve the *brāhmaṇa*, and do not disobey him by feeling proud of being the wife of a king." However, when she understood the decision of the king, she replied, "O my dear king! Since you have decided to give up your life by burning yourself along with our son, I shall follow you and relieve myself of these unbearable sufferings. For any wife this is certainly the most recommended act."

The king placed the dead body of his son on the pyre; then he and the queen meditated upon almighty God for some time. Indra and other demigods including the demigod of *dharma* appeared instantaneously when they learned about the king's plan. Viśvadeva (god of the world), Marut-gaṇāḥ (masters of the wind), Lokapālā (governors of the different planets), the eleven Rudras and so on, along with all the sages including Sage Viśvāmitra, then arrived on the scene. Viśvāmitra came with the desire to grant anything the king might desire. The demigod Dharma said to the king, "You need not die. You have pleased everyone by setting an example with your acts of tolerance, self-control, truth and observance of your promise." Indra, the king of demigods, said with great satisfaction, "O fortunate one! By your penance, you, along with your wife and son, have conquered all the eternal *puṇya-lokas* (heavenly planets attained by means of merit). Therefore, all three of you may now depart for heaven. You have achieved that place that is most difficult for human beings to attain." He then sprinkled nectar on the dead body of the prince lying on the pyre and flowers rained from the heavens while *dundubhis* (kettledrums) resounded throughout the sky. Prince Rohita rose up from the pyre, relaxed and smiling, as healthy and fresh as he was in Ayodhyā.

The king embraced his son and he, along with his queen, regained his original glory, grace and beauty. They wore beautiful clothes and were decorated with garlands. When Indra asked the king to leave for heaven with his wife and son, Hariścandra replied that he could not proceed unless his master, the *caṇḍāla*, would allow him to. At that moment, Dharmadeva appeared and told him that he had disguised himself as that *caṇḍāla*, and had shown him Caṇḍāla-purī (Caṇḍāla City) with the aim of appraising the king's *dharma-niśtha* (dedication to righteousness). Then, Indra again asked the king to leave for heaven, but Hariścandra refused, saying, "The people of Kauśala (Ayodhyā) are grieving for their king, so I cannot leave them like that. Unless they also get the right to go to heaven, I will not go." Demigod King Indra interjected, "The people of Kauśala have committed an act of sin as well as an act of virtue, so how can they be allowed to go to heaven alongside their king without proper evaluation?" King Hariścandra then proposed to donate the fruits of all his *puṇyā* (pious acts) to them. Indra replied, "*Tathāstu*! So be it!" Thus, Indra, Dharmadeva, Sage Viśvāmitra and other *brāhmaṇas* went to Ayodhyā and informed the people about the return of King Hariścandra and that, because of his good deeds, they would all go to heaven. The people of Ayodhyā were greatly pleased to learn this. The great King Hariścandra then crowned his son Rohita as the new king and sent him to Ayodhyā along with many well-wishers. He was awarded great glory, the scope of which is sought after even by the demigods. At that time, Śukrācārya composed a verse glorifying the charity and patience of Hariścandra. The verse is as follows:

aho titikṣāmahatāmyamaho dānaphalam mahat
yadāgato hariścandro mahendrasya salokatāṁ

This verse vividly illustrates the superlative piety of Hariścandra's actions. He did not lose his courage or power even after donating his kingdom to Viśvāmitra. On being ordered by his then master, the *caṇḍāla* Vīrabāhu, to kill a woman, the king stubbornly refused though he was prepared to perform any other tough task such as fighting someone as powerful as Devarāja Indra, or Yakṣas and Kinnaras (sons of Kuvera, the lord of wealth), and deliver their wealth to him, rather than commit the heinous act of killing a woman. A ruler should be of worthy character because when a kingdom is handed over as a gift to an unworthy person, such a person cannot protect and rule over it. After donating his kingdom to Viśvāmitra, and when prompted to give further *dakṣiṇā*, the king invited the people of Vārāṇasī to purchase his queen in order to raise the required sum of money, but no one came forward. Therefore, Viśvāmitra had to come in the guise of *brāhmaṇa* to buy the queen and prince. When the king offered himself for sale, again no one came forward, so Dharmaraja had to come in the guise of a *caṇḍāla* to buy him by paying the required amount of money. The above incidents prove that the king's righteousness was of the highest order and something rarely to be seen in this world. In the *Sabha-parva* section of the *Mahābhārata*, written by Śrī Kṛṣṇa-dvaipāyana Vedavyāsa, it is mentioned that, during an assembly headed by Indra, Sage Nārada uttered the name of only one king, Hariścandra, and, upon hearing only this name, King Yudhiṣṭhira asked, "O great soul! What penance did Hariścandra perform to acquire a status equivalent to that of Indra?" Sage Nārada replied, "Hariścandra was king of all the kings and they all bowed before him. He won over Saptadvīpa (seven islands or continents) while riding his golden chariot and fighting with his weapons. After conquering all the kings on earth, he performed a great *rājasūya-yajña* and gladly donated five times whatever anyone asked of him. When the *yajña* was completed, he happily gave away food and a variety of wealth to the *brāhmaṇas*. Therefore, he achieved the kind of glory that is unattainable by thousands of kings. O Kaunteya (son of Kuntī)! Your father Pāṇḍu was also amazed at the glory of Hariścandra. He wishes you also to perform a *rājasūya-yajña* so you might also achieve matchless glory like that of Hariścandra."

In *Śrīmad Bhāgavatam*, Śrī Śukadeva Gosvāmī has mentioned Hariścandra:

yo 'nityena śarīreṇa satāṁ geyaṁ yaśo dhruvam
nācinoti svayaṁ kalpaḥ sa vācyaḥ śocya eva saḥ
hariścandro rantideva uñchavṛttiḥ śibir baliḥ
vyādhaḥ kapoto bahavo hy adhruveṇa dhruvaṁ gatāḥ
(*Śrīmad Bhāgavatam* 10.72.20-21)

"Those who do not use their mortal bodies for such acts as are praised by devotees, are to be pitied and are condemned. King Hariścandra, Rantideva, Uñchavṛtti (Sage Mudgala), Śibi, Bali, Vyāsa, Kapot and many others in the past, went to the planet of Dhruva (Dhruvaloka) with their mortal bodies."

To conclude the story of King Hariścandra, Śrīla Viśvanātha Cakravartīpāda writes in his commentary:

viśvāmitrānṛṇyāya hariścandro bhāryātmajādi
sarvaṁ vikrīya svayaṁ caṇḍālatāṁ prāpto'nya
nirviṇṇah sah ayodhyāvāsibhirjaneḥ svargaṁ gataḥ

King Nāhuṣa

Śrī Nāhuṣa was a noble king belonging to the Lunar Dynasty.[3] His father's name was Āyu and his mother's name was Svarbhanvi. Candra's (presiding deity of the moon) son was Buddha, Buddha's son was Purūravā (famous as the first king of the Lunar Dynasty) and Āyu was the son of Purūravā. In the *Viśvakośa*,[4] Nāhuṣa's wife is designated as Aśoka Sundarī, whereas in the Bengali Dictionary of Āśutoṣa Deva, her name is mentioned as Virajā. King Nāhuṣa had six sons, named Yati, Yayāti, Śaryāti (also known as Saṁyāti), Āyati, Viyati and Kṛti respectively. King Nāhuṣa was a righteous and noble king who eliminated all the evil from his kingdom by his exemplary administration. Thus, the people of his empire felt safe and happy. He was enormously powerful and succeeded in killing the atrocious demon Tunda, and thus acquired all sorts of opulence in the three worlds. Due to his numerous pious deeds (*puṇyā*), he became free from all sinful reactions, even after killing a cow out of ignorance. Due to the fruits of his pious deeds, King Nāhuṣa also reigned in heaven.

Once upon a time, Cyavana Ṛṣi undertook a vow to remain underwater for meditation in Prayāga. It so happened that some fishermen came there with the intention of catching

3 Candra-vaṁśa: the Lunar Dynasty, or family lineage of Candra, the demigod of the moon (family and descendants of Janaka, Kuru, Yadu, etc.). Atri, one of seven famous sages (Saptarṣis), was born of Brahmā's desire (*mānasa-putra*), and Candra is his son. The Seven Sages are: Marichi, Atri, Angira, Pulaha, Kratu, Vaśiṣṭha and Pulastya.

4 *Encyclopedia of Sanskrit Literature*, compiled by Śrī Nagendranath Basu in the Bengali language.

fish but, coincidently, they also caught the *ṛṣi* and later sold him to King Nāhuṣa for an appropriate price.

One time, Indra, the king of the demigods, hid inside the stem of a lotus at Mānasarovara for one thousand years under the protection of Goddess Lakṣmī. He did this to free himself from the sinful reaction of killing the *brāhmaṇa* (*brahma-hatya*) by the name Viśvarūpa at the time of killing the demon Vṛtrāsura. During that period, the demigods and sages requested King Nāhuṣa to preside over heaven and offered him Indra's crown. However, King Nāhuṣa became so absorbed in the opulence of heaven that he developed the desire to enjoy the wife of Indra, Śacī-devī. Observing Nāhuṣa's negative transformation, Bṛhaspati (spiritual master of the demigods), the demigods and great sages were shocked and worried to see this distressing development. All of their efforts to stop Nāhuṣa went in vain. Śacī-devī then took shelter of Bṛhaspati who promised to protect her. He advised her to tell Nāhuṣa that she was ready to fulfill his desire, provided that he should come to her on a palanquin carried by saintly persons.

Śacī-devī sent this proposal to Nāhuṣa, who, blinded by lust, agreed to go to her on a palanquin carried by the sages who had crowned him king of heaven. While carrying Nāhusa, the sages, who thought this to be some sort of stunt, engaged in a discussion among themselves about certain Vedic hymns, which disturbed Nāhuṣa's sitting posture. Thus, while he changed to a more comfortable posture, Nāhuṣa's foot accidently touched the head of Sage Agastya. Agastya became furious and cursed Nāhuṣa, "May you transform into a member of the reptile species!" Due to the power of that curse, the king's body immediately changed into the body of a snake and fell down to Dvaita Forest:

pitari bhraṁśite sthānād indrāṇyā dharṣaṇād dvijaiḥ
prāpite 'jagaratvaṁ vai yayātir abhavan nṛpaḥ
(*Śrīmad Bhāgavatam* 9.18.3)

"Due to his immoral behavior toward Śacī-devī and the curse of Sage Agastya, Nāhuṣa was degraded to the status of a python. Consequently, his son Yayāti became the king."

tāvat triṇākaṁ nahuṣaḥ śaśāsa vidyā-
tapo-yoga-balānubhāvaḥ
sa sampad-aiśvarya-madāndha-buddhir
nītas tiraścāṁ gatim indra-patnyā
(*Śrīmad Bhāgavatam* 6.13.16)

Nāhuṣa was afraid and tearful, and repeatedly begged for forgiveness at Agastya's feet. Out of compassion, Sage Agastya said, "King Yudhiṣṭhira will free you from this curse. You will achieve liberation from the snake species when he answers some of your questions correctly."

This episode of Nāhuṣa's liberation is described in detail in the *Mahābhārata*, *Vana-parva* (the Pāṇḍavas' stay in the forest), Chapters 79-81. One day, when the Pāṇḍavas were staying in Dvaita Forest, Bhīmasena went hunting and fell into the grip of a great python. To his surprise, even after repeated attempts, he failed to free himself. Then he asked the python, "Who are you? Introduce yourself!" The snake said, "I am starving and want to eat you." Unfazed by the snake's reply, Bhīma was not worried for his own life, but about his brother's safety in this forest full of snakes and demons. Meanwhile, King Yudhiṣṭhira was observing various bad omens. The delay in Bhīma's return made him anxious. After having assigned Dhanañjaya (Arjuna) to protect Draupadī, and Nakula and Sahadeva to protect the *brāhmaṇas*, he took Sage Dhaumya (Yudhiṣṭhira's head priest and the son of Sage Asita) along with him in search of Bhīma.

After walking a long distance, they saw Bhīma trapped in the grip of a four-fanged python, which had a very large cave-like mouth and gold-colored skin. Bhīma explained everything to them, so Yudhiṣṭhira asked the snake to introduce himself, upon which the python replied, "I am Nāhuṣa, the son of one of your ancestors, King Āyu of the Lunar Dynasty. I previously attained the opulence of all the three worlds as a result of my penance and *yajñas*, and eventually became the ruler of heaven as well. I was so filled with pride due to attaining such opulence and respect that I arranged for a thousand *brāhmaṇas* to carry me on a palanquin. The sages, demigods, Gandharvas,[5] Rakṣasas,[6] and all others used to pay me taxes. I was so powerful and impressive that others were rendered lusterless by the mere sight of me. One day when Sage Agastya was carrying my palanquin, my foot unknowingly touched him. The sage became enraged, and he cursed me to become a snake. After I repeatedly prayed to him for forgiveness, he told me that you would rescue me upon my posing some questions to you. Now here you are, so if you answer my questions correctly, I will let Bhīmasena go and my curse will be lifted."

Yudhiṣṭhira asked him, "What kind of queries? What must I do?" Thus, the python requested him to answer his first two questions:

1. "Who is a *brāhmaṇa*?"
2. "What is *vedya* (worthy to be known)?"

Yudhiṣṭhira then replied:

1. "The true *brāhmaṇa* is one who possesses truthfulness, charity, tolerance, kindness, penance and mercy."
2. "Almighty God is *vedya*. He is devoid of mundane happiness and sorrow. If one knows Him, he or she is never unhappy."

Nāhuṣa, in the form of a python, was pleased that Yudhiṣṭhira had correctly answered his questions. He thought: *"A courageous and intelligent man usually becomes immoral because of pride, and I myself have been an example of this."* Thus, after Yudhiṣṭhira had answered his questions, Nāhuṣa released Bhīmasena and, as promised, Nāhusa's curse was lifted and he received a transcendental body:

haihayo nahuṣo veṇo
rāvaṇo narako 'pare
śrī-madād bhraṁśitāḥ sthānād
deva-daitya-nareśvarāḥ
(*Śrīmad Bhāgavatam* 10.73.20)

"In the past, Haihaya (Kārtavīrya), Nāhuṣa, Veṇa, Rāvaṇa, Narakāsura and many other demons, kings, and demigods fell from the

5 The heavenly court musicians of Indra.
6 Man-eating demons.

path of righteousness due to the pride of their wealth and position."

It is mentioned in the *Manu Saṁhitā* that Nāhuṣa had fallen from his position due to false pride:

veno vinaṣṭo avinayātnahuṣaścaiva pārthivaḥ
(*Manu Saṁhitā* 7.41)

In the *Ṛk Saṁhitā* (1.31.11, 10.63.1), Nāhuṣa is described as the son of Āyu and the father of Yayāti.

King Duṣyanta

In *Śrīmad Bhāgavatam*, Chapter 20 of the 9th Canto, Śrī Śukadeva Gosvāmī addresses King Parīkṣit in the following way: "Hey Bharata!" He then proceeds to describe the history of Pūru and his descendant Duṣyanta. Purūravā is the originator of the Lunar Dynasty. The son of Pūru was Janamejaya, and his son was Pracinvāna. The sons and grandsons in the line of Pracinvāna were respectively: Pravīra, Manusyu, Cārupada, Sudyu, Hugava, Saṁyāti, Ahaṁyāti, Raudrāśva, Ṛteyu, Rantināva, Sumati and Rebhi. Mahārāja Duṣyanta is the famous Lunar Dynasty king who was the son of Rebhi. Buddha was the father of Purūravā, and Candra was the father of Buddha. Atri was the father of Candra. Atri is also known as the son born from the mind's desire (*manasā-putra*) of Brahmā. In the *Harivaṁśa Purāṇa* it is stated that Duṣyanta was the son of Surodha (father) and Updanavi (mother):

dauṣmanter bharatasyāpi śāntanos tat-sutasya ca
yayāter jyeṣṭha-putrasya yador vaṁśo 'nukīrtitaḥ
(*Śrīmad Bhāgavatam* 12.12.26)

Śukadeva Gosvāmī addressed Parīkṣit Mahārāja as "Hey Bharata!" because Bharata, the son of Duṣyanta, was the ancestor of both the Kurus and Pāṇḍavas. Śrila Kṛṣṇa-dvaipāyana Vedavyāsa has written about King Duṣyanta in the 9th Canto of *Śrīmad Bhāgavatam*. He is described here in brief as follows:

While hunting in a forest, King Duṣyanta came upon the *āśrama* (hermitage) of Sage Kaṇva. There, Śakuntalā, a beautiful woman, captivated him. Since the Pūru Dynasty is famous for consisting of followers of the path of virtue, Duṣyanta asked her to introduce herself. She told him, "I am the daughter of Sage Viśvāmitra and the Apsarā (heavenly dancing girl), Menakā, and have been left in the forest by my mother. Thus, I was raised by Kaṇva Muni." Śakuntalā then offered to serve the king in many ways. The king took her to be of royal blood and, as such, accepted her as his wife. They married secretly in the Gandharva style, i.e. the *gandharva-vivāha-rīti*, or marriage by mutual consent without a ceremony, and the king then returned to his kingdom. Śakuntalā eventually gave birth to the mighty Bharata, and Sage Kaṇva performed the birth rites for him. Bharata was so powerful that during his childhood he would catch lions and play with them. His great power was due to the fact that Bharata was a partial expansion of Supreme Lord Hari. Śakuntalā then went to King Duṣyanta with her son, but the king initially refused to accept them both. However, when he heard a booming voice from the sky ordering him to keep them, he accepted Śakuntalā as his queen and Bharata as his son:

pitary uparate so 'pi cakravartī mahā-yaśāḥ
mahimā gīyate tasya harer aṁśa-bhuvo bhuvi
(*Śrīmad Bhāgavatam* 9.20.23)

"That famous Bharata became the powerful emperor of seven islands after the death of his father, Duṣyanta. He was known as a partial representation of Lord Hari."

The *Mahābhārata* presents the following description: During the rule of King Duṣyanta, who was the foremost forefather of the Kauravas and renowned for his bravery, the kingdom enjoyed great happiness. Once, Duṣyanta went hunting in the forest with his soldiers. Walking amid his soldiers, he appeared as brilliant as Indra, the king of the demigods. On entering the deep forest, he saw a very beautiful garden with equally beautiful rows of trees, and all the wild animals such as deer, lions and elephants ran away as the soldiers moved about, gleefully creating chaos. Mystics, celestial musicians, celestial dancers, monkeys and damsels of heaven used that forest as a playground. The king then became hungry and tired due to excessive labor. Gradually, he came across an uninhabited area where he stumbled upon the *āśrama* of Sage Kaṇva, the son of Sage Kaśyapa. The beauty of the *āśrama* enchanted him. He took off his royal paraphernalia and went inside with his ministers and priests, leaving his soldiers outside. After walking some distance within the *āśrama*, he left them as well and ventured further on his own. He reached the River Mālinī at the far end of the *āśrama*. Seeing no one, he called out to see if anyone was there. Hearing his cries, a girl as beautiful as Goddess Lakṣmī emerged from the *āśrama* and welcomed him. She offered water at his feet and when the king asked for Sage Kaṇva, she asked him to wait for some time. The extreme beauty of the girl captivated the king, so he asked her to introduce herself. She said, "I am the daughter of Sage Kaṇva." The king thought: *"Sage Kaṇva is a celibate, so how could she be his daughter?"* Thus the king asked her to elucidate, upon which Śakuntalā replied, "Once upon a time, Sage Viśvāmitra was performing severe penance to a degree that made Indra fearful, so he sent the beautiful Apsarā Menakā to distract him. Menakā expressed to Indra her fear of the power and anger of Viśvāmitra, but she could not disobey Indra's order, so she asked him for his help by dint of Vāyu, the demigod of air. Indra agreed, and with the help of favorable winds, she managed to distract Viśvāmitra and eventually engaged in sexual activity with him. As a result of this, a beautiful girl was born. After accomplishing her mission, she abandoned the newborn girl on the banks of River Mālinī and returned to Indraloka, the abode of Indra. Birds of various species surrounded and protected the newborn girl from the wild carnivorous animals that roamed the forests. Just when all the birds were protecting the baby girl, Sage Kaṇva arrived at the bank of the river to take a bath. To his surprise, he discovered a helpless girl amid the flock of birds, so he took the child to his *āśrama* and began taking care of her. As per the scriptures, one who gives birth, who saves the life, or who provides food is understood to be a father. As she was surrounded and protected by the *śakun* (birds) in the lonely forest, she was named Śakuntalā."

After listening to her story, the king took her to be the equivalent of any princess and thus proposed to her. She did not agree immediately, but asked him to wait for her guardian father, Sage Kaṇva, to return. Upon the return of her protector, the king narrated everything to him. Then Sage Kaṇva informed the king that, out of six accepted types of marital rites for the warrior class, a marriage ceremony according to the tradition of the Gandharvas would be an acceptable and valid form of marriage. Śakuntalā then said, "I will marry the king if he promises that the son born out of our union will be the only prince and heir to his empire." The king agreed to the terms. Before leaving for the capital, he promised her that he would send his army to escort her there. However, when the king returned to his capital, he had a sudden change of heart. He now felt unhappy and anxious for the act he had done. Śakuntalā was mortified by the king's behavior, and Sage Kaṇva, by dint of his mystical powers, understood everything when he saw her distress. Thus, he reassured her, "My dear daughter, do not worry. The *gandharva-vivāha-rīti* is a lawful, valid and acceptable kind of marriage for those of the warrior class. This holds true especially in the case of Duṣyanta, who is a righteous and great king. I hereby predict that you shall give birth to a saintly and courageous boy, who will rule the earth." Thus, as predicted by Sage Kanva, Śakuntalā gave birth to a brilliant baby boy after three years of marriage. The sages then performed the *jātakarmādi-saṁskāra* (rite performed just after birth). The child grew up to be so fearless and brave that, from the age of six, he would bind lions, elephants and other varieties of wild animals to trees, and then proceed to play with them. As the sages observed the remarkable deeds performed by this powerful boy, they named him Sarvadamana (all-powerful, one who can control all).

After some time, Śakuntalā took her son to King Duṣyanta in Hastināpura, as per the instructions of Sage Kaṇva. The disciples of Sage Kaṇva who accompanied Śakuntalā returned to the *āśrama* after relating the events to the king. Śakuntalā told the king about their son, reminded him of his promise and requested him to declare Sarvadamana as the princely heir. Although Duṣyanta recalled everything, he said, "O wicked woman! Whose wife are you? I do not have any relationship with you. Please go away from here!" Upon hearing the harsh words of the king, she felt ashamed and became almost senseless, but she also became angry and morose because of the king's behavior. She understood that the king was simply pretending not to know her, despite being well aware of the facts. After composing herself, she said, "O King! If you wish to abandon me, I shall willingly go back to the *āśrama*, but it will not be right for you to abandon the son born from your own wife." The king became furious when he heard this, and harshly replied, "This boy is not my son. Women are known to lie. How could a child of such a young age turn out to be as strong and robust as a *śāla* (teak) tree? Menakā gave birth to you, Śakuntalā, when she was subjugated by lust; thus you might have followed in your mother's footsteps!"

Śakuntalā replied, "My birth is superior to that of yours, but if you do not believe in truth then I shall be on my way. However, before I leave I want you to know that it was not my intention to meet and become involved with you. Even though you may not want to accept my son, he is still destined to become the ruler of the whole planet." As Śakuntalā prepared to leave, a booming voice was heard resounding from the sky. "O Duṣyanta! Take care of your

son. Do not disobey Śakuntalā. You have to care for and bring up this son according to our instructions. Know that, for this reason, this boy will be known as Bharata (cherished)."

Upon hearing these instructions from the celestial voice, the king was joyful and asked his ministers and priests, "Did you all hear the celestial voice? Let it be known beyond any doubt that this boy is my son! If I would have accepted that boy as my son on the basis of Śakuntalā's words alone, the people might have doubted the royalty of my son, but now all doubt has been removed." Thus, King Duṣyanta spiritedly accepted Bharata as his son. He then proceeded to explain to Śakuntalā that he behaved the way he did in order to eradicate any confusion, suspicion and gossip that an illegitimate child taking over the rule of the empire would cause. Later, this Bharata became the mighty emperor of earth and performed many sacrificial fires like the king of the demigods, Indra. Sage Kaṇva also asked Bharata to perform various *yajñas*, to which he donated generously. The current and past glory of the nation Bharata (modern-day India, derived from Bhārata-varṣa—the land of King Bharata) is attributed to that same King Bharata. His predecessor dynasty is known as the Bhārata Dynasty.

The narration of Duṣyanta's character in *Abhijñana Śakuntalām* by the poet Kālidāsa, as given in the *Viśvakośa* (encyclopedia), is different from that given in the *Mahābhārata*. The *Viśvakośa* mentions that, as per the *Mahābhārata*, Duṣyanta had deserted Śakuntalā by cunningly stating that he did not remember anything due to being afraid of criticism by his people. However, according to Kālidāsa in *Abhijñana Śakuntalām*, it is mentioned that he forgot Śakuntalā due to a curse by Sage Durvāsā, and thus thought that by accepting Śakuntalā, he might become deviated from righteous conduct in the future. He thought: *"I do not know this woman, so if I accept her as my wife, my conduct will be unrighteous, especially as she is pregnant."* Śakuntalā planned to show the marital ring given by him, but she failed to do so, whereupon the king became very suspicious of her. Śakuntalā then returned to her *āśrama* in disgrace.

In *Mahābhārata* we find that Śakuntalā abused the king with absolute shamelessness, using many harsh insults such as "crooked," etc. but in Kālidāsa's narration she is presented as a paragon of elegance and modesty.

King Nṛga

Vaivasvata Manu is the son of the demigod Sūrya, the presiding deity of the sun, and Manu's son is Mahārāja Ikṣvāku, who is widely known as the originator of the Solar Dynasty (Sūrya-vaṁśa). Mahārāja Nṛga was born in the Ikṣvāku Dynasty. In the *Anuśāsana- parva* of *Mahābhārata*, where Bhīṣma instructs Yudhiṣṭhira, it is mentioned that the extent of the glory of King Nṛga and his attainment of heaven due to a donation of a large number of cows is beyond comparison with donations given by other kings.

One can find details about King Nṛga in the 64th Chapter, 10th Canto, of *Śrīmad Bhāgavatam*. Bānāsura was the eldest among the hundred sons of Bali Mahārāja. He was devoted to Lord Śiva and used to please him by playing different musical instruments with his thousand hands. Demigods such as Indra were like servitors to him. He had a daughter named Ūṣā. Once, having seen Ūṣā in the company of Aniruddha (grandson of Lord Kṛṣṇa), Bānāsura arrested Aniruddha, which ultimately resulted in a battle with Lord Kṛṣṇa, who chopped off all of Bānāsura's hands except four, and spared his life when so requested by Lord Śiva. By the grace of Lord Kṛṣṇa he became one of the chief associates of Lord Rudra (Śiva). Śrī Kṛṣṇa took Aniruddha and Ūṣā to Dvārakā-purī, where the residents greeted them.

One day in Dvārakā, Sāmba (son of Jāmbavatī), Pradyumna, Cāru, Bhānu, Gada and others went to a forest to take a stroll and, after various activities, felt tired and became thirsty. As they searched for water they looked inside a dry well and saw a peculiar creature lying there that resembled a hill. After some time, they concluded that this creature was a huge chameleon. They became compassionate when they saw the awful condition of the chameleon and tried to pull it out of the well with the help of ropes, but all their efforts were in vain. Finally they went to Śrī Kṛṣṇa and told Him everything. Lord Kṛṣṇa, accompanied by the Yādavas, approached the well and lifted out the chameleon easily, using only His left hand. By the mere touch of the Lord's hand, the chameleon acquired a transcendental body.

Although Śrī Kṛṣṇa knows everything, He, in order to display human qualities and values, asked the former chameleon, "How did you become a chameleon and how did your lizard body transform into a heavenly body?" Upon hearing the questions of Lord Śrī Kṛṣṇa he replied, "I am the son of Ikṣvāku and was the famous King Nṛga. No one was able to compete with me as far as donations and charity are concerned. I donated thousands of milking cows to pious *brāhmaṇas* and performed many fire sacrifices. I also created numerous ponds and dug many wells. Once, I donated a cow to a *brāhmaṇa*, but after some time the cow came back to my place and mingled with the other cows. Being completely unaware of this, I donated that cow to some other *brāhmaṇa*. Suddenly, the original owner of the cow, the first *brāhmaṇa*, arrived and was furious to find his cow was now in the hands of another *brāhmaṇa*. Thus, he laid his claim for the cow, and an argument ensued between them. When news of the argument reached me, I tried to settle the dispute by offering one lakh (100 thousand) cows in exchange for that single cow. I apologized for my mistake but my apologies fell on deaf ears, resulting in both *brāhmaṇas* leaving the cow and going away in anger. I passed away after some time, and a Yamadūta (messenger of the demigod of death) then took me to Yamarāja (the demigod of death). Yamarāja asked me what I would like to avail myself of first, the good or bad fruits accruing from my good or bad deeds, respectively. When I learned that there would be unending results of my numerous pious acts, whereas in contrast I had only a few results of sins to undergo, I decided to endure the bad fruits first. As a result, I became a chameleon and fell into this well."

After relating this introduction, King Nṛga sang the glories of Lord Kṛṣṇa and boarded a celestial plane to heaven.

In order to teach a lesson to all, Lord Kṛṣṇa explained that even the most magnanimous of persons is compelled to suffer if he or she steals something owned by a *brāhmaṇa*. There may be an antidote for poison, but there is no escaping from the sinful act of stealing from a *brāhmaṇa*. Fire can be extinguished by water, but the suffering resulting from robbing from a *brāhmaṇa* can destroy a whole dynasty:

brahma-svaṁ duranujñātaṁ
bhuktaṁ hanti tri-pūruṣam
prasahya tu balād bhuktaṁ
daśa pūrvān daśāparān
(*Śrīmad Bhāgavatam* 10.64.35)

"If a person enjoys a *brāhmaṇa's* property without first receiving due permission, that illicit behavior destroys three generations of his family. Even worse, if he takes it by force or gets the government or other outsiders to help him usurp it, then ten generations of his ancestors and ten generations of his descendants will be destroyed."

rājāno rāja-lakṣmyāndhā nātma-pātaṁ vicakṣate
nirayaṁ ye 'bhimanyante brahma-svaṁ sādhu bāliśāḥ
(*Śrīmad Bhāgavatam* 10.64.36)

"If a king, blinded due to being falsely proud of his power or wealth, thinks it appropriate to usurp the belongings of a *brāhmaṇa*, he in fact invites hell. Such a fool cannot foresee his own downfall."

gṛhṇanti yāvataḥ pāṁśūn krandatām aśru-bindavaḥ
viprāṇāṁ hṛta-vṛttīnāṁ vadānyānāṁ kuṭumbinām
rājāno rāja-kulyāś ca tāvato 'bdān niraṅkuśāḥ
kumbhī-pākeṣu pacyante brahma-dāyāpahāriṇaḥ
sva-dattāṁ para-dattāṁ vā brahma-
vṛttiṁ harec ca yaḥ,
ṣaṣṭi-varṣa-sahasrāṇi viṣṭhāyāṁ jāyate kṛmiḥ
na me brahma-dhanaṁ bhūyād
yad gṛdhvālpāyuṣo narāḥ,
parājitāś cyutā rājyād bhavanty udvejino 'hayaḥ
(*Śrīmad Bhāgavatam* 10.64.37-40)

"If a king loots money from generous *brāhmaṇas* who have dependent families, and if those *brāhmaṇas* grieve and cry, the king and his royal family will have to suffer in the hell known as Kumbhīpāka for the number of years equivalent to the number of dust particles wetted by the *brāhmaṇas'* tears dropped to the earth. More so, if a person steals a *brāhmaṇa's* property, gifted by his own self or by someone else, he will take birth as a worm in feces for sixty thousand years. People who desire to take possession of a *brāhmaṇa's* wealth become short-lived and bring about their own ruin. They lose their kingdoms and become snakes that cause anxiety to others."

The *Mahābhārata* (*Anuśāsna-parva*, Chapter 70) also gives a description of King Nṛga. There is no difference between the accounts given in *Mahābhārata* and *Śrīmad Bhāgavatam*. It is known from the description in the *Mahābhārata* that when Nṛga was falling down to earth, he heard Dharmarāja saying, "Lord Vāsudeva will deliver you. After one thousand years, the fruits of your sins will be redeemed, and you will go to the eternal planets."

At the end of this narration Lord Vāsudeva says, "It is not proper to take away the wealth of a *brāhmaṇa* knowingly. It destroys truth, just as a *brāhmaṇa's* cow brought about downfall and suffering to King Nṛga."

yaḥ sva-dattāṁ parair dattāṁ hareta sura-viprayoḥ
vṛttiṁ sa jāyate viḍ-bhug varṣāṇām ayutāyutam
(*Śrīmad Bhāgavatam* 11.27.54)

"Anyone who steals the property of the demigods or the *brāhmaṇas*, whether originally given to them by himself or someone else, must live as a worm in stool for one hundred million years."

King Yayāti

Mahārāja Yayāti was born in the Candra-vaṁśa (Lunar Dynasty) and was the second of the six sons of Mahārāja Nāhuṣa. The life of Mahārāja Yayāti has been described in the *Rāmāyaṇa*, *Mahābhārata*, *Śrīmad Bhāgavatam* and *Viṣṇu Purāṇa*. Mahārāja Nāhuṣa turned into a snake and fell down to the Dvaita Forest due to the curse of Sage Agastya. His eldest son renounced the world, and thus his second son, Yayāti, took the reins of the kingdom into his own hands. Although he belonged to the warrior class (*kṣatriya*), he married Devayānī, the daughter of the *brāhmaṇa* Śukrācārya. This unusual incident is described in the *Ādi-parva* of the *Mahābhārata*, wherein the episode of Kaca and Devayānī is given. A brief summary is as follows:

The demigods sent Kaca, the son of Bṛhaspati, to Śukrācārya to learn the technique of *mṛta-sañjīvanī* (reviving the dead) but when the demons learned about this plan, they killed Kaca and fed him to the dogs and wolves. Śukrācārya then used this *mṛta-sañjīvanī* technique to revive him but the demons dissected and burned him again, and finally threw his ashes into the ocean. However, upon Devayānī's request, Śukrācārya again brought Kaca back to life, thereby greatly incensing the demons, who killed Kaca one more time and burned his body, but this time they mixed his ashes with wine. They then offered this concoction to Śukrācārya, who unknowingly drank it. Kaca came back to life in the stomach of Śukrācārya, who revived him again upon the request of his daughter Devayānī. Kaca informed Śukrācārya that he was in his stomach. Since there was no way out, Śukrācārya taught Kaca the technique of *mṛta-sañjīvanī* and told him to come out by dissecting his (Śukrācārya's) stomach, and to revive him afterward using the technique he had learned. Kaca did everything he was told and accepted Śukrācārya as his spiritual master, serving him along with his daughter Devayānī, sincerely and single-mindedly for a long time. Both Śukrācārya and Devayānī were pleased with his loving service and became very fond of him. When Devayānī put forth a marriage proposal to Kaca, he turned her down because he thought this to be unethical. Upon being refused, Devayānī became furious and hence cursed him by saying, "The *mṛta-sañjīvanī* you have learned will be fruitless!" Kaca countered her by saying, "I accept your curse, but this technique will bear fruit when used by someone trained in it by me, and you will not get a *brāhmaṇa* husband." By the Lord's arrangement, it was Kaca's curse that forced Devayānī to marry Yayāti of the warrior class.

In the 9th Canto, 18th Chapter, of *Śrīmad Bhāgavatam*, the circumstances under which Devayānī married King Yayāti are described as follows:

One day, Śarmiṣṭhā, the daughter of Vṛṣaparvā (king of the demons), and Devayānī, the daughter of Śukrācārya (spiritual master of the demons), along with hundreds of their girlfriends, were strolling in an extremely beautiful and magnificent garden where bumblebees were hovering around trees laden with flowers. Having spotted a nice pond, they took off their clothes and entered the water. While playing in the pond, the girls suddenly saw Lord Śiva passing by, seated on the back of his bull, along with his wife Pārvatī. Ashamed of being naked in front of Lord Śiva, the girls quickly came out of the water and covered themselves with their garments. However, unknowingly, Śarmiṣṭhā took Devayānī's clothes, and for this inappropriate action Devayānī insulted Śarmiṣhta by saying, "You have put on my dress just like a dog snatching clarified butter meant for use in a sacrifice. We are among the qualified *brāhmaṇas*, who are accepted as the face of the Supreme Personality of Godhead. We are of those who always keep the Absolute Truth within the core of their hearts and instruct those following the path of good fortune—the path of Vedic civilization. They are the only worshipable objects within this world and, due to this, not only are they offered prayers and worship by the great demigods who are the directors of the various planets, but even by the Supreme Personality of Godhead Himself. We are even yet more respectable because we belong to the dynasty of Bhṛgu, whereas your father, being among the demons, is our disciple. Therefore, how dare you wear my clothes? You are forbidden even to touch our clothes, just as a *śūdra* is forbidden to touch the *Vedas*."

Upon hearing Devayani's cruel words, Śarmiṣṭhā became very angry and replied, "You beggar, without understanding your position, you unnecessarily talk so much. Did not all of you wait at our door, depending on us for your livelihood like crows? Now I will teach you a lesson!" Having spoken these spiteful words, Śarmiṣṭhā then took away Devayānī's garments, pushed her into a well and left her there.

Meanwhile, by providence, King Yayāti, who was on a hunting trip nearby, went to that well to drink some water and spotted Devayānī inside it. Seeing Devayānī naked in the well, King Yayāti immediately handed her his own upper cloth and, being very kind to her, lifted her out. Using words saturated with love and affection, Devayānī said to King Yayāti, "O great hero, you have accepted my hand. Let me not be touched by others, for our relationship

as husband and wife has been made possible by God's arrangement and not by any human being. Kaca, the son of the learned scholar Bṛhaspati, cursed me by saying that I would not get a *brāhmaṇa* for a husband. Therefore, O mighty-armed one, our relationship has been arranged by providence." Because this type of marriage (*pratiloma*— between a man from the warrior class and a woman from the priestly class) is not sanctioned by the scriptures King Yayāti did not like it, but because it was arranged by providence and he was attracted by Devayānī's beauty, he accepted her request. Thereafter, when the learned king returned to his palace, Devayānī returned home crying and told everything to her father, Śukrācārya. Upon hearing this, his mind became very much aggrieved due to having to deal with such mundane affairs, and he condemned the profession of priesthood while praising the profession of *uñcha-vṛtti* (collecting grains from the fields). He then left home with his daughter to go to the palace of Vṛṣaparvā, the father of Śarmiṣṭhā.

Afraid of being cursed by his spiritual master Śukrācārya, the king of demons, Vṛṣaparvā, met him on the way and fell at his feet, begging for forgiveness. Śukrācārya calmed down and told the demon king, "It is not possible for me to ignore my daughter's plight, and so it will be very beneficial for you to fulfill Devayānī's desire." Vṛṣaparvā thus asked Devayānī, "What is your desire?" She told him, "Śarmiṣṭhā and her friends must accompany me as my maidservants whenever and wherever I marry by the order of my father." Vṛṣaparvā was aware that Śukrācārya's displeasure would bring danger, and that his pleasure would bring material gain. Therefore, in order to please Śukrācārya and his daughter, he readily surrendered his own daughter Śarmiṣṭhā and her thousand friends to Devayānī as her maidservants.

When Śukrācārya married Devayānī to Mahārāja Yayāti, he noticed that since Śarmiṣṭhā was a princess, she had the ability to lure the king toward her, so he cautioned Yayāti not to become romantically involved with Śarmiṣṭhā. Though Śarmiṣṭhā was serving Devayānī as a maidservant, she felt like revolting against her. She was waiting for an appropriate opportunity to seduce Yayāti, and that moment came when Devayānī gave birth to a son. Upon seeing Devayānī with a nice son, Śarmiṣṭhā approached King Yayāti and requested him to have a son with her. Yayāti was cautious due to Śukrācārya's warning, but he fulfilled her desire by considering her request to be the will of God. Devayānī gave birth to two sons: Yadu and Turvasu, and Śarmiṣṭhā gave birth to three sons: Druhya, Anu and Pūru. When Devayānī learned that her husband was also the father of Śarmiṣṭhā's sons, Devayānī became frenzied with extreme anger and returned to her father. Out of fear of Śukrācārya's wrath, King Yayāti followed her in an attempt to make her stay, but failed to appease her. After learning from his daughter what had happened, Śukrācārya cursed Yayāti to become old, weak and ugly. However, despite this, Yayāti stayed humble and respectfully said to Śukrācārya, "This curse will deprive Devayānī more than me." Realizing the adverse affects of the curse, Śukrācārya blessed the king that, by his own desire, he would be able to regain his youth by exchanging his old age for someone else's youth. After receiving blessings from Śukrācārya, King Yayāti approached his eldest son, Yadu, and asked him for his youth, but he refused by stating that one cannot detach one's self from material comforts without getting a chance to enjoy them. Yayāti then asked Turvasu, Druhya and Anu to exchange their youth for his old age but, due to a lack of education in religious principles along with the misconception that their youth would be everlasting and the only means of experiencing pleasure, they all refused. In the end, Yayāti made this proposal to his youngest and most virtuous son, Pūru. Considering the order of his father to be his first priority, he agreed and said, "It is proper to obey one's father, as one is known to be the most virtuous son if he fulfills his desires without being asked. One who fulfills his father's desires when asked to do so is known as a decent son (neither the best, nor the worst), but the son who performs his duty irreverently is the worst. However, one who refuses his father's order is considered to be his father's stool." Thus, Pūru happily accepted the old age of his father. King Yayāti began enjoying his pursuits with his regained youth, and became the ruler of the entire earth planet, consisting of seven islands. He took care of his people just as a father cares for his sons. Devayānī always engaged herself to please him by various means. Yayāti performed grand fire sacrifices, during which he donated large sums of money in charity in order to offer his prayers unto Lord Hari. Nevertheless, he was not satisfied, even after enjoying all varieties of material pleasure for a thousand years.

After enjoying the sensuousness of women and other material pastimes for a long time, he eventually realized that all those pleasures and comforts were but momentary and abominable. When he finally renounced all material luxuries after realizing the folly of them, he made up a story of a goat couple, based on his own actions, and narrated that story to his wife as follows:

"A he-goat was wandering in a forest in search of his favorite foodstuff when he saw a she-goat stuck in a well. He pulled her out of the well, inspired by his own desire to enjoy her. The she-goat accepted him as her husband, and after some time, when the she-goat saw her husband with another she-goat, she became very envious. Thus she immediately left him and went to her previous master, a *brāhmaṇa*. When the *brāhmaṇa* learned about the ill treatment his she-goat had received, he disabled the sexual ability of the he-goat, but later for the sake of his own interest the *brāhmaṇa* restored the he-goat's sexual power. That he-goat then resumed enjoying all sorts of sensuality with his wife for many years, but was still not satisfied." After relating this story to Devayānī, the king explained, "I was almost like that he-goat. All material foodstuffs, gold, jewels, women, money or any other objects cannot fulfill and satisfy one's desires. Rather, one's desires will only ever increase by trying to fulfill them:

na jātu kāmaḥ kāmānām upabhogena śāmyati
haviṣā kṛṣṇa-vartmeva bhūya evābhivardhate
(*Śrīmad Bhāgavatam* 9.19.14)

"Just as adding *ghee* (clarified butter) to a fire does not extinguish the fire, but instead increases it more and more, so the endeavor to satisfy one's lusty desires by continuously fulfilling them can never be successful"

When a man is free from envy and does not desire ill fortune for anyone, he is equipoised. To such a person, everything appears to be blissful. Those who seek true happiness give up sense gratification promptly, understanding it to be the cause of extreme distress. Otherwise, even when one has become an invalid due to old age, one will still be unable to give up one's desire for sense gratification. The senses of a lusty person can destroy him or her at any moment. Therefore, one who desires actual happiness must give up such insatiable desires, which are the cause of all tribulations:

mātrā svasrā duhitrā vā nāviviktāsano
bhavet balavān indriya-grāmo vidvāṁsam api karṣati
(*Śrīmad Bhāgavatam* 9.19.17)

"One should not even allow oneself to sit on the same seat as one's own mother, sister or daughter because sense attraction is so strong that even one who is very advanced in knowledge may become agitated by lusty desires."

King Yayāti's desires were not fulfilled even after a thousand years of enjoying sense gratification. On the contrary, his hunger for fulfillment only increased. The path of passion is not the path of peace. After experiencing the truth, he renounced the world and engaged himself in remembering the pastimes of the Lord. One who has abandoned striving for material happiness knows that, whether good or bad, in this life or the next, on this planet or the heavenly planets, it is temporary and full of suffering. Such a person is understood to be an *ātmārāma* (one who takes pleasure in *ātmā*—the soul). One should always remember that perishable material objects are the cause of bondage to the material world.

Thus, Mahārāja Yayāti preached to his wife accordingly and took back his old age from his youngest son, Pūru. King Yayāti gave the southeast to his son Druhyu, the south to his son Yadu, the west to his son Turvasu and the north to his son Anu. In this way, he divided the kingdom and Pūru was crowned as the king of all wealth and treasures of the earth. After having divided his kingdom among his sons in a satisfactory way, Yayāti renounced the world and left for the forest to perform penance. Though accustomed to a luxurious life, and having enjoyed worldly pleasures for many years, Yayāti did not hesitate even for a moment to renounce the world. He performed severe penance and became an associate of God. Devayānī understood the purport of her husband's comic narrative of the goats.

Therefore, she also decided to renounce the world by giving up all her worldly comforts, taking them to be objects of illusion, and devoted herself totally to Kṛṣṇa. In this mood, she eventually left her mortal body.

The *Ādi-parva* of *Mahābhārata* also illustrates the story of King Yayāti. The story is given in detail in Chapters 76 through 86. Unfortunately, it is not possible to discuss all the details in this present brief composition, but what follows are specific excerpts of those chapters deemed worthy of the reader's attention:

Śarmiṣṭhā said, "Your father is a bard of demons who continually sings and begs. He accepts donations, whereas others glorify my father, who gives alms and never accepts anything from anyone." When Śukrācārya learned from Devayānī of these harsh words that Śarmiṣṭhā had spoken to her, he consoled her by saying, "You are neither the daughter of one who begs and accepts charity nor the daughter of one who glorifies others—you are the daughter of a person who should actually be glorified. I have enormous strength and control all the objects of heaven and earth. One who tolerates all blasphemy can rule or control the whole world and one who conquers his anger by applying forgiveness is best among men." However, Devayānī was not satisfied with her father's reassurance. Thus, she challenged him by saying, "It is not justified to excuse a disciple who does not behave like a disciple."

Śukrācārya, the best among the Bhṛgus, went to Vṛṣaparvā and told him, "The fruits of bad *karma* (action) or sin may not be immediate, but the consequences of such activity must definitely be faced at some point in time. When one eats bad or unhealthy food, one will fall ill, if not immediately, then after some time. Similarly, the unjust actions or sins of parents may not affect the parents themselves, but will definitely punish their sons and grandsons. You have killed the son of Bṛhaspati, Kaca, who was a righteous and pious servitor of his own master—an innocent *brāhmaṇa*. As a consequence of this sin, Devayānī almost died today due to the instrumental role of Śarmiṣṭhā." After listening to Śukrācārya, Vṛṣaparvā took his words as if Śukrācārya would unleash demons, so he satisfied him with humble words and prayers that succeeded in changing Śukrācārya's plan.

Devayānī adopted various methods to seduce Yayāti into accepting her as his wife, but did not succeed. He told her, "A *brāhmaṇa's* anger is more harmful and deadly than the sharpest sword, and more poisonous than a cobra's poison. A sword or a snake's poison can kill only one person, but a *brāhmaṇa's* wrath can destroy whole kingdoms and dynasties. Therefore, I cannot accept you as my wife unless your father, Śukrācārya, betroths you to me." When Devayānī heard the king's reasons for not marrying her, she spoke to her father, who immediately came to give away Devayānī in marriage to King Yayāti. He asked the king to accept Devayānī as his wife, and so the king agreed under the condition that Śukrācārya would grant him a boon. He requested, "Please grant that the impious act between a low-caste person and a high-caste person will not affect me."[7] After many years of married life, Devayānī became pregnant and gave birth to a son. Śarmiṣṭhā also decided to accept King Yayāti as her husband, as she was still unmarried. King Yayāti explained to her that Śukrācārya had cautioned him from engaging in such an act, but she seduced him by stating various scriptural references and explaining logically that under

7 *varṇa-saṅkara*—children born out of a union forbidden by the scriptures, i.e., the union of a low-caste male and high caste female.

special circumstances one may lie. Thus, in the name of *dharma* (religious principles), King Yayāti fulfilled her wish. In the *Mahābhārata* it is mentioned that, later, King Yayāti went on a hunting trip, and once more approached the same well in the forest from which he had pulled out Devayānī, while looking to quench his thirst during an earlier hunting excursion. This time he saw Devayānī accompanied by Śarmiṣṭhā and her two thousand maidservants. He asked them who they were, so Devayānī told him about herself and Śarmiṣṭhā in brief. The king said his name was Yayāti and that, as he had been hunting for a long time, he felt thirsty and thus had come there to quench his thirst. Then, as the king was about to leave, Devayānī approached him and proposed that he should accept her as his wife, along with her two thousand girlfriends and maidservant Śarmiṣṭhā. The latter happenings have already been narrated.

According to the *Śrīmad Bhāgavatam*, Devayānī learned about the sons of Śarmiṣṭhā from her husband, but the *Mahābhārata* differs here. As per the *Mahābhārata*, Devayānī saw three heavenly looking children playing with King Yayāti while she was taking a stroll in a forest. Wondering who those boys were, she asked her husband, "My dear husband, who are those princely looking boys you are playing with? Their appearance is very similar to yours." When the king did not reply, she asked the boys their names, the name of their father and that of his dynasty.

The children instantly pointed toward the king and told her that their mother was Śarmiṣṭhā. Then they ran toward the king playfully, but found that the king was morose and did not respond to them. They began to cry and ran to their mother. As Devayānī had observed the loving exchange between the children and their father, she understood everything and felt sad. The further narration of the *Mahābhārata* and the *Śrīmad Bhāgavatam* is similar. The *Mahābhārata* defines Śukrācārya's curse as: "O righteous King! You have considered unrighteousness as a virtue. Therefore, may that most dreaded old age conquer you soon." When King Yayāti said that he did this not to satisfy his lust but to fulfill the obligation of *dharma*, Śukrācārya answered that still he should have taken permission from him. He furthermore told the king that it is incorrect to lie about *dharma*.

In the *Mahābhārata* we also find details of the coronation of Pūru as follows:

Mahārāja Yayāti addressed a gathering of *brāhmaṇas*, distinguished citizens and ministers, saying, "I am not going to give my kingdom to my eldest sons, as they did not obey me. If a son acts against his father's wishes, he is not considered to be a son. However, the son who is humble and obeys his mother and father, while working for their welfare, is the true son. Yadu, Turvasu, Druhya and Anu did not obey me, whereas Pūru did. Though being the youngest, Pūru is actually the appropriate heir to my kingdom. Śukrācārya has also instructed me to appoint him." The descendants of Yadu, Turvasu, Anu and Pūru are known as Yādava, Bhoja, Mleccha and Paurava respectively. From the *Mahābhārata* it is known that, after relinquishing his position as the ruler and by crowning Pūru as king and heir to the throne, Mahārāja Yayāti resided in heaven for a few days. This was possible due to the result of the pious fruits he had accumulated while performing penance. During his stay in heaven, Indra once asked him who else was as powerful as he (Yayāti). Yayāti then replied that there was no one else as powerful as himself among the humans, Gandharvas, demigods and saints. Upon hearing such a proud and egotistical statement, Indra told him that with those words he had insulted them all, and was therefore unworthy of remaining in heaven. Thus, Indra directed him to leave heaven, after which King Yayāti prayed to Indra, "I am not worried about leaving heaven, but please allow me to stay in the company of sages and devotees." Indra gave his consent. The sage Aṣṭaka[8] saw Yayāti while Yayāti was being removed from heaven due to Indra's curse, and asked him, "Who are you, and why have you been expunged from heaven?" Yayāti told him in all earnestness that he had insulted all living beings and thus had fallen down from heaven. A brief summary of the long discussions held between Yayāti and the followers of Aṣṭaka is as follows:

Yayāti said, "An older person is worthy of respect by the *brāhmaṇas*." Aṣṭaka replied, "The scriptures confirm that a person who is more learned and has performed more penance deserves respect from *brāhmaṇas*." Yayāti then countered by saying, "One may feel proud after becoming learned or performing severe penance, and that pride will surely take one to hell. Wise persons are never proud of themselves. I have been ejected from heaven because of my pride. I accumulated enough pious fruits to stay there, but all of them were destroyed by my pride. A wise person will learn a lesson by examining my life." Thus, Mahārāja Yayāti discussed many topics with the followers of Aṣṭaka. Those who might be keen to learn more about this topic are kindly requested to study this portion of the *Mahābhārata* relating these events. Aṣṭaka asked Yayāti to return to heaven on the basis of the fruits accumulated by his pious deeds, but he refused. Yayāti had many discussions with King Śibi as well. Śibi proposed to give the fruits of his pious deeds to Yayāti for his return to heaven, but Yayāti declined the offer. Aṣṭaka's followers became curious when they saw Yayāti reject the offer. They asked Yayāti who he was and who his father was. They further told him that no one on this earth, whether a *brāhmaṇa* or a *kṣatriya*, could perform the kind of act that he had performed. By way of introduction, Yayāti told them he was the son of Nāhuṣa and the father of Pūru. His name was Yayāti, the ruler of earth. Aṣṭaka and the followers of Aṣṭaka were his nearest and dearest, as he was their maternal grandfather. Yayāti further told them that all the saints and planets might become worthy of being worshiped by virtue of their determination to uphold truth only. Then Yayāti took leave from his grandsons and left for heaven, as the glory of his pious actions became known throughout the universe. Everyone's problems may be resolved by reading about this story of Yayāti. In the Saṁhitās (stanzas) of the *Ṛg Veda*, Yayāti's life story is given:

manuṣyavadagneḥ aṅgirāśvādamgiro
yayāti vat pūrvavachuche
(*Ṛg Veda* 1.31.17)

8 Aṣṭaka was a pious king whose father was Viśvāmitra. Yayāti's daughter Mādhavi was his mother. Thus, Yayāti was Aṣṭaka's maternal grandfather. (*New Bengali Dictionary*, by Āśutoṣa)

King Śāntanu

tataś cākrodhanas tasmād devātithir amuṣya ca
ṛkṣas tasya dilīpo 'bhūt pratīpas tasya cātmajaḥ
devāpiḥ śāntanus tasya bāhlīka iti cātmajāḥ
pitṛ-rājyaṁ parityajya devāpis tu vanaṁ gataḥ
abhavac chāntanū raja prāṅ mahābhiṣa-saṁjñitaḥ
yaṁ yaṁ karābhyāṁ spṛśati jīrṇaṁ yauvanam eti saḥ
śāntim āpnoti caivāgryāṁ karmaṇā tena śāntanuḥ
(*Śrīmad Bhāgavatam* 9.22.11-14)

"From Ayutāyu came a son named Akrodhana, and his son was Devātithi. The son of Devātithi was Ṛkṣa, the son of Ṛkṣa was Dilīpa and the son of Dilīpa was Pratīpa. The sons of Pratīpa were Devāpi, Śāntanu and Bāhlīka. Devāpi left the kingdom of his father and went to the forest. Therefore, Śāntanu became the king. Śāntanu, who in his previous birth was known as Mahābhiṣa, had the ability to transform anyone's body from old age to youth simply by the touch of his hands. Since he bestowed peace or calm upon all, he became known as Śāntanu."

Once, there was no rainfall in the kingdom for twelve years, so the king consulted his learned *brāhmaṇa* advisors, who told him, "This is your fault, since you are enjoying the property of your elder brother. For the elevation of your kingdom and home, you should return the kingdom to him." As such, keeping the welfare of the citizens in mind, Śāntanu went to the forest to convince his brother to reign over the kingdom, but his head-minister Aśvavāra undertook a shrewd endeavor to try and retain Śāntanu as king.

To prevent Devāpi from taking over the kingdom, Aśvavāra devised a plan and sent some learned *brāhmaṇas* to meet with Devāpi before Śāntanu could reach him, so as to make Devāpi unfit for kingship. Convinced by the advice of the *brāhmaṇas*, Devāpi thwarted the request of Śāntanu. According to the Vedic injunctions, this disqualified Devāpi from being the rightful heir to the throne. Under these circumstances, Śāntanu again became the king and Indra, being pleased, showered rains. The *Ādi-parva* of *Mahābhārata* gives a detailed description of Mahārāja Śāntanu. A synopsis of this is as follows:

In Dvāpara-yuga, Śāntanu was the famous twenty-first king of Hastināpura, who belonged to the Lunar Dynasty. His father was King Pratīpa and his mother was Sunandini, the daughter of Śevyarāja. In his previous birth, King Śāntanu was the famous King Mahābhiṣa who was born in the dynasty of King Ikṣvāku. He had performed one thousand *aśvamedha-yajñas* as well as one hundred *rājasūya-yajñas* and, as a result of these *yajñas,* had attained Brahmāloka, the abode of Lord Brahmā. Once upon a time, many demigods and sages, along with King Mahābhiṣa, were gathered near Lord Brahmā when the demigoddess Gaṅgā arrived. As she approached the assembly, her upper garment blew away due to a strong wind. Everyone in the assembly felt embarrassed and lowered their heads, but King Mahābhiṣa shamelessly continued to stare at her. Brahmā did not like this and cursed him, saying, "Leave this place and take birth on Mṛtyuloka (planet of death—earth)!" However, upon receiving this curse, Mahābhiṣa requested Brahmā for the favor that he might be born as the son of King Pratīpa, to which Brahmā agreed.

Gaṅgādevī felt attracted toward Mahābhiṣa. She kept thinking about him and along the way, she met the Eight Vasus, namely Dhruva, Soma, Anala, Anila, Dhāra, Pratyūṣa, Prabhāva and Aha (Dyau). According to the *Mahābhārata*, Ganadeva cursed these Vasus to take human forms. Vaśiṣṭha, the son of the demigod Varuṇa, was, like the well known Āpava, the *manasā-putra* (son born from the mind's desire) of Lord Brahmā, and one of the Sapta-ṛṣis (Seven Sages). Cursed by Nimi, Vaśiṣṭha lost his body but, by Brahmā's instructions, he was born again as the son of Varuṇa and Mitra.

He had his hermitage on one side of the great mountain, Sumeru, which was a most pleasant place. The wish-fulfilling cow, Kāma-dhenu, was born from a *surabhi* cow with the co-operation of Sage Kaśyapa. Sage Vaśiṣṭha accepted Kāma-dhenu as *homa-dhenu.*[9] She was free to graze

9 The cow whose milk is used exclusively for *homa*, or fire offerings to the gods.

and move around the beautiful surroundings of Tapovana, the place of performing penances.

Once upon a time, the Eight Vasus were wandering there with their wives. When one of them, Dyau, learned about the glory of Kāma-dhenu from his wife, he abducted the cow along with her calf. Vaśiṣṭha searched for Kāma-dhenu but could not locate her, so he used his mystical powers to see that the Vasus had abducted her. He cursed the Eight Vasus to take birth on the earth planet. The sons of Vasu apologized and prayed for mercy, which pleased the sage, who said, "You will be relieved of this curse within a year of your birth but, because of his faulty actions, Dyau will have to live for a very long time as a human and will not be able to have any children. However, he will be pious and learned, with a predisposition to always work to please his father."

Due to the curse of Brahmā, King Mahābhiṣa took birth as Śāntanu, the second son of King Pratīpa, who ruled the entire earth. Once, the great king, Pratīpa, was performing austerities on the banks of the Gaṅgā. Suddenly Gaṅgādevī emerged from her waters and sat on the right part of his lap. He did not accept her as his wife but as his daughter-in-law, so he told her that she should accept his son as her husband. As destiny has its ways, Mother Gaṅgā met the accursed Eight Vasus. They told Gaṅgādevī about the curse and requested her to enable them to be born of her, and then drown them in her waters immediately after birth, so that they would be liberated. That is why Mother Gaṅgā drowned all her sons except Dyau in her waters, as per the instructions of Sage Vaśiṣṭha. Dyau, while appearing as the son of Śāntanu, became famous as Devavrata and Gāṅgeya.

Once upon a time, Śāntanu, while hunting along the banks of River Gaṅgā, stumbled upon a very beautiful maiden, whose looks enchanted him. As per destiny, he was attracted to her and expressed his desire to take her as his wife. Remembering the prayers of the Vasus, Gaṅgādevī was pleased, and replied that her consent depended on the condition that the king was not to question her activities, whether good or bad. Furthermore, should the king object to any of her activities, she would immediately leave him.

The king agreed to her terms and they were wed. The king was pleased by her kindness and devotion to him. In due course of time, eight sons were born of Gaṅgādevī and Śāntanu. However, the queen would immediately throw her newborn sons into the river after their birth, drowning them all, which made the king feel highly offended in his heart. Despite this, being bound by his promise, he could not question Gaṅgā.

When Mother Gaṅgā had thrown seven sons into the river, Śāntanu felt so upset and angry that, when the eighth son was born, he could not tolerate the situation any further and stopped Gaṅgā, thereby saving the child. It was the arrangement of providence that he had not stopped her earlier. Unable to drown her eighth son, she addressed the king, "I will not kill this son of yours, but as you have broken your promise, I will not live with you. I am Gaṅgā, the daughter of Sage Jahnu. I married you to fulfill the desire of the demigods. Your sons are not ordinary human beings; they are the Eight Vasus who were born as humans due to a curse of Sage Vaśiṣṭha. Nevertheless, no persons other than us were eligible to be their parents. You have attained eternal glory by having the Eight Vasus as your sons. I promised them that I would liberate them from their human bodies immediately after birth. That is why I drowned them. However, due to my request, and as desired by Vaśiṣṭha, the eighth son shall live with you and you shall raise him. This child has a one eighth part of each of the Vasus."

Thereafter, Mother Gaṅgā disappeared along with Śāntanu's son. On earth, this eighth Vasu was known as Dyau, Śāntanu's son Devavrata, or Gāṅgeya. Mahārāja Śāntanu became very sad after the disappearance of Gaṅgā and his son.

One day, Mahārāja Śāntanu, while hunting and managing to strike a deer with his arrow, reached the bank of River Bhāgīrathī. Upon his approach, he was amazed to find that a colossal, charming prince had blocked the flow of river water with a net of arrows. He saw Gaṅgā there, so he asked her who the prince was. She replied, "O King! He is the same eighth son who was born out of your union with me. He has become exceptionally proficient in weaponry and well versed in the *Vedas*, so please accept your offspring now." King Śāntanu accepted and took his son back to his kingdom, where he made him the prince.

One day, King Śāntanu saw an extremely beautiful girl as he was walking along the banks of River Yamunā, so he asked her who she was. She told him that she was the daughter of Dhivara Rāja (King of Fishermen), and that she had come there to sail as per the instructions of her father. Thereafter, the king approached her father and introduced himself. He then expressed his desire to take Dhivara Rāja's daughter as his wife. Her father agreed on the condition that the king would give his kingdom to the son born from her womb, thereby depriving his first son of this privilege. This inappropriate condition confused the king and he became morose, as he really desired to have this woman as his wife, yet the idea of depriving his first son of inheriting the kingdom seemed unbefitting to him. The learned Devavrata was a very intelligent boy, so therefore he observed the moroseness of his father and asked him for the reason for his worries. When he learned the exact cause of his father's apprehension, Devavrata immediately went to Dhivara Rāja and requested him to hand over his daughter Satyavatī to the king. Dhivara Rāja said, "O Devavrata! Mahārāja Śāntanu wants to marry my daughter, but he is worried that no other woman can give birth to a son as brave and intelligent as you. Therefore, if you become unhappy and angry about this issue, the son born from his other wife, whether he be a demigod or a man, a celestial singer or a demon, will be unable to sustain his life." After a long discussion, Dhivara Rāja said that he would not agree to the proposal unless he was fully assured that the son born from the union between his daughter and the king would become the next ruler, and would have no threat from Devavrata or any other son born to him.

Understanding the feelings of Dhivara Rāja, and for the happiness of his father, Devavrata, the son of Mother Gaṅgā, took an oath in the presence of warriors and Dhivara Rāja, saying, "O Dhivara Rāja! Only the son born to your daughter will become king and, to eliminate the possibility of my son becoming king, I shall observe celibacy and never marry." After this, King Śāntanu married the daughter of Dhivara Rāja, Satyavatī, who was also known as Yojanagandha (she whose fragrance could be smelled over the span of a *yojana* – approx. 8 miles). From that day onward, Devavrata came to be known as Bhīṣma, a name given to him by the sages and demigods because he took such an obstinate (*bhīṣham*) oath.

In due course of time, two brave sons named Citrāṅgada and Vicitravīrya were born to Satyavatī from Śāntanu. Bhīṣma enthroned Citrāṅgada as king, but he died in a war with Gandharva Rāja, so Vicitravīrya was crowned king:

dekhah sāntoyā grāma-kuṇḍa sunirmala
śāntanu munir tapasyara sthala
(*Bhakti-ratnākara* 5.1450)

dekhaha 'sāntoyā' nama grāma shobha kare
etha śāntanu muni āradhe kṛṣṇere
(*Bhakti-ratnākara* 5.1404)

During circumambulation of the 84 *krośas* of Śrī Vrajamandala, organized by Śrī Caitanya Gauḍīya Math, our devotees visit the *kutīra* (hermitage, small hut) of Bhīṣma's father, Sage Śāntanu. In the local language, Śāntanu Kunda (pond) is known as "Santoya." Santoya is near Bahulāvana.[10]

10 Śāntanu Kunda is about three and half miles from Maholi. As one crosses the bridge of Śāntanu Kunda, one reaches the proximity of the Śāntanu Bihari temple located on a high hill, and by climbing some steps one can approach it. In this temple one can have a glimpse of Śāntanu Bihari's Kṛṣṇa deity, with Śrī Rādhikā on His left and the deities of Laddu Gopāla, Śālagrāma and Mahāvirājī. Being very old and untended, the water in Śāntanu Kunda is not fit for drinking and appears to be of green color due to being full of weeds.

King Janaka

There were two famous kings called Janaka:

The first King Janaka: The grandson of Nimi and son of Mithi or Mithilā was Janaka. He was famous as Videha Janaka and was the founder of the royal dynasty Videha. The term "Videharāja" signifies the kings of North Bihar, or Mithilā.

rāmasya kośalendrasya caritaṁ kilbiṣāpaham
nimer aṅga-parityāgo janakānāṁ ca sambhavaḥ
(*Śrīmad Bhāgavatam* 12.12.24)

"*Śrīmad Bhāgavatam* narrates the sanctifying pastimes of Lord Rāmacandra, the king of Kosala, King Nimi abandoning his material body and the birth of the descendants of King Janaka."

The second Janaka is the father of Sītā, the wife of Lord Rāma. The meaning of the name Sītā is the furrow made by a plow. When King Janaka was plowing a field, from the front of his plow (*sīra*) appeared a daughter who was thus named Sītādevī. Janaka was also known as Śīradhvaja.

The First King Janaka

In the 9th Canto of *Śrīmad Bhāgavatam*, written by Śrī Kṛṣṇa-dvaipāyana Vedavyāsa Muni, the life of Videharāja Janaka has been described and is summarized as follows:

In the dynasty of Nimi, the son of Ikṣvāku named Brahmajña (one who has knowledge and understanding of Brahman), Janaka and other sages and saintly kings appeared. Mahārāja Nimi appointed Vaśiṣtha as the head priest for a *yajña*, but the king of the demigods, Indra, had already appointed him to perform some rites elsewhere. Therefore, he went to perform

Indra's *yajña* and asked King Nimi to wait for his return. The king of Videha, Nimi, kept quiet, and since he was learned and realized the uncertainty of life, he did not wait for the return of Vaśiṣṭha and began performing the sacrifice with another head priest.

When Vaśiṣṭha returned after completing Indra's *yajña* and found that his disciple Nimi had started the *yajña* without him, he cursed him by saying, "May the material body of Nimi, who considers himself to be learned, immediately be destroyed." Being cursed without a valid reason, Nimi counter-cursed Sage Vaśiṣṭha that his body might also be destroyed.

After this altercation, the spiritually advanced Nimi gave up his body. Vaśiṣṭha followed suit and took another birth from the womb of Urvaśī, out of her union with Mitra and Varuṇa. As Nimi had left his body while performing the *yajña*, the priests performing the *yajña* preserved his body in fragrant substances and prayed to the demigods present there by saying, "If you possess divine powers and are satisfied with us, then please bring our King Nimi back to life."

The demigods gave their blessings and promptly King Nimi woke up from death and said to the assembled sages, "The wise who leave this dreadful body do not crave for bodily pleasures; they desire only to serve the lotus feet of God, so I do not desire this awful body. In water, fish and similar creatures fear larger fish. Similarly, everyone in a human or any other body will always fear death."

When they heard what King Nimi was saying, the sages became anguished, as they had just prayed to the demigods to bring Nimi back to life; yet Nimi was not keen to accept the body but rather rejected it as a source of grief and greed. As a solution to the problem, the demigods said, "Videharāja Nimi may either live in a symbolic body or as a transcendental body, on the eyelids of human beings as per his will." Considering that there might be anarchy in the kingdom without the king, the saints began to churn the body of King Nimi and, as a result, produced a son.

Since he was born under unusual circumstances, he was named Janaka. Also, because he was born from a lifeless body he was named Videha, and since he was born as a result of a churning process, he was also known as Mithi. The city established by him was known as Mithilā, and his son was Udavasu.

The kings of Videha or Mithilā-purī are celebrated with the title of Rāja Janaka. *Śrīmad Bhāgavatam* mentions that Lord Balarāma stayed at the house of King Janaka of Mithilā-purī during Dvāpara-yuga. When Duryodhana, the son of Dhṛtarāṣṭra, learned that Śrī Balarāma was not staying with Lord Kṛṣṇa, he exploited this opportunity and learned from Him various techniques and tricks of fighting with a mace.

taṁ dṛṣṭvā sahasotthāya maithilaḥ prīta-mānasaḥ
arhayāṁ āsa vidhi-vad arhaṇīyaṁ samarhaṇaiḥ
(*Śrīmad Bhāgavatam* 10.57.25)

"The king of Mithilā immediately rose from his seat when he saw Lord Balarāma approaching. With great love, the king honored Lord Balarāma by offering Him elaborate worship, as stipulated by scriptural injunctions."

Details about King Janaka are given in the *Śatapatha Brāhmaṇa* of the *Śukla Yajurveda*, *Chandogya Upaniṣad*, *Mahābhārata*, *Harivaṁśa*, *Śrīmad Bhāgavatam* and various other Vedic scriptures. According to the *Śatapatha Brāhmaṇa* he was a king of Videha or Mithilā-purī. The *Rāmāyaṇa* mentions two Janakas. One was the son of Mithi and father of Udāvasu, and the other was the son of Hrasvaromā and the father of Sītā.

The Second King Janaka

According to the *Viṣṇu Purāṇa*, Śīradhvajaḥ Janaka was a famous king belonging to the Lunar Dynasty. His father was Hrasvaromā and his son was Bhānumān.

tataḥ śīradhvajo jajñe yajñārthaṁ karṣato mahīm
sītā śīrāgrato jātā tasmāt śīradhvajaḥ smṛtaḥ
(*Śrīmad Bhāgavatam* 9.13.18)

"From Hrasvaromā came a son named Śīradhvaja (also called Janaka). When Śīradhvaja was plowing a field, from the front of his plow appeared a baby girl named Sītādevī, who later became the wife of Lord Rāmacandra. Thus, he was known as Śīradhvaja." According to the *Śrīmad Bhāgavatam*, Kuśadhvaja was the son of Śīradhvaja Janaka.

In the *Rāmāyaṇa* it is mentioned:

atha me kṛṣataḥ kṣetraṁ lāṅgalād utthitā mama
kṣetraṁ śodhayatā labdhvā nāmnā sīteti viśrutā
bhūtalād utthitā sā tu vyavardhata mamātmajā
vīryaśulketi me kanyā sthāpiteyam ayonijā
(*Vālmīki Rāmāyaṇa* 1.66.13-14)

"One day, as King Janaka was plowing the ritual field, a baby girl appeared from the front of his plow. As she had emerged from the *śīra* (furrow), people called her Sītā. She was raised as the daughter of King Janaka, and he vowed to give her in in marriage to a bridegroom of proven prowess."

After the killing of the Tāḍakā demoness, Sage Viśvāmitra went to the royal assembly of King Janaka with Rāma and Lakṣmaṇa. When Mahārāja Janaka offered his respects to Sage Viśvāmitra and asked him the purpose of his arrival, the sage asked the king to marry Sītā to Rāma. The king also wished to do the same, but he had already made the vow that, if somebody wished to marry Sītā, he would have to certify his valour. Devavrāta, the forefather of King Janaka, possessed a bow formerly used by Lord Mahādeva (Śiva), which he had acquired at the time of a fire sacrifice performed by Dakṣa. As a descendant of Devavrāta, King Janaka was in possession of that bow, which was so large and heavy that it was impossible for an ordinary person to string it. King Janaka decided that he would marry Sītā to the first person able to string Lord Mahādeva's bow. Rāmacandra learned about this difficulty with the bow of Janaka, just as He also came to know that many renowned and brave kings had failed in their attempts to perform this feat. Being the Supreme Lord Himself, Lord Rāmacandra strung the bow with the greatest of ease and even managed to effortlessly break it in two as well. King Janaka and other brave persons in his assembly were astonished to witness such a great act. When King Daśaratha received the news, he went to Videha-nagari along with his entourage. King Janaka married Sītā to Rāma during the Uttara Phalguni Nakṣatra (specific astrological alignment).

The story of King Janaka is given in the *Kalki Purāṇa* as well as the *Harivaṁśa Purāṇa*, wherein the details of Narakāsura are mentioned. As instructed by Sage Nārada, King

Janaka performed a fire sacrifice and a baby girl appeared from the site of the *yajña*. The demigoddess Bhūmi (earth) gave this beautiful baby girl to Janaka, saying, "In Treta-yuga, when a son is born to this girl after the death of Rāvaṇa, Janaka should take that son." King Janaka took care of that boy for fifteen years and nine months and then gave him to the demigoddess earth when she approached him. Demigoddess earth told the boy (Narakāsura) that King Janaka was not his actual father, but that Lord Viṣṇu in the form of Varāha was his father.

In *Devī Bhāgavatam*, wherein the details of Śukadeva Gosvāmī are given, a description of King Janaka is also found. The details about the birth of Śukadeva Gosvāmī, the son of Sage Vedavyāsa, are as follows:

A celestial dancer by the name Ghṛtācī approached Sage Vyāsadeva. Seeing her, the sage became disturbed, but the celestial beauty disappeared by assuming the form of a parrot. However, the sage was still experiencing pangs of attraction toward her, so to mitigate his passion, he rubbed two dry pieces of wood together, resulting in a fire that brought about the appearance of a beautiful baby boy. Then the demigoddess Gaṅgā-devī came there and bathed the boy herself. Celestial trumpets sounded and the demigods showered flowers. Since Ghṛtācī had disappeared in the guise of a parrot (*śuka*), the sage named his son Śukadeva. The child began to grow like a bright tongue of fire, and Sage Vyāsadeva began the performance of various rituals for his son. After the conclusion of those rituals, the child attained an understanding of the knowledge contained in the Vedic scriptures, so he accepted Bṛhaspati as his spiritual master. After completing his *brahmacarya* training period as a young celibate, Śukadeva returned to Vyāsadeva, whereupon Vyāsadeva asked him to get married. However, the extremely detached Śukadeva had no such desire to marry. Although Vyāsadeva tried in so many ways to convince him of the benefits of this, he failed. Therefore, he narrated the *Śrīmad Bhāgavatam* (the most essential scripture) to him, and then sent him to King Janaka, who convinced him to marry by his clever use of logic. Though Śukadeva agreed to marry, he nonetheless left family life behind and departed for Mount Kailāsa to perform penance.

Śukadeva from the *Devī Bhāgavatam* and from the *Śrīmad Bhāgavatam* are different persons. Śukadeva Gosvāmi, who narrated the *Śrīmad Bhāgavatam* to King Parikśit at the time of the king's death, never married.

Some of the arguments put forward by King Janaka to Śukadeva in favor of married life were as follows:

At an immature stage of *yoga* one may feel that one has full control of all one's senses. This, however, is nothing but an illusion. No one can fully control the senses, as all are engulfed by the clutches of *māyā* (external potency of the Supreme Lord). The unconquerable senses might even cause great sages to deviate from the path of righteousness. Thus, there is nothing unusual if sensual desires should subvert the objective of an adolescent. Therefore, it is healthy to marry and satisfy the senses.

It is very difficult to live alone in a forest. Such environments are populated by wild animals, and the five material elements (earth, water, fire, air and ether) are present everywhere. Where is there a place where one can avoid all mortal objects? One will also have the burden of the necessity of food in a forest. Even if someone decides to live without food, one will need a stick as well as a deerskin to cover one's body.

A person with any doubt in his mind cannot achieve stability; only a person who is without doubt can become stable. Therefore, only a truly enlightened person can remain detached from desires while living among the objects of desire.

Śrīla Bhakti Siddhānta Sarasvatī Gosvāmī Ṭhākura has professed that solitude is better than living among non-devotees, but always associating with pure devotees of the Lord is much more beneficial than living in a solitary place. While living alone one might meditate on worldly matters due to one's previous impressions, which may cause one to fall from the righteous path. On the other hand, maintaining association with pure devotees will sanctify the heart. That is why Śrīla Prabhupāda established many temples, because without the association of pure devotees, one might not realize one's actual benefit:

yaṁ pravrajantam anupetam apeta-kṛtyaṁ
dvaipāyano viraha-kātara ājuhāva
putreti tan-mayatayā taravo 'bhinedus
taṁ sarva-bhta-hṛdayaṁ munim ānato 'smi
(*Śrīmad Bhāgavatam* 1.2.2)

"When Śukadeva Gosvāmī left home to take *sannyāsa*, he left without undergoing the sacred thread ceremony or the ceremonies usually observed by the higher castes. Thus, Vyāsadeva cried out in fear of separation from him, 'O my son!' However, only the trees, which were absorbed in the same feelings of separation, echoed in response to the grieving father."

The above verse composed, by Śrī Sūta Gosvāmī, proves that Śukadeva from the *Devī Bhāgavatam* and the *Śrīmad Bhāgavatam* are not the same. That said, we might add that not everyone agrees about the authenticity of the *Devī Bhāgavatam*.

King Bharata

There are three famous *mahārājas* named Bharata, all of whom are described as follows:

There was a King Bharata who was the son of Nābhi and Ṛṣabhadeva (*śaktyāveśāvatāra*[11] of the Lord) and the oldest of their one hundred sons. India is known as Bhārata-varṣa from his name only. Earlier, this country was known as Ajanābha-varṣa.

There was another Bharata, who was a partial expansion of Lord Rāmacandra. He had all the sixty attributes of Lord Viṣṇu and is counted among the twenty-five *līlā-avatāras* and ten manifestations of Godhead, Śrī Hari. This Mahārāja Bharata, the brother of Śrī Rāma, appeared in the Solar Dynasty, whose members, in succession, are: The sun-god Vivasvān, Vaivasvata Manu, Ikṣvāku, Māndhātā, Triśaṅku, Hariścandra, Rohita, Mahārāja Sagara, Asamañjasa, Aṁśumān, Dilīpa, Bhagīratha, Aśmaka, King Bālika (Nārīkavaca), Khaṭvāṅga, Dīrghabāhu, Raghu, Aja and King Daśaratha. Śrī Bharata, the partial expansion of Godhead, was born out of the union of King Daśaratha and Kaikeyī.

The son of the famous King Duṣyanta of the Lunar Dynasty was also known as Bharata, a partial expansion of the Lord. His mother was Śakuntalā and he appeared in the hermitage of Sage Kaṇva. He exhibited extraordinary powers during childhood, so sages named him Sarvadamana (one who is able to control everyone). He is the forefather of Kuru and the Pāṇḍavas, so the Pāṇḍavas are sometimes addressed as "O Bhārata!" He was a great king

11 Empowered *avatāra*—a descent/manifestation of the Lord's extraordinary power.

and he performed many fire sacrifices like King Indra.

Jaḍa Bharata

King Bharata the son of Ṛṣabhadeva became Jaḍa later in life. He began to rule the earth following the orders of his father, who had installed him on the throne. Bharata Mahārāja married Pañcajanī, the daughter of Viśvarūpa, and ruled the citizens perfectly as father and grandfather. Mahārāja Bharata had five sons with his wife Pañcajanī. These sons were named Sumati, Rāṣṭrabhuta, Sudarśana, Āvaraṇa and Dhūmraketu.

King Bharata performed various kinds of sacrifices with great faith and offered the results to the Supreme Personality of Godhead, Vāsudeva (Lord Kṛṣṇa), for His satisfaction. Therefore, being purified by ritualistic sacrifices, the heart of Mahārāja Bharata was completely uncontaminated and his devotional service unto Vāsudeva increased day after day.

By virtue of his devotion, he learned that devotees such as Nārada always think of the transcendental form of Supreme Lord Vāsudeva within their hearts. The Lord's transcendental form is decorated with the Śrīvatsa, the Kaustubha Jewel and a flower garland. His hands hold a conchshell, disc, club and lotus flower. Destiny arranged for Mahārāja Bharata to enjoy material opulence for ten million years. When that period ended he retired from family life, divided his wealth among his sons, left his opulent paternal home and started for Pulahāśrama, which is situated in Haridvara.

The purity of the place of penance of Sage Pulaha was maintained due to the presence of River Gaṇḍakī. King Bharata lived alone in the forest and regularly offered his prayers to Lord Vāsudeva with *tulasī* leaves, water, flowers and fruits, which removed the threefold material miseries from his heart, thus allowing him to attain devotion unto the lotus feet of Lord Vāsudeva.

One day, after bathing in River Gaṇḍakī, King Bharata, while chanting the names of the Lord, saw a thirsty and pregnant deer on the banks of the river. While the deer was drinking water from the river, she heard the roar of a nearby lion and jumped across the river to save her life. She gave birth while in the air and, unfortunately, died. The newborn deer fell into the water and began drifting down the river helplessly. The king felt compassion for the fawn since it had lost its mother, so he rescued the baby deer and brought it to his hut and raised it with great care. He treated the animal with fervent affection and was cautious to protect it from wild beasts.

However, due to excessive attachment to the deer, his normal routine and daily rites were adversely affected and, in a very short time, he began to neglect all his religious duties. He developed the idea that his foremost duty was to take care of the deer, so he always meditated

on the deer while walking, eating, bathing and so on. Due to this wrongful thinking, he fell from his path of penance. He had abandoned all worldly objects and had come to the forest in order to meditate upon Lord Hari, but now he had developed intimacy with a young deer, which made him deviate from his purpose. He treated the deer like a son. One day, he could not find the deer in the house and started crying, "O deer! O deer!" and then he died. While dying he saw the young deer sitting next to him, so King Bharata grieved for him as though he were his own son. As he was thinking about the deer at the time of his death, he was given the body of a deer in his next birth.

However, despite being reborn as a deer he did not forget his past. He vividly remembered his worship of God and the fact that he had failed to attain salvation in his previous birth due to his attachment to a young deer. He grieved whenever he recalled how he had left his relatives and kingdom in order to perform penance and focus on almighty God, yet his attachment to a young deer had diverted him from his worship, causing him to take birth as a deer. He did not reveal his grief and resultant detachment to anyone, and departed from his mother and Kālañjara Mountain (where he was born as a deer) to go to the place of Sage Pulastya at Śālagrāma. There, he associated with the sages and began to wait for death. He shunned attachment to anything and anyone, fearing that bad association might result in rebirth in a lower species. He relinquished his life by entering the water of a river once he was free from the reaction of being attached to a deer.

Bharata was then reborn from the younger wife of a *brāhmaṇa*, whose lineage was that of Aṅgirāsa. He vividly recalled his previous births, and thus was wary of unfavorable association with relatives, despite being born in a *brāhmaṇa* family. He meditated upon the lotus feet of the Lord and adopted the outward appearance of a mentally deficient, deaf, dumb and blind person. Out of affection for his son, his father performed his *upanāyana* ceremony (acceptance of the sacred thread) and taught him about all the priestly procedures and rites. Bharata began to behave in such a way that his father would consider him useless, leading him to ask him to leave home. His father could not make him proficient in chanting the Gāyatri *mantra* even after four months of training and began to worry about his son's future.

When Bharata's father died, his mother left him and his sister in the custody of his stepmother and immolated herself on her husband's funeral pyre. Afterwards, his stepbrothers paid no attention to his educational needs. They were unaware of the importance of devotion toward God, and thus were unable to comprehend the covered glories of Bharata. Bharata was undisturbed by the poor behavior of mean and foolish people. Even when they made fun of him he would reply as if he were mad. He ate whatever he got for his work while receiving no monetary remuneration, and sufficed with whatever was given to him in charity. He never did anything for the satisfaction of his senses and always meditated upon God without hankering for honor, dishonor, happiness or sorrow. He was healthy and strong despite all the odds; he never wore any special clothes during the various seasons; he would sleep on the bare ground; he shunned bathing and appeared dirty and shabby even though, in his heart, he was a simple soul, pure and bright. Foolish people avoided him because of his outward appearance. He roamed around with an undisturbed mind even when insulted by hostile people, and would stay in rice fields just as his brothers had asked him to. They gave him broken rice, mustard seeds, sesame seeds, oil cake, husk and burned food. However, he ate everything as if it were nectar.

One day, the leader of a gang of dacoits (bandits) captured a man to offer to Goddess Kālī as a sacrifice so he might be blessed with a son. However, the man escaped and the dacoits went to search for him. Instead, they caught Bharata, who was protecting the rice fields from deer and pigs during the night. They bathed him, dressed him, gave him a garland made of sandalwood according to the prescribed rites, and chanted sacrificial prayers to Kālī. Then they prepared the weapon to be used for the sacrifice. Killing is permitted in specific emergency situations but the killing of a *brāhmaṇa* is always forbidden.

The impending killing of the pious and devoted Bharata was unacceptable to God. Goddess Kālī was agitated by the lustrous halo of Jaḍa Bharata. Her face turned fearsome due to extreme anger, and she emerged from her effigy while making loud laughing sounds. Beheading the dacoits with her sword, she and her devoted maids drank the blood oozing from their throats.

Those who commit violence against good and pious men suffer. God protects those devotees who seek His shelter, who are not proud of the body and who love all living beings. The pure devotees of the Lord remain undisturbed, even at the time of death.

Once, the king of the Sauvira and Sindhu region, Rahuguna, was travelling on a palanquin to the dwelling place of Sage Kapila. Upon approaching the banks of River Ikṣumatī, the chief palanquin bearer felt the need for the help of another palanquin bearer. They began looking for someone and found Bharata. They saw him as fit for the job due to his being strong, healthy and well built. They forcefully engaged him in lifting the palanquin but Bharata was unaccustomed to the work and was cautious not to crush any insects under his feet, so he was unable to keep pace with the other bearers. This made the palanquin unstable and the king uncomfortable. Rahuguna asked the bearers to be careful. The bearers were scared and told the king that it was not their fault because the instability was due to the new bearer, who was unable to keep pace with them, hence causing the king discomfort. The king was pious by nature but still he became angry. He taunted Bharata and sarcastically said, "Are you tired? It appears that you are unable to walk properly since you have walked for so long. You have become old. Is there no life left in you?" The egoless Bharata was undisturbed by the king's comment and he continued to bear the load of the palanquin on his shoulder.

When the palanquin shook again, the king became furious and shouted, "What are you doing? Do you not know anything? I am your master. You are insulting me by not obeying my orders. You seem incapable of learning

without the need for punishment!" Bharata remained equipoised with a smile on his face, and he bestowed his mercy upon the king by saying, "I am different from the body and am not the bearer of the palanquin, so I do not feel tired. Since the destination of my body is not the same as that of my soul, carrying this load is no trouble to me. My body may have physical dimensions, but I have none. Physical weakness, fatigue, mental pain, sickness, thirst, desire, fear, jealousy, passion, sleep, anger, grief, affection and so on develop when one develops a false ego. I do not identify myself with the body, so I do not have any of those feelings. I am not born and I do not die. Anything measurable has a beginning and end, so this relationship of king and servant is not everlasting. With the passing of time, it may happen that the kingdom is lost and a servant may become the king and the king may become a servant. The thought that I am a king or I am a servant falls under materialistic behavioral practice. Who is the king? Who is the servant? If I am a vagabond in this world then punishing me will be of no use, because if a mad person is punished he may become more arrogant. Also, if I am an enlightened man, then punishing me will be of no value." When he heard these wise words from Bharata, the king's false ego of being a king was nullified. He descended from the palanquin, and fell at the feet of Bharata while begging for mercy.

King Rahūgaṇa was unafraid of Indra, but he feared the contempt of a *brāhmaṇa*. He wanted to know who Bharata was, so he enquired from him whether he was the pious Sage Kapila roaming in disguise to test an individual's ability. He asked how an innocent family man, attached to material objects, could come to discern the actual nature of Bharata's esoteric glory. An offense against a pure devotee like Jaḍa Bharata can destroy anyone, even a powerful man possessing powers equivalent to Śiva.

The knowledge-filled discussions between Jaḍa Bharata and King Rahūgaṇa are narrated in detail in the 5th Canto of *Śrīmad Bhāgavatam*, Chapters 11–14. Some relevant quotations are as follows:

na yāvad etan mana ātma-liṅgaṁ
saṁsāra-tāpāvapanaṁ janasya
yac choka-mohāmaya-rāga-lobha-
vairānubandhaṁ mamatāṁ vidhatte
(*Śrīmad Bhāgavatam* 5.11.16)

"The mind is the root cause of all miseries in the material world. So long as this fact is unknown to the conditioned living entity, he has to accept the miserable condition of the material body and wander within this universe in different positions. The mind is affected by disease, lamentation, illusion, attachment, greed and enmity, and thus it creates bondage and a false sense of intimacy with the material world."

The 12th Chapter says:

rahūgaṇaitat tapasā na yāti na
cejyayā nirvapaṇād gṛhād vā
na cchandasā naiva jalāgni-sūryair
vinā mahat-pāda-rajo-'bhiṣekam
(*Śrīmad Bhāgavatam* 5.12.12)

"The perfect stage of devotional service cannot be attained unless one is blessed to bathe in the dust of the feet of great devotees. One cannot attain the Supreme Lord without the mercy of His devotees. It is never attained by *tapasya* (austerity), the Vedic process of worship, acceptance of the renounced order of life, discharge of the duties of household life, the chanting of Vedic hymns, the performance of penance in the hot sun, the performance of penance within cold water or the performance of penance near a blazing fire."

Sage Jaḍa Bharata has described in detail the fearful miseries of this world in the 13th and 14th Chapters:

rahūgaṇa tvam api hy adhvano 'sya
sannyasta-daṇḍaḥ kṛta-bhūta-maitraḥ
asaj-jitātmā hari-sevayā śitaṁ
jñānāsim ādāya tarāti-pāram
(*Śrīmad Bhāgavatam* 5.13.20)

(Sage Jaḍa Bharata said to King Rahūgaṇa,) "You are living in this material world following the path of sense gratification. Abandon acts of punishing others and make friendship with all. O King! Give up attraction to sense objects and take up the sword of knowledge sharpened by devotional service. Then, you will be able to cut the hard knot of material bondage by engaging your senses in serving Lord Hari, and will attain liberation from this material world."

kvacid āsādya gṛhaṁ dāvavat priyārtha-
vidhuram asukhodarkaṁ
śokāgninā dahyamāno bhṛśaṁ nirvedam upagacchati.
(*Śrīmad Bhāgavatam* 5.14.15)

"This world is exactly like a blazing forest fire. There is no trace of happiness in this world. Pain is the only result of all the pleasures of this world. Being entangled in material life, the conditioned soul is burned by the fire of lamentation. Sometimes he considers himself very unfortunate and sometimes he claims that he suffers because he performed no pious activities in his previous life. Thus, he always remains morose."

While describing the glory of Sage Bharata, Śukadeva Gosvāmī told King Parīkṣit that, just as a fish cannot move like Garuḍa (eagle carrier of Lord Viṣṇu), up until now no king has been able to completely follow the path laid down by Sage Bharata, the son of Ṛṣabha. A person who hears and follows the glorious and beneficial character of Bharata attains his desired fruits.

Bharata, the Son Of King Daśaratha

khaṭvāṅgād dīrghabāhuś ca raghus
tasmāt pṛthu-śravāḥ
ajas tato mahā-rājas tasmād daśaratho 'bhavat
tasyāpi bhagavān eṣa sākṣād brahmamayo hariḥ
aṁśāṁśena caturdhāgāt putratvaṁ prārthitaḥ suraiḥ
rāma-lakṣmaṇa-bharata-śatrughnā iti saṁjñayā
(*Śrīmad Bhāgavatam* 9.10.1-2)

"Dīrghabāhu was the son of Mahārāja Khaṭvāṅga, and Dīrghabāhu's son was the celebrated Mahārāja Raghu. From Mahārāja Raghu came Aja, and Aja was the father of the great personality Mahārāja Daśaratha. Being prayed for by the demigods, the Supreme Personality of Godhead appeared as Rāma along with His expansions—Lakṣmaṇa, Bharata and Śatrughna—as the four sons of Mahārāja Daśaratha."

The *Śrī Viṣṇu-dharmottara* states that Rāma, Lakṣmaṇa, Bharata and Śatrughna were *avatāras* of Vāsudeva, Saṅkarṣaṇa, Pradyumna and Aniruddha respectively. Also, the *Padma Purāṇa* states that Rāmacandra was an *avatāra* of Nārāyaṇa; and Lakṣmaṇa, Bharata and Śatrughna were respectively Śeṣa, Cakra and Śaṅkha (conchshell in the hand of Śrī Nārāyaṇa). It is further mentioned in Vālmīki's *Rāmāyaṇa* that Daśaratha was graced with these four forms of the Lord as his sons due to his performance of a *putraśreṣṭhī-yajña* under the guidance of Sage Śṛṅgi. That *yajña* was performed on the advice of Sage Vaśiṣṭha and was arranged by the king's chief minister, Sumantra.

King Daśaratha had three queens, Kauśalyā, Kaikeyī and Sumitra. Bharata was born to Kaikeyī, the daughter of the king of Kaikeya, at the auspicious time of the Pushya Nakṣatra and Mīna Lagna astrological configuration. By Viśvāmitra's grace, Bharata was married to Mandavi, the elder daughter, and Śatrughna to

Śrutakīrti, the younger daughter of Kuśadhvaja, who was the younger brother of saintly King Janaka. Lord Rāmacandra and Lakṣmaṇa were married to Sītā and Ūrmilā, the daughters of Janaka, in the presence of the saints Viśvāmitra, Vaśiṣṭha and Śatānanda. After the marriages, when King Daśaratha was returning to Ayodhyā with Rāma, Lakṣmaṇa, Bharata and Śatrughna and their brides, he was alarmed to see Paraśurāma, the son of Jamadagni, who had a large body and long hair, and was known as the slayer of the warrior class. Daśaratha breathed a sigh of relief when Lord Rāmacandra tied the string to the bow given to Him by Paruśarāma and robbed him of his effulgence. Then they all left for Ayodhyā.

Bharata mostly stayed at his maternal grandfather's place and was very affectionate toward Śatrughna, the son of Queen Sumitra. After his marriage, Bharata took him along to his maternal grandfather's house. Rāma, Lakṣmaṇa, Bharata and Śatrughna were each blessed with two sons. Rāma had Lava and Kuśa, Lakṣmaṇa had Aṅgada and Citraketu, Bharata had Takṣa and Puṣkala, and Śatrughna had Subāhu and Śrutasena. *Viśvakoṣa* affirms that the name of Bharata's son Puṣkala is Puṣkara.

When King Daśaratha decided to coronate his eldest son, Rāma, as the king, Kaikeyī, the second wife of King Daśaratha, under the influence of her maidservant Manthara, asked him to fulfill two promises he had made to her earlier when she saved his life. She first asked him to exile Rāma to the forest for fourteen years and, as the second stipulation, she wanted her son Bharata to reign as king. Daśaratha had intense love for Rāma and could not live without Him. Despite his attachment to Rāma, he was bound by his promise, and was unable to stop Rāma from going into exile. However, Rāma solved this dilemma by happily going into exile of His own accord after learning about his father's promise. King Daśaratha later died from the severe pain of separation. Thus, Lord Rāma became known as Maryāda Puruṣottama (one who establishes the dignity of moral codes).

These events also troubled Bharata, who began to experience very frightful dreams. When a messenger from Ayodhyā arrived with the bad news of his father's death, he immediately went to Ayodhyā and performed the last rites for him. Then, his father's ministers asked him to sit on the throne, but he refused. He was disturbed to hear of the adverse attitude of his mother toward his father and elder brother. Being deprived of the service of Lord Rāma due to his mother, he rejected her company:

gurur na sa syāt sva-jano na sa syāt
pitā na sa syāj jananī na sā syāt
daivaṁ na tat syān na patiś ca sa syān
na mocayed yaḥ samupeta-mṛtyum
(*Śrīmad Bhāgavatam* 5.5.18)

"If a spiritual master cannot liberate his disciple from the path of repeated birth and death by guiding him toward the path of devotion, he is not a spiritual master."

There are several examples of this: King Bali, who gave up the association of his spiritual master Śukrācārya; Vibhīṣaṇa, who gave up the company of his brother Rāvaṇa; Prahlāda, who left his father, Hiraṇyakaśipu; Bharata, who rejected his mother, Kaikeyī; Khaṭvāṅga, who gave up the demigods; and the wives of priests performing *yajña* who gave up their husbands. All these personalities recognized such association as harmful.

Bharata was totally devoted to his elder brother, Rāma. He went to Citrakūṭa Mountain to bring Lord Rāmacandra back to Ayodhyā but seeing Rāma dressed as a mendicant in tree bark with His hair tied in thick locks, he became dejected and hurt. Rāma would not agree to renege on his father's promise and return to Ayodhyā, despite Bharata's pleading. Bharata then took the sandals of Lord Rāma, placed them on his head and carried them to Nandigrāma. He installed the sandals on the royal throne and began ruling Ayodhyā as per his brother's instructions. He himself led a life of celibacy with total detachment.

It is described in the Bengali *Rāmāyaṇa* written by Krittivasi, that Śrī Lakṣmaṇa exhibited pastimes of unconsciousness when struck by Meghanāda's artillery. At that time, Śrī Hanumān went to Gandhamādana Mountain to bring the Sañjīvanī herb to cure Lakṣmaṇa. However, he was unsuccessful in locating the herb, so he lifted the whole mountain and brought it back. While he was traveling through the sky on his return to Laṅkā with the mountain, he passed over Nandigrāma, near Ayodhyā, and the shadow of the mountain fell upon the place where the sandals of Lord Rāmacandra were placed. According to biographies in the *New Bengali Dictionary*, by Āśutoṣa Deva, it is written that Bharata's maternal grandfather's house was in Nandigrāma. The darkness caused by the shadow cast over the sandals annoyed Bharata, so he struck Hanumān with an arrow given to him by Śatrughna. Hanumān fell to the earth with the Gandhamādana Mountain. When they heard Hanumān reciting the name "Rāma," Bharata and Śatrughna approached him and asked him about the welfare of Lord Rāma, Śrī Lakṣmaṇa and Śrīmatī Sītā. They became apprehensive when they learned about Lakṣmaṇa's injury. To ensure that Hanumān reached Laṅkā quickly, Bharata lifted Hanumān along with the mountain, Gandhamādana, a hundred *yojanas* in the sky with his arrow.

After completing his fourteen years of exile and winning over Laṅkā, Śrī Rāmacandra reached the residence of Sage Bhāradvāja on the fifth day of the lunar fortnight. He inquired about the welfare of the people of Ayodhyā, His mother and brother Bharata. Sage Bhāradvāja told Him that Bharata had long rope-like hair and was living like a hermit, waiting anxiously for His return. He further told Him that Bharata was ruling over Ayodhyā by keeping Śrī Rāma's sandals in front of him. Śrī Rāmacandra sent Hanumān to find out about Bharata. Śrī Hanumān went to Nandigrāma, situated at a distance of one *krośa* (approx. two miles) from Ayodhyā, in the guise of a human. He observed that Śrī Bharata had become very weak and dull, had grown long hair and was living like a recluse, due to being overwhelmed by the pain of separation from Śrī Rāma. He was ruling over Ayodhyā with Śrī Rāmacandra's sandals in front of him. Therefore, Śrī Bharata was overwhelmed with joy and embraced Hanumān upon learning about the return of Lord Rāma.

Śrī Rāmacandra went to Ayodhyā with Śrīmatī Sītā, Śrī Lakṣmaṇa, Śrī Hanumān, Śrī Sugrīva and Śrī Vibhīṣaṇa in a celestial aircraft. The people of Ayodhyā along with Brahmā and the other demigods were very pleased to witness their arrival. However, Lord Rāmacandra was unhappy to see Bharata dressed as a recluse, sleeping on a grass mat and eating only barley boiled in cow urine.

When Lord Rāma arrived in Ayodhyā, Bharata greeted Him with prayers and other forms of reception. All such details are given by Sage Śrī Kṛṣṇa-dvaipāyana Vedavyāsa in the 10th Chapter of the 9th Canto of *Śrīmad Bhāgavatam*:

bharataḥ prāptam ākarṇya
paurāmātya-purohitaiḥ
pāduke śirasi nyasya rāmaṁ
pratyudyato 'grajam

nandigrāmāt sva-śibirād
gīta-vāditra-niḥsvanaiḥ
brahma-ghoṣeṇa ca muhuḥ
paṭhadbhir brahmavādibhiḥ

svarṇa-kakṣa-patākābhir
haimaiś citra-dhvajai rathaiḥ
sad-aśvai rukma-sannāhair
bhaṭaiḥ puraṭa-varmabhiḥ

śreṇībhir vāra-mukhyābhir
bhṛtyaiś caiva padānugaiḥ
pārameṣṭhyāny upādāya
paṇyāny uccāvacāni ca
pādayor nyapatat premṇā
praklinna-hṛdayekṣaṇaḥ
(*Śrīmad Bhāgavatam* 9.10.35-38)

"When Lord Bharata learned that Śrī Rāmacandra was returning to Ayodhyā, He immediately placed Lord Rāmacandra's wooden sandals upon his head and came out from his camp at Nandigrāma. Lord Bharata was accompanied by ministers, priests and other respectable citizens, as well as by professional musicians vibrating pleasing musical sounds and learned *brāhmaṇas* loudly chanting Vedic hymns. Following in the procession were chariots drawn by beautiful horses harnessed with golden ropes. These chariots were decorated with flags featuring golden embroidery along with other flags of various sizes and dazzling patterns. There were soldiers bedecked with golden armor, servants bearing betel nuts and many well-known beautiful maidservants. Numerous servants followed on foot, holding umbrellas, whisks, different grades of precious jewels and other paraphernalia befitting a royal reception. He was overwhelmed, and a stream of tears flowed from his eyes as he met his elder brother, Lord Rāmacandra. He placed the Lord's sandals in front of Rāma and stood there with folded hands, tears streaming from his eyes. Lord Rāma also became overwhelmed and, as he held Bharata close to his chest, the tears flowing from the Lord's eyes soaked Bharata."

King Bharata possessed an extraordinary character. People of contemporary times cannot imagine such characteristics. The leaders of current times never hesitate to perform mean acts in order to protect their right to power. A good government is not possible in kingdoms dominated by selfish rulers. One can learn from the pastimes of Śrī Rāma and Śrī Bharata how real leaders should act.

Yudhajita, the king of Kaikeya, sent Sage Gārgaya, the son of spiritual master Sage Aṅgirā, to Lord Rāmacandra. Śrī Rāmacandra came forward with His brothers to welcome him and to ask him what the purpose of his visit was. Sage Gārgaya told Him that King Yudhajita, the maternal uncle of Bharata, was keen to win the wonderful state of Gandharva across the river Sindhu (Indus), so as to make it an internal part of his kingdom. The son of the king of that state had assembled three *crores* (30 million) of Gandharva soldiers for its protection. Only Śrī Rāmacandra could defeat them.

When Lord Rāma learned about the desire of the sage and Śrī Yudhajita, He immediately assigned Bharata to the task. Śrī Bharata immediately took leave to conquer the state of Gandharva, along with his sons Takṣa, Puṣkala, the infantry and so on. Various carnivorous animals such as lions and tigers, as well as boars and demons from Ayodhyā, also joined the troops. Yudhajita and his army joined

Bharata as he reached the Kaikeya country after fifteen days. They attacked the Gandharva nation and fought a ferocious battle for seven days, but neither side could win. Then Śrī Bharata fired a weapon called Saṁvarta and killed all of the thirty million brave Gandharvas instantaneously. Bharata, who was totally devoted to his elder brother, Śrī Rāma, divided the Gandharva nation into two parts and established two beautiful cities named Taxila and Puṣkalavati. He ordered Takṣa to become the ruler of Taxila and Puṣkala to become the ruler of Puṣkalavati. Bharata returned to Ayodhyā after five years. Śrī Rāmacandra was pleased to hear about all of this.

As per the desire of Śrī Bharata, Lord Rāma enthroned Aṅgada and Candraketu, the sons of Lakṣmaṇa, as the kings of Karupatha and Candrakanta respectively. Bharata went with Candraketu to Candrakanta and stayed there for one year. Thus, Bharata spent ten thousand years in the service of Lord Rāma. Lord Rāma was in pain due to His separation from Lakṣmaṇa, so He decided to leave for the forest after crowning Bharata as king. The people of Ayodhyā became senseless and Bharata became imbalanced when they heard about the Lord's decision. Bharata was not keen on becoming a king at the expense of separation from Lord Rāma. According to Bharata's desire, Rāmacandra crowned Kuśa as the king of southern Kuśala, and Lava as the king of northern Kuśala. Bharata followed Rāmacandra and disappeared on the banks of the pious River Sarayū.

Bharata, the Son of King Duṣyanta

This Bharata was the son of King Duṣyanta, a famous king of the Lunar Dynasty. His mother was Śrīmatī Śakuntalā, the daughter of Sage Viśvāmitra, who was brought up at the house of Sage Kaṇva. Bharata (Duṣyanta's son) was a part of a partial expansion of the Supreme Lord:

pitary uparate so 'pi cakravartī mahā-yaśāḥ
mahimā gīyate tasya harer aṁśa-bhuvo bhuvi
(*Śrīmad Bhāgavatam* 9.20.23)

When Mahārāja Duṣyanta passed away from this planet, his son became the emperor of the world, the proprietor of the seven islands. He is referred to as a partial representation of the Supreme Personality of Godhead in this world. A detailed description of the birth of King Bharata has been given in the chapter about King Duṣyanta.

Sage Kaṇva had predicted that a powerful boy would be born to Śakuntalā and would rule the whole planet. Śrī Bharata gained immense power and, when he was only six years old, would catch hold of wild beasts such as lions, tigers, elephants, wild boars and wild buffalos from the forest, tie them to a tree and proceed to play with them. Sage Kaṇva named him Sarvadamana upon observing his exceptional acts.

Instructed by Sage Kaṇva, Śakuntalā came to King Duṣyanta with the boy but the king had forgotten the events, so he refused to accept the boy as his son. King Duṣyanta had married Śakuntalā according to the Gandharva rituals with the condition that her son would be the only prince and heir to his empire. She felt dejected by the king's treatment, but before leaving she said, "My son will rule the earth, though the king has not accepted him." At that instant, a celestial voice said, "O King! Śakuntalā speaks the truth. Do not disobey her. Accept this son of yours, and take care of him." After this the boy was named Bharata because the celestial voice had proclaimed, "Take care, take care!"

Thus, King Duṣyanta accepted his wife Śakuntalā and son Bharata. Not only this, but when the time came he performed Bharata's coronation as Prince Regent. After becoming ruler of the world with its seven islands, Bharata performed many *yajñas* just like Indra. He performed one hundred *aśvamedha-yajñas* on the banks of River Yamunā, three hundred on the banks of River Sarasvatī and four hundred on the banks of River Gaṅgā. After these, he performed one thousand *aśvamedha-yajñas*, one hundred *rājasūya-yajñas* and thousands of *vājapeya-yajñas*. He also performed *yajñas* arranged by Sage Kaṇva, wherein large donations were given.

According to some, this country is known as Bhārata after King Bharata and that the glories of Bhārata (India) spread because of him. His predecessors are also known as Bhārata. In the 20th Chapter of the 9th Canto of *Śrīmad Bhāgavatam*, Sage Vyāsadeva has described the wonderful glories of Śrī Bharata, the son of Duṣyanta.

On his left hand there was a mark of a disc and, on both feet, there were marks of *padma-*

kośa (lotus buds). Upon becoming the emperor of earth, he offered his prayers unto the Lord by performing two hundred and fifty *aśvamedha-yajñas* at all places, from the basins of River Gaṅgā at Gaṅgā Sagara, up to the place of the river's origin. He astonished all kings by roping in 3,300 horses in a *yajña*. He even surpassed the glory of the demigods and attained the Supreme Lord:

bharatasya mahat karma
na pūrve nāpare nṛpāḥ
naivāpur naiva prāpsyanti
bāhubhyāṁ tridivaṁ yathā
(*Śrīmad Bhāgavatam* 9.20.29)

"One cannot approach the heavenly planets simply by the strength of his arms, for who can touch the heavenly planets with his hands? So, similarly, one cannot imitate the wonderful activities of Mahārāja Bharata. No one could perform such activities in the past, nor will anyone be able to do so in the future."

King Bharata had three queens belonging to the kingdom of Vidarbha. They always wanted Bharata's son to be as strong and magnanimous as he was, because if this did not happen then the king might desert them, considering them to be lacking in ethical behavior. Therefore, they would kill their sons as soon as they were born. Consequently, the king performed a *marutyaga-yajña*.

By this *yajña*, the Marutaganas were pleased and blessed Bharata with a son named Bhāradvāja who was born from the union of Bṛhaspati and Mamatā. Mamatā deserted Bṛhaspati due to considering the boy to be worthless, but the Marutaganas brought up the child and then gave him to King Bharata to prevent the destruction of his dynasty.

King Māndhātā

Manu's son Ikṣvāku was the first king of the Solar Dynasty. Among the descendants of King Ikṣvāku, there was a famous king by the name Yuvanāśva. His son, King Māndhātā, was the forefather of King Hariścandra, King Sagara, King Bhagīratha, King Khaṭvāṅga, King Daśaratha and Lord Śrī Rama.

Sage Kṛṣṇa-dvaipāyana Vedavyāsa has described the appearance of King Māndhātā in the 9th Canto of *Śrīmad Bhāgavatam*. King Māndhātā's paternal grandfather was Senajit or Prasenajit, and Senajit's son was Yuvanāśva. It so happened that Yuvanāśva was unable to conceive a son, though he had one hundred wives. For this reason he was unhappy, so he decided to live in the forest with his wives. However, the sages felt compassionate when they heard of the miserable condition of the king, and performed an *indra-daivata-yajña* to grant him a son.

One night, the king felt very thirsty and was unable to control this urge. To quench his thirst, he went to the place where the sages were performing the *yajña* but, at that time, all the sages were sleeping and, as destined, Yuvanāśva drank the water actually meant for his wives, which the sages had empowered by means of specific *mantras*. So, when the sages woke up, they found that the empowered water was missing and began looking for the person who had drunk it. It caused some anxiety when they learned that Yuvanāśva had drunk the water but, upon reflection, they considered that this was an unavoidable act of fate.

Destiny is final and the conditioned souls cannot perform or act on their own. The sages offered their obeisances unto the lotus feet of omnipotent Lord Hari, the controller of all. The water, imbued with power by the *yajña*, caused Yuvanāśva to have a son. Thus, at the appropriate time, a son having the symptoms of a great king came tearing out of the right side of the stomach of King Yuvanāśva, and began to cry immediately after taking birth. This worried the saints, as they wondered: "*Who will feed the baby now?*"

At that instant, the presiding demigod of the *yajña*, Indra, appeared and lovingly said to the infant, "Dear child! Please do not cry! You may feed from me." Then Indra placed his index finger into the child's mouth to feed him. Since Indra asked the baby, "*Mā dhātā?*" ("Accept me, or drink from me?"), the son of Yuvanāśva was named Māndhātā. The child began to suck Indra's nectarlike index finger and grew up healthy and strong within a day. By the blessings of the *brāhmaṇas*, Yuvanāśva never died and obtained mystical powers as the result of his penance. His son Māndhātā became extremely powerful and even dacoits like Rāvaṇa feared him. Thus, Indra gave him another name—Trasaddasyu ("one who intimidates thieves and rogues").

After some time, Māndhātā became the ruler of the whole planet. He worshiped Lord Viṣṇu, the presiding lord of *yajña*, by performing many fire sacrifices, accompanied by large donations.

yāvat sūrya udeti sma yāvac ca pratitiṣṭhati
tat sarvaṁ yauvanāśvasya māndhātuḥ kṣetram ucyate
(*Śrīmad Bhāgavatam* 9.6.37)

"All places, from where the sun rises on the horizon, shining brilliantly, to where the sun sets, are known as the possession of the celebrated Māndhātā, the son of Yuvanāśva."

King Māndhātā married Bindumatī, the daughter of Śaśabindu, and she gave birth to three sons and fifty daughters. The three sons were called Pūrukutsa, Ambarīṣa and

Mucukunda (a great mystic *yogī*). King Hariścandra appeared in the dynasty of Pūrukutsa. Sage Saubhari married the fifty daughters of King Māndhātā and, by virtue of his mystical powers, the sage exhibited greater opulence than King Māndhātā, which even surprised Māndhātā.

The above description of King Māndhātā is given in the *Viṣṇu Purāṇa* also. The exceptional character of Mucukunda, the son of King Māndhātā, is narrated in the 10th Canto of *Śrīmad Bhāgavatam*:

sa ikṣvāku-kule jāto māndhātṛ-tanayo mahān
mucukunda iti khyāto brahmaṇyaḥ satya-saṅgaraḥ
(*Śrīmad Bhāgavatam* 10.51.14)

"Mucukunda was the name of this great personality, who was born in the Ikṣvāku Dynasty as the son of Māndhātā. He was devoted to the brāhminical culture and was always truthful."

King Mucukunda

śaśabindor duhitari bindumatyām adhān nṛpaḥ
pūrukutsam ambarīṣaṁ mucukundaṁ ca yoginam
teṣāṁ svasāraḥ pañcāśat saubhariṁ vavrire patim
(*Śrīmad Bhāgavatam* 9.6.38)

"Māndhātā begot three sons from the womb of Bindumatī, the daughter of Śaśabindu. These sons were Pūrukutsa, Ambarīṣa and a great mystic yogi Mucukunda. These three brothers had fifty sisters who all accepted the great sage Saubhari as their husband."

King Mucukunda appeared in the Solar Dynasty[12] and was King Māndhātā's youngest son. It is mentioned in *Śrīmad Bhāgavatam*:

sa ikṣvāku-kule jāto māndhātṛ-tanayo mahān
mucukunda iti khyāto brahmaṇyaḥ satya-saṅgaraḥ
(*Śrīmad Bhāgavatam* 10.51.14)

"Mucukunda was the name of this great personality, who was born in the Ikṣvāku Dynasty as the son of Māndhātā. He was devoted to the brāhminical culture and was always truthful."

On the request of the demigods and their king, Indra, King Mucukunda saved them from the cruelty of the demons for a long period of time, while foregoing sleep. When the demigods appointed Kārtikeya as the protector of heaven, they thought not to bother King Mucukunda anymore and, being satisfied with his services, they said to him, "O King! You have not slept for a long time and have suffered much pain to protect us, so please take rest. You have forsaken even your kingdom on earth, Mṛtyuloka (where death prevails), to take care of us and have discarded all pleasures for that cause. Please understand that your son, wife, ministers and people of your kingdom have died during this period of time. Kāla (time) kills all living entities in due course. Dear King! We are pleased by your service and wish to bless you. We can give you anything except liberation, because only Lord Viṣṇu can award liberation to someone."

King Mucukunda offered respects to the demigods and requested that he be allowed to sleep, as he had not slept for a long time. Since

12 Vivasvāna (god of the sun) was the father of Vaivasvata Manu, Ikṣvāku was the son of Vaivasvata Manu, and in Ikṣvāku's succession Yuvanāśva was a famous king of the Solar Dynasty. Yuvanāśva's son was King Māndhātā.

they were committed to granting whatever he might ask of them, they agreed to his unusual request and granted him sleep for a long period of time, while further stating that whoever would dare to wake him would instantaneously burn to ashes. After receiving this boon, the king took permission from the demigods and entered a cave to sleep.

The powerful Jarāsandha, the son of King Vrīhidratha, was king of the Magadha region. He was born from two mothers, and each gave birth to a half of his body. A female demon called Jara joined the two parts and thus he was named Jarāsandha. He had received a blessing that he would not die unless his body was cut exactly into two parts and thrown away. King Kaṁsa married Jarāsandha's two daughters Asti and Prāpti, but when Kṛṣṇa killed Kaṁsa, Jarāsandha became a foe of Kṛṣṇa. Jarāsandha attacked Mathurā seventeen times, but Kṛṣṇa always triumphed.

Sage Garga got a powerful son by the blessings of Lord Mahādeva. He was known as Kālayavana as he was brought up by a Yavana (low-caste) king. Jarāsandha formed a friendship with Kālayavana with the help of Śiśupāla's friend Śālva. Jarāsandha inspired Kālayavana to attack Mathurā, and when he did so, Śrī Kṛṣṇa exhibited a pastime of fleeing to Dvārakā, which made Kālayavana believe that Kṛṣṇa was afraid of his power. When Kālayavana saw Kṛṣṇa for the second time, he ran after Him. Śrī Kṛṣṇa tricked him by pretending to run away, and brought him to the cave where King Mucukunda was sleeping. When the Lord reached the spot, He disappeared. Kālayavana, experiencing great difficulty in locating Kṛṣṇa, kicked the person sleeping there, thinking him to be Kṛṣṇa. As soon as Mucukunda woke up and opened his eyes, Kālayavana got burned to ashes. Mucukunda was then amazed to see the effulgent form of Śrī Kṛṣṇa, and immediately offered obeisances unto His lotus feet, saying, "Your brilliant effulgence overwhelms my strength and I am unable to have an uninterrupted view of You, despite all my efforts. O Exalted One! You are the object of worship of all living beings."

Jarāsandha and Kālayavana could not attain enlightenment even though they saw Śrī Kṛṣṇa with their own eyes because they were without devotion. However, the devoted and religious Mucukunda was able to realize and recognize the Supreme Personality of Godhead by His mercy. Śrī Kṛṣṇa began to explain Himself. "King Mucukunda! In the past you worshiped Me intensely to win My favor. Therefore, I have appeared before you in this cave and have shown you My real self." Śrī Kṛṣṇa told the king to ask for a boon. Mucukunda, considering Kṛṣṇa to be Nārāyaṇa, offered his obeisances and praised Him in thirteen verses. The following two verses should be given special attention:

labdhvā jano durlabham atra mānuṣaṁ
kathañcid avyaṅgam ayatnato 'nagha
pādāravindaṁ na bhajaty asan-
matirgṛhāndha-kūpe patito yathā paśuḥ
(*Śrīmad Bhāgavatam* 10.51.46)

"O Unconquerable One, that person has an impure mind who, despite having somehow or other automatically obtained the rare and highly evolved human form of life, does not worship Your lotus feet. Like an animal that has fallen into a blind well, such a person has fallen into the darkness of a material home."

bhavāpavargo bhramato yadā bhavej
janasya tarhy acyuta sat-samāgamaḥ
sat-saṅgamo yarhi tadaiva sad-gatau
parāvareśe tvayi jāyate matiḥ
(*Śrīmad Bhāgavatam* 10.51.53)

"When the material life of a wandering soul has ceased, O Acyuta, he may attain the association of Your devotees and, when he associates with them, there awakens in him devotion unto You, who are the goal of the devotees and the Lord of all causes and their effects."

Satisfied by Mucukunda's words, Śrī Kṛṣṇa said, "Though I enticed you with benedictions, your mind was not overcome by material desires. May you thus possess ceaseless, desireless devotion toward Me. May you wander this earth meditating on Me because you followed the principles of a *kṣatriya* and killed living beings while hunting and performing other duties in your previous birth. Thus, you must vanquish the sins incurred by carefully executing penances while remaining surrendered to Me. O King! In your next life you will become an excellent *brāhmaṇa* and certainly come to Me alone. At that time, you shall no longer have the desire for sense enjoyment."

Many years had passed since Mucukunda went to sleep in the mountain cave. When he awoke and came out of the cave, he realized that no one he knew was alive anymore. Thus nobody recognized him. With a saddened heart he turned toward the Himālayas and performed strict penance and eventually exhibited the pastime of disappearance.

Bhīṣma

śalaś ca śāntanor āsīd gaṅgāyāṁ bhīṣma ātmavān
sarva-dharma-vidāṁ śreṣtho mahā-bhāgavataḥ kaviḥ
(*Śrīmad Bhāgavatam* 9.22.19)

"From Śāntanu, through the womb of his wife named Gaṅgā, came Bhīṣma, the exalted, self-realized devotee and learned scholar."

When Sage Vaśiṣṭha cursed the Eight Vasus to take birth as humans, they pleaded to be rescued. Then Sage Vaśiṣṭha said, "All of you will be freed from this curse within a year, except for Dyau. Dyau will stay on earth for a long time due to his improper actions. He will not mate with any woman and thus will not produce any children. He will be pious, learned in all the scriptures and will always try to please his father." Dyau, born from the union of Śāntanu and Gaṅgā, became famous as Devavrata and Gangeya (son of Gaṅgā). Devavrata took an oath, in front of warriors and Dhivararāja, (fisherman king) that the son born from the womb of Dhivararāja's daughter would be heir to the kingdom. To ensure this, he vowed that he would not marry and would observe lifelong celibacy. From that day, sages and demigods called him Bhīṣma due to his firm oath. When the demigods heard Devavrata's oath, they showered flowers from the sky.

To please his father, Devavrata brought Satyavatī, the daughter of the fisherman king, and offered her to his father as a bride. Śāntanu was very pleased with Devavrata and blessed him with a boon that death would only come to him when he himself desired it.

Śāntanu and Satyavatī had two sons, Citrāṅgadā and Vicitravīrya. After Śāntanu's death, Citrāṅgadā became the king but was later killed by a Gandharva. So, after performing Citrāṅgadā's last rites Bhīṣma made Vicitravīrya the king but, due to his tender age, he was king in name only. Therefore, as desired by his mother, Satyavatī, Bhīṣma looked after the kingdom. He was the bravest of the brave.

Kāśīrāja (king of Kāśī) arranged a *svayaṁvara* ceremony for the marriage of his three daughters named Ambā, Ambikā and Ambālikā, Bhīṣma went there, kidnapped them and brought them to his city. Nobody dared to oppose his action. Ambikā and Ambālikā were married to Vicitravīrya, but Bhīṣma released Ambā when he discovered her inclination toward Śālva.

Unfortunately, Vicitravīrya left for the heavenly abode before he could develop any relationship with his newlywed wives. Satyavatī became sad and miserable due to the death of her son and completed the last rites for him, along with her daughters-in-law. She wondered what would then happen to their dynasty.

She expected Bhīṣma to be obedient to her and assumed he would obey any of her instructions. Thus, one day, Satyavatī affectionately said to Bhīṣma, "Dear son! You are the only hope of Śāntanu's royal dynasty and are the only one who can offer anything to your deceased ancestors; only you can perform the necessary rites. You know all the scriptures and I understand that you will obey me. Vicitravīrya was your brother and was also very dear to you. He passed away without giving birth to a son, but the two brides you brought for him are young, beautiful, qualified and keen to give birth to a son. I am your mother and I ask you to beget sons with them in order to save this dynasty. At the same time, become king and rule this country."

After listening to Mother Satyavatī, Bhīṣma said, "O mother! Whatever you say is right undoubtedly, but you are aware of my oath of celibacy. I took that oath for you and I cannot neglect it. I repeat that I can abandon the three worlds and renounce the kingdom of the demigods, but I cannot divert from the truth. Even if the demigods or Dharmarāja himself (demigod of righteous justice) were to abandon *dharma*, still I wouldn't divert from virtuous conduct. Everything will be ruined if *dharma* should be obliterated. Please give serious thought to this. We are not here to wreak destruction and a warrior is to be highly condemned if he does not observe *dharma*. Therefore, it is impossible for me to do this. May you please engage a pure *brāhmaṇa* to accomplish what you desire."

Observing Bhīṣma's attitude, she did not press him any further. She prayed, and finally Sage Kṛṣṇa-dvaipāyana Vedayāsa agreed to have children with the two sisters. Dhṛtarāṣṭra was born from Ambikā, and Pāṇḍu was born from Ambālikā. Pāṇḍu went on to have five sons and Dhṛtarāṣṭra had one hundred sons. Bhīṣma raised all of them.

While on a pilgrimage, Bhīṣma associated with Sage Pulastya. Śrīla Bhakti Vinoda Ṭhākura, in his book *Navadvīpa-dhāma Māhātmya*, mentions that Bhīṣma came to Jahnudvīpa in Navadvīpa and associated with Sage Jahnu. Bhīṣma taught King Yudhiṣṭhira what he had learned from Sage Jahnu.

Bhīṣma chose the side of the Kauravas in the war between the Kauravas and Pāṇḍavas. He took an oath before Duryodhana and the other Kauravas that he would kill ten thousand enemy soldiers every day, and as promised, he fought for ten days. Although he fought for the Kauravas, he had special love for the Pāṇḍavas.

Śrī Kṛṣṇa broke His own oath of not lifting a weapon during the battle, out of love for His devotee Bhīṣma, who had promised to break Kṛṣṇa's oath. Kṛṣṇa took a weapon in His hand in order to uphold the oath of His devotee Bhīṣma. Bhīṣma was overwhelmed by the Lord's vast affection for him and thus glorified the Lord with many verses.

To exact revenge on Bhīṣma, Ambā took her next birth as the son of the king of Pañcāla, Drupada. In this life he was known as Śikhaṇḍī, who was a eunuch. Bhīṣma would drop his weapons in Śikhaṇḍī's presence because he would not fight with women or eunuchs. Arjuna decided to take advantage of this, so after consultation with Śrī Kṛṣṇa, he asked Śikhaṇḍī to stand in front of Bhīṣma. Śikhaṇḍī did so and Bhīṣma dropped his weapons. Arjuna then pierced the weaponless Bhīṣma with his arrows. Bhīṣma fell down and lay on a bed of arrows. As he had been given the boon of choosing his own moment of death, he did not die during *dakṣiṇa-ayanam*, the time when the sun passes on the southern side.

When he felt thirsty, Duryodhana and others brought him cold water, but Bhīṣma refused to take it. When he asked Arjuna for water, Arjuna pierced the earth with his arrow and a spring of water came from the hole. Bhīṣma then drank water from that spring. This incident demonstrates that Bhīṣma was more affectionate toward the Pāṇḍavas.

After the battle, King Yudhiṣṭhira visited Grandfather Bhīṣma, who was lying on the bed of arrows. Yudhiṣṭhira asked some questions that Bhīṣma answered expertly. He provided very clear answers to the most difficult subjects queried by King Yudhiṣṭhira. These questions and answers are described in detail in the 9th Chapter of the 1st Canto of *Śrīmad Bhāgavatam* and in the *Śānti-parva* of *Mahābhārata*.

When even a small piece of glass pierces any human being, he trembles with pain, but Bhīṣma was indifferent to the pain caused by hundreds of arrows piercing him while lying on a bed of arrows. This is not an ordinary thing and proves that his body was transcendental. In such a condition, he explained the complex elements of *dharma* to King Yudhiṣṭhira.

śrī-bhagavān uvāca
ittham etat purā rājā bhīṣmaṁ dharma-bhṛtāṁ varam
ajāta-śatruḥ papraccha sarveṣāṁ no 'nuśṛṇvatām
nivṛtte bhārate yuddhe suhṛn-nidhana-vihvalaḥ
śrutvā dharmān bahūn paścān
mokṣa-dharmān apṛcchata
tān ahaṁ te 'bhidhāsyāmi deva-vrata-makhāc chrutān
jñāna-vairāgya-vijñāna-śraddhā-bhakty-upabṛṁhitān
(*Śrīmad Bhāgavatam* 11.19.11-13)

The Supreme Personality of Godhead, Lord Kṛṣṇa, said, "My dear Uddhava, just as you are now inquiring from Me, similarly, in the past, King Yudhiṣṭhira, who considered no one his enemy, inquired from the greatest of the upholders of religious principles, Bhīṣma,

~ Bhīṣma ~

while all of us were carefully listening. When the great battle of Kurukṣetra had ended, King Yudhiṣṭhira was overwhelmed by the death of many beloved well-wishers and, thus, after listening to instructions about many religious principles, he finally inquired about the path of liberation. I will now speak unto you those religious principles of Vedic knowledge, detachment, self-realization, faith and devotional service that were heard directly from the mouth of Bhīṣmadeva."

In the descriptions of Lord Kṛṣṇa's pastimes in the 10th Canto of *Śrīmad Bhāgavatam*, Sage Kṛṣṇa-dvaipāyana Vedavyāsa has mentioned Bhīṣma's name in many places. The discussions between Yamarāja and his messengers in the 6th Canto confirm that Bhīṣma is counted among the twelve great personalities (*mahājanas*):

svayambhūr nāradaḥ śambhuḥ
kumāraḥ kapilo manuḥ
prahlādo janako bhīṣmo balir vaiyāsakir vayam
dvādaśaite vijānīmo dharmaṁ bhāgavataṁ bhaṭāḥ
guhyaṁ viśuddhaṁ durbodhaṁ
yaṁ jñātvāmṛtam aśnute
(*Śrīmad Bhāgavatam* 6.3.20-21)

(Yamarāja said,) "O messengers! Lord Brahmā, Nārada, Lord Śiva, the Four Kumāras, Lord Kapila [son of Devahūti], Svāyambhuva Manu, Prahlāda Mahārāja, Janaka Mahārāja, Grandfather Bhīṣma, Bali Mahārāja, Śukadeva Gosvāmī and I myself know the real religious principle, which is known as *bhāgavata-dharma*. It is very confidential and difficult for ordinary human beings to understand, but if one is fortunate enough to understand it, he is immediately liberated and thus returns home, back to Godhead."

During the month of Māgha (January–February), when the sun moved toward the northern hemisphere, on the day of Śuklāṣṭamī, the 8th day of lunar movement toward the phase of the full moon, Bhīṣma meditated upon Kṛṣṇa by words and heart, and left the world while remembering Him:

sūta uvāca
kṛṣṇa evaṁ bhagavati mano-vāg-dṛṣṭi-vṛttibhiḥ
ātmany ātmānam āveśya so 'ntaḥśvāsa upāramat
sampadyamānam ājñāya bhīṣmaṁ brahmaṇi niṣkale
sarve babhūvus te tūṣṇīm vayāṁsīva dinātyaye
tatra dundubhayo nedur deva-mānava-vāditāḥ
śaśaṁsuḥ sādhavo rājñāṁ khāt petuḥ puṣpa-vṛṣṭayaḥ
(*Śrīmad Bhāgavatam* 1.9.43-45)

Sūta Gosvāmī said, "Thus, as Bhīṣmadeva meditated upon Śrī Kṛṣṇa, the Supreme Personality of Godhead, with his mind, speech, sight and actions, he became silent and his breathing stopped. Knowing that Bhīṣmadeva had merged into the unlimited eternity of the Supreme Absolute, all present there became silent like birds at the end of the day. Thereafter, both men and demigods sounded drums in honor and respect, and from the sky fell showers of flowers."

King Citraketu

āsīd rājā sārvabhaumaḥ śūraseneṣu vai nṛpa
citraketur iti khyāto yasyāsīt kāmadhuṅ mahī
(*Śrīmad Bhāgavatam* 6.14.10)

"O King Parīkṣit, in the province of Śūrasena there was a king named Citraketu, who ruled the entire earth. During his reign, the earth produced all the necessities for life."

śūraseno yadupatir mathurām āvasan purīm
māthurāñ chūrasenāṁś ca viṣayān bubhuje purā
(*Śrīmad Bhāgavatam* 10.1.27)

These verses mention the province of Śūrasena. Formerly, King Śūrasena, the chief of the Yadu Dynasty, was ruling the places known as Mathurā and Śūrasena. Since Mathurā and Śūrasena have been mentioned together, it is quite likely that Śūrasena was adjacent to Mathurā.

King Citraketu had ten million wives but had no children because all his wives were barren. He was very wealthy since childhood and possessed all luxuries but was unhappy because he had no children. Royal splendor, wealth and beautiful wives could not provide him any happiness

However, he engaged himself in the service of saints and sages. He was acquainted with many famous sages and they used to visit his home. One day, Sage Aṅgirā came to his palace. The king welcomed the sage by washing his feet and offering him prayers and food. When the sage was comfortably seated, the king sat at his feet and the sage asked, "O King! Are you all right? Are you well protected and served by your ministers, secretaries, people, fort, army, law-and-order and friends? Are they and your sons working according to your wishes? I am not sure why, but it seems that you are unhappy. Is there anything you do not have, as you appear to be extremely worried?"

King Citraketu replied, "O perfect sage! You know everything external and internal regarding embodied conditioned souls. A person afflicted by hunger and thirst cannot be satisfied by offerings of garlands and sandalwood. Similarly, how can I be satisfied with my kingdom and opulence when I am childless? Please save my forefathers and me from hellish life by enabling me to have a son." When the king said this, Sage Aṅgirā, who was born of Lord Brahmā's mind, performed a sacrifice by offering oblations of sweet rice to the demigod Tvaṣṭā. Aṅgirā gave the remnants of the *yajña* to Queen Kṛtadyuti, who was the first and most qualified queen. He told the king that he would have a son who would be the cause of both joy and grief.[13]

By this, the sage meant that this son would give happiness upon birth and sorrow at the time of death. However, the king misunderstood and assumed that his son would be highly virtuous. The king thought that by "joy" and "grief" the sage meant that his son would be virtuous but proud of royal luxuries.

Kṛttikādevī (Mother Pārvatī) conceived a child named Skanda (Kārtikeya) after receiving the semen of Lord Śiva from Agni. Similarly, Kṛtadyuti became pregnant from Citraketu after eating remnants of sweet rice from the *yajña* performed by Aṅgirā and gave birth to a baby boy. The people of Śūrasena were delighted to see the baby boy after waiting such a long time. Seeing the child, the king engaged learned *brāhmaṇas* in offering benedictions to him and performaning the birth ceremony. He donated gold, silver, clothes, ornaments, land, horses, elephants and six hundred million cows to the *brāhmaṇas*. Additionally, to ensure a long life for the prince, the king donated to others whatever they sought.

When a poor man gets some money after undergoing much difficulty, his affection for his wealth increases daily. In the same way, when King Citraketu finally received a son, his love for the child grew excessively, day by day. As Kṛtadyuti had given birth to a son, his love for her increased in comparison to the other queens, who, taking this as an insult by the king, became jealous of Kṛtadyuti.

Lamenting, they said, "Oh! How fortunate is the woman bearing a son! Damned be our

13 Vaiṣṇavas have commented that Sage Aṅgirā actually visited King Citraketu to give him transcendental knowledge but the king desired something comparatively insignificant, a son.

birth and life, as we could not bear a son. The woman who engages herself in the service of her master remains satisfied. Due to our bad luck, we are treated as maidservants to the maidservant." However, even after giving birth to a son, Kṛtadyuti was not at peace as she observed the jealousy of her co-wives. On the other side, as the feelings of hatred and jealousy increased in the other queens, they lost their wisdom intelligence and their hearts turned cruel. Unable to tolerate the insult of the king, they poisoned the young prince. Queen Kṛtadyuti never thought even in her wildest dreams that the other queens would go that far.

She assumed that her son was sleeping and continued her household work, but the prince did not get up for a long time, so she sent a maid to bring him to her. The maidservant approached the prince and, upon observing him to be senseless, fell to the ground screaming. After hearing her loud cries, the queen ran over to her and when she saw the dead prince, she immediately fell unconscious. Hearing their loud weeping, all the residents of the palace gathered at the scene of the tragedy. They too started weeping when they became aware of what had happened. With crocodile tears, the culprit queens also pretended to cry.

When King Citraketu heard the news, he could not stand properly and stumbled again and again while walking to see the dead child. Relatives followed him and, surrounded by *brāhmaṇas*, he was taking deep breaths. He fainted as he drew near the body of his son and was unable to speak after regaining his senses, as his throat was choked. Queen Kṛtadyuti observed the pathetic condition of her husband due to the death of the only son of their dynasty. She screamed like a *kurarī* bird (female osprey), the sound of which could have even melted a stone, and thereby increased the grief of those near and dear.

"Alas, O Providence, O Creator! You are certainly inexperienced in creation, for during the lifetime of a father You have caused the death of his son, thus acting in opposition to Your creative laws. If You are determined to contradict these laws, then You are certainly the enemy of the living entities and never merciful. You may say that there is no law that a father must die in the lifetime of his son and that a son must be born in the lifetime of his father, since everyone lives and dies according to his or her own destiny. However, if destiny is so strong that birth and death depend upon it, there is no need of a controller—no need of God. Furthermore, if You say that a controller is needed because the material energy does not have the power to act, then one may answer that if the bonds of affection You have created are disturbed by fruitive action, no one will raise children with affection. Rather, everyone will cruelly neglect their children and gradually creation will cease."

Overcome with grief, she continued to gaze upon her son and repeated the words, "My dear son, I am helpless and very much aggrieved; you should not give up my company. Just look at your lamenting father. We are helpless because without a son we will have to suffer the distress of going to the darkest hellish regions. You are our only hope to save us from this. Therefore, I request you not to proceed any further with the merciless Yama (god of death). My dear son, you have slept a long time. Now please arise. Your playmates are calling you to play. Since you must be very hungry, please get up and suck my breast and dispel our lamentation. I am certainly most unfortunate, for I can no longer see your gentle smile, as you have closed your eyes forever. I therefore conclude that you have been taken from this planet to another, from where you will not return. My dear son, I can no longer hear your pleasing voice." When the king heard the queen speaking like this, he became very anxious, and wept loudly. All the people of the city were struck senseless due to the sudden unfortunate incident.

Understanding the sorry state of King Citraketu, Sage Aṅgirā, accompanied by Sage Nārada, went to him. They saw King Citraketu lying as though dead, near the body of his son, due to excessive grief. Knowing well that this is how the external potency of the Lord casts a spell on living souls, they consoled the king with the following words: "O King! Who is it you are grieving for? If you say he is your son and you are his father, then was this relationship there since the beginning of time? Is it still existing now? Will it be there in the future? The sand particles caught in a flowing river unite for some time and later separate. Similarly, we living beings come together and later separate with the passage of time. If one sows seeds, it does not mean he or she will definitely get a plant or sprouts. Sometimes seeds are damaged, and so it is not advisable to grieve for bodily relatives. All the living beings in this universe that are together now were not together in their previous births and will not be together after death. Therefore, you should consider these relationships to be non-eternal, non-existent and false like a dream. The Lord creates living beings like a father, cares for them like a king and kills them like a snake. In this world, a father, king and snake are all dependent. It is a separate subject that under the influence of *māyā* (external potency of the Lord) they develop the false ego of being a doer. Just as a seed becomes a fruit and yields many new seeds, so, similarly, a son is born from the bodies of his mother and father. By this it can be understood that, as the basic elements of the material body are eternal, the living entity that appears within these material elements is also eternal."

Enlightened by the instructions of Nārada and Aṅgirā, King Citraketu became hopeful with knowledge. Wiping his shriveled face with his hand, the king began to speak. "You have both come here dressed like *avadhūtas*, liberated persons, to cover your real identities. I see that of all men, you are the most elevated in consciousness; you know everything as it is. Just to benefit materialists like us, who are always attached to sense gratification, and just to dissipate our ignorance, you wander on the surface of the globe according to your desire. O great souls, I have heard of many eminent and perfect persons. Are you one among Sanat-kumāra, Nārada, Ṛbhu, Aṅgirā, Devala, Asita, Apāntaratamā (Vyāsadeva), Mārkaṇḍeya, Gautama, Vaśiṣṭha, Bhagavān Paraśurāma, Bhagavān Kapila, Śukadeva, Durvāsā, Yājñavalkya, Jātukarṇa, Aruṇi, Romaśa, Cyavana, Dattātreya, Āsuri, Patañjali, Sage Dhaumya, Sage Pañcaśikha, Hiraṇyanābha, Kauśalya, Śrutadeva and Ṛtadhvaja? I am as foolish as a village animal because I am immersed in the darkness of ignorance."

Then Sage Aṅgirā replied, "O King! I am that Sage Aṅgirā, who gave you a son as per your desire, and this is the son of Lord Brahmā, Sage Nārada. You are a devotee of God and it astonishes me that, despite being a knowledgeable person, you are overcome by grief. You are lamenting for something that is not worthy of grief. We came to bless you after much deliberation. When I came to you last time, I could have given you transcendental knowledge but you were more concerned about progeny and asked me for a son. Now you have experienced the difficulties that one has to suffer as a father. You have lost your son and are lamenting over it. All the sources of material pleasure like wife, house, wealth, kingdom, prosperity and other objects for sense pleasure are non-eternal and false like a dream. Kingdom, opulence, army, ministers and servants are all ultimately a source of sorrow and pain, and attachment to them causes fear and illusion. While contemplating the objects of the senses, various types of desire arise to perform actions that are binding. False ego is the cause of the three types of suffering, i.e., self-inflicted (*adhyātmika*), inflicted by others (*adibhautika*) and inflicted by demigods (*adhidaivika*). With a calm and stable mind, you must ask yourself, 'Who am I? Where have I come from and where will I go?' You are not meant to suffer sorrow and illusion. I insist that you give thought to what I have said and discard the illusory conception that 'I am this body.'"

Sage Nārada said to King Citraketu, "Please compose yourself and accept a *mantra* I wish to impart to you. You will be able to have an audience with Lord Saṅkarṣaṇa if you chant this *mantra* properly for seven nights. In former days, Lord Śiva and other demigods took shelter of the lotus feet of Saṅkarṣaṇa. Just as burning wood results in fire, in the same way the experience of being a demigod, a human and other endless states of mind such as birth, growth, decay, destruction and other characteristics of the body appear to be that of the soul. Sometimes, in our dreams, we experience the fear of a lion or cobra due to our physical conditioning. Likewise, the activities of the body seem to be those of the real self. In deep sleep the body's senses and false ego are absent, so one does not experience the world. Similarly, the enlightened souls are free of false ego and do not identify with the body. Therefore, they are liberated from worldly events or material existence."

Sage Nārada observed that King Citraketu still had some attachment for his son, even after the sage had preached so much to him. Thus, Sage Nārada brought the king's son back to life. In order to clear all the doubts of the king and his relatives, Sage Nārada inspired the boy to preach to his father. Sage Nārada said to the prince, "O soul! May good come to you! Please rise and observe how much your parents and other relatives are grieving due to your death. Your life span is not yet over. Please return to your body and enjoy the comforts of royal life along with your relatives and rule this kingdom."

The prince replied, "I have taken many births as a result of my *karma*. In which of my births were these people my parents? In the never-ending flow of this world, we meet in various circumstances. Our relationships keep on changing as relative, friend, foe and sometimes none of these. Just as money keeps on changing hands, similarly the soul keeps on changing parents. In this world, the relationship between any two souls is temporary. Of course, as long as the relationship lasts, the affection between the two exists and when the relationship ends, the affection vanishes. The

soul is eternal. The body takes birth, not the soul. A father has control over his son as long as he is alive and after death the relationship between father and son ceases to exist. The soul neither takes birth nor dies. The soul cannot be damaged or destroyed. The conditioned soul develops a false ego under the spell of the Lord's external potency and becomes attached to material objects. The living beings suffer due to their attachment toward material objects and this attachment develops due to a lack of knowledge of the self."

King Citraketu and his family members were surprised to hear such glorious words from his dead son. Their sorrow disappeared and they stopped grieving. The queens who had killed the son of Kṛtadyuti felt ashamed of their sinful act. After understanding the words of Sage Aṅgirā, they all abandoned the desire to get a son, realizing the pain associated with becoming a mother. They went to the banks of River Yamunā and prayed to become free from the reaction of the sin of killing a young boy. Due to association with Sage Aṅgirā and Sage Nārada, King Citraketu was liberated from the dark well of worldly relations. After this, he performed rites such as bathing in the Yamunā, and then went to Nārada and Aṅgirā. Nārada was pleased with him and gave him the following *mantra*:

oṁ namas tubhyaṁ bhagavate vāsudevāya dhīmahi
pradyumnāyāniruddhāya namaḥ saṅkarṣaṇāya ca
namo vijñāna-mātrāya paramānanda-mūrtaye
ātmārāmāya śāntāya nivṛtta-dvaita-dṛṣṭaye
(*Śrīmad Bhāgavatam* 6.16.18-19)

"O Lord, O Supreme Personality of Godhead, who are addressed by the *oṁkāra* (*praṇava*), I offer my respectful obeisances unto You. O Lord Vāsudeva, I meditate upon You. O Lord Pradyumna, Lord Aniruddha and Lord Saṅkarṣaṇa, I offer You my respectful obeisances. O Reservoir of Spiritual Potency, O Supreme Bliss, I offer my respectful obeisances unto You, who are self-sufficient and most peaceful. O Ultimate Truth, One without a Second, You are realized as Brahman, Paramātmā and Bhagavān and are therefore the reservoir of all knowledge. I offer my respectful obeisances unto You."

Then Nārada and Aṅgirā left for Brahmāloka. Surviving only on water, King Citraketu chanted for one week the mantra that Nārada gave him. By following the sage's instructions, Citraketu achieved rulership of the planet of the Vidyādharas as an intermediate by-product of his advancement in spiritual knowledge. Thereafter, he attained the shelter of the lotus feet of Anantadeva, which is the ultimate goal. As the ultimate fruit of his penance, Lord Saṅkarṣaṇa appeared before him. The Lord was of fair complexion, dressed in blue attire, had bright eyes, a smiling face and was surrounded by great souls like Sanat-kumāra. Just by virtue of his having an audience with the Lord, all the reactions of of Citraketu's sins were destroyed. He offered his obeisances unto the Lord with a pure heart and eyes filled with tears due to his devotion. His throat became choked with ecstasy, which prevented him from chanting the glories of the Lord. He then controlled his thoughts and senses, regained his composure and continued to chant the glories of the *saccidānanda* (eternally existent, all-knowing and all-blissful) Lord, who is the spiritual master of all and the personification of devotional scriptures such as Nārada-pañcarātra.

Lord Saṅkarṣaṇa was pleased with the glorifications offered by Citraketu and thus revealed Himself to him. He reassured Citraketu that he had achieved perfection, and then after instructing him, the Lord disappeared. Citraketu began traveling in outer space as the head of the Vidyādharas. He boarded a transcendental airplane provided by Lord Viṣṇu and, along with Vidyādharas and Cāraṇas, he took off to visit Sumeru Mountain and other places.

One day while traveling, he saw Pārvatī sitting on the lap of Lord Mahādeva while surrounded by Siddhas, Cāraṇas and an assembly of sages. Lord Mahādeva was a good friend of King Citraketu and they used to exchange jokes with each other. Citraketu was well aware of Lord Mahādeva's transcendental position but seeing him with Pārvatī on his lap and embracing her in front of the sages like an oridinary man, he thought that people would misunderstand Lord Mahādeva's pastimes and commit an offense. Thus, he joked with Lord Mahādeva and said, "How amazing it is that Lord Mahādeva, although a great master of austerity, is embracing his wife openly in the midst of an assembly of great saints!" Lord Śiva smiled and remained silent, as did all the members of the assembly. But this joke infuriated Mother Pārvatī and she cursed the king to become a demon.

After hearing this curse, King Citraketu descended from the plane and approached Pārvatī. He offered his obeisances to her and said, "O goddess! I happily accept this curse. You have wrongly cursed me. Even though I have not committed any offense to you and Lord Mahādeva, I have been cursed due to my previous *karma*. You are not responsible for this. I know that this is not going to harm me. Living entities suffer pain and pleasure according to their previous actions. Neither I nor any friend or foe is the cause of this pain and pleasure, though the ignorant may blame others for their sufferings. The living entity, influenced by the threefold *guṇas* (modes or qualities of material nature), is himself the cause of his suffering, so what is a curse and what is a blessing? What is heaven and hell and happiness and sorrow? After all, none of these are real. The Lord creates embodied beings with the assistance of His *māyā* potency. Ignorance is the cause of bondage, and enlightenment is the cause of liberation. *Sattva-guṇa* gives pleasure and *rajo-guṇa* is the cause of pain. The omnipresent Lord is equal to all. He does not favor or dislike anyone. Therefore, how could such a detached person become angry? While living in ignorance, under the spell of *māyā*, the living entity performs pious or impious deeds that lead to pleasure, pain, good, bad, bondage, liberation, birth and death. Therefore, I shall not ask you to liberate me from this curse. I meant no offense but please forgive me."

Lord Mahādeva and Mother Pārvatī were pleased by Citraketu's words. After this, the king boarded the plane and left. Lord Mahādeva and Mother Pārvatī were amazed to see Citraketu unperturbed by the curse. Lord Mahādeva then glorified the devotees of the Supreme Lord. He spoke to Mother Pārvatī in the presence of the assembly and said, "Devotees of Supreme Lord Nārāyaṇa do not fear anything. They see heaven, hell, and liberation as the same. Living under the influence of *māyā* causes bondage, which leads one to suffer pain, pleasure, birth, death, curses and blessings, etc. As one might think that the sorrow and happiness in a dream are real or, due to ignorance, mistake a rope for a snake, then similarly, material pain and happiness are suffered due to ignorance. One who has pure devotion for Lord Vāsudeva need not take shelter of anyone else. If I consider Lord Brahmā, the Aśvini Kumāras, Sage Nārada and other saints independent from the Lord, then I shall not be able to understand His actual identity. God is partial to no one and harbors no enmity toward anyone. Citraketu is a dear devotee of the Lord and sees all as equal. It is quite normal for a devotee like Citraketu to be unperturbed; it is not unusual in any way. We are both devotees of Lord Saṅkarṣaṇa and live like friends. Harsh yet well-intentioned talks are common among friends. Rather, this gives pleasure and motivates *sakhya-rasa*. It seems that you cursed him in a moment of anger."

King Citraketu could have cursed Mother Pārvatī but, being a devotee of the Lord, he was tolerant. He accepted Mother Pārvatī's curse with humility. Due to her curse, King Citraketu next appeared as a demon from the *dakṣiṇāgni-yajña* performed by Sage Tvaṣṭā, and became known as the learned Vṛtrāsura.

Though King Citraketu was born as a demon, his devotion was not lost. This can be understood from his speech to Devarāja Indra. The devotional feelings of Vṛtrāsura are vividly described in the *Śrīmad Bhāgavatam* 6.11.22-27.

"The name of one of the ten sons of Lord Kṛṣṇa's wife Jāmbavatī was Citraketu."

"The name of one of the two sons of Lord Lakṣmaṇa was Citraketu." (SB 9.11.12)

King Citraketu of Śūrasena is mentioned in verse 9.24.40 of *Śrīmad Bhāgavatam*:

"The name of one of the two sons of Devabhaga, the brother of Vasudeva, was Citraketu."

Also, one finds the following reference in verse 4.1.39-40 of *Śrīmad Bhāgavatam*:

"Ūrjā, the wife of Vaśiṣṭha, one of the Saptarṣis (Seven Sages), gave birth to seven sons, including Citraketu. Later on they became known as the pious Saptarṣis."

The name Citraketu appears in other scriptures also.

King Bhagīratha

dilīpas tat-sutas tadvad aśaktaḥ kālam eyivān
bhagīrathas tasya sutas tepe sa sumahat tapaḥ
(*Śrīmad Bhāgavatam* 9.9.2)

"Like Aṁśumān himself, his son Dilīpa was also unable to bring the Gaṅgā to this material world, and he also became a victim of death in due course of time. Then, Dilīpa's son, Bhagīratha, performed very severe austerities to bring the Gaṅgā to this material world."

The first king of the Solar Dynasty was Vaivasvata Manu's son Ikṣvāku. Māndhātā, Pūrukutsa, Trasaddasyu, Amaraṇya, Haryaśva, Tribandhana, Triśaṅku, Hariścandra, Rohita, Harita, Campa, Sudeva, Vijaya, Bharuka, Vṛka and Bāhuka all belonged to the Ikṣvāku Dynasty. Being troubled by enemies, Bāhuka went to the forest with his wife, but died there. When Bāhuka's pregnant wife prepared to die together with her husband, Sage Urva forbade her to do so. The other wives of Bāhuka were envious of her and, in order to eliminate the child in her womb, they fed her a type of poison (*gara*). Thus, she gave birth to a son who was born with *gara*, so he was named Sagara. On the advice of Sage Urva, King Sagara performed an *aśvamedha-yajña*, but Indra kidnapped the horse that was intended for the *yajña*.

King Sagara had two wives—Sumatī and Keśinī. *Mahābhārata* states that his wives were named Vaidarbhī and Śaibyā. When the sons of Sumati went looking for the stolen horse that was intended for the *yajña*, they first dug up the earth and formed the *sagara* (ocean). After a long search they found the horse standing next to Lord Kapila. Mistakenly, they took Him to be the thief of the horse. When they expressed their anger toward Him, they were all burned to ashes by the fire in their own bodies due to their offense:

na sādhu-vādo muni-kopa-bharjitā
nṛpendra-putrā iti sattva-dhāmani
kathaṁ tamo roṣamayaṁ vibhāvyate

jagat-pavitrātmani khe rajo bhuvaḥ
(*Śrīmad Bhāgavatam* 9.8.12)

"It is sometimes argued that the sons of King Sagara were burned to ashes by fire emanating from the eyes of Kapila Muni. This statement, however, is not approved by greatly learned persons because Kapila Muni's body is completely in the mode of goodness, and therefore cannot manifest the mode of ignorance in the form of anger, just as the pure sky cannot be polluted by the dust of the earth."

Mahābhārata narrates this episode as follows:

Once, King Sagara desired a son, so in order to obtain the blessings of Lord Mahādeva, he performed severe penance. Soon after, Mahādeva was pleased and gave King Sagara a boon that he would get 60,000 sons from one wife but they would all die together, and he would get a brave son from his second wife. Thus, as promised by Lord Mahādeva, 60,000 sons were born from Vaidarbhī and, from Śaibyā, one son as bright as Kārtika was born. The mother and father named this son Asamañjasa.[14] Asamañjasa's son, Aṁśumān, went to Kapila Muni in search of the horse in order to secure salvation of his ancestors. Having arrived there, he found the *yajña* horse and the ashes of the sons of Sumati. Aṁśumān started glorifying Lord Kapila and, by doing so, managed to satisfy Him. Lord Kapila then gave him permission to take the horse but, as Aṁśumān kept on standing before Him, Kapiladeva understood that he wanted to ask for something more. When Lord Kapila learned of his wish, He told him that his ancestors would be liberated if they were offered the oblation water of Mother Gaṅgā. After this, Aṁśumān paid his obeisances to Lord Kapila and returned to his father. King Sagara completed the *yajña*, gave his kingdom to Aṁśumān and left for the heavenly abode. Despite many great efforts, Aṁśumān's son Dilīpa failed to bring the Gaṅgā to the earth. After the death of Dilīpa, his son Bhagīratha decided to perform penance in order to bring the Gaṅgā.

Being pleased by Bhagīratha's penance, Mother Gaṅgā appeared before him to grant him a benediction. Thus, Bhagīratha requested her to descend to earth for the salvation of his ancestors. Then Mother Gaṅgā replied, "To fulfill your wish I shall descend to earth, but I shall require a competent person on the earth to curb the force and velocity of my fall; otherwise I shall pierce the earth planet and enter Pātāla, the lower planetary system. Actually, I do not wish to descend to earth, because humans will wash away their sins by taking a dip in my waters, thereby maligning me. If that should occur, then how will I attain liberation from all those sins?" Therefore, King Bhagīratha countered her with two arguments:

1) Pure-hearted sages will take away all the accumulated sins by bathing in your waters, because Lord Hari, the destroyer of all sins, resides in their hearts.

2) The all-prevailing Lord Śiva, who is non-different from and most dear to the Supreme Lord, will endure the pressure of your flow.

After that, Bhāgīratha resolutely performed penance in order to receive the mercy of Lord Śiva. When Lord Śiva became pleased by his penance, he appeared before him. Thus, Bhāgīratha requested him to endure the flow of the Gaṅgā, to which Rudra agreed. So, when the Gaṅgā finally descended to earth, Śiva took her on his head and the noble King Bhāgīratha took the Gaṅgā to the place where his forefathers were burned to ashes. Bhāgīratha mounted a

14 In the *Mahābhārata* version of Kaliprasanna Singha, the son born from Śaibyā is named Asamañjā.

swift chariot while blowing his conch[15] and

---

15 Śrīla Saccidananda Bhaktivinoda Ṭhākura states in his book *Navadvīpa-dhāma Māhātmya* that King Bhagīratha founded Gaṅgā-nagara in Antardvīpa. The history of Gaṅgā-nagara is as follows: Bhagīratha was traveling in his chariot, blowing his conch so that Gaṅgā would follow him, but when they reached Navadvīpa, she stopped. When King Bhagīratha looked back, he was startled because he did not see her behind him anymore. So, he went back to Gaṅgā-nagara and performed penance there. Satisfied by his penance, Mother Gaṅgā appeared and the king prayed for the salvation of his ancestors. To this, Mother Gaṅgā replied that she would come to Navadvīpa in the month of Māgha since Lord Śrī Gaura Hari would appear on Pūrṇimā in the month of Phālguna. On that same day that she will break her fast, and moving on for the deliverance of his ancestors at the end of Phālguna.

While glorifying Jahnudvīpa, Śrīla Bhaktivinoda Ṭhākura states that when Bhagīratha came to Jahnudvīpa with the Gaṅgā, Sage Jahnu became angry and swallowed the Gaṅgā because his *ācamana* cup (part of *pañca-pātra* – utensils used for offering prayers at the time of *sandhyā*) had been swept away by the current of the Gaṅgā. When Bhagīratha did not see Gaṅgā anymore, he offered prayers to Sage Jahnu and the sage then brought out the Gaṅgā by cutting off a part of his body. Therefore, one of the names of Gaṅgā is Jāhnavī. According to the *Rāmāyaṇa*, Sage Jahnu brought the Gaṅgā out through his ear. According to the Harivaṁśa, sages have described Gaṅgā as the daughter of Sage Jahnu. In Amarārtha-candrikā, the following names of Gaṅgādevī are mentioned: Gaṅgā, Viṣṇupadī, Jahnu-tanayā, Sura-nimnagā, Bhāgīrathī, Tripathagā, Trisrotas and Bhīṣmas.

In the *Encyclopedia of Sanskrit Literature*, we find the following names: Viṣṇupadī, Jahnu-tanayā, Sura-nimnagā, Bhāgīrathī, Tripathagā, Trisrotāḥ, Bhīṣmasū, Arghya-tīrtha, Tīrtha-rāja, Tridaśa-dīrghikā, Kumārasū, Saridvarā, Siddhāpagā, Swargāpagā, Svarapagā, Svāpagā, Ṛṣikalpa, Haimavatī, Svarvāpī, Haraśekharā, Nandinī,

Mother Gaṅgā will follow him, purifying all places in the process. By the mere touch of the water of the Gaṅgā, the sons of Sagara were at once freed from all their sins, and they left for heaven. Mother Gaṅgā descended to earth because of Bhagīratha; thus she is also known as Bhagīrathī. In this context, Sage Vedavyāsa has glorified the Gaṅgā in three verses:

yaj-jala-sparśa-mātreṇa brahma-daṇḍa-hatā api
sagarātmajā divaṁ jagmuḥ
kevalaṁ deha-bhasmabhiḥ
bhasmībhūtāṅga-saṅgena svar yātāḥ sagarātmajāḥ
kiṁ punaḥ śraddhayā devīṁ sevante ye dhṛta-vratāḥ
na hy etat param āścaryaṁ svardhunyā yad ihoditam

Alakanandā, Sita-Sindhu, Adhvagā, Ugraśekhara, Siddha-sindhu, Svarga-saridvarā, Mandākinī, Jāhnavī, Puṇyā, Samudra-subhagā, Svarnadī, Sura-dīrghikā, Sura-nadī, Svardhunī, Jyeṣṭhā, Jahna-sutā, Bhīṣma-jananī, Śubhrā, Śailendrajā, Bhavāyanā and others.

pṛthvī gaṅgāya bhaviṣyatyantimo kalau

"River Gaṅgā will disappear before the destruction of the earth at the end of Kali, the last age."

According to the Brahma-vaivarta Purāṇa, River Gaṅgā will remain in Kali-yuga for 5,000 years.

Along the way at Cakradaha, while Bhagīratha was taking Mother Gaṅgā toward the sea, a wheel of his chariot got stuck in the earth. This place had earlier been known as Pradyumna-nagara, the place where Lord Pradyumna killed the demon Śambarāsura. As his chariot wheel got stuck in the earth there, the place became famous as Cakradaha. In the local accent, Cakradaha is pronounced as "Cakdaha." Cakdaha is a railway station of the Eastern Railways. Śrīla Jagadiśa Paṇḍita, an associate of Lord Caitanya Mahāprabhu, brought a deity of Lord Jagannātha from Puruṣottama-dhāma and installed it at Yaśara Śrīpaṭ near the Cakdaha Railway Station. Later on, the Founder-Ācārya of Sree Chaitanya Gaudiya Math, His Divine Grace Śrīla Bhakti Dayita Mādhava Gosvāmī Mahārāja, established a branch there.

ananta-caraṇāmbhoja-prasūtāyā bhava-cchidaḥ
(*Śrīmad Bhāgavatam* 9.9.12-14)

"Because the sons of Sagara Mahārāja committed a great sin, the heat of their bodies had increased, and they were burned to ashes. However, by the mere touch of the water of the Gaṅgā, the sons of Sagara Mahārāja were elevated to the heavenly planets. Therefore, what is to be said of a devotee who worships Mother Gaṅgā faithfully with a determined vow? One can only imagine the benefit that accrues to such a devotee. Because Mother Gaṅgā emanates from the lotus toe of Lord Hari, she is able to liberate one from material bondage. Therefore, whatever is described herein about her is true, and in no way an exaggeration."

In the *Vana-parva* of *Mahābhārata*, the detailed story of King Sagara, the episode of King Bhagīratha bringing Mother Gaṅgā to earth and the salvation of the Sagara Dynasty are described. The narration in *Mahābhārata* is almost identical to that of *Śrīmad Bhāgavatam*.

However, we do find differences in the narration of Vālmīki's *Rāmāyaṇa*, which is that Mother Gaṅgā appeared as a result of the union between Himālaya and Manorama, or Maina (daughter of Sumeru). The demigods prayed to the Himālaya demigod and received River Gaṅgā as a donation.[16] Lord Brahmā kept River Gaṅgā in his water pot (*kamaṇḍalu*), and when Bhagīratha learned that River Gaṅgā was contained in the water pot of Brahmā, he left his kingdom at the disposal of his ministers and performed penance to please Brahmā. After one thousand years of penance, Brahmā, along with all the demigods, appeared before Bhagīratha, who disclosed the purpose of his penance to him. After hearing of his desire, Brahmā told him that the earth would not be able to bear the force of Mother Gaṅgā's water and, in order to curb her force, one would first have to please Lord Mahādeva.

Bhagīratha performed penance for a year, and managed to please Lord Mahādeva, who thereafter accepted his prayer and agreed to bear the falling water of the Gaṅgā. Āśutoṣa Mahādeva is easily pleased. When Gaṅgā Devī learned that Śiva was going to curb her stream of water falling from the heavens, she decided to descend to earth with great force and enter the lower planets along with Mahādeva. Śiva was wary when he learned of this resolve, so as Gaṅgā descended, Śiva trapped her in the locks

16 According to the *Krittivasi Rāmāyaṇa* in the Bengali language, the demigods took Gaṅgā Devī in order to marry her to Lord Śiva. Menakā (Maina) was unable to see Gaṅgā Devī, and thus cursed her. Due to the curse, Gaṅgā Devī changed to the element of water.

of his hair. Gaṅgā Devī could not escape in spite of her many efforts, and when Bhagīratha did not see Gaṅgā, he became anxious and prayed to Śiva. Then, Lord Śiva merged Gaṅgā into Bindu-sarovara. Seven streams of the Gaṅgā emerged from Bindu-sarovara. On the eastern side were three streams: Hlādinī, Pāvanī and Nalinī. On the western side there were three streams: Vankaśu, Sita and Sindhu. The remaining stream followed Bhagīratha and came to be known as Bhāgīrathī. From the narration of the *Rāmāyaṇa* one learns that two daughters were born from Maina, the wife of Himālaya. The elder daughter was Gaṅgā Devī and the younger was Umā Devī. To ensure the success of a certain task of the demigods, Himālaya sent Gaṅgā Devī to Surloka, the higher planetary system. Umā attained Rudra as her husband after performing great penance. The husband of Gaṅgā is also Mahādeva.

bhagīrathena sā nītā tena bhāgīrathī smṛtā
ityeva kathitaṁ sarvaṁ gaṅgopākhyānam uttamaṁ
(*Brahma-vaivarta Purāṇa*)

When Bhagīrathī touched the sea, the sons of Sagara ascended to heaven. Since Gaṅgā Devī emerged from the lotus foot of Lord Viṣṇu, she is also known as Viṣṇupadī. The etymological meaning of Gaṅgā is *gamyate brahma-padamanayā gam-gan* (*Gamyad-yoga*, Verse 1.122). According to the encyclopedia: *gacchatīti gam-gan-ṭāp* (*Viśvakośa*).

Sage Durvāsā

nigudha niścayam dharme yaṁ
tam durvāsāsaṁ viduh
(*Mahābhārata – Ādi* 1.104.5)

In the *Mahābhārata*, it is mentioned that he who is determined on the path of *dharma* is known as Durvāsā. This Durvāsā is a partial expansion of Lord Śiva. He is counted among the Saptarṣis and is the son of Sage Atri:

marīcir atry-aṅgirasau pulastyaḥ pulahaḥ kratuḥ
brahmaṇo manasā putra vaśiṣṭhas ceti sapta te
(*Viśvakośa*)

marīcimatryaṅgirasau pulastyaṁ pulahaṁ kratum
pracetasaṁ vaśiṣṭhaṁ ca bhṛguṁ nāradameva ca
(*Manu Saṁhitā* 1.35)

Since Sage Atri accepted Anusūyā, the daughter of Sage Kardama, as his wife, she is the mother of Durvāsā:

atreḥ patny anasūyā trīñ jajñe suyaśasaḥ sutān
dattaṁ durvāsasaṁ somam ātmeśa-
brahma-sambhavān
(*Śrīmad Bhāgavatam* 4.1.15)

Anasūyā, the wife of Sage Atri, gave birth to three very famous sons: Soma, Dattātreya and Durvāsā—partial representations of Lord Brahmā, Lord Viṣṇu, and Lord Śiva respectively. This is narrated in the 4th Canto of *Śrīmad Bhāgavatam*. Here follows a summary of the life of Sage Durvāsā:

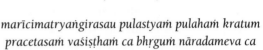

When Lord Brahmā ordered Sage Atri to populate the world after marrying Anasūyā, Sage Atri and his wife went to perform severe austerities in the valley of Ṛkṣa Mountain. The great sage focused his mind by means of *yogic* breathing exercises and, by controlling all his attachments, stood on one leg for one hundred years, surviving on nothing but air. He was thinking: "*May the Lord of the universe, of whom I have taken shelter, kindly be pleased to offer me a son exactly like Him.*" While Sage Atri was engaged in performing severe austerities, a blazing fire emanated from his head by virtue of his breathing exercises and that fire was seen by the respective principal deities of the three worlds. At that time, the three deities Brahmā, Viṣṇu and Mahādeva approached Sage Atri, accompanied by denizens of the heavenly planets such as the Apsarās, Gandharvas, Siddhas, Vidyādharas and Nāgas.

Sage Atri was overwhelmed with joy when he obtained an audience with Śrī Rudra, holding a trident in his hand, on his bull Nandi, with Śrī Brahmā on his swan, holding a *kamaṇḍalu* (water pot) in his hand, and with Śrī Viṣṇu on Garuḍa, holding His *cakra* in His hand. Sage Atri offered prayers in a melodious voice and, being satisfied by the glories sung by Sage Atri, Brahmā, Viṣṇu and Śiva told him that their partial expansions would appear in his house as his sons and would become famous throughout the three worlds:

somo 'bhūd brahmaṇo 'ṁśena datto viṣṇos tu yogavit
durvāsāḥ śaṅkarasyāṁśo nibodhāṅgirasaḥ prajāḥ
(*Śrīmad Bhāgavatam* 4.1.33)

"Thereafter, from the partial representation of Brahmā, the god of the moon, Soma, was born; from the partial representation of Viṣṇu, the great mystic Dattātreya was born; and from the partial representation of Śiva, Durvāsā was born."

As he was a partial expansion of Lord Śiva, Sage Durvāsā was effulgent and had a short temper. He accepted Kandali, the daughter of Sage Aurva, as his wife. Sage Urva held fire on his own forehead and obtained a son as effulgent as fire. Urva's son was Aurva. When Aurva tried to ignite the earth, Śrī Brahmā threw him in the ocean and since then Aurva became famous as Badavanala.

Durvāsā's wife was born from the thigh of her father. As per destiny, Kundali was also short-tempered and strict by nature. Sage Durvāsā was dissatisfied with her behavior and vowed at the time of marriage that he would excuse one hundred offenses of his wife, but no more than that. As promised, Śrī Durvāsā tolerated one hundred of his wife's offenses, but immediately after she had committed a hundred offenses, he became angry and cursed her, due to which Kanduli turned to ashes. When Sage Aurva learned of his daughter's ill fate, he cursed Sage Durvāsā, saying, "Let Sage Durvāsā's false ego be destroyed!"

As a result of this curse, Sage Durvāsā's pride was destroyed when he confronted King Ambarīṣa. In the 9th Canto of *Śrīmad Bhāgavatam*, Śrī Kṛṣṇa-dvaipāyana Vedavyāsa has narrated in detail the incident between Ambarīṣa Mahārāja and Sage Durvāsā. That chapter glorifies the superiority of a devotee in comparison to a *brāhmaṇa* renunciant. Śrīla Viśvanātha Cakravartī Ṭhākura has described Sage Durvāsā's character differently in his purport. There he says that Sage Durvāsā cursed Ambarīṣa Mahārāja in anger just to reveal Ambarīṣa's glory. Sage Durvāsā had ten thousand disciples.

The *Uttara-khaṇḍa* of the *Rāmāyaṇa* reveals that Sage Durvāsā was also the reason why Lord Rāma abandoned Lakṣmaṇa. A brief summary of the incident is as follows:

Once, in the disguise of a sage, time personified (Kāla-pūruṣaḥ) came to have an audience with Lord Rāmacandra. He wanted to have a private discussion with Him, so he set the condition that anyone who might observe him talking or overhear the discussion would be killed by Lord Rāma. When Lord Rāma agreed to the terms, he began the discussion.

Śrī Lakṣmaṇa was asked to stand guard at the door. Lord Rāma had told Śrī Lakṣmaṇa, "If anyone should enter while My discussions with Kāla-pūruṣaḥ are going on, I will kill that person."

During that time, Sage Durvāsā arrived at the door and told Śrī Lakṣmaṇa that he wanted to meet Lord Rāma immediately. Śrī Lakṣmaṇa informed the sage that the Lord was busy and that he would have to wait. This annoyed Sage Durvāsā, who said, "I must meet Lord Rāmacandra immediately, or else I shall curse this entire kingdom, city, you, your brothers and all their offspring." Lakṣmaṇa became scared when He heard of this impending curse, and the frightened Lakṣmaṇa reckoned that although He didn't mind if He were to be killed, at least all the others should not be cursed. Therefore, Lakṣmaṇa went inside where Śrī Rāmacandra and Kāla-pūruṣaḥ were engaged in a discussion and relayed the message about the arrival of Sage Durvāsā, the son of Atri. Then, Kāla-pūruṣaḥ (Kāla-pūruṣaḥ was the son of the sun-god and the grandson of Brahmā), who was sent by Brahmā, left that place. Śrī Rāmacandra offered obeisances to Sage Durvāsā and inquired about the purpose of his arrival. Sage Durvāsā told Him that he had completed a fast of one thousand years, and therefore wanted to take some food. Śrī Rāmacandra thus offered him food to his satisfaction. After this, Śrī Rāmacandra abandoned Lakṣmaṇa while in consultation with Sage Vaśiṣṭha.

Śrīmad Bhāgavatam describes the incident of Śrī Durvāsā cursing Indra:

śrī-śuka uvāca
yadā yuddhe 'surair devā badhyamānāḥ śitāyudhaiḥ
gatāsavo nipatitā nottiṣṭheran sma bhūriśaḥ
yadā durvāsaḥ śāpena sendrā lokās trayo nṛpa
niḥśrīkāś cābhavaṁs tatra neśur ijyādayaḥ kriyāḥ
(*Śrīmad Bhāgavatam* 8.5.15-16)

Śukadeva Gosvāmī said, "When the *asuras*, with their serpent weapons, severely attacked the demigods in a battle, many of the demigods fell and lost their lives. Indeed, they could not be revived. At that time, O King, Durvāsā Muni had cursed the demigods, the three worlds were poverty-stricken, and therefore ritualistic ceremonies could not be performed. The effects of this were very serious."

The history of Durvāsā cursing Indra goes as follows:

Once, while Indra was riding on the back of Airāvata,[17] he came across Sage Durvāsā, who, out of pleasure, offered his own flower garland to Indra. But Indra, filled with the pride of prosperity, threw the garland on the head of Airāvata and the garland fell down and was crushed under the feet of Indra's elephant carrier. This aggrieved Sage Durvāsā, so he cursed Indra to lose his opulence. Due to this curse, Indra, along with the three worlds, became entirely lusterless. The accursed Indra, along with the demigods, approached Lord Brahmā to find a solution to this problem. Śrī Brahmā then prayed to Śrī Hari for the welfare of the demigods, and so the Lord appeared and instructed them to appeal for a truce with the demons so they could churn the *kṣīra-sāgara*[18] together, by using the serpent Vāsuki, and Mandāra-parvata[19] as the means to churn the ocean. By their collective effort and the support of the Lord, they were able to churn the ocean and produce the nectar of immortality that would restore the luster of the demigods. Most of the demons never had any intention of sharing the nectar, so they snatched the jug of nectar right out of the hands of Dhanvantari,[20] who had collected it. However, in the end, being favored by the Lord, the demigods were able to drink all the nectar that resulted from the churning process and became immortal, regained their luster and lost all their fear. This

17 Airāvata: a magnificent white elephant.

18 Kṣīra-sāgara: the ocean of milk.

19 Mandara-parvata: a large mountain named Mandara.

20 Dhanvantari: a plenary manifestation of Lord Viṣṇu.

incident has been described in detail in the 8th Canto of the *Bhāgavatam*, from the 5th through the 9th Chapters.

"Due to Durvāsā's curse, Duṣyanta abandoned Śakuntalā." (*Viśvakośa*)

As per the *Mahābhārata*, Śūrasena had an extremely beautiful daughter named Pṛthā. Vasudeva was the son of Śrī Śūrasena. The son of Śūrasena's father's sister was Kuntībhoja. King Kuntībhoja was childless and Śūrasena was under oath that he would give his first child to Kuntībhoja. Since Pritha, the daughter given by Śūrasena, was brought to Kuntībhoja's place, she became known as Kuntī. At her father's place, Kuntī was appointed as a servitor of the *brāhmaṇas* and other guests. Pritha satisfied Sage Durvāsā (who has control over his senses, observes fasts, is short-tempered and well versed in *dharma*) by serving him suitably. With the possibility of her remaining childless in the future, Sage Durvāsā gave her specific *mantras* and blessed her that whichever demigod she would choose to call upon with those *mantras* would bless her to beget a son. Kuntī, being a virgin, thus worshiped the sun-god, Sūrya, and was blessed with a son, Karṇa. After her marriage, she called upon the demigod of *dharma*, as per the desire of her husband, to beget another son, Yudhiṣṭhira. Then she begot Bhīma by calling upon Vāyu, the demigod of air, and then Arjuna by calling upon Indra.

Due to the blessings of Durvāsā conferred upon Śrīmatī Rādhārāṇī, the food She prepared tasted like nectar:

kata upahāra āne, hena nāhi jāni
rāghavera ghare rāndhe rādhā-ṭhākurāṇī
durvāsāra ṭhāñi teṅho pāñāchena vara
amṛta ha-ite pāka tāṅra adhika madhura
(*Śrī Caitanya-caritāmṛta Antya* 6.115-116)

Once, Sage Durvāsā came to the house of Rādhā's father, Śrī Vṛṣabhānu. At that time, he was pleased by the service of Śrīmatī Rādhārāṇī and blessed Her that whatever will be cooked by Śrīmatī Rādhārāṇī will be more delicious than nectar. It will increase the life-span of whoever eats it.

In the Uttara section (1st section) of the *Gopāla-tāpanī Upaniṣad* in the *Atharva Veda*, details about Sage Durvāsā are given. Therein, the pastimes of Śrī Kṛṣṇa, the cowherd damsels of Vraja and Śrī Durvāsā are narrated by Śrī Brahmā.

The *gopīs* (cowherd damsels of Vṛndāvana) asked Śrī Kṛṣṇa to which *brāhmaṇa* they should offer food so that their wishes would be fulfilled. Śrī Kṛṣṇa told them that offering food to Sage Durvāsā would fulfill their desires. Then the resident women of Vraja said, "O Lord! How shall we cross the Yamunā River?" Śrī Kṛṣṇa told them, "If you go to the banks of the Yamunā and tell Yamunā that Śrī Kṛṣṇa is a *brahmacārī* (celibate), then Yamunā will pave the way."

The *gopīs* replied, "O Gopīnātha! You enjoy so many pastimes with the cowherd damsels, so how are You a celibate?"

Śrī Kṛṣṇa said, "There is no reason to doubt it. Just by remembering Me, an impure person becomes pure, one who is not strict in rituals becomes strict, and a sense-enjoyer becomes a renunciant. Now, if by remembering Me the water of that overflowing river retreats, what is so strange about it?"

Therefore, the *gopīs* went to Yamunā with complete faith in the words of Śrī Kṛṣṇa and spoke thusly, "Kṛṣṇa is a strict *brahmacārī*." Upon hearing these words, and as promised by Kṛṣṇa, Yamunā parted her waters and allowed the *gopīs* to cross. Upon reaching Durvasa Muni's *āśrama*, the *gopīs*, after offering him their due respects, presented him with all the sumptuous foodstuffs they had brought with them. They served him with sweet rice cooked in milk (*khīr*) and rice cooked in clarified butter (*ghṛtānna*) among other dishes, and thus satisfied his hunger. After eating the food, Sage Durvāsā gave them permission to go home.

Then the *gopīs* said, "O sage! How shall we cross Yamunā?" The sage replied, "I live on eating only sacred *durva* grass (tender grass); therefore, by remembrance of me the daughter of the demigod of the sun, Yamunā, will surely give you passage."

When they heard what Durvāsā said, their leader, Śrīmati Rādhārāṇī (Gandharvī), asked, "Dear sage! Please explain to us how Kṛṣṇa is a *brahmacārī* and how after eating so much food you are calling yourself an eater of only sacred *durva* grass?"

To this question of the main *gopī*, Durvāsā Muni replied, "Kṛṣṇa resides in all five of the basic elements of nature (earth, water, fire, air and space) and in all material sense objects. Besides this, Śrī Kṛṣṇa is a non-doer under all circumstances, so therefore He is a non-enjoyer—a *brahmacārī*. Kṛṣṇa, in His form as Paramātmā, is the witness of everything." With these words of wisdom, Sage Durvāsā expressed the nature and non-enjoying aspect of Supreme Lord Śrī Kṛṣṇa.

Śrīla Viśvanātha Cakravartī has explained as follows why Durvāsā proclaimed himself as the eater of sacred *durva* grass after eating so much food: *durvāsinaṁ durvāsasam munir atmaramam ityartham.* This means that Sage Durvāsā is situated in complete self-realization; therefore, either eating some material food or not eating at all is entirely the same thing to him. He can eat an enormous quantity of food but can just as easily live for many days without eating anything whatsoever. He does not have any hankering for or attachment to anything material.

Sage Durvāsā and his disciples visited the Pāṇḍavas in Kāmyavana during their period of exile to request food from them, but since they had just run out of food, Śrī Kṛṣṇa came and exhibited transcendental pastimes in order to save the Pāṇḍavas from being cursed by Durvāsā. This is all narrated in the *Mahābhārata*. A summary of this episode is as follows:

The Pāṇḍavas were forced to live in exile in the forest after they were tricked during a gambling match. Duryodhana, Duḥśāsana and Śakuni had planned to bring harm to the Pāṇḍavas. Once, in Dvaita Forest, the Gandharvas imprisoned Duryodhana, but Arjuna secured his release. Ever since that incident, Duryodhana and his peers felt insulted and, due to their intense jealousy, became increasingly engaged in devising a plan to inflict injury upon the Pāṇḍavas. One day, Sage Durvāsā, accompanied by his ten thousand disciples, went to the palace of Duryodhana. Duryodhana was pleased to see them and, with the intention of destroying the Pāṇḍavas, began to serve the volatile Durvāsā and his disciples. Pleased by the services rendered by Duryodhana, Durvāsā, after a number of tests, expressed his desire to bestow a boon upon Duryodhana. Then Duryodhana asked the sage, "O Sage Durvāsā! Along with your ten thousand disciples, you should visit the Pāṇḍavas in a state of hunger in Kāmyavana, right after Draupadī has taken her food."

Durvāsā agreed to fulfill this wish and, to keep his promise, Durvāsā, along with all his disciples, went to the Pāṇḍavas right after Draupadī had taken her meal. Durvāsā was hungry at that time. Yudhiṣṭhira Mahārāja bowed before him, welcomed him in accordance with proper protocol and invited him with his ten thousand disciples to come and take food.

Sage Durvāsā accepted the invitation, but first went to River Deva to bathe (the local residents of Kāmyavana in Vraja say that Vimala Kunda is River Deva). After inviting the sage,

King Yudhiṣṭhira became worried after he found out that Draupadī had already taken her meal. Feeling apprehensive that the Pāṇḍava Dynasty would be ruined if cursed by Durvāsā, who was known for his furious nature, Draupadī became morose and anxiously began to meditate upon the Lord. At that time, Śrī Kṛṣṇa was taking rest and Queen Rukmiṇī was fanning Him with a cāmara (a yak-tail fan). Śrī Kṛṣṇa is omnipresent and the destroyer of the suffering of His devotees. Therefore, although He was reclining on His bed in Dvārakā, He heard the call of His devotee far away and immediately appeared before Draupadī in Kāmyavana, saying, "Draupadī! I am very hungry. Please give Me food quickly."

Given the serious circumstances, it was quite surprising that Draupadī laughed when Śrī Kṛṣṇa asked her for food. She said, "I do not have any food. On top of that, Sage Durvāsā is our guest today with his ten thousand disciples and they are all hungry! After having taken a dip in the river and performing their rituals, they are all going to come here for food. The Pāṇḍava Dynasty will be destroyed by Durvāsā's curse and that will inevitably happen if we are unable to feed them."

Then Śrī Kṛṣṇa said, "I do not have time to hear more from you. I am suffering from hunger, so give Me food quickly."

Draupadī had received a special pot from the sun-god. Before Draupadī took the food from that pot, any number of guests could be fed to his or her heart's content from it, but this would not be so if Draupadī had taken her food from it.

During the course of discussion, Śrī Kṛṣṇa made Draupadī fetch the unusual pot and then took a small piece of vegetable stuck to it, ate it with water, and said, "*Tṛptosmi* (I am satisfied)!"

As soon as Śrī Kṛṣṇa was satisfied, Sage Durvāsā and his disciples, who were taking a dip in the river, began to burp as if they had overeaten. The sage was surprised to learn that he and the others suddenly did not feel hungry anymore. He knew that the Pāṇḍavas would offer him varieties of food even if he came uninvited. So, now, having been invited to their place, if he and his disciples did not return, it could be interpreted as an offense unto the feet of the devotees (in this case the Pāṇḍavas). Sage Durvāsā was afraid of the devotees ever since he had once offended King Ambarīṣa. He had suffered tremendously for his offense, being chased all over the universe and scorched by the Lord's Sudarśana-cakra. So, in order to solve his dilemma, the sage asked his disciples to take rest, assuming that they would surely start feeling hungry again after some time. He thought, *"At that time, we will go to the Pāṇḍavas."* Meanwhile, Śrī Kṛṣṇa sent Bhīma to fetch Durvāsā and his disciples after they failed to show up on time. Upon hearing Bhīma calling out for them, Durvāsā Ṛṣi and his disciples quickly ran away to avoid detection. When they finally did arrive the next day, they were received with an accordingly adequate welcome.

The *Viśvakośa* states that Sage Durvāsā was like an intoxicated person, and that therefore he could do anything at any time. On some days he would eat an amount of food that could have fed him for many days, while on other days he would eat only the smallest amount, yet to his complete satisfaction. One day, while eating very hot *khīr* (*pāyasa*: sweetened milk-rice), the sage asked Śrī Kṛṣṇa if He would smear the uneaten remainder on His body. Śrī Kṛṣṇa complied with Durvāsā's request, but out of devotion, the *brāhmaṇa* sage did not ask Kṛṣṇa to rub the *khīr* on His feet. Then, Śrī Kṛṣṇa rubbed some of the *khīr* on the body of

Lady Rukmiṇī, and upon seeing this, Durvāsā tied her to a chariot to pull it instead of a horse. Durvāsā then boarded the chariot and began to hit her with a stick as though she were a horse. After pulling the chariot for some time, Lady Rukmiṇī became very tired. This angered Durvāsā, so he descended from the chariot and began to walk south. When prayed to, and feeling pleased by the calm and collected response of Śrī Kṛṣṇa, he told Him, "You have conquered anger, so by my blessings You will become very dear to all. However, You did not rub *khīr* on the soles of Your feet and this has saddened me. Nevertheless, as a result, Your entire body, excluding the soles of Your feet, has now become impenetrable."

Durvāsā was the principal sage among the saints by whose curse the Yādava Dynasty was destroyed in the Pindāraka region, near Dvārakā. In the 1st Chapter of the 11th Canto of *Śrīmad Bhāgavatam*, the names of many saints are mentioned, but in the *Viśvakośa*, Sage Durvāsā alone has been described as the curse-giver. By his curse only, a mallet, which destroyed the dynasty of the Yadus, appeared in the false womb of Sāmba.

It is inferred that Sage Durvāsā was the most furious among all sages, so that is why his name only is mentioned. According to the description in *Śrīmad Bhāgavatam*, Viśvāmitra, Asita, Kaṇva, Durvāsā, Bhṛgu, Aṅgirā, Kaśyapa, Vāmadeva, Atri, Vaśiṣṭha, Nārada and other sages were present at Pindāraka. A brief description of the incident can be found in *Śrīmad Bhāgavatam*. Lord Śrī Kṛṣṇa arranged for a great war between the Kurus and the Pāṇḍavas, in order to reduce the number of people present on earth, while He simultaneously resolved to set in motion the destruction of His own dynasty through the curse of a *brāhmaṇa*, which was instigated by means of a prank.

As per the desire of Śrī Kṛṣṇa, Viśvāmitra and the other saints gathered in the Pindāraka region near Dvārakā. While playing, the sons of the Yādavas also arrived at the site and the young boys played a prank on the saints. They dressed up Prince Sāmba, the son of Jāmbavatī, as a pregnant woman, making him wear women's clothing and bloating his belly. Then they mischievously took him to the gathering of the sages and said, "O sages! You are all-knowing, so please tell us which child this pregnant lady will bear?"

The sages, being very annoyed by their mischief, invoked a curse. "This lady will give birth to a mallet that will destroy the Yadu Dynasty." At that moment, a mallet came out of the fake belly of Sāmba. Frightened, they took the mallet to King Ugrasena and told him everything. The king told them to grind the mallet into powder and throw it into the sea. They then did what the king had instructed.

However, a fragment of the mallet remained and was swallowed by a fish, while the powder was swept to the seashore by the waves and turned into shrubs. Eventually, a fisherman caught the fish and retrieved the piece of mallet from its stomach. A hunter then found the small piece of mallet and fixed it on the tip of an arrow. Although omniscient Śrī Kṛṣṇa knows all, He did not do anything to prevent this. On the contrary, He supported the proceedings.

In *Śrīmad Bhāgavatam*, 11th Canto, Chapter 30, the pastimes relating to the destruction of the Yadu Dynasty are described. When they noticed many bad omens, the Yādavas, as per the advice of Śrī Kṛṣṇa, abandoned Dvārakā and went to the Prabhāsa region on the bank of River Sarasvatī. There, enchanted by the external potency of Śrī Kṛṣṇa, they started drinking a huge amount of *maireya*, a type of wine. Becoming intoxicated, they lost all their discrimination and began to fight among themselves. After all their weapons were destroyed, they started to fight with the reeds that had grown from the mallet powder, and eventually they were all killed. Elsewhere, Śrī Kṛṣṇa and Śrī Balarāma exhibited Their disappearance pastimes with the support of a hunter. The consequences of making a mockery of saints are most destructive. This incident is the perfect example to teach how careful we should be in our dealings with saints. Foolish persons are destroyed when they ignore this.

Sage Agastya

The *Ṛg Veda* states that Sage Agastya is the son of Varuṇa and Mitra (the demigods of the ocean and the sun). Sage Agastya was born from an earthen pot and was of diminished stature, so one of his initial names is Māna.

Later, when he crushed the pride of the mountain Vindhya, he got the name Agasti.

vālmīkiś ca mahā-yogī valmīkād abhavat kila
agastyaś ca vaśiṣṭhaś ca mitrā-varuṇayor ṛṣī
(*Śrīmad Bhāgavatam* 6.18.5)

"By the semen of Varuṇa, the great mystic Vālmīki took birth from an anthill. Bhṛgu and Vālmīki were specific sons of Varuṇa, whereas Agastya and Vaśiṣṭha Ṛṣis were the common sons of Varuṇa and Mitra, the tenth son of Aditi."

It is surprising to know that even the demigods are not liberated if their dynasty is discontinued. Sage Agastya did not wish to marry, but, one day, he saw that his forefathers were dangling in a well upside down. He was bewildered and asked his forefathers the reason for this. They said, "We are your ancestors and we shall be liberated if you protect the dynasty." (*Mahābhārata*, *Vana-parva*, Chapter 96, as mentioned in *Viśvakośa*)

Sage Agastya abandoned his vow of celibacy and decided to marry in order to liberate his ancestors. However, he found no one worthy enough to marry him. With the power of his mind, he mentally accumulated the different parts of various beings that he found to be the most beautiful, and created an imaginary girl by assembling those beautiful parts. At that time, the king of Vidarbha was performing penance in order to get a child. Sage Agastya gave that imagined girl to the king and, in due course of time, the king of Vidarbha was blessed with a beautiful girl (the girl produced by Sage Agastya's mental prowess). The beauty of the girl pleased the king and *brāhmanas* and she was given the name Lopamudrā. In the same way that the glow of the star Rohiṇī outshines all other stars, Lopamudrā began to shine among one hundred girls and one hundred maidservants. Lopamudrā possessed a superlative character and good manners, and was more beautiful even than celestial women. The king of Vidarbha became tired of looking for an appropriate match for his daughter, as he had been unable to find one after searching for a long time.

At this time, Sage Agastya felt that Lopamudrā was suitable for family life, so he went to the king of Vidarbha and presented his proposal to marry Lopamudrā. The king was shocked to hear the proposal but was afraid that the great sage would curse him if he did not agree. Therefore, the king put this proposal before his daughter to see her opinion; sensing her father's fear, she said, "Father, you need not worry about me. You may give me to Sage Agastya and become free of anxiety." Hearing this, the king gave the girl to Sage Agastya, who accepted Lopamudrā as his wife and Lopamudrā abandoned her royal clothes and ornaments according to her husband's wishes and dressed herself in old torn clothes and deerskin as well as clothes made from the bark of trees; at the same time she agreed to accept his strict rules and regulations. Then, Sage Agastya, along with his newlywed wife, went to a bank of the Gaṅgā and began performing severe penance. Lopamudrā engaged herself in the service of her husband with love and devotion and Sage Agastya was satisfied by this service. However, he realized that Lopamudrā had a desire to acquire as much wealth as her father. Thus, he went to King Śrutvarśa, then to King Bradhnaśva and, after that, to King Trasaddasyu (the son of Pūrukutsa) and asked them for the opulence Lopamudrā sought, but they said that their income and expenses were similar and that they did not have the capacity to give such wealth. In addition, they said, "O *brāhmaṇa*! The demon Ilvala is the richest man on earth; let us all go to him and ask him for riches."

As the demon Ilvala saw Sage Agastya, accompanied by kings, coming toward him, he arranged for their welcome and inquired as to the reason for their visit. Ilvala used to kill *brāhmaṇas* with the help of his younger brother, Vātāpi. By his mystical powers, Vātāpi would take the form of a ram and then Ilvala would cut up that sheep and feed it to the sages or *brāhmaṇas*. After the sages had eaten, Ilvala would call Vātāpi and then, at that time, Vātāpi would come out of the stomach of the sages. In this way, he had killed many *brāhmaṇas* and sages.

hrādasya dhamanir bhāryā-sūta vātāpim ilvalam
yo 'gastyāya tv atithaye pece vātāpim ilvalaḥ
(*Śrīmad Bhāgavatam* 6.18.15)

"The wife of Hlāda was named Dhamani. She gave birth to two sons, named Vātāpi and Ilvala. When Agastya Muni became Ilvala's guest, Ilvala served him a feast by cooking Vātāpi, who was in the shape of a ram."

With the intention of killing Sage Agastya, he asked Vātāpi to take the form of a sheep and then proceeded to feed Sage Agastya. When the kings became aware of his intention, they became morose and almost unconscious. However, Sage Agastya told the kings not to worry. He promised them, "You have no need to worry as I am going to digest Vātāpi after eating him." Then he ate all the things that were offered to him by Ilvala. After Sage Agastya had finished eating, Vātāpi did not come out of the stomach of Sage Agastya despite being called repeatedly by his brother. Only some air passed from the lower portion of the body of Sage Agastya with a thunderous sound. Then Sage Agastya laughed and informed Ilvala that he had digested his brother, so how could he possibly come out?

Ilvala was distraught when he learned that Sage Agastya had digested Vātāpi. He became terrified and began to tremble. He called upon his family members and, along with them, with folded hands, inquired about the purpose of the visit of the sage and kings. To this, Sage Agastya asked him to give enormous wealth to the kings and himself without inflicting any damage on anyone. When Ilvala became aware of the desire of the sage, immediately he arranged to satisfy their request. The sage also revealed to Ilvala his knowledge of the many hidden desires of Ilvala's mind. Thus, Ilvala was compelled to provide to the sage immense wealth along with a golden chariot pulled by two horses, named Virava and Surava. The kings and Sage Agastya then proceeded to board the chariot with all the wealth, and swiftly reached the sage's *āśrama*. Then, all the kings took permission from Sage Agastya and departed to their respective destinations.

Sage Agastya fulfilled the desire of Lopamudrā. Lopamudrā prayed to her husband for a child and, in response to this, Sage Agastya said, "I am satisfied by your service." He then asked Lopamudrā, "Do you want a hundred or a thousand sons, each with the capability of ten persons, or ten sons, each with the capability of a hundred persons, or one son with the capability of defeating a thousand people?"

Lopamudrā expressed her desire to have one son, full of all virtues, wisdom and strength. After fulfilling her desire, Sage Agastya went to the forest. This child took seven years to develop in the womb of Lopamudrā. After the completion of seven years, the exceptionally brilliant poet Dridhasyu came out of her womb and approached his father while reciting *Saṅgopaniṣad.* He would always collect firewood for his father, even since early childhood. Due to this, he became famous as Idhmavāha:

īḍamānam bharamajahre idhmavāha stato bhavat
(*Mahābhārata*, *Vana-parva* 99.23-27)

Sage Agastya was overwhelmed to see that this son was even more virtuous than himself. By giving birth to such an excellent son, he had secured the liberation of his ancestors. Since that time, the place where he lived is renowned as Agastyāśrama. In the 28th Chapter of the 4th Canto of *Śrīmad Bhāgavatam*, Sage Agastya narrates the story of the daughter of the king of Vidarbha. In this story, in a very ornamental linguistic style, he describes the effect of the association of the devotees of Lord Kṛṣṇa. This is done with reference to Idhmavāha, Dṛḍhacyuta and other sages:

agastyaḥ prāg duhitaram upayeme dhṛta-vratām
yasyāṁ dṛḍhacyuto jāta idhmavāhātmajo muniḥ
(*Śrīmad Bhāgavatam* 4.28.32)

Sage Agastya married the first-born daughter of Malayadhvaja (an avowed devotee, i.e., a fully surrendered devotee of Lord Kṛṣṇa). From her a son was born, whose name was Dṛḍhacyuta. The name "Dṛḍhacyuta" means "one who is not interested in attaining Satyaloka or other higher planets," or it can mean "one who is detached from the comforts of this world or heaven, devoid of any desire for liberation, of pure heart and dedicated to service unto Lord Kṛṣṇa without interest in any other means or objects of worship." The name of another son of Sage Agastya was Idhmavāha. The name "Idhmavāha" refers to one who carries wood for burning in a sacrifice when approaching a spiritual master. Therefore, Sage Agastya is also known as Idhmavāhātmājah. "Idhmavāhātmājah" means *idhma vāhāh ātmāja yasya tadrisah* ("one who has realized the real nature of the soul").

Sage Agastya had a number of hermitages (*āśramas*), including one in the Daṇḍakāraṇya Forest where he gave guidance to Lord Śrī Rāmacandra. According to *Mahābhārata*, he had an *āśrama* in Gayā also.

Sage Agastya had unique power due to his severe penance. He dried up the ocean to fulfill the desire of the demigods. He destroyed the two demons Ilvala and Vātāpi. When Vindhyācala decided to block the path of the sun, he crushed his pride. When Lord Rāmacandra visited his *āśrama* in Daṇḍakāraṇya, he presented the Lord with the bow of Lord Viṣṇu, an infallible arrow given by Brahmā, inexhaustible quivers and a sword. He was extremely intelligent, yet he still used to carry the palanquin of King Nāhuṣa. One day, when the king was taking a ride on a palanquin, his foot touched the sage. This offended Sage Agastya and he cursed King Nāhuṣa to turn into a snake (*Vana-parva* of *Mahābhārata—Viśvakośa*).

After crushing the ego of Vindhya Mountain, Sage Agastya took up residence at Dakṣiṇatya. The people of the Draviḍa region learned many things from him. European scholars have concluded that Sage Agastya was from Tibet. Sage Agastya now resides as a celestial star in the southern sky (*Viśvakośa*).

Sage Agastya was the spiritual master of Vindhya Mountain. Due to his own false ego, Vindhya Mountain stopped the movement of the sun. As a result, all the demigods prayed to Sage Agastya for help. Sage Agastya went to Vindhya and, when Vindhya offered obeisances to his spiritual master, Sage Agastya asked him to stay in the same position and continue to remain so until his return. Then Sage Agastya went to the south and never returned. Since that time, Vindhya Mountain could not stop the movement of the sun by raising his head or peak. This incident occurred on the first day of the month of Bhādra. Thus, this day is known as Agastya-yātrā (*Mahābhārata, New Bengali Dictionary* of Āśutoṣa Deva).

The incident where Sage Agastya dehydrated the ocean is mentioned in *Mahābhārata*, of which a summary now follows:

During Satya-yuga there was a group of ferocious demons known as Kālakeya. The leader of this group of demons was Vṛtrāsura. When the demigods were terrorized and tormented by the Kālakeya demons, they approached Lord Brahmā, who directed them to go to the extremely merciful Sage Dadhīci. He further instructed them to beg from Dadhīci his bones, from which they were to prepare a highly potent weapon (*vajra*). The king of the demigods, Indra, would then kill Vṛtrāsura with that weapon. Thus, when the demigods approached Sage Dadhīci, he gave them his bones and Viśvakarmā used them to prepare a weapon for Indra. When Indra approached Vṛtrāsura, a ferocious battle ensued between the demigods and demons. During this conflict, Indra killed Vṛtrāsura with the weapon prepared from the bones of Sage Dadhīci.

The demons were scared by the death of Vṛtrāsura and jumped into the ocean, filled with fishes and crocodiles. They were accustomed to devouring sages and wreaking destruction during the nocturnal hours. Due to their habit of killing *brāhmaṇas* at night and hiding in the sea during the daytime, people began to flee out of fear. The king of the demigods, Indra, along with the other demigods, took refuge of Śrī Nārāyaṇa.

Lord Śrī Nārāyaṇa told them, "The ferocious demons, the Kālakeyas, are destroying the world from their base in the ocean. In order to kill them, someone needs to dry up the ocean, and Sage Agastya has this capability." As instructed by Lord Nārāyaṇa, the demigods approached Sage Agastya and prayed to him to do away with the ocean. As a result of this prayer, Sage Agastya came to the seashore and angrily drank all the water. The demigods were amazed to see him perform such a herculean task. When the demigods were killing the Kālakeya demons by means of their celestial weapons, many of the Kālakeya demons entered the lower planetary system (Pātāla) by tunneling through the earth.

An incident is mentioned in the 4th Chapter of the 8th Canto of *Śrīmad Bhāgavatam* where Sage Agastya cursed King Indradyumna of

Pandya State to become an elephant. A brief description is as follows:

King Indradyumna was following devotional practices and had taken a vow of silence while staying at an *āśrama* he had built at Malayācala. During that time, Sage Agastya and his disciples came to King Indradyumna's *āśrama*. Since he was engaged in deep meditation, he could not provide an adequate reception and welcome to Sage Agastya. This annoyed the sage, so he cursed him that he might become a *stabdha-matiḥ gaja* (dull elephant). This is how King Indradyumna got the body of an elephant due to the curse of the sage:

śrī-śuka uvāca
evaṁ śaptvā gato 'gastyo bhagavān nṛpa sānugaḥ
indradyumno 'pi rājarṣir diṣṭaṁ tad upadhārayan
āpannaḥ kauñjarīṁ yonim ātma-smṛti-vināśinīm
hary-arcanānubhāveṇa yad-gajatve 'py anusmṛtiḥ
(*Śrīmad Bhāgavatam* 8.4.11-12)

(Śukadeva Gosvāmī then said,) "My dear King, after Agastya Muni had thus cursed King Indradyumna, the sage left that place along with his disciples. Since the king was a devotee, he endorsed Sage Agastya's curse because it was the desire of the Supreme Personality of Godhead. Therefore, in his next life he got the body of an elephant but, due to his prior devotional service, he still remembered how to perform worship and offer prayers to the Lord."

In the 23rd Chapter of the 5th Canto of *Śrīmad Bhāgavatam*, it is stated that Sage Agastya resides on the upper chin of the dolphin-shaped Śiśumāra planetary system.

According to the 84th Chapter of the 10th Canto of *Śrīmad Bhāgavatam*, at Kurukṣetra during a solar eclipse, seeing how much the Lord's consorts loved their husband, the *gopīs* were struck with wonder. At that time, Sage Nārada and other sages had come to have an audience with Lord Kṛṣṇa. Sage Agastya was among them.

Agastya is revered as the *brāhmaṇa* who brought the Sanskrit speaking civilization to South India, and drank and digested the ocean. When the Vindhya mountain range would not stop growing, Agastya crossed it to the south direction and commanded it to cease growing until his return; he still has not returned (*Encyclopedia Britannica*, Volume 20.540).

Sage Aṅgirā

Sage Aṅgirā was conceived in the mind of Śrī Brahmā; hence, he is known as the *manasā-putra* of Śrī Brahmā. He is counted among the Saptarṣis (Seven Sages). It is described in the 3rd Canto of *Śrīmad Bhāgavatam* that Śrī Brahmā produced ten sons to expedite the creation of the material universe:

marīcir atry-aṅgirasau pulastyaḥ pulahaḥ kratuḥ
bhṛgur vasiṣṭho dakṣaś ca daśamas tatra nāradaḥ
(*Śrīmad Bhāgavatam* 3.12.22)

"(The Saptarṣis all took birth from the different parts of Śrī Brahmā:) Nārada appeared from the lap of Śrī Brahmā, Dakṣa appeared from his toe, Vaśiṣṭha appeared from his life span, Pulastya came from his navel, Aṅgirā from the mouth, Atri from the eyes, and from his mind came Marīci."

The wife of Sage Aṅgirā was Śubha (Śraddhā) and Bṛhaspati was his son. He also had six daughters named Bhanumati, Rākā, Sinīvālī, Arviśvatī, Haviśvatī and Puṇyājanika (Kuhū).

Mahābhārata mentions that, once, Sage Aṅgirā performed intense penance and, due to its profound effect, the effulgence from his body engulfed the whole world. It so happened that the fire demigod, Agni, was performing penance at the same time. Due to the overwhelming nature of the results of Sage Aṅgirā's penance, Agni thought that he had lost his luster and wrongly assumed that Śrī Brahmā had created another powerful fire. However, eventually he realized that Sage Aṅgirā had become so radiant that he was responsible for spreading this competing heat across the universe.

When Sage Aṅgirā saw the demigod of fire, he said, "O Agni! Please take on the form of fire and perform your own duty. I shall be your son." Thus, Agni assumed the form of fire and Aṅgirā became Agni's son, taking the name Bṛhaspati (*Viśvakośa*).

In the *Vana-parva* of *Mahābhārata* is an account of a question and answer session between Śrī Vaiśampāyana and Śrī Janamejaya. The old history narrated by Sage Mārkaṇḍeya in answer to Yudhiṣṭhira Mahārāja, is given in brief as follows:

In ancient times Sage Aṅgirā performed severe penance in his *āśrama*. Due to the powers thus accumulated, Sage Aṅgirā became so bright that he was illuminating the entire world. At that time, Agni was also performing penance but was upset because he could not get the desired results. He was unable to comprehend the reason behind this and could only draw the conclusion that, due to his indulgence in penance, his power of fiery effulgence had disappeared. He thought that Śrī Brahmā had therefore created another fire for the benefit of the people of the world.

The fire demigod Agni then contemplated how he could get back his fire potency, and thus meditated to discern the cause of its loss. As a result, he realized that Sage Aṅgirā was radiating so much heat that it extended to nearby planets. This scared Agni, so, hesitatingly, he went to Sage Aṅgirā and when Sage Aṅgirā saw Agni, he said, "O Agni! Śrī Brahmā created you in the form of fire to remove the darkness, and you are well known throughout the universe. Therefore, please resume your position and give welfare to all the three worlds in the form of fire." Then Agni said, "At this moment you have become *hutāśana* (another name for fire) and I am no longer glorious. Everyone will recognize you as the maintainer instead of me. I am abandoning the quality of fire; you are foremost and I am secondary."

To this, Sage Aṅgirā said, "O Agni! You give welfare to the people by accepting offerings made in *yajñas*, so please adopt me as your first son." Agni agreed and Aṅgirā became his son known as Bṛhaspati. This Bṛhaspati is the spiritual master of all the demigods. The demigods agreed to what Sage Aṅgirā had spoken.

According to the *New Bengali Dictionary*, written by Āśutoṣa Deva, Sage Aṅgirā attained Bṛhaspati as his son due to the blessing of the demigod Agni. The name of the elder son of Sage Aṅgirā was Utathya.

After being cursed by a *brāhmaṇa* boy, King Parīkṣit abandoned his kingdom and went to Sukartāla on the banks of the Gaṅgā, where he sat meditating on the lotus feet of Śrī Kṛṣṇa while fasting until death. At that time, the munificent sages that purify the world came there with all their disciples, including Atri, Vaśiṣṭha, Cyavana, Śaradvān, Ariṣṭanemi, Bhṛgu, Aṅgirā, Parāśara, Viśvāmitra, Paraśurāma (son of Gādhi), Utathya, Indrapramada, Subāhu, Medhātithi, Devala, Ārṣṭiṣeṇa, Bhāradvāja, Gautama, Pippalāda, Maitreya, Aurva, Kumbhayoni, Agastya, Kṛṣṇa-dvaipāyana Vedavyāsa and Śri Nārada. *Śrīmad Bhāgavatam* mentions that these and other sages and saints gathered there, with Sage Aṅgirā being one of them.

The 4th Canto of Śrimad *Bhāgavatam* states that Kardama Muni handed over his nine daughters to the nine great sages, who created the population of the world. He was instructed to do so by Lord Brahmā. Kardama Muni gave his daughter Kalā to Marīci, and another daughter, Anasūyā, to Atri. He delivered Śraddhā to Aṅgirā, and Havirbhū to Pulastya. He delivered Gati to Pulaha, the chaste Kriyā to Kratu, Khyāti to Bhṛgu, and Arundhatī to Vaśiṣṭha. Aṅgirā's wife, Śraddhā, gave birth to four daughters, named Sinīvālī, Kuhū, Rākā and Anumati:

śraddhā tv aṅgirasaḥ patnī
catasro 'sūta kanyakāḥ
sinīvālī kuhū rākā
caturthy anumatis tathā
(*Śrīmad Bhāgavatam* 4.1.34)

In the Svārociṣa era (*manvantara*), Sage Aṅgirā had another two sons. One of them was known as Utathya, and the other was the learned scholar Bṛhaspati.

According to the 5th Canto of *Śrīmad Bhāgavatam*, Jaḍa Bharata was the son of a *brāhmaṇa* born in the lineage of Aṅgirā. It is known from the 6th Canto of *Śrīmad Bhāgavatam*, where Prajapati Dakṣa has discussed the subject of the creation of life, that Dakṣa willingly dedicated his two daughters, named Svadhā and Satī, to Sage Aṅgirā. Svadhā wished to obtain all the Pitās (departed ancestors) as her sons, and Satī desired the Atharvāṅgirasa *Veda* as her son:

prajāpater aṅgirasaḥ
svadhā patnī pitṝn atha
atharvāṅgirasaṁ vedaṁ
putratve cākarot satī
(*Śrīmad Bhāgavatam* 6.6.19)

In the description of King Citraketu, Sage Aṅgirā is also mentioned. It is stated that when Sage Aṅgirā came to discuss transcendental knowledge with King Citraketu, the king expressed a desire to have a son instead of gaining transcendental knowledge. At that time, Sage Aṅgirā blessed him with a son who would be a source of happiness as well as sorrow. Then, on the death of that son, Sage Aṅgirā came with Śrī Nārada and consoled the king.

From the description given in the 8th Chapter of the 8th Canto of *Śrīmad Bhāgavatam*, it is known that when Mother Lakṣmī appeared as a result of the churning of the milk ocean by the demigods and demons, she accepted the Lord as her husband. The Lord took her on His chest. At that time, Sage Aṅgirā glorified the Lord, along with Brahmā, Rudra and others.

It is known from the 6th Chapter of the 9th Canto that Mahārāja Ambarīṣa had three sons, respectively named Virūpa, Ketumān and Śambhu. The son of Virūpa was Pṛṣadaśva, and his son was Rathītara. Rathītara had no sons, but when he requested the favor of the great sage Aṅgirā, the sage bestowed him several glorious sons. Sage Aṅgirā was also among the sages who arrived during the solar eclipse at Kurukṣetra mentioned earlier.

According to the 11th Chapter of the 11th Canto, Sage Aṅgirā was among the sages present in the Piṇḍāraka region who cursed the Yadu Dynasty with destruction.

The 11th Chapter of the 12th Canto of *Śrīmad Bhāgavatam* describes the presiding deity of the sun and the other six associates of the Supreme Lord for each month of the year. There, we find that Indra as the sun-god, Viśvāvasu as the *gandharva*, Śrotā as the *yakṣa*, Elāpatra as the *nāga*, Aṅgirā as the sage, Pramlocā as the *apsarā* and Varya as the *rākṣasa* rule the month of Nabhas (Śrāvaṇa).

Sage Kaśyapa

Brahmā was born from the lotus flower growing from the navel of Mahāviṣṇu's expansion, Garbhodakaśāyī Viṣṇu, who is resting on the waters of the Causal Ocean (*mahat-tattva*). Marīci took birth from the mind of Lord Brahmā, and Kaśyapa appeared from the womb of the daughter of Dakṣa Mahārāja, fathered by Marīci. From Kaśyapa and Aditi, Vivasvān took birth:

marīcir manasas tasya jajñe tasyāpi kaśyapaḥ
dākṣāyaṇyāṁ tato 'dityāṁ vivasvān abhavat sutaḥ
(*Śrīmad Bhāgavatam* 9.1.10)

The birth of Sage Kaśyapa is detailed in the 1st Chapter of the 4th Canto of *Śrīmad Bhāgavatam*.

patnī marīces tu kalā suṣuve kardamātmajā
kaśyapaṁ pūrṇimānaṁ ca yayor āpūritaṁ jagat
(*Śrīmad Bhāgavatam* 4.1.13)

"Kardama Muni's daughter Kalā, who was married to Marīci, gave birth to two children, whose names were Kaśyapa and Pūrṇimā. Their descendents are spread all over the world."

śrī-śuka uvāca
tataḥ prācetaso 'siknyām anunītaḥ svayambhuvā
ṣaṣṭiṁ sañjanayām āsa duhitṝḥ pitṛ-vatsalāḥ
(*Śrīmad Bhāgavatam* 6.6.1)

"Thereafter, at the request of Lord Brahmā, Prajāpati Dakṣa, who is known as Prācetasa, begot sixty daughters from the womb of his wife, Asiknī. All the daughters were very affectionate to their father." Prācetasa gave thirteen of his daughters to Sage Kaśyapa. The population of the entire universe is produced from the wombs of the wives of Sage Kaśyapa, and to hear their names is very auspicious:

punaḥ prasādya taṁ somaḥ kalā lebhe kṣaye ditāḥ
śṛṇu nāmāni lokānāṁ mātṝṇāṁ śaṅkarāṇi ca
atha kaśyapa-patnīnāṁ yat-prasūtam idaṁ jagat
aditir ditir danuḥ kāṣṭhā ariṣṭā surasā ilā
muniḥ krodhavaśā tāmrā surabhiḥ saramā timiḥ
timer yādo-gaṇā āsan śvāpadāḥ saramā-sutāḥ
(*Śrīmad Bhāgavatam* 6.6.24-26)

The names of the wives of Sage Kaśyapa are Aditi, Diti, Danu, Kāṣṭhā, Ariṣṭā, Surasā, Ilā, Muni, Krodhavaśā, Tāmrā, Surabhi, Saramā and Timi. All the aquatics took birth from the womb of Timi; ferocious animals such as tigers and lions took birth from the womb of Saramā; buffalo, cows and other animals with cloven hooves took birth from the womb of Surabhi; from the womb of Tāmrā eagles, vultures and other large birds of prey took birth and from the womb of Muni the Apsarās took birth. The serpents known as Dandaśūka, as well as other serpents and insects such as mosquitoes, were born from the womb of Krodhavaśā, while all varieties of creepers and trees were born from the womb of Ilā. The Rākṣasas, bad spirits, were born from the womb of Surasā, while the Gandharvas were born from the womb of Ariṣṭā. Horses and other animals whose hooves are not split were born from the womb of Kāṣṭhā. From the womb of Danu appeared the Dānavas; Diti gave birth to the Daityas, and the demigods took birth from the womb of Aditi. The names of the principal sons of Aditi are as follows: Vivasvān, Aryamā, Pūṣā, Tvaṣṭā, Savitā, Bhaga, Dhātā, Vidhātā, Varuṇa, Mitra, Śatru and Urukrama.

Sage Kaśyapa is the grandson of Śrī Brahmā and is the son of Marīci and his wife Kalā. Some say that Sage Kaśyapa had seven wives, and others say he had thirteen wives, who are described as mothers of the demigods, demons, serpents, birds and so on. He took birth on this earth after being cursed by Śrī Brahmā when he stole the cow of Varuṇa (mentioned in the *New*

Bengali Dictionary of Āśutoṣa Deva). This great sage, Kaśyapa, was also present at the time of Arjuna's birth. He was given the whole world as a present from Paraśurāma and eventually he requested Paraśurāma to leave the world. His other name is Ariṣṭanemi. He lives on the northern side of the universe.

The birth of Hiraṇyākṣa and Hiraṇyakaśipu from the womb of Diti, the wife of Kaśyapa, is described in the 3rd Canto of *Śrīmad Bhāgavatam* as follows:

During the evening time, Diti, the daughter of Dakṣa Prajāpati, asked her husband, Kaśyapa, for a son. Sage Kaśyapa told his wife that he would fulfill her desire after the evening but Diti was unable to control her passion, and so she kept on pressing her husband to fulfill her desire. In the end, Sage Kaśyapa finally succumbed to her plea but she learned from her husband that her actions would bear her two ill-natured and cruel sons, who would be killed by others. Hearing this, Diti prayed to her husband to bestow the benediction that only the Supreme Lord would kill her sons. Sage Kaśyapa agreed to her request. Those two sons of Diti were Hiraṇyākṣa and Hiraṇyakaśipu. Sage Kaśyapa informed Diti that a great devotee by the name of Prahlāda would appear in the house of Hiraṇyakaśipu. When Kaśyapa told her that her own grandson would become a great devotee, Diti was pacified.

The description of the birth of the forty-nine Marutas is detailed in the 6th Canto of *Śrīmad Bhāgavatam*, which mentions that Lord Viṣṇu killed Hiraṇyākṣa and Hiraṇyakaśipu in order to help Indra, the king of the demigods. Hearing of the death of her two sons, Diti lamented her loss and grew vengeful. Thus, she endeavored to please her husband by means of her service, after which she begged from him the boon of giving her a son who would kill Indra. The plan worked, but when the sage heard his wife's request, he became very much aggrieved. Associating with a woman can be dangerous, as is revealed here. A woman's heart is therefore sometimes compared to the sharp edge of a knife. Sage Kaśyapa lamented falling for her charms, which had provided the incentive for him to grant such an impious boon to her, but in order to uphold *dharma*, he kept his word and advised Diti to observe the vow of strictly following the Vaiṣṇava principles (devotion to Supreme Lord Viṣṇu). If she should do so, then she would get a son who would be able to kill Indra. However, he also warned her that if there should be any mistake in the rituals, she would instead get a son who would be a friend of the demigods and a supporter of Indra.

As advised by her husband, Diti engaged herself in observing this vow. Meanwhile, Indra came to know about the desire of Diti, so in the name of serving her, he began to look for mistakes in her practices, but could not find any fault. Once, however, being very tired, Diti neglected to wash her mouth, hands and feet after eating, and went to sleep during the evening twilight. Finally, finding a fault, Indra, who possesses all mystic powers,[21] entered Diti's womb while she was sleeping and, with the help of his thunderbolt, cut the embryo into seven pieces and then cut each of those pieces into seven pieces. Thus, the forty-nine Marutas were born. As a result of failing to properly observe her vow of following the Vaiṣṇava principles, Diti's sons, the Marutas, became friends of the demigods instead of the demons.

The description of hearing the glories of the Gajendra-mokṣana episode in *Śrīmad Bhāgavatam* 8.4 tells us that, by remembrance of the wives of Sage Kaśyapa (daughters of Dakṣa), all the sins of human beings are destroyed. According to the 7th Chapter of the

21 *Yoga-siddhis* such as *aṇimā* and *laghimā*.

8th Canto, both Sage Kaśyapa's godly sons born from his wife Aditi as well as the demonic sons born from his wife Diti churned the Kṣīra-sagara (Ocean of Milk) to get the nectar of immortality. The churning process had the demigods and demons holding opposite ends of Vāsuki, the king of serpents, using him as a rope to spin the churning stick, Mount Mandara, as instructed by Lord Ajita.

kaśyapo 'trir vaśiṣṭhaś ca viśvāmitro 'tha gautamaḥ
jamadagnir bhāradvāja iti saptarṣayaḥ smṛtāḥ
(*Śrīmad Bhāgavatam* 8.13.5)

"Kaśyapa, Atri, Vaśiṣṭha, Viśvāmitra, Gautama, Jamadagni and Bhāradvāja are known as the Seven Sages."

atrāpi bhagavaj-janma kaśyapād aditer abhūt
ādityānām avarajo viṣṇur vāmana-rūpa-dhṛk
(*Śrīmad Bhāgavatam* 8.13.6)

"In this *manvantara* (period of time) of the reign of a Manu, the Supreme Personality of Godhead appeared as the youngest of all the Ādityas, known as Vāmana, the dwarf. His father was Kaśyapa and His mother was Aditi."

In the 8th Canto of *Śrīmad Bhāgavatam*, it is described in detail that Lord Vāmana appeared, taking Sage Kaśyapa as His father and Aditi as His mother, in order to complete a task of the demigods. A recapitulation of the event is given as follows:

Bali regained his life by the grace of his guru, Śukrācārya, after Indra, the king of the demigods, had killed him. He became extremely effulgent after successfully performing the *viśvajīta-yajña* with the blessings of the *brāhmaṇas* belonging to the Bhṛgu Dynasty. He then launched an attack on the heavenly planets. Observing and experiencing the strength of Bali Mahārāja, Indra went to Bṛhaspati, the *guru* of the demigods, and sought advice on how to deal with the situation. Acting upon the instructions of Bṛhaspati, Indra and the other demigods fled from heaven and began to live clandestinely in space. Bali Mahārāja thereafter occupied heaven and became the ruler of the three worlds. Due to affection for their disciple, the *brāhmaṇas* of the Bhṛgu Dynasty arranged for one hundred *aśvamedha-yajñas*, all of which were performed by Mahārāja Bali.

Aditi,[22] the mother of the demigods, was saddened to see her sons having to live in hiding, without a kingdom. Meanwhile, after a long period of time, Kaśyapa Ṛṣi returned home, having completed austerities. Surprised at finding his house so lusterless and his wife so weak and pale, he asked Aditi what had happened. Upon inquiry, Aditi revealed everything to him and requested him to act, so that the demigods (and thus her sons) would regain the heavenly kingdom. In this context, two sermons given by Sage Kaśyapa regarding the duty of a householder are worthy of attention:

api vātithayo 'bhyetya kuṭumbāsaktayā tvayā
gṛhād apūjitā yātāḥ pratyutthānena vā kvacit
(*Śrīmad Bhāgavatam* 8.16.6)

"I hope that you did not fail to properly receive the uninvited guests that came to your house who, thereupon, returned home due to being unattended because you were too much focused on your own family."

gṛheṣu yeṣv atithayo nārcitāḥ salilair api
yadi niryānti te nūnaṁ pherurāja-gṛhopamāḥ
(*Śrīmad Bhāgavatam* 8.16.7)

22 Two of Kaśyapa Ṛṣi's wives, Diti and Aditi, are mentioned here in connection with this topic. The sons of Diti are the demons and the sons of Aditi are the demigods. The demons and the demigods are stepbrothers.

"Homes from which guests go away without having been received even with an offering of a little water are like those holes in the fields that are the homes of jackals."

Aditi, the mother of the demigods, appealed to Kaśyapa Muni to help the demigods regain heaven and other opulences from the demons; however, Sage Kaśyapa did not take her request seriously. He said, "See how the illusory energy of Lord Viṣṇu is so powerful that the entire world is bound by affection for children! The demigods are our friends and the demons are our enemies; this vision of the duality of friend and enemy only occurs to those who are infatuated by the illusory energy (*māyā*) of the Supreme Lord. Due to their forgetfulness of the Supreme Lord, people experience the negation of knowledge (*viparīta-buddhi*) regarding their own constitutional position, and consequently they are subject to all sorts of troubles and difficulties. Actually, all are engaged in a mutual interrelationship of love by dint of their relationship with the Supreme Lord. A pure understanding of knowledge does not include any vision of enmity. My advice to you is that you should give up your bodily misidentification along with your false sense of relations, and worship Hari with full dedication. Lord Vāsudeva appears in the pure heart of a *jīvātmā*. Lord Hari can fulfill all the desires of all souls. Any devotional service unto the Supreme Lord never goes to waste, whereas all other means are incomparable to devotional practice."

Mother Aditi took the teachings of her husband to heart, but nonetheless she persistently requested that her sons should regain the kingdom of heaven. Sage Kaśyapa took this as a sign of the Lord's desire, so he advised his wife to observe a fast for twelve days[23] by drinking only milk. Sage Kaśyapa explained to Mother Aditi, "None other than Lord Keśava will be able to fulfill your desire." He thus instructed her that, in addition to fully devoted worship of the lotus-eyed Śrī Hari, she should survive on milk alone, during the bright fortnight of the moon in the month of Phālguna. Mother Aditi observed the fast as per her husband's instructions. Thereafter, fulfilling the words of Sage Kaśyapa, Lord Nārāyaṇa appeared before Mother Aditi as Śyāmasundara (sweet and dark complexioned) dressed in yellow garments and in a four handed form.

"Oh! What incredible power do the words of Sage Kaśyapa possess?" Mother Aditi was filled with great bliss and love upon obtaining an audience with the Lord. Satisfied by the prayers offered by Mother Aditi, the Lord gave

23 One celestial day is equal to one year of the human beings, i.e., 365 days.

her the boon that, by appearing as her son, He would fulfill her desire. After this, at an auspicious time, the Lord appeared in the heart of Kaśyapa Ṛṣi while he was in a state of trance. Kaśyapa then imparted divine knowledge to Aditi through initiation.

When Lord Brahmā understood that the Supreme Personality of Godhead was now within the womb of Aditi, he began to offer prayers to the Lord by reciting transcendental names (*guhya-stotra*). Then, on the twelfth day of the month of Śrāvaṇa, at the very auspicious moment of the Abhijita star, Lord Nārāyaṇa appeared from the womb of Aditi as Śyāmasundara-pītāmbara (dark complexioned, sweet and dressed in yellow garments) holding a conch, disc, club, and lotus. Kasyapa Ṛṣi and Mother Aditi became filled with great bliss upon seeing the beautiful dwarf form of Vāmana, and were completely overwhelmed with affection for their child. All the birth *saṁskāras* (purificatory rituals) of the child were performed according to the scriptural directions. At the sacred thread ceremony (*upanayana-saṁskāra*) of Vāmanadeva, the sun-god himself instructed Him in the *gāyatrī-mantra*, Bṛhaspati presented Him with the sacred thread, Kaśyapa gave Him a straw belt (a girdle), Mother earth gave Him a deerskin to sit on and the moon-god, who is the king of the forests, gave Him a *brahma-daṇḍa* (the staff of a *brahmacārī*). Mother Aditi gave Him a *kaupīna* cloth (sacred undergarment) and an umbrella, Lord Brahmā gave Him a waterpot, the Seven Sages offered Him *kuśā* grass, Sarasvatī gave Him a string of *rudrākṣa* beads, Kuvera gave Him a pot for begging alms and Bhagavatī, the mother of the universe, gave Him alms.

After the *upanāyana-saṁskāra* ceremony, Lord Vāmanadeva fulfilled the desire of Mother Aditi by begging from Bali an amount of land equal in size to three of His steps, in the field known as Bhṛgukaccha. The Lord tricked Bali by dint of His unlimited powers and spanned beyond the three worlds using only two steps, thereby returning the heavenly realm to the demigods. Upon Bali's request, Vāmanadeva placed His third and final step on Bali Mahārāja's head, thereby supremely blessing him and allowing Bali to fulfill his promise. Sage Kaśyapa was among the sages present at Pindaraka-kṣetra by whose curse the Yadu Dynasty was destroyed. Sage Kaśyapa possessed the ability of absorbing poison, as told in *Śrīmad Bhāgavatam*:

takṣakaḥ prahito viprāḥ kruddhena dvija-sūnunā
hantu-kāmo nṛpaṁ gacchan dadarśa pathi kaśyapam
taṁ tarpayitvā draviṇair nivartya viṣa-hāriṇam
dvija-rūpa-praticchannah kāma-rūpo 'daśan nṛpam
(*Śrīmad Bhāgavatam* 12.6.11-12)

"O learned *brāhmaṇas*, the snake-bird Takṣaka, who had been sent by the angry son of a *brāhmaṇa*, was moving toward the king to kill him when on his way he encountered Kaśyapa Muni. Takṣaka flattered Kaśyapa by presenting him with valuable offerings and thereby stopped the sage, who was expert in counteracting poison, from protecting Mahārāja Parīkṣit."

Sage Kaśyapa is one of the six great *ācāryas* mentioned in the *Śrīmad Bhāgavatam*, 7th Chapter, 12th Canto. The personality of Sage Kaśyapa is described in the *Harivaṁśa Purāṇa* and *Mahābhārata*, written by Sage Śrī Kṛṣṇa-dvaipāyana Vedavyāsa.

Sage Parāśara

Sage Parāśara was the son of Śrī Śakti (son of Śrī Vaśiṣṭha) and his wife Adṛśyanti:

parāsuḥ sa yatastena vaśiṣṭhaḥ sthāpito muniḥ
garbhasthena tato loke parāśara iti smṛtiḥ
(*Mahābhārata* 1.176.3)

parāsorāśāsanaṁ avasthānam yena sa parāśaraḥ āṅg
pūrvācchāsateḥ ūran
(Nīlakaṇṭha commentary on *Mahābhārata*)

"While in the womb of his mother, his grandfather Vaśiṣṭha desired to die, hence he was named Parāśara."

Details about Sage Parāśara are given in the *Ādi-parva* of *Mahābhārata* Chapters 175-182. A brief description is given as follows in *Viśvakoṣa*:

Among the hundred sons of Sage Vaśiṣṭha, Śakti was the best. He was married to Adṛśyanti. Once, when Śakti was strolling through a forest, King Kalmāṣapāda[24] of the Ikṣvāku Dynasty became tired from his hunting excursion and, while looking for a place to rest, happened upon Śakti, who was traversing the same path. The path treaded by Śakti was very narrow, to the degree that only one person at a time could pass through. Therefore, the king asked Śakti to step back, but he refused to do so and a quarrel erupted. The king became furious and, under the control of his false ego, acted like a demon and struck Śakti with his whip. The strike of the whip injured Śakti, who broke into a senseless fury and cursed the king thusly: "I am a sage and you have hit me as though I were a demon, so may you therefore become a demon from this day onward!" However, the king had already been cursed by another saint to become a demon, so he immediately assumed a demonic form and devoured Śakti on the spot. Furthermore, Kalmāṣapāda devoured all the remaining sons of Vaśiṣṭha as well. In this way, the hundred sons of Vaśiṣṭha were killed. Actually, the hundred sons of Vaśiṣṭha were brought to ruin by the cunningness of Viśvāmitra. Overcome with grief as a result of this, Vaśiṣṭha attempted suicide several times but somehow failed to succeed to do so. While returning to his *āśrama,* he suddenly heard the distinct sound of the chanting of the *Vedas* from the western direction. He asked, "Who is reciting the *Vedas* there?"

Śakti's wife replied, "Please understand that this voice uttering the *Vedas* belongs to my twelve-year-old son still residing in my

24 In the 9th Chapter of the 9th Canto of *Śrīmad Bhāgavatam* the details about Kalmāṣapāda are as follows: Sudāsa's son King Saudāsa was the husband of Damayantī, also known as Madayantī. Some called Saudasa "Mitrasaha," while others called him "Kalmāṣapāda." Because of his past crimes, Saudāsa was cursed by Vaśiṣṭha to become a *rākṣasa.* This incident is decribed thus:

One day while hunting, Saudasa killed a man-eating demon, but spared the life of the demon's brother. To avenge his brother's death, that demon began to work as a cook at the king's palace. One day, when Śrī Vaśiṣṭha visited the king's palace, the demon in the guise of a cook served him human flesh. When the mystic, Vaśiṣṭha, noticed that he was being served an inedible substance, he cursed King Saudasa to become a man-eating demon. Later, when he learned that this heinous action was not the king's doing, but that of his demon servant, he observed a twelve-year-long fast so as to lift the curse from the innocent king. King Saudasa had already taken water into his hand with which he planned to curse Śrī Vaśiṣṭha in return, but his wife stopped him from doing so. King Saudasa then looked in all the ten directions, the sky, earth and all places full of life, but he could not decide where to throw the water. Having no other recourse, he dropped the cursed water onto his own feet. This transformed his good nature into that of a demon, and his feet turned black as an effect of dropping the cursed water on them. Thus he became known as Kalmāṣapāda. As he tolerated and agreed with the words of his wife, he also came to be known as Mitrasaha.

womb." When Vaśiṣṭha learned that Adṛśyanti was pregnant he was ecstatic, and in that mood he returned to his house. While he was on his way, a demon attacked Adṛśyanti. Therefore, Vaśiṣṭha uttered a mantra and threw water on the demon, thereby redeeming him from the curse. Upon regaining his human form, it turned out to be King Kalmāṣapāda of the Ikṣvāku Dynasty. When Vaśiṣṭha finally returned to his *āśrama*, Adṛśyanti gave birth to a son as bright as Śakti. Vaśiṣṭha performed all his initial birth rituals (*jāta-karma-saṁskāra*). Since this son was in the womb when, in his mind, Vaśiṣṭha desired to die, he named him Parāśara.

From his birth Parāśara understood that Vaśiṣṭha was his father. One day he addressed Vaśiṣṭha as his father in front of Adṛśyanti, who became filled with emotion and, as a result, her voice became choked up. Therefore, Parāśara said, "Mother, why are you crying?" As she caressed her son she said, "My dear son, the one you are taking as your father is actually not your father but your grandfather. One of the demons ate your father in the forest." Upon learning this, Parāśara decided to destroy all the worlds. Observing his resolve, Sage Vaśiṣṭha instructed him about transcendental knowledge, hoping that this would relieve him of his anger and sinful plans, but Parāśara did not agree and his wrath remained unpacified.

Out of animosity toward the whole demon community, he performed a sacrifice to kill all *rākṣasas* (demons). Remembering the death of his father, Śakti, he began to kill the whole demon community, including women, children, the elderly and others, while performing the sacrifice. Earlier, Vaśiṣṭha had objected to his decision to destroy all the worlds, upon which Parāśara had then relented somewhat, but Sage Vaśiṣṭha did not stop him this time. Later, Pulastya, Pulaha and other saints came to Parāśara as representatives of the *brāhmaṇas* and said to him, "Dear friend, not all the demons are complicit in the killing of your father by their kind. Therefore, by indiscriminately killing all those demons, even the ones who had no part in your father's killing, you are unnecessarily destroying the creation. So, we request that you might end this sacrifice and become free of this horrible act of killing. This is not the nature of *brāhmaṇas* and saints, as they are peaceful in their behavior. Being angry, you are destroying ordinary persons by performing this sacrifice. The demon that devoured your father was not guilty; your father was destined to go to the heavenly abode from this planet due to his own fault; otherwise that demon would not have been able to eat your father. Viśvāmitra was just an instrument in the course of events. Your father, his brothers and King Kalmāṣapāda are all residing with the demigods in heaven. Your grandfather Vaśiṣṭha is aware of everything. Now please stop this sacrifice and may you thus be blessed with the best of all things."

As requested, Parāśara stopped the sacrifice, and transferred the fire that was established and intended for the destruction of the *rākṣasas*, to the forests in the north of the Himālayas. Even now, that same fire burns *rākṣasas*, trees and rocks every year. The compiler of all the *Vedas*, Sage Śrī Kṛṣṇa-dvaipāyana Vedavyāsa, is the son of Parāśara:

tataḥ saptadaśe jātaḥ satyavatyāṁ parāśarāt
cakre veda-taroḥ śākhā dṛṣṭvā puṁso 'lpa-medhasaḥ
(*Śrīmad Bhāgavatam* 1.3.21)

"Thereafter, the seventeenth *avatāra* (divine manifestation) of Godhead, Śrī Vyāsadeva, appeared in the womb of Satyavatī through Parāśara Muni, and divided the one *Veda* into several branches and sub-branches, seeing that the people in general were less intelligent."

At the time when King Parīkṣit came to Śukaratala on the banks of River Gaṅgā and began observing the *prayopaveśana* fast, Parāśara was among the pious sages who arrived there. The names of the saints mentioned in *Śrīmad Bhāgavatam* 1.19.9-10 are Atri, Cyavana, Śaradvān, Ariṣṭanemi, Bhṛgu, Vaśiṣṭha, Parāśara, Viśvāmitra, Aṅgirā, Paraśurāma, Utathya, Indrapramada, Idhmavāhu, Medhātithi, Devala, Ārṣṭiṣeṇa, Bhāradvāja, Gautama, Pippalāda, Maitreya, Aurva, Kavaṣa, Kumbhayoni, Dvaipāyana and the great personality Nārada.

vicitravīryaś cāvarajo nāmnā citrāṅgado hataḥ
yasyāṁ parāśarāt sākṣād avatīrṇo hareḥ kalā
(*Śrīmad Bhāgavatam* 9.22.21)

"Citrāṅgada, whose younger brother was Vicitravīrya, was killed by a Gandharva who was also named Citrāṅgada. Satyavatī, before her marriage to Śāntanu, gave birth to the master authority of the *Vedas*, Vyāsadeva, known as Kṛṣṇa-dvaipāyana, who was begotten by Parāśara Muni."

As per *Śrīmad Bhāgavatam* 12.6.48-49, the directors of the universe, led by Brahmā and Śiva, requested the Supreme Personality of Godhead, the protector of all the worlds, to save the principles of religion. The almighty Lord, exhibiting a divine spark of a portion of His plenary portion, then appeared in the womb of Satyavatī as the son of Parāśara. In this form named Kṛṣṇa-dvaipāyana Vedayāsa, he divided the *Veda* into four parts.

Sage Maitreya said to Vidura:

sāṅkhyāyanaḥ pāramahaṁsya-mukhyo
vivakṣamāṇo bhagavad-vibhūtīḥ
jagāda so 'smad-gurave 'nvitāya
parāśarāyātha bṛhaspateś ca
provāca mahyaṁ sa dayālur ukto muniḥ
pulastyena purāṇam ādyam
so 'haṁ tavaitat kathayāmi vatsa
śraddhālave nityam anuvratāya
(*Śrīmad Bhāgavatam* 3.8.8-9)

"The great sage Sāṅkhyāyana was the chief among the transcendentalists, and when he was describing the glories of the Lord in terms of *Śrīmad Bhāgavatam*, it so happened that my spiritual master, Parāśara, and Bṛhaspati both heard him. The great sage Parāśara, as aforementioned, being so advised by the great sage Pulastya, spoke unto me the foremost of the *Purāṇas* (*Bhāgavata Purāṇa*). I shall also describe this before you, my dear son, according to what I heard, because you are always my faithful follower."

Lord Saṅkarṣaṇa spoke the purport of *Śrīmad Bhāgavatam*, the slayer of the sorrow of souls, to the great sage Sanat-kumāra. Sanat-kumāra, in turn, when requested by Sāṅkhyāyana Muni, explained *Śrīmad Bhāgavatam* to him.

A description of Śrī Kṛṣṇa-dvaipāyana Vedavyāsa Muni is also given in *Devī Bhāgavatam*. A summary of it is as follows:

Sage Parāśara arrived on the banks of the Yamunā while going on a pilgrimage across the country. Desiring to cross Yamunā River, he sought help from a fisherman. However, the fisherman was busy doing some work, and thus asked his daughter Matsyagandha to take the sage across the river instead. As instructed by her father, Matsyagandha began rowing the boat, but when they reached the middle of the river, providence arranged for loving emotions to develop in Sage Parāśara even though the body of Matsyagandha stank of dead fish. However, by the blessings of Sage Parāśara, she turned into a beautiful damsel and her foul odour was transformed into the cooling smell of sandalwood. She became Yojanagandha, meaning that her fragrance could be smelled as far away as a *yojana*, which is approximately eight miles. As per her desire, Sage Parāśara created a dense mist around them and blessed her that she would not lose her virginity despite their union. The son born from her womb would be as bright and virtuous as he was and her bodily odor would always remain as it now was. The union of Matsyagandha with Sage Parāśara was an act of providence and, by their union, the world-famous sage Śrī Kṛṣṇa-dvaipāyana Vedavyāsa appeared as a partial expansion of the Lord at a very auspicious moment. As soon as he appeared, Sage Vedavyāsa sought permission to leave home. His mother tried to stop him, but in most respectful words Sage Vedavyāsa told his mother that whenever she would remember him, he would appear before her.

Sage Vedavyāsa began to perform penance as soon as he appeared. Sage Parāśara compiled a *saṁhitā* of twelve chapters known as *Parāśara Saṁhitā*, which details the duties to be performed during Kali-yuga:

kṛte tu mānavo dharmāstretāyāṁ gautama smṛtah
dvāpare śaṅkhalikhitou kalau parāśara smṛtah

"In Satya-yuga the *dharma* as instructed by Manu is to be followed, in Treta-yuga that instructed by Gautama, in Dvāpara-yuga the *dharma* instructed by Śankha and Sage Likhita is to be followed, and in Kali-yuga only the words of Parāśara are to be followed."

King Śibi

In *Śrīmad Bhāgavatam*, King Bali told his guru, Śukrācārya:

śreyaḥ kurvanti bhūtānāṁ sādhavo dustyajāsubhiḥ
dadhyaṅ-śibi-prabhṛtayaḥ ko vikalpo dharādiṣu
(*Śrīmad Bhāgavatam* 8.20.7)

"Great souls like Dadhīci and Śibi sacrificed their lives for the welfare of others, so where is the need to deliberate on the decision to give away this earth in sacrifice? What objections can one make against this?"

Jarāsandha said to Bhīma, Arjuna and Śrī Kṛṣṇa, who were all disguised as *brāhmaṇas*:

yo 'nityena śarīreṇa satāṁ geyaṁ yaśo dhruvam
nācinoti svayaṁ kalpaḥ sa vācyaḥ śocya eva saḥ
hariścandro rantideva uñchavṛttiḥ śibir baliḥ
vyādhaḥ kapoto bahavo hy adhruveṇa dhruvaṁ gatāḥ
(*Śrīmad Bhāgavatam* 10.72.20-21)

"Those possessing a mortal body that do not strive to gain eternal glory as eulogized by sages are considered to belong among the most unworthy and shameless people. In the past many great souls like Hariścandra, Rantideva, Uñchavṛtti Mudgala, Śibi, Bali, the legendary hunter and pigeon, and many others have attained the permanent by means of the impermanent."

King Śibi was born in the Lunar Dynasty. King Yayāti had five sons—Yadu, Turvasu, Anu, Druhyu and Pūru. Among them, Anu's son was Sabhānara, Sabhānara's son was Kālanara, Kālanara's son was Sṛñjaya, Sṛñjaya's son was Janamejaya, Janamejaya's son was Mahāśāla, Mahāśāla's son was Mahāmanā and Mahāmanā's son was Uśīnara. Uśīnara had four sons—Śibi, Vara, Kṛmi and Dakṣa. Śibi was the eldest. (*Śrīmad Bhāgavatam* 9.23.1-4)

Śibi had four sons—Vṛṣādarbha, Sudhīra, Madra and Kaikaya. King Śibi was religious and charitable. In *Mahābhārata* (*Vana-parva*, Chapter 196) a detailed account of King Śibi is given by Sage Kṛṣṇa-dvaipāyana Vedavyāsa, which is now summarized:

Once, the demigods decided to go to earth to test the religiosity and gentleness of King Śibi, the son of Uśīnara. As such, Agni and

Indra arrived on the earth planet. Agni assumed the form of a pigeon and Indra took the form of a bird of prey. So, Indra, as an eagle, started chasing after Agni, who had taken the form of a pigeon. Meanwhile, King Śibi was sitting on his divine throne. Then, all of a sudden, the frightened pigeon fell on the king's lap to save himself. Observing the pigeon's act of surrender, the king's priest told the king, "This pigeon has taken shelter of you in order to protect itself from an eagle. On the other hand, the wise say that when a pigeon falls on one's body it is considered a bad omen. One may however donate wealth in order to clear oneself of the consequences of this bad omen." Hearing this, the pigeon said in a grieved voice, "O my rescuer! O great soul! I am not an ordinary pigeon! Please don't think that my falling in your lap is a bad omen for you. I am actually a *muni* (sage) and I have taken birth in this body of a pigeon because of the fruits of my *karma*. I am properly educated, celibate, a performer of penance and free of sins; I teach the *Vedas* and have reached perfection in reciting Vedic hymns. It will not be proper for you to hand over to the eagle a learned *brāhmaṇa*, who has taken shelter of you to save his life." Meanwhile, the eagle that had been chasing the pigeon also arrived on the spot and said, "O King! This pigeon has revealed his previous birth to you and I feel that in your previous birth you were born from this pigeon. Therefore, you are now protecting this pigeon, assuming it to be your father. However, I must tell you that I am starving, so I wonder whether or not it is proper for you to hinder me in trying to fulfill the urges of my belly?" King Śibi was astonished upon hearing the pigeon and the eagle speak, and he wondered how they, in spite of being birds, were able to speak perfect Sanskrit. He thought: "*These two are both qualified and, given the circumstances, it is a matter of careful deliberation on how I should deal with them.*"

After carefully contemplating the situation, King Śibi said, "One who hands over the fearful and surrendered into the hands of an enemy will not attain liberation whenever such a time should arrive. It will not rain in his kingdom and the seeds won't sprout even though they have been planted at the appropriate time. A person who offers a frightened refugee to an enemy will have his child die in childhood, his ancestors will never attain a place in heaven and the demigods will refrain from accepting anything offered by him. Indra and other demigods will attack such a person with their weapons like the Vajra (thunderbolt) and others. Therefore, instead of surrendering this pigeon to you, I want to make you an offer. I shall ask the people of my dynasty to give you the cooked flesh of an ox; instead of this pigeon. My people will deliver substantial volumes of flesh to your residence."

Hearing the appropriate argument and subsequent offer of the king, the eagle replied, "O King! I will not eat the flesh of an ox, therefore please hand over the pigeon to me." The king then replied, "I will ask my people to give you the ox complete with all body parts intact, but you may not kill this pigeon."

As the eagle did not agree to this proposal, King Śibi resolutely said, "O beautiful eagle, this pigeon is tenable by me like the *saṁyukta-yajña*. I may give up my life, but I will not return this pigeon to you, so please do not waste your time trying to achieve this. Therefore, please make me a proposition—anything that may both please my people and serve your purpose as well." The eagle thus replied, "O King! If you cut the flesh from your right thigh equal in proportion to the pigeon and give it to me, this pigeon will be free and my purpose will be served. Simultaneously, your ancestors will also praise you."

The king accepted this proposition and proceeded to cut off a piece of flesh from his right thigh, and placed it on one of the plates of the balance with the pigeon on the other plate as a counterweight. The balance tipped over to the side of the pigeon. King Śibi thus cut off another piece of flesh, this time from another body part, and placed it on the balance, but still the pigeon weighed more. In this manner, he sliced the flesh from all parts of his body, but its weight could not match the weight of the pigeon. Then, as a last measure, the king sat himself down on the balance. The eagle was astonished not to see a single sign of anger, repentance, grief or worry in the king, and so the eagle vanished, saying, "The king has achieved the pigeon's release." Since the eagle had vanished so suddenly, the king asked the pigeon about the true identity of the eagle, as no one but the Lord would be able to perform such an act.

The pigeon replied, "I am the god of fire, Agni, and the eagle was the holder of the Vajra weapon, the husband of Śacī, Indra. O King! You are the best among the sons of Sauratha. We descended from the heavenly planets in order to test you, and in order to protect me you cut off the flesh of your own body with a sword. I am going to make all those parts pious, enchanting and pleasantly fragrant with a golden hue. You will become glorious and rule over your people. A man will be born from your side and his name will be Kapotroma. Your son will be the most superb among all the followers or descendants of Sauratha."

In *Mahābhārata*, *Vana-parva*, Chapter 131, where details about Uśīnara, the father of Śibi, are mentioned, it is stated that the above incident took place with King Uśīnara. Śibi's exalted personality has also been described in the *Agni Purāṇa*.

Mahābhārata, *Vana-parva*, Chapter 197, describes that during the *aśvamedha-yajña* of Viśvāmitra's son King Aṣṭaka, his three brothers Pratardana, Vasumana, and Uśīnara's son Śibi, came there as well. However, on the way to the *yajña* they encountered Sage Nārada. During the discussion that followed, they posed a question to Sage Nārada. "Who among us will become fallen, and who will go to heaven?" In reply to this Nārada said, "Śibi will go to heaven and I shall become fallen, as I am not like Śibi." Thus he humbly described Śibi.

One day, a *brāhmaṇa* came to beg grains from Śibi. Śibi asked, "What type of grains are you begging?" The *brāhmaṇa* said, "You must kill your son named Vṛṣāgarbha (some call him Vṛṣādarbha), perform his rites, prepare food and wait for me." As instructed by the *brāhmaṇa*, the king killed his son, performed his *saṁskāra*, cooked food, kept it in utensils that he carried on his head and thus began to search for the *brāhmaṇa*. Meanwhile, a man came and informed him that the *brāhmaṇa* that he was looking for was angry and was setting fire to Dhanagāra, Astragāra, Astraśala and Hathiśala. The king was not disturbed by this bad news and appeared indifferent. Upon finding the *brāhmaṇa*, he walked up to him and said, "Dear *brāhmaṇa*, your food is ready and served. Take as you please." Although the *brāhmaṇa* had very well heard the king, he did not reply. When the king requested him again to take the food, he remained silent for some time and then asked the king to eat.

As requested by the *brāhmaṇa*, the king sat down to eat. As soon as the king began to eat, the *brāhmaṇa* took hold of his hand and expressed his faith in the king with the following words, "O King, you have control over your anger; therefore you can do anything for the service of a *brāhmaṇa*." After that, the king saw his son standing before him, looking like a demigod, while the *brāhmaṇa* had vanished. The Lord Himself had come disguised as a *brāhmaṇa* in order to test King Śibi. When his ministers questioned his actions, the king told them that he did not act for fame, wealth or enjoyment, as only the path treaded by gentlemen is praiseworthy.

Sage Mārkaṇḍeya

Śrīmad Bhāgavatam, Canto 4, Chapter 1, affirms that Mārkaṇḍeya, Vedaśirā, Śukrāgarbhā and other famous personalities appeared as descendants of the dynasty of Brahmā's son Bhṛgu. Bhṛgu was married to Khyāti, a daughter of Dakṣa. She gave birth to two sons, named Dhātā and Vidhātā, and a devotee daughter, named Śrī. The sage known as Meru had two daughters, named Āyati and Niyati, whom he gave in charity to Dhātā and Vidhātā. Dhātā's wife Āyati gave birth to Mṛkaṇḍa, and Vidhātā's son was Prāṇa. Mārkaṇḍeya was the son of Mṛkaṇḍa and Vedaśirā of Prāṇa.

It is thus written in *Mārkaṇḍeya Purāṇa* that Mārkaṇḍeya was born from the union of Mṛkaṇḍa and Manasvini. In this Purāṇa, Dhūmāvatī is described as a wife of Mārkaṇḍeya, and Vedaśirā is described as his son.

Also in *Mahābhārata*, his father's name is given as Mukandu and his mother's name as Damorna. He has narrated a Purāṇa under his own name. There was no other who lived as long as Sage Mārkaṇḍeya, due to being blessed with an extraordinarily long life span (*cirañjīvi*) by Lord Viṣṇu. Whatever he saw, he narrated to Yudhiṣṭhira (*Skanda Purāṇa*). He would dispell doubts related to the *Purāṇas* and other scriptures, as mentioned in the *New Bengali Dictionary* of Āśutoṣa.

It is customary to pray to him while performing rituals on birthdays or other *saṁskāras*:

dvibhujaṁ jatilāṁ saumyaṁ suvṛddhāṁ cirañjīvinam
mārkaṇḍeyam naro bhaktyā pūjayecch cirāyuṣam
(*Tithi-tattva* by Raghunandana Bhaṭṭācārya)

The story of Sage Mārkaṇḍeya is also described in *Nṛsimha Purāṇa* and *Padma Purāṇa*. The narrative in *Śrī Nṛsimha Purāṇa* is as follows:

Bhṛgu's son was Mṛkaṇḍu. Mṛkaṇḍu had a son by the name of Mārkaṇḍeya. When his son was born, he was grieved to learn that his son would not live for more than twelve years. When Mārkaṇḍeya enquired as to the reason for his father's sorrow, he answered him, "My son, I have just learned that you will die at age twelve." On hearing this, Mārkaṇḍeya told his father, "You need not worry, dear father, I shall act in such a way that I will defeat death and live a long life." After this, Sage Mārkaṇḍeya took permission from his mother and father to leave for the forest to perform penance. In the forest he installed a deity of Viṣṇu and resolved to perform severe penance. He thus defeated death by the power of penance and attained a long life.

In *Padma Purāṇa* it is mentioned that when Sage Mṛkaṇḍu was performing penance with his wife, a son named Mārkaṇḍeya was born. However, Sage Mṛkaṇḍu's joy soon turned into sorrow when he learned that this son would die at the age of eight. Therefore, at the time of his son's *upanayana-saṁskāra* (sacred thread ceremony), Mṛkaṇḍu asked his son to offer obeisances to the sages. Ever since then Mārkaṇḍeya would always do as he was told. Meanwhile, the Saptarṣis (Seven Sages) came there and Mārkaṇḍeya bowed his head before them with devotion. Observing the respects offered by the child, these seven sages were pleased and blessed him thus: "May you have *cirāyu*, or an extraordinarily long life span." Later, when they learned that the child was destined to live for a very short time, they became morose and worried. Therefore, they took the child with them and approached Brahmā. Brahmā bestowed longevity on the child after learning the unfortunate details from the Saptarṣis. Mārkaṇḍeya then returned home after receiving the boon of long life from Brahmā.

One of the eighteen *Purāṇas* written by Śrī Vedavyāsa is *Mārkaṇḍeya Purāṇa*. This Purāṇa begins with Svayambhū[25] Brahmā instructing Mārkaṇḍeya. By reading or listening to this Purāṇa, one will increase his life span, all his desires will be fulfilled and all his sins will be destroyed.

In the discussions between Yudhiṣṭhira and Nārada in *Śrīmad Bhāgavatam* 7.1, an incident is described about Jaya and Vijaya, the doorkeepers of Vaikuṇṭha who were cursed to take three births. In their second births during Treta-yuga they appeared as Rāvaṇa and Kumbhakarṇa. Lord Rāmacandra killed them and they then appeared during Dvāpara-yuga as Śiśupāla and Dantavakra. During that discussion, Śrī Nārada inspired King Yudhiṣṭhira to hear the glories of Lord Rāma from Sage Mārkaṇḍeya:

tatrāpi rāghavo bhūtvā
nyahanac chāpa-muktaye
rāma-vīryaṁ śroṣyasi tvaṁ
mārkaṇḍeya-mukhāt prabho
(*Śrīmad Bhāgavatam* 7.1.44)

Śrīmad Bhāgavatam 12.8-12 describes the personality of Mārkaṇḍeya Ṛṣi. Sage Śaunaka was born in the Bhṛgu Dynasty (*Mahābhārata*, *Anuśāsana-parva*, 30th Chapter) and Sage Mārkaṇḍeya was also born in that dynasty. Therefore, Sage Śaunaka naturally became curious to hear about Sage Mārkaṇḍeya. He asked Sūta Gosvāmī, "Everyone says that Sage Mārkaṇḍeya possesses a very long life. How has this come to pass? At the time of universal destruction, only Sage Mārkaṇḍeya was left. However, that best among all descendants of the Bhṛgu Dynasty has taken birth in our dynasty during this *kalpa* (time span) only. I have also heard that when he was wandering around alone in the causal ocean at the time of annihilation, he saw a divine personality who was sleeping on a leaf of a banyan tree and had taken the form of a child. O great sage, we are bewildered and enchanted. You are the knower of the *Purāṇas*, so kindly remove our lack of understanding."

Here follows a brief summary of Śrī Sūta Gosvāmī's answer:

At the time of his *upanayana-saṁskāra* by his father, Sage Mārkaṇḍeya took an oath of celibacy and began to worship Śrī Hari.

25 One who is born without a father and mother.

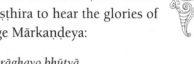

His worship lasted for the duration of six *manvantaras*. It is often observed that whenever anyone takes to performing strong penance, the demigods become afraid of losing their position and thus try to obstruct that penance. A similar occurrence took place here as well. During the seventh *manvantara*, Indra, the king of the demigods, sent Kāmadeva (Cupid) and his associates to disrupt the penance of Sage Mārkaṇḍeya. Gandharvas (celestial musicians) tried to seduce him with songs and music while Apsarās (celestial female dancers) performed alluring dances. The spring season, greed and lust all performed their beguiling acts, as well as other servants of Indra who played many tricks to shake Mārkaṇḍeya's resolve. Kāmadeva shot a five-headed arrow with his bow, but failed to get the attention of the sage. The servants of Indra performed many inappropriate acts, but later when they felt the fiery heat of the sage's penance, they all ran away. The power of the sage's penance was such that even Cupid was defeated and fled. After this, Lord Śrī Hari appeared in the guise of the twins Nara-Nārāyaṇa, who were so much pleased by the penance of Sage Mārkaṇḍeya that They appeared before him to bestow Their mercy upon him. Out of the two deities of Lord Śrī Hari known as Nara-Nārāyaṇa, one was white complexioned and the other was dark. Both were four-armed and Their eyes were like lotuses. One wore a deerskin and the other was wearing tree-bark. Both were full of many virtues and were being worshiped by many demigods. When Mārkaṇḍeya Ṛṣi saw them, he got up and offered his obeisances and prayers with great devotion. Then, to please the Lord, he sang His glories. A part of that composition goes:

nānyaṁ tavāṅghry-upanayād apavarga-mūrteḥ
kṣemaṁ janasya parito-bhiya īśa vidmaḥ
brahmā bibhety alam ato dvi-parārdha-dhiṣṇyaḥ
kālasya te kim uta tat-kṛta-bhautikānām
(*Śrīmad Bhāgavatam* 12.8.43)

"My dear Lord, even Lord Brahmā, who enjoys his exalted position for the entire duration of the universe (*dvi-parārdha*), fears the passage of time, so what to speak of those conditioned souls whose bodies Lord Brahmā creates. They encounter fearful dangers at every step of their lives. I do not know of any relief from this fear except shelter at Your lotus feet, which are the very form of liberation."

Satisfied by the glories sung by Sage Mārkaṇḍeya, the Lords expressed Their desire to bless him. In his turn, Mārkaṇḍeya Ṛṣi expressed his desire to see the external potency of the Lord. Nara-Nārāyaṇa agreed to this desire and returned to Badarikāśrama. Mārkaṇḍeya went back to his *āśrama* and began his normal life again. He wondered how he would ever be able to see the external potency of the Lord. Engrossed in Agni, Sūrya, Candra, Prithvi, Vāyu, Akāśa and Ātmā, he meditated upon Hari, and began to see Hari in everything and everywhere. Out of love, he began to worship the Supreme Lord by offering Him various items mentally. Sometimes he would become so absorbed in tasting the nectar of *prema* (ecstatic love of God) that he would commit mistakes in his regular worship.

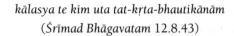

One day, he was performing *sandhyā-vandana* on the banks of River Puṣpabhadrā when suddenly a strong wind began to blow. Clouds covered the sky, driven by strong winds, and heavy rain began to pour down along with the sound of thunder. Slowly, floodwaters full of crocodiles accumulated and became very fearful as their strong waves submerged the earth. Sage Mārkaṇḍeya, along with *svedaja*, *aṇḍaja*, *udbhijja*, and *jarāyuja*,[26] while undergoing suffering caused by lightning, water and the oppressive heat of the sun, was aghast to see the earth becoming more and more submerged in water. Due to the continuous heavy rainfall, the ocean submerged the islands, nations and even mountains with the aid of very strong winds. When the three worlds were eventually fully submerged in water, Sage Mārkaṇḍeya was the only one left. Thus, he began to traverse the water blindly and uselessly. He was surrounded by great darkness while hunger and thirst made him desperate. All the while, large aquatic animals such as crocodiles, whales, *timingalas*[27] and others were troubling him, along with strong winds that impaired him. Eventually, he fell unconscious. Sometimes he would nearly drown in strong whirlpools and at other times the aquatics would harass and attack him. Sometimes he would become sorrowful and at other times he would become ignorant. Sometimes he felt sad and at other times he felt cheerful. Sometimes he became frightened and at other times he became afflicted by disease. So many times he underwent the painful suffering that awaits one at the time of death. In this way, roaming the waters and suffering from Lord Viṣṇu's *māyā*, many thousands of years passed.

Then one day he discovered a mound of earth on which a delicate banyan tree bearing leaves and fruits had grown. On the northeastern side of that banyan tree was a leaf, and on that leaf a very unique child was lying down, dispelling the darkness by His effulgence. The color of the child was dark just like a *mahā-marakata-maṇi* (precious sapphire). His lotus face was very beautiful; His neck was marked with three horizontal lines; His chest was broad; His nose was perfectly shaped; He had beautiful eyebrows and fine-looking, quivering locks of hair. His beautiful and enchanting ears were red like pomegranate flowers; the corners of His eyes were red; His lips were red like coral and caused His nectarean smile to give off a reddish glow; He had the most beautifully shaped navel and his stomach was shaped like the leaf of a pipala tree. This dazzling child was sucking the toes of His own feet, holding them with the beautiful fingers of His hands. The sage was amazed to observe this. All his tiredness vanished at once, simply by catching a mere glimpse of that child. He thus felt cheerful at heart. As a result of his excitement, he could no longer close his eyes.

He became very curious upon seeing this child and walked up to Him to learn about His identity. However, as he came within close proximity of the child, he suddenly found himself drawn into the body of the child when He inhaled, just as a miniscule fly would be drawn in, and in this way he entered the body of the child. Immediately upon arriving inside

26 *Jarāyuja*: living entities born from wombs; *aṇḍaja*: living entities born from eggs; *svedaja*: living entities born from perspiration; *udbhija*: living entities sprouted from seeds.

27 *Timingala*: an aquatic so large that it can swallow whales.

the body of the child, he saw the whole world situated there, just as it had been before the annihilation. He was amazed and enchanted to see everything there. He saw all the things and necessities of life in vivid shape—so much so that he saw the Himālayas and Puṣpabhadrā River where he had an audience with Nara-Nārāyaṇa; he saw his own *āśrama* as well. While he was thus engrossed in observing all such places, he was hurled out with the exhalation of the child and was plunged back into the ocean of annihilation. After some time, he again saw the same banyan tree on that mound of earth and the same child who was now asleep with His lips open, bearing a nectar-like smile. He then contemplated that perhaps this child was none other than Adhokṣaja Śrī Hari. Feeling affection for Him, Sage Mārkaṇḍeya wanted to embrace the child. Therefore, with great effort he approached the child but He vanished before he could embrace Him. With the sudden disappearance of the child, Sage Mārkaṇḍeya found himself standing in his *āśrama* as before, and the banyan tree and waters of annihilation had vanished.

While traversing the sky with his consort Pārvatī Devī, Lord Śiva saw Sage Mārkaṇḍeya in deep meditation. When Mother Pārvatī observed the effort of the sage, she requested her husband, Mahādeva, to bless Mārkaṇḍeya with mystical powers. Mahādeva thus approached him at the request of Mother Pārvatī. When he saw Lord Mahādeva in front of him, Sage Mārkaṇḍeya abandoned his *samādhi* and began to worship Mahādeva, the master of the three worlds, and his faithful consort, Pārvatī. Lord Śiva in turn glorified the devotees of the Lord and offered Sage Mārkaṇḍeya any boon he wanted. Sage Mārkaṇḍeya requested that he be blessed with unwavering devotion unto Lord Śrī Hari, His devotees and Lord Maheśvara. Mahādeva was pleased to hear this pious request and blessed him with agelessness, deathlessness, glory, knowledge of the three modes of time (past, present and future), detachment and complete mastership of the *Purāṇas*.

In the book *Orissa ka Māhātmya* it is written that Sage Mārkaṇḍeya had an audience with Lord Puruṣottama (Śrī Jagannātha Deva) upon exiting the mouth of the sleeping child who was lying on the leaf of a banyan tree. Thus, the sage understood that Śrī Puruṣottama-kṣetra is eternal and not affected by annihilation. Sage Mārkaṇḍeya constructed a *sarovara* (pond) and its *ghāṭa* (bank) in the *vāyu-koṇa* (northwestern quarter) of the banyan tree as ordained by Lord Jagannātha, and he also worshiped the Lord's dearmost devotee, Lord Śiva. Even today at Purī, Mārkaṇḍeśvara Mahādeva and Mārkaṇḍeya Sarovara are well worth seeing.

Śrīla Bhakti Vinode Ṭhākura has mentioned Sage Mārkaṇḍeya in his *Śrī Navadvīpa-dhāma Māhātmya* in the chapter glorifying Śrī Godruma-dvīpa (one of the nine islands in Navadvīpa, West Bengal—the area of *kīrtana*) as follows:

In Dvāpara-yuga, Indra, the king of the demigods, could not understand the real identity of Śrī Kṛṣṇa, the son of Nanda Mahāraja. Śrī Kṛṣṇa stopped Indra's *yajña* and began Govardhana-pūjā. This annoyed Indra, who thus created such heavy rains that they submerged the whole of Vraja. Śrī Kṛṣṇa lifted Govardhana Mountain and saved the residents of Vraja. Afterward, Indra realized his mistake and approached the Lord with a *surabhi* cow to apologize to Him, and thus worshiped Śrī Kṛṣṇa at Govinda-kunda near Govardhana. In this glorious Kali-yuga, Lord Kṛṣṇa, accepting the complexion and mood of Śrīmatī Rādhārāṇī, appeared as Lord Gaurāṅga in Navadvīpa. Meditating on this, Indra vowed that he would not repeat such a silly offense again, and thus asked Śrī Kṛṣṇa to bless him in such a way that he might not commit any offense during Kali-yuga at the time of Śrī Caitanya's pastimes. Śrī Kṛṣṇa agreed and made him fearless. Before the appearance of Śrī Caitanya Mahāprabhu in Navadvīpa-dhāma, Indra arrived at Godruma-dvīpa with his *surabhi* cow to perform *bhajana* (worship) of Śrī Gaurāṅga Mahāprabhu. This island has been named Godruma-dvīpa because the *surabhi* cow stayed under the banyan (*aśvattha*) tree.

Mārkaṇḍeya, the son of Mṛkaṇḍa, was blessed with a lifespan of seven *kalpas* (cycles of universal creation and destruction). At the time of universal destruction, when the whole earth was immersed in water, he, while helplessly swimming, took shelter at Navadvīpa-dhāma and rested there. That is because sixteen *krośas* (approximately thirty-two-mile-wide) Nadia-dhāma was not immersed in water. The *surabhi* cow was living in Godruma-dvīpa and fed milk to Mārkaṇḍeya, giving him new life when he was unconscious and suffering due to hunger and thirst. As he regained his strength by taking the milk of the *surabhi* cow, he glorified her. He narrated the dire consequences of having a lifespan of seven *kalpas* and related his personal sufferings. The *surabhi* cow preached to him, saying that all his sorrow would cease by performing devotion of Śrī Gaurāṅga Mahāprabhu and that, by doing so, all his desires would be fulfilled.

It is known from *Śrīmad Bhāgavatam*, 84th Chapter, 10th Canto, that Kuntī, Subhadrā and other royal queens during their gathering at Kurukṣetra at the time of the solar eclipse were amazed to see the love of the cowherd damsels (*gopīs*) for Śrī Kṛṣṇa. At Kurukṣetra, when the cowherd damsels had come to meet Śrī Kṛṣṇa, Śrī Vyāsadeva, Śrī Nārada and many other sages had also come there to have an audience with Śrī Kṛṣṇa. Among those saints was Sage Mārkaṇḍeya.

Sage Aṣṭāvakra

In his book *Bhakti-ratnākara*, Śrī Narahari Cakravartī Ṭhākura (Śrī Ghanaśyāma Dāsa), while describing the holy places in Mathurā-mandala, the land of Śrī Kṛṣṇa, visited by the associates of Lord Caitanya such as South Indian Śrīmad Rāghava Gosvāmī as well as Śrīnivasa Ācarya and Śrīla Narottama Ṭhākura, remarks:

ae āṭasu'- grāme mahā-kautuka haila
aṣṭāvakra muni etha tapasya karila
(*Bhakti-ratnākara* 5.1620)

"In Āṭasu-grāma, Saint Aṣṭāvakra performed austerities."

aṣṭakrītvo vakraḥ vrittau saṅkyasujartha
para (aṣṭanaḥ sañjñāyāṁ) iti dīrgha
(Ṛṣi Viśeṣa *Viśvakoṣa*)

Sage Śrī Kṛṣṇa-dvaipāyana Vedavyāsa has described Sage Aṣṭāvakra in the discussions between Sage Lomaśa and King Yudhiṣṭhira as related in the *Mahābhārata*, *Vana-parva*, Chapters 132-134. Sage Uddhālaka's son was Śvetaketu, who was celebrated as the greatest and wisest of experts in the science of mantra. Śvetaketu had an audience with Goddess Sarasvatī in human form. During the lifetime of Sage Uddhālaka, his son Śvetaketu and Sage Kahoda's son Aṣṭāvakra were the most knowledgeable persons on earth regarding Brahman. Sage Aṣṭāvakra's father was Kahoda and his mother was Sujātā. Śvetaketu was the brother of Sujātā. In the material sense,

Śvetaketu and Aṣṭāvakra were related as maternal uncle and nephew.

When Yudhiṣṭhira Mahārāja inquired from Sage Lomaśa about Aṣṭāvakra Muni, he replied that Sage Uddhālaka had a well-known disciple named Kahoda who stayed in the house of his master for a long time, serving him and studying all the scriptures. Being pleased with him, Uddhālaka gave him complete knowledge of the scriptures. In fact, he was so pleased that he gave his daughter Sujātā (Sumatī according to some) in marriage to him. The sage's daughter became pregnant, and the child in her womb became expert in all Vedic scriptures and grew effulgent like fire.

One day, while in the womb of his mother, he was listening to his father's recitation of the *Vedas* and said to his father, Kahoda, "O father! What you have recited the whole night was pronounced incorrectly. By your mercy only, I have been able to learn all the four *Vedas* and other scriptures, and I am telling you that your recital of the *Vedas* was incorrect."

Sage Kahoda was sitting with his disciples at that time and felt insulted by hearing such words from his unborn son. He thus cursed his son by saying, "Since you have insulted me while still in the womb, may your body be bent in eight places." Therefore, the child was born with a body that was crooked in eight places (eight physical deformities) and became known as Aṣṭāvakra.

Aṣṭāvakra's maternal uncle Śvetaketu was as wise and virtuous as Aṣṭāvakra. Sujātā was suffering intensely because of the child growing in her womb. For want of money she told her husband privately, "I do not have enough money to make arrangements for the birth of my son." After hearing these pitiful words from his wife, Sage Kahoda went to King Janaka to acquire some wealth. However, he ended up drowning himself after suffering a defeat in a debate with the learned Bandi in Janaka Mahārāja's assembly. When Uddhālaka learned about the fate of his son-in-law, he asked his daughter Sujātā not to tell anything to Aṣṭāvakra. Sujātā honored her father's request. When Aṣṭāvakra Muni was born, he took Uddhālaka as his father and Śvetaketu as his brother and treated them accordingly. One day when Aṣṭāvakra was twelve years old, he saw Śvetaketu sitting on the lap of Uddhālaka. Aṣṭāvakra said, "You are not his son; I am his son." Śvetaketu firmly protested this allegation and said, "You are mistaken; he is not your father." This made Aṣṭāvakra suspicious and he then asked his mother, "Who is my father? If Uddhālaka is not my father, then where is my real father?" The Aṣṭāvakra's queries grieved Sujātā and she thus revealed everything to him.

Aṣṭāvakra went to Śvetaketu at night and said, "Many amazing things are heard about the *yajña* of King Janaka." Therefore, he proposed a visit there and they both left for the *yajña*. On the way, Aṣṭāvakra met the king, who blocked their path. Having reached a deadlock situation, Sage Aṣṭāvakra said, "In the absence of a *brāhmaṇa*, this path could be used by the blind, the deaf, women, load-carrying persons, or the king. However, if a *brāhmaṇa* is present then he should be allowed to pass first." The king then stepped aside to let them through. Upon reaching the site where the *yajña* of King Janaka was taking place, the gatekeeper blocked their path. When Aṣṭāvakra complained about this to the king, the gatekeeper said, "O son of a *brāhmaṇa*! We are merely prisoners working under the orders of our superiors. In this assembly young *brāhmaṇas* are not allowed to enter; only elderly learned *brāhmaṇas* may enter." In order to secure entry into the assembly of King Janaka, Aṣṭāvakra argued with the gatekeeper for a long time. While arguing, Sage Aṣṭāvakra said, "A man cannot become wise or learned only by becoming old. Those who are of firm determination, who have attained equilibrium by means of the instructions of the *Vedas*, who are dedicated servants of their respective spiritual masters, who are controllers of their senses and who have attained the peak of knowledge are actually learned and wise, regardless of age. The tree that is small and lean, but full of fruits, shall be called big. A person should not be considered mature on consideration of bodily size alone. It is not true that a person becomes mature only when the hair on the head turns gray. The demigods consider the one who is wise to be mature, even though that person may be very young.

"People cannot be termed as best simply because of their old age, white hair, being extremely rich or having many friends. One who dedicates himself to the study of all *Vedas*, along with their many branches, is definitely considered great." Sage Aṣṭāvakra explained to the gatekeeper that he had come to the assembly to meet the most learned there, and to defeat such a person. The gatekeeper was very surprised to hear such statements from the very young *brāhmaṇa* and said to him, "Child, you are just twelve years old, so how will you enter the conference of such respected and learned men? However that may be, let me think of a way to let you enter."

After this, Sage Aṣṭāvakra addressed King Janaka and said, "O King! You are the best in this assembly. I am observing all the signs of prosperity in you. Before you, only Yayāti was as opulent a king as you are. I have heard that at your court the learned scholar Bandi defeats other learned wise men in debates on the scriptures, thereby forcing them to end their lives by drowning in water. Therefore, after hearing this, I have come here to discuss Brahman. Where is this Bandi? If he meets me, I shall kill him." The king was not happy to hear Aṣṭāvakra's words and said, "Being unaware of the powers of your opponent Bandi, you are thinking you can defeat him. Many *brāhmaṇas* have recognized his authority after debating with him. Whenever *brāhmaṇa* opponents meet him, those *brāhmaṇas* see themselves as fireflies in front of the sun."

During this discussion with Sage Aṣṭāvakra, King Janaka asked him many questions, including: "Who sleeps with open eyes? Who remains stationary after taking birth? Who is without a heart? Who grows rapidly?"

Upon receiving the correct answers, the king was surprised and said to Sage Aṣṭāvakra, "I think you are not human and that you are a demigod. You are certainly not a child. Nobody can stand up to you in debate. Thus, I give you my permission so that you may go and meet Bandi."

The topics of discussion between Bandi and Aṣṭāvakra based on the scriptures are described in detail in *Mahābhārata* but, bearing in mind the length of this book, this topic will not be elaborated upon.

In the end, Aṣṭāvakra defeated Bandi in all respects. Observing the power of Sage Aṣṭāvakra, Janaka was amazed and said, "I heard your transcendental words. You are beyond the mundane, as you have defeated Bandi in debate. Therefore, in order to fulfill your desires, I shall dispense with Bandi." Aṣṭāvakra Muni asked the king, "If the demigod Varuṇa is the father of Bandi, then why not drown him in your pond? You should drown him in water." When Bandi heard this, he said, "If I am Varuṇa's son, then I do not fear water, but Aṣṭāvakra will see his father Kahoda right here in a moment." As soon as he said this, all the drowned *brāhmaṇas*, after being worshiped by Varuṇa, appeared in the assembly of King Janaka. Kahoda regained his previous form and said to the king, "O Janaka! This is why people seek a son. My son was able to accomplish what I could not. A weak man might have a healthy son, a fool might have a wise son and an illiterate might have a learned son."

Bandi then emerged from the pond and, after taking permission from King Janaka, entered the ocean. The *brāhmaṇas* offered prayers to Sage Aṣṭāvakra, after which he left for his house together with his father. Aṣṭāvakra's father asked him to enter River Samaṅgā in front of his mother, so, as instructed by his father, Sage Aṣṭāvakra entered the river, and as soon as he took a dip, his limbs became straight and he emerged from the river with a normal body. From that day on he also became known as Samaṅgā. But still he was more commonly known as Aṣṭāvakra, though he now possessed a regularly shaped body.

The discourse given to King Janaka by Aṣṭāvakra Muni is known as the Aṣṭāvakra Saṁhitā. King Bhagīratha got divine limbs by the blessings of Sage Aṣṭāvakra.

The wives of Lord Kṛṣṇa were kidnapped by dacoits due to a curse of Sage Aṣṭāvakra and the details about Aṣṭāvakra are described differently in the *Brahmā-vaivarta Purāṇa*, *Śrī Kṛṣṇa Janma Khaṇḍa*, Chapter 30.

His real name was Devala, and he was the son of Sage Asita. Once, while he was performing penance in a cave of Gandhamādana Mountain, a celestial beauty named Rambhā approached him for union. When the sage refused her offer, she cursed him and his body became crooked (*New Bengali Dictionary* by Āśutoṣa Deva).

In *Brahmā-vaivarta Purāṇa*, Śrīmatī Rādhikā asks Kṛṣṇa, "Who is that effulgent sage with an extremely lowly and ill-shaped figure, whose limbs are all crooked and whose skin is black colored?" Śrī Kṛṣṇa replied, "That is Sage Aṣṭāvakra, famous in the three worlds for his brilliance."

It is said that when he went to an assembly, the people present there laughed when they saw his crooked limbs. Seeing them laughing loudly, he said, "Today I have come to an assembly of cobblers, who care only about the external features of skin and ignore the internal features."

Śrīla Rūpa Gosvāmī has warned in his *Upadeśāmṛta* that a great saint does not consider the apparent faults and bodily features of pure devotees:

dṛṣṭaiḥ svabhāva-janitair vapuṣaś ca doṣair
na prākṛtatvam iha bhakta janasya paśyet
gaṅgāmbhasāṁ na khalu budbuda-phena-paṅkair
brahmā-dravatvam apagacchati nīra-dharmaiḥ
(*Upadeśāmṛta* 6)

"Gaṅgā water does not lose its spiritual power when sometimes bubbles or foam appear on its surface due to the nature of water. Similarly, one should ignore the superficial defects of a devotee having a body born in a low family, a bad complexion, a deformed body, or a diseased or infirm body, because a devotee never identifies with the body. Devotees should never be seen from a materialistic point of view. According to ordinary vision, such imperfections may seem prominent in the body of a Vaiṣṇava devotee but, despite such seeming defects, the body of a Vaiṣṇava devotee cannot be polluted."

In the same context, Śrīla Bhakti Siddhānta Sarasvatī Gosvāmī Ṭhākura has written: "One may commit an offense against a pure devotee when one fails to understand the actions of such a pure devotee, who has developed a keen interest in the pastimes of the Supreme Lord (*jata-ruci*)."

One may not get good results if one makes fun of the activities of mystical *sādhus*, pure devotees or a *guru*. One should never consider them lowly. Therefore, considering a pure devotee to be a conditioned soul or one's disciple, and then trying to correct his or her actions, is a major offense.

King Ikṣvāku

ikṣumakati vyāpnoti ku-aca atvāñcā
athavā ikṣum śābdaṁ akatiti ikṣa ak-uṇa

"Ikṣvāku, the son of Vaivasvata Manu, was the first of the kings belonging to the Solar Dynasty. He had one hundred sons, of whom Vikukṣi was the eldest. Ikṣvāku was the first king of Ayodhyā." (*Viśvakoṣa*)

King Ikṣvāku was the ancestor of Lord Rāmacandra:

imaṁ vivasvate yoga proktavān aham avyayam
vivasvān manave prāha manur ikṣvākave 'bravīt
(*Bhagavad-gītā* 4.1)

"The Personality of Godhead, Lord Śrī Kṛṣṇa, said: I instructed this dispassionate, imperishable science of *yoga* to the sun-god, Vivasvān, and Vivasvān instructed it to Manu, the father of mankind, and Manu in turn instructed it to Ikṣvāku."

In the 1st Chapter of the 9th Canto of *Śrīmad Bhāgavatam*, Śrī Śukadeva Gosvāmī narrates the story of King Ikṣvāku's previous dynasty to Parīkṣit Mahārāja, which is as follows:

Brahmā was born from the navel of the Lord resting on the waters of annihilation. Then from Brahmā's mind Marīci appeared, and from Marīci came Kaśyapa. After this, from the union of Kaśyapa Ṛṣi and Aditi, Vivasvān was born. Śrāddhadeva Manu was born from the union of Vivasvān and Saṁjñā. Śrāddhadeva Manu was married to Śraddhā, and Ikṣvāku was their legitimate child:

tato manuḥ śrāddhadevaḥ saṁjñāyām āsa bhārata
śraddhāyāṁ janayām āsa daśa putrān sa ātmavān
ikṣvāku-nṛga-śaryāti- diṣṭa-dhṛṣṭa-karūṣakān
nariṣyantaṁ pṛṣadhraṁ ca
nabhagaṁ ca kaviṁ vibhuḥ
(*Śrīmad Bhāgavatam* 9.1.11-12)

"O King, best of the Bhārata Dynasty, from Vivasvān, from the womb of Saṁjñā, Śrāddhadeva Manu was born. Śrāddhadeva Manu, having conquered his senses, begot ten sons in the womb of his wife Śraddhā. The names of these sons were Ikṣvāku, Nṛga, Śaryāti, Diṣṭa, Dhṛṣṭa, Karūṣaka, Nariṣyanta, Pṛṣadhra, Nabhaga and Kavi."

Śrāddhadeva Manu begot these ten sons similar to himself by worship of Lord Śrī Hari. Among them Ikṣvāku was the eldest and greatest. The description of the birth of Ikṣvāku from the nostrils of Manu is mentioned in *Śrīmad Bhāgavatam*:

kṣuvatas tu manor jajñe ikṣvākur ghrāṇataḥ sūtaḥ
tasya putra-śata-jyeṣṭhā vikukṣi-nimi-daṇḍakāḥ
(*Śrīmad Bhāgavatam* 9.6.4)

"The son of Manu was Ikṣvāku. One time when Manu sneezed, Ikṣvāku was born from Manu's nostrils. King Ikṣvāku had one hundred sons, of whom Vikukṣi, Nimi and Daṇḍakā were the most prominent."

Kṛṣṇaṣṭāmī (8th day of the dark fortnight) of the months of Māgha, Pauṣa and Phālguna is famous as Aṣṭaka, as related in the 9th Canto of *Śrīmad Bhāgavatam*. In some scriptures, the offering of meat to one's forefathers is prescribed on such dates. On one such date Ikṣvāku instructed his son Vikukṣi to bring pure meat. Complying with his father's orders he went to the forest and killed many deer and rabbits.

He became tired because of the great effort expended, and started to feel hungry. He could not think of anything but hunger. After some time, he could not tolerate the hunger any longer and ate one of the rabbits, giving the remaining meat to his father after returning to his house. Ikṣvāku sent that meat to Vaśiṣṭha for a *saṁskāra* to offer as an oblation to the forefathers. Sage Vaśiṣṭha could judge with his non-material eyes that the meat was polluted and therefore not suitable for *śrāddha* (last rites).

Being informed of this by Sage Vaśiṣṭha, King Ikṣvāku questioned Vikukṣi, who told him everything. When Ikṣvāku learned about his son's sinful act, he became angry and ordered Vikukṣi to leave his kingdom. He became detached from the world after rejecting his son. He associated with his spiritual master, Sage Vaśiṣṭha, and became a *yogī*, discarding all royal comforts. After this, Ikṣvāku attained liberation after leaving his body by means of *yoga*.

Vikukṣi returned after the death of his father and began to rule the earth. He worshiped Lord Śrī Hari by means of *yajña* and became known as Śaśāda: *śaśāda iti nāmnā khyātaḥ imām pṛthvīm saśāta palāyana*. This incident has also been described in the *Viṣṇu Purāṇa*, written by Vedavyāsa Muni.

In the last verse of Chapter 12, Canto 9, of *Śrīmad Bhāgavatam*, Sage Śrī Kṛṣṇa-dvaipāyana Vedavyāsa has stated the consequences of the annihilation of the Ikṣvāku Dynasty during Kali-yuga:

ikṣvākūṇām ayaṁ vaṁśaḥ
sumitrānto bhaviṣyati
yatas taṁ prāpya rājānaṁ
saṁsthāṁ prāpsyati vai kalau
(*Śrīmad Bhāgavatam* 9.12.16)

"The last king in the dynasty of Ikṣvāku will be Sumitra; after Sumitra there will be no more sons in the dynasty of the sun-god, and thus the dynasty will end."

King Mucukunda is described as Ikṣvākunandana (son of Ikṣvāku) in the first verse of Chapter 52 of the 10th Canto of *Śrīmad Bhāgavatam*. He may have been mentioned in this way because he appeared in the Ikṣvāku Dynasty, and due to him Ikṣvāku became famous. Actually, King Mucukunda was the son of Mahārāja Māndhātā of the Ikṣvāku Dynasty. In this context the arrival of Kali-yuga is mentioned in *Śrīmad Bhāgavatam*:

śrī-śuka uvāca
itthaṁ so 'nagrahīto 'nga kṛṣṇenekṣvāku nandanaḥ
taṁ parikramya sannamya niścakrāma guhā-mukhāt
saṁvīkṣya kṣullakān martyān paśūn vīrud-vanaspatīn
matvā kali-yugaṁ prāptaṁ jagāma diśam uttarām
(*Śrīmad Bhāgavatam* 10.52.1-2)

Śukadeva Gosvāmī said, "My dear king, thus graced by Lord Kṛṣṇa, Mucukunda circumambulated Him and bowed down to Him. Then, the beloved descendant of Ikṣvāku, Mucukunda, exited through the opening of the cave. Seeing that the size of all the human beings, animals, trees and plants was severely reduced, and thus realizing that the age of Kali was at hand, Mucukunda left for the north."

In *Viśvakoṣa* the name of another King Ikṣvāku is mentioned, but he is different from Ikṣvāku of the Solar Dynasty. He is mentioned as the king of Varanasi. There is an unusual story about him. One day, Subandhu, the king of Varanasi, had a dream that his bedroom was filled with sugarcane. When he awoke, he saw that his dream was true. All the canes dried in due course of time except one. Subandhu consulted astrologers to inquire about the reason behind this, and they told him that a child would be born out of sugarcane, and that the child would be his son. The words of the astrologers came true and indeed a child was born by piercing the Ikṣu (sugarcane). As the child was inside the Ikṣu he was named Ikṣvāku. This Ikṣvāku became the king of Varanasi after the death of Subandhu. His principal queen was Alinda, who gave birth to Kuśa. (*Viśvakoṣa*)

The meaning of Ikṣvāku in *Amarartha Candrika* is given as: *ikṣvākuh kaṭutumbīsyāta*, meaning that *ikṣvāku* is the name of bitter gourd.

Sage Māṇḍavya

āni-śulagram tadukto māṇḍavyaḥ
(*Ṭīkā Nīlakantha*)

In the 107th Chapter of the *Ādi-parva* of *Mahābhārata*, Sage Vaiśampāyana relates the activities of Ani Māṇḍavya in reply to a question of Janamejaya.

In times gone by there lived a *brāhmaṇa*, Sage Māṇḍavya, who was learned, intelligent, truthful and a great yogi. That *brāhmaṇa* was silently performing penance with his hands raised for a very long time, under a tree next to the main gate of his *āśrama*. At that time, some dacoits came there with looted items and, being chased by the guards of the city, hid themselves in his *āśrama*. When the guards arrived they inquired from the sage about the dacoits, but Sage Māṇḍavya did not reply. As they did not receive any response, the guards went inside the *āśrama* and found the dacoits hiding there with the stolen goods. They bound the dacoits to bring them to the king. The guards were also suspicious of Sage Māṇḍavya and thought him to be one of the accomplices of the dacoits, as they had found them in his *āśrama* and, above all, he had given no response to their query about the dacoits. Thus, they arrested him and took him with them. In ancient times people abided by the law and followed *dharma*. They did not harm anybody by framing him or her with false charges. So, if any charge was framed against anyone, the king would consider it true and pronounce punishment. Therefore, the king gave the order to kill the dacoits and Sage Māṇḍavya, even without questioning the sage. The royal soldiers hanged everyone as ordered and returned the loot to the king. All died through hanging, apart from the great mystic Māṇḍavya Ṛṣi, who did not die even though he was kept hanging for a long time and not given anything to eat. He held onto his life and, using the power of penance, called upon his fellow sages. Those sages came to him in the form of birds and transformed themselves back to their original forms when they approached Sage Māṇḍavya. The sages felt morose to see him hanging yet engaging in penance even in that state, and inquired about the reason for his torment. Sage Māṇḍavya replied to the sages, "It would be wrong to blame others for my suffering. I do not know what I have done, but surely I and no one else am the cause of it."

A royal personage was astonished to see him alive and undisturbed even after hanging for such a long time and having been pierced with a *śula* (spear or spike), so he informed the king. The king was fearful when he heard this and, having realized his mistake, he then rushed to the sage and prayed for forgiveness. Sage Māṇḍavya was pleased to hear the humble words of the king. The king himself pulled the sage off the *śuli* (hanging stage) but even after many attempts, he could not take out the *śula* from his body so he then cut away the weapon's protruding part. Sage Māṇḍavya continued performing penance despite having part of the lance still in him. He won all the rare, pious planets as fruits of his penance. As he carried within him the front part of the *śula*, which is called *āni*, he became famous as Ani Māṇḍavya.

One day, learned Sage Māṇḍavya went to Yama-purī, the abode of the demigod Dharma. When he saw Dharmarāja seated there he condemned him and asked him what he had done to cause him to be hanged and to stay hanging for such a long time. He further said that he would demonstrate the power of his penance.

Dharmarāja replied that during Māṇḍavya's childhood he had pierced the back of an insect with a sharp twig. That is why the sage had to suffer so much. The sage was furious to hear this and said, "O Dharmarāja! You have given me such a harsh punishment for a sin committed by me during childhood. I therefore curse you to be born in a low-caste and I hereby make a law that one may not suffer the fruits of his bad *karma* until one reaches fourteen years of age. One shall bear the fruits of the sins committed only after this age." Due to this curse, Dharma

took birth as Vidura in a low-caste. Maitreya Ṛṣi said to Vidura:

māṇḍavya-śāpād bhagavān prajā-saṁyamano yamaḥ
bhrātuḥ kṣetre bhujiṣyāyāṁ jātaḥ satyavatī-sutāt
(*Śrīmad Bhāgavatam* 3.5.20)

"I know that you are now Vidura due to a curse given by Māṇḍavya Muni and that formerly you were King Yamarāja, the great controller of living entities after their death. You were begotten by the son of Satyavatī, Vyāsadeva, with the maid, who was accepted as a wife by his brother Vicitravīrya."

In another incident, the devoted wife of a leper *brāhmaṇa* nullified Sage Māṇḍavya's curse:

kuṣṭhī-viprera ramaṇī, pativratā-śiromaṇi,
pati lāgi' kailā veśyāra sevā
stambhila sūryera gati, jīyāila mṛta pati,
tuṣṭa kaila mukhya tina-devā
(*Caitanya Caritāmṛta, Antya-līlā* 20.57)

In his commentary on this verse, Śrīla Bhaktivedanta Svami Mahārāja narrates the incident as follows:

"The *Āditya Purāṇa*, *Mārkaṇḍeya Purāṇa* (15.19) and *Padma Purāṇa* tell about a *brāhmaṇa* who was suffering from leprosy but had a very chaste and faithful wife. He desired to enjoy the company of a prostitute, and therefore his wife went to her and became her maidservant, just to draw her attention to his service. When the prostitute agreed to associate with him, the wife brought her leprous husband to the prostitute's house. When the leper, the sinful son of a *brāhmaṇa*, saw the chastity of his wife, he finally abandoned his iniquitous intentions. However, while coming home, he unintentionally touched the body of Māṇḍavya Ṛṣi, disturbing his meditation, thus the sage cursed him to die at sunrise. Because of her chastity, his wife was very powerful. Therefore, when she heard about the curse, she vowed to stop the sunrise. Because of her strong determination to serve her husband, the three deities Brahmā, Viṣṇu and Maheśvara, were very happy and gave her the benediction that her husband would be cured and brought back to life. This example is given herein to emphasize that a devotee should engage himself or herself exclusively for the satisfaction of Kṛṣṇa, without personal motives. This will make life successful."

Śrila Bhaktivinoda Ṭhākura writes in his *Amṛta-pravāha-bhāṣya* that the real purpose of the living being's life is to have firm faith in unalloyed devotion to Supreme Lord Kṛṣṇa. This will result in the development of the highest taste.

Vidura

As explained previously, due to the curse of Sage Ani Māṇḍavya, Yamarāja took birth as Vidura in the *śūdra* (lower) caste.

Vicitravīrya of the Kuru Dynasty had two queens, Ambikā and Ambālikā. Dhṛtarāṣṭra was born to Ambikā and Pāṇḍu to Ambālikā:

kṣetre 'prajasya vai bhrātur mātrokto bādarāyaṇaḥ
dhṛtarāṣṭraṁ ca pāṇḍuṁ ca viduraṁ cāpy ajījanat
(*Śrīmad Bhāgavatam* 9.22.25)

"Bādarāyana Śrī Vyāsadeva, following the order of his mother, Satyavatī, begot three sons—Dhṛtarāṣṭra, Pāṇḍu and Vidura—from the two wives of his childless brother Vicitravīrya, i.e., Ambikā, Ambālikā and a maid-servant respectively."

When Ambikā's mother-in-law, Satyavatī, asked her to again visit Vyāsa, she did not go but instead sent a beautiful maidservant dressed in Ambikā's clothes. Therefore, Yamarāja took birth as Vidura from the womb of that maidservant.

maitreya uvāca
sādhu pṛṣṭaṁ tvayā sādho lokān sādhv anugṛhṇatā
kīrtiṁ vitanvatā loke ātmano 'dhokṣajātmanaḥ
naitac citraṁ tvayi kṣattar bādarāyaṇa-vīryaje
gṛhīto 'nanya-bhāveṇa yat tvayā harir īśvaraḥ
māṇḍavya-śāpād bhagavān prajā-saṁyamano yamaḥ
bhrātuḥ kṣetre bhujiṣyāyāṁ jātaḥ satyavatī-sutāt
bhavān bhagavato nityaṁ sammataḥ sānugasya ha
yasya jñānopadeśāya mādiśad bhagavān vrajan
(*Śrīmad Bhāgavatam* 3.5.18-21)

Śrī Maitreya said, "O Vidura, all glory unto you. You have inquired from me about the greatest of all goodness, and thus have shown your mercy to the people of the world. Supreme Lord Śrī Kṛṣṇa is your life and, because of this, your glory will spread across the worlds. It is not at all amazing that you have whole-heartedly accepted the Lord without deviation of thought, for you were born due to the blessings of Vyāsadeva. Your good self is one of the eternal associates of the Supreme Personality of Godhead. Therefore, before leaving, the Lord asked me to instruct you about transcendental knowledge."

Vidura was expert in politics, economics and *dharma*; he was peaceful, devoid of greed and anger, and could clearly discern the results of actions. Due to his virtue of being capable of foreseeing consequences, he saved the Pāṇḍavas from many dangers. He was present as the main assistant of Yudhiṣṭhira Mahārāja at the *rājasūya-yajña*. The great Bhīṣma married Vidura to a beautiful young daughter of Mahāpati Ḍevaka, a *śūdra*. With her, Vidura begot humble sons with qualities as good as his.

When Dhṛtarāṣṭra tricked Yudhiṣṭhira by sending him to the city of Vāraṇāvata with the intention of killing him by burning in the

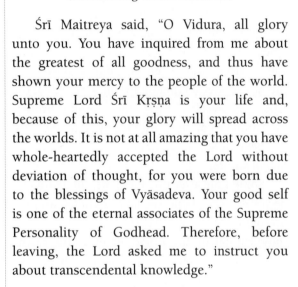

Lākṣagṛha (house of lacquer) under the ill advice of Duryodhana, the Pāṇḍavas escaped from the danger due to the timely advice and expertise of the wise Vidura. He advised Yudhiṣṭhira to keep an open path all around the house in such a way that they would encounter no obstacle in vacating the house if required, even during the dark of night. He further told him that if any confusion occurred in finding the desired direction, they could navigate their way by observing the position of the stars in the sky. After giving many such wise instructions to the Pāṇḍavas, he sent one of his most reliable tunnel diggers to Vāraṇāvata City to dig a tunnel from the center of Lākṣagṛha, where the Pāṇḍavas were staying. His timing was perfect, and when the day arrived that the house was set aflame by their enemies, the Pāṇḍavas saved their lives by escaping through the tunnel as advised by Vidura. This incident has been described in detail in the *Ādi-parva* of *Mahābhārata*.

Some time after this incident, the Pāṇḍavas became very famous when they attained limitless wealth, married Draupadī, established their capital in the kingdom of Indraprastha and performed a *rājasuya-yajña*. Then, due to extreme jealousy, the proud Duryodhana planned to do them harm and take away their kingdom. Śakuni instigated in him the thought of defeating them in a game of dice. Therefore, Duryodhana proposed his plan to Dhṛtarāṣṭra, who, being excited by it, discussed it with Vidura. Vidura, who was far-sighted and expert in politics, mentioned the great problems that might arise in the future because of this proposal. With many well-presented arguments, he recommended not to proceed with such a plan. But it was of no use, since Dhṛtarāṣṭra would always consider Vidura's good advice incorrect or as recommendations that were not in his favor. Vidura was a practitioner of justice; thus he never acted against the Pāṇḍavas. Nonetheless, Dhṛtarāṣṭra deputed him against his desire and asked him to go to Indraprastha to invite Yudhiṣṭhira and others to Hastināpura to play a game of dice, without heeding any of his advice. As a consequence of this game of dice, the Pāṇḍavas lost everything and had to forgo the kingdom. At this time also Vidura made many attempts to save the Pāṇḍavas, but could not succeed.

Dhṛtarāṣṭra became gravely silent on the day before the beginning of the great battle of Kurukṣetra, as he wondered what would happen. He could not decide what to do or what not to do. He then called Vidura and told him, "Vidura, I am suffering from the fire of worry. Now I am unable to sleep. Therefore, please advise me what is good for us at this hour." The intelligent Vidura preached to him the whole night about the path of righteousness and virtue. Since it went on for a whole night, this *Prastava-mulaka* chapter is given as the *Prajagara-parva* chapter in *Mahābhārata*. In this chapter, Vidura slightly softened the attitude of the selfish and greedy Dhṛtarāṣṭra by his meaningful teachings, but did not succeed fully. Dhṛtarāṣṭra told Vidura, "I have fully grasped the deep meaning of your extremely accurate logic-filled sermons, but what is the use of understanding? I lose my power to think properly as soon as I remember Duryodhana. This causes me to understand that no one can dare to go against fate. Fate is foremost, and any endeavor to go against it is in vain."

After this, Duryodhana welcomed Śrī Kṛṣṇa appropriately when He arrived at Hastināpura as a messenger, and invited Him to stay for lunch, but Śrī Kṛṣṇa declined and said, "A messenger accepts offers of food only after completing his job. A person accepts food from others either when invited with affection or if he or she needs help. I am yet to accomplish my task. I am neither obligated by some problem, nor invited out of sincere love. Therefore, I do not consider it appropriate to accept any invitation other than at the house of the impartial, religious-minded, rightful and wise Vidura." And so the Lord went to the house of Vidura, which is an extremely rare occurrence even for great yogis. Upon observing that Śrī Kṛṣṇa was in his house, Sage Vidura was greatly pleased and offered prayers by means of his words, body and other items. He then offered the Lord varieties of relishable food and drinks.

Vidura exhibited the pastimes of a pauper. Captured by the pure devotion of Vidura, Lord Śrī Kṛṣṇa, with great love, accepted bananas, banana skin, fragments of rice and dry bread at the house of Vidura, in preference to all the four types of tasty items that could be chewed, sucked, licked or drunk, offered by a non-devotee.

Devotees give different accounts of this incident at various places. For example, once, King Duryodhana organized a function at his palace. Although Duryodhana felt jealous of Śrī Kṛṣṇa, in order to follow etiquette, he invited Śrī Kṛṣṇa as well. Considering it proper to fulfill the obligation, Śrī Kṛṣṇa came to the house of Duryodhana. King Duryodhana displayed false feelings and offered the Lord a seat at a level equal to himself, requesting Him to eat many tasty items. Since Duryodhana was a non-devotee, Śrī Kṛṣṇa did not eat even a single piece of the items offered. He said, "I am not hungry. I am completely full. I did not come here to eat; I only came to maintain the dignity of the invitation." Then Śrī Kṛṣṇa left and went to the house of Śrī Vidura. At that time, Śrī Vidura was not there, as he had gone to collect alms. Śrī Vidura's wife was alone. Upon seeing His devotee, His hunger flared and He repeatedly asked Vidura's wife to give him something to eat. The wife of Vidura offered her obeisances to the Lord and wept with anxiety. She told Him that her husband was not at home and that there was nothing to eat. Śrī Kṛṣṇa saw a bunch of raw bananas in a corner of the house. Pointing to them, Śrī Kṛṣṇa requested Vidura's wife to give him a banana immediately. Finding no other way, Vidura's wife pulled a half ripe banana from the bunch and, overwhelmed by her excessive emotions, she peeled the skin off it and dropped the banana while giving banana skin to Śrī Kṛṣṇa. Exactly at that instant Śrī Vidura arrived. Unexpectedly having Śrī Kṛṣṇa as a guest, he offered his obeisances and tears began to flow from his eyes. He struck his hand on his head when he observed that Śrī Kṛṣṇa was eating the banana skin instead of the banana, and said to his wife, "O silly woman! You have destroyed everything; you have offered the banana skin to Śrī Kṛṣṇa instead of the banana." However, Śrī Kṛṣṇa then said to Vidura, "I eat neither the banana nor the banana skin. I eat the substance offered lovingly by a devotee."

patraṁ puṣpaṁ phalaṁ toyaṁ
yo me bhaktyā prayacchati
tad ahaṁ bhakty-upahṛtam
aśnāmi prayatātmanaḥ
(*Bhagavad-gītā* 9.26)

"If one offers Me with love and devotion, a leaf, a flower, fruit or water, I will accept it."

bhaktera dravya prabhu 'kāḍi' 'kāḍi' khāya
abhaktera dravya prabhu 'ulaṭi' nā cāya
(*Śrī Caitanya-bhāgavata, Madhya*, 9.185)

In the pastimes of Śrī Caitanya, His associate Śridhara exhibited the pastime of being poor like Vidura. Lord Caitanya Mahāprabhu used to go and snatch food from him and would not go anywhere else:

cāri danḍa kalaha kariyā
tabe se kiniye dravya ardha-mūlya diyā
satyavādī śrīdhara yathārtha mūlya bole

ardha-mūlya diyā prabhu nija haste tole
uṭhiyā śrīdhara dāsa kare kārākāri
eimata śrīdhara-ṭhākurera hurāhuri
(*Śrī Caitanya-bhāgavata, Madhya* 9.163-165)

"Mahāprabhu would lovingly argue for two hours every day with His devotee Śridhara. During that discussion, honest Śrīdhara would quote an appropriate price for vegetables and, knowingly, Mahāprabhu would ask him to sell at half of that price. When denied by Śridhara, Mahāprabhu would snatch the vegetables. Then both of them used to hold the vegetables and push each other."

A devotee in western India has sung: *duryodhana ke meva tyage saga vidura ghar khayo,* which means, "Satisfied with the devotion of Vidura, Śrī Kṛṣṇa discarded the royal food offered by Duryodhana and ate the fragments of rice that Vidura had collected when he went to beg alms." (Āśutoṣa Deva's *New Bengali Dictionary*)

īśvarera kṛpā jāti-kula nahin mane
vidurer ghare kṛṣṇa karila bhojane
(*Śrī Caitanya-caritāmṛta, Madhya Līlā* 10.138)

"The mercy of the Supreme Personality of Godhead is not restricted to the jurisdiction of caste and creed. Vidura was a *śūdra*, yet Kṛṣṇa accepted lunch at his home."

āpane śūdrār putra vidurer sthāne
anna māgi' khāilena bhaktir kāraṇe
(*Śrī Caitanya-bhāgavata, Madhya* 26.11)

"Vidura was a son of a *śūdra*. But due to the fact that he possessed devotion, the Lord begged food from him."

In the 10th Chapter of the 1st Canto of *Śrīmad Bhāgavatam* it is described in detail how Yudhiṣṭhira became the king of the whole planet, including the oceans, with the help of Śrī Kṛṣṇa, how people lived happily during Yudhiṣṭhira's reign and how Śrī Kṛṣṇa went to Hastināpura and Dvārakā with Arjuna and the Yādavas after completing three *aśvamedha-yajñas*. After this, the birth of King Parīkṣit is also described. When Vidura arrived at Hastināpura after his pilgrimage, the grief-stricken Pāṇḍavas felt rejuvenated. Yudhiṣṭhira Mahārāja offered prayers to Vidura with great respect and said: "As birds protect their young ones under the shadow of their own wings, similarly, you have saved us and our mother from drinking poison, burning in the Lākṣagṛha and other dangers. We are fortunate that you remember us."

bhavad-vidhā bhāgavatās tīrtha-bhūtāḥ svayaṁ vibho
tīrthī-kurvanti tīrthāni svāntaḥ-sthena gadābhṛtā
(*Śrīmad Bhāgavatam* 1.13.10)

"My lord, devotees like your good self are truly holy places personified. Devotees purify the holy places, which are maligned by the sins of sinners. Because you carry the Personality of Godhead within your heart, you turn all regions into places of pilgrimage."

When Yudhiṣṭhira Mahārāja asked Vidura about his pilgrimage and the welfare of the Yādavas, he explained all about his pilgrimage but did not reveal the destruction of the Yadu Dynasty. He stayed at Hastināpura for some time with the intention of liberating his elder brother Dhṛtarāṣṭra by providing him some knowledge of *tattva* (principle of truth), and for the sake of love of all others.

The question might arise how Vidura was qualified to preach knowledge of *tattva* since he was low-caste, but this can be explained by the following verse:

abibhrad aryamā daṇḍaṁ yathāvad agha-kāriṣu
yāvad dadhāra śūdratvaṁ śāpād varṣa-śataṁ yamaḥ
(*Śrīmad Bhāgavatam* 1.13.15)

"While Vidura played the part of a *śūdra*, having been cursed by Maṇḍūka Muni, Aryamā[28] officiated at the post of Yamarāja to punish those who committed sinful acts."

Yamarāja accepted the body of a *śūdra* for one hundred years due to the curse of Sage Māṇḍavya. Therefore, Vidura was not a *śūdra* in reality, even though he was born in a low-caste family.

After attaining the right to rule, Yudhiṣṭhira Mahārāja along with his brothers began to live like the demigods. Meanwhile, bad times came quietly. Vidura realized that the lives of all were going to end shortly, so he advised his elder brother to quit the world, saying, "Now that all-destroying *kāla* (time) has arrived, not only your wealth but also your very life will go. Your father, brothers, friends and sons are all dead and now time has come for you. Furthermore, you are now old; you are blind by birth and you are toothless and hard of hearing. You constantly suffer from a choking cough. I am amazed that you are still engaged in sense pleasure. Oh! What is this hope in all living beings that they are going to live forever?"

When he failed in his attempt to distract Dhṛtarāṣṭra from material attachments, Vidura told his materially arrogant brother, "You are staying in a house that is not yours. Bhīma killed all your sons. How disgraceful it is that you have to survive on the grains offered by them. You sent them to Lākṣagṛha, you made arrangements for them to be given poison, you made arrangements to insult their wife, you captured their land and wealth and now you are living on the food provided by them. It is better to die than to live in this way." Vidura added, "That person is learned who leaves home while meditating upon Śrī Hari. Such a person is actually a superior human being."

Upon being slighted and advised by his brother, Dhṛtarāṣṭra regained some of his original self-awareness and curtailed his sense of attachment to his relatives. He left for the Himālayas, and Gāndhārī, the daughter of King Subala and devoted wife of Dhṛtarāṣṭra, followed her husband. Then Vidura departed from Hastināpura. When Yudhiṣṭhira Mahārāja was unable to find Dhṛtarāṣṭra, Gāndhārī or Vidura, he became anxious. At that time, Śrī Nārada Gosvāmī arrived and consoled him.

At the end of the 2nd Canto of *Śrīmad Bhāgavatam* it is stated that Sage Śaunaka and other sages requested Śrī Sūta Gosvāmī to relate the conversation between Sage Maitreya and Śrī Vidura on the topic of transcendental knowledge. This is described in the 3rd and 4th Cantos of *Śrīmad Bhāgavatam*. The following is a brief summary of that narration:

Śrī Vidura observed that Dhṛtarāṣṭra was spellbound by affection for his sons; thus he would follow neither Śrī Kṛṣṇa's advice, nor his own. In addition to this, Vidura felt that Dhṛtarāṣṭra had motivated the insult to him by Duryodhana and others. He became morose and, rejecting his company, left for pilgrimage. After visiting many sites of pilgrimage, he reached the banks of River Yamunā. There he met the devotee Uddhava, the disciple of Bṛhaspati. After some discussion, when Śrī Vidura expressed his desire to hear *catur-ślokī Bhāgavatam* (original four verses of *Bhāgavatam*), Śrī Uddhava advised him to approach Sage Maitreya. Inspired by Śrī Uddhava, Śrī Vidura met Śrī Maitreya on the banks of River Bhāgīrathī. Śrī Vidura posed many questions on elementary topics to Sage Maitreya, as described in detail in the 3rd and 4th Cantos of *Śrīmad Bhāgavatam*. When Śrī Vidura was satisfied with the answers

28 Aryamā is one of the twelve Ādityas, and therefore it was quite possible for him to take charge of the office of Yamarāja during his absence for one hundred years in the form of Vidura.

to his questions, he offered his obeisances to the sage and returned to Hastināpura to meet his relatives.

When requested by Śrī Kṛṣṇa, Śrī Akrūra came to Hastināpura to learn about the well-being of the Pāṇḍavas. Vidura and Kuntīdevī told him about the misdeeds of Dhṛtarāṣṭra's sons against the Pāṇḍavas. On remembering Lord Kṛṣṇa, when Kuntīdevī began to cry, Śrī Akrūra and the famous Vidura consoled her:

sama-duḥkha-sukho 'krūro viduraś ca mahā-yaśāḥ
sāntvayām āsatuḥ kuntīṁ tat-putrotpatti-hetubhiḥ
(*Śrīmad Bhāgavatam* 10.49.15)

"Both Akrūra, who shared Queen Kuntī's distress and happiness, and the illustrious Vidura consoled the queen by reminding her of the extraordinary way her sons had taken birth."

The sons were born of heavenly gods (Dharma, Vāyu and Indra respectively) and thus

could not be vanquished like ordinary mortals. In fact, there was the distinct possibility of their supreme welfare in the near future.

When Dhṛtarāṣṭra left home, Dharmarāja Yudhiṣṭhira went to his *āśrama* to meet him. He inquired from Dhṛtarāṣṭra about the penances of Mother Kuntī, elder mother Gāndhārī, Uncle Vidura, etc. The details given by Dhṛtarāṣṭra about Śrī Vidura are described in *Viśvakoṣa* as follows:

The blind King Dhṛtarāṣṭra said, "Dear son! Everyone is living satisfactorily while performing his or her righteous and religious duties, but the most intelligent Vidura has become very weak, as he is performing severe penance and is not taking anything."

Once, some *brāhmaṇas* had an audience with Vidura in the forest. While they were conversing, they saw naked Śrī Vidura, his body covered with layers of dust and his long hair turned into matted locks. He was standing at some distance. That great soul glanced once at the *āśrama* and immediately went farther away. After seeing this, the religious Yudhiṣṭhira ran after him. Sage Vidura was about to enter into the deep forest. Observing this, Dharmarāja compassionately called out, "O great soul! I am your dear Yudhiṣṭhira. I have come to meet you." Śrī Vidura stood in a composed mood leaning against a tree. Yudhiṣṭhira approached him and said, "O my object of worship, I am your most beloved Yudhiṣṭhira; I have come to meet you." Śrī Vidura did not reply but looked directly at Dharmarāja. By his mystical powers he locked his eyes with those of Yudhiṣṭhira, body to body, life to life, organs to organs, and entered his body. Vidura's body then became stiff and dead like a wooden statue and remained leaning against that tree. After this, Yudhiṣṭhira felt more powerful than previously, and he could recall all that was told to him by Śrī Vyāsadeva.

As Yudhiṣṭhira was about to cremate the body of Vidura, a celestial sound was heard, which said, "Mahārāja! Do not set fire to the body of Vidura. He has attained *yati-dharma* (become a renunciate, a *sannyāsī*). He may attain the Sāntānikā planets. Therefore, do not grieve for him." Thus, on hearing that divine voice, Dharmarāja Yudhiṣṭhira abandoned his intent to cremate Vidura's body and returned to Dhṛtarāṣṭra's *āśrama*.

The pastimes of Vidura's disappearance by entering the body of Yudhiṣṭhira have also been narrated in the *Āśramavasika-parva* of *Mahābhārata*.

Sage Vaśiṣṭha

Vaśiṣṭha was born from the life breath of Śrī Brahmā. He is one of the Saptarṣis (Seven Sages) and his wife Arundhatī is the daughter of Sage Kardama. According to the *Kurma Purāṇa*, Sage Vaśiṣṭha had seven sons and one daughter:

vaśiṣṭhashca tayorjayam sapta putrān jijanata
kanyanca puṇḍarīkākṣam sarva śobhā-samanvitam
(*Kurma Purāṇa*, Chapter 12)

According to the *Ṛg Veda*, Śrī Vaśiṣṭha appeared from the union of Urvaśī with Mitra (sun) and Varuṇa. When Mitra and Varuṇa beheld the Apsarā, Urvaśī, at a sacrifice, their seed fell from them. It fell on many places, into an earthen pot, into water, and on the ground. Sage Vaśiṣṭha was produced on the ground, while Agastya was born in the earthen pot and the radiant Matsya appeared from the water. The *Ṛg Veda* explains that Varuṇa transformed Śrī Vaśiṣṭha into a sage.

We may understand from the *Ṛg Veda* that Vaśiṣṭha and his successors were the priests of King Sudāsa. (*Viśvakoṣa*)

Vaśiṣṭha is the son of Brahmā and is one of the Seven Sages. When he cursed Nimi to lose his body, Nimi cursed him in a similar way. Thus, as instructed by Śrī Brahmā, he was reborn from the seed of Mitra and Varuṇa. He begot one hundred sons, one of which was Śakti, with his wife Arundhatī. A dispute over the wish-fulfilling cow, Nandinī, erupted between him and Viśvāmitra. As a consequence of this, King Kalmāṣapāda was transformed into a demon when cursed by Śakti, and ate Vaśiṣṭha's hundred sons, including Śakti, when instigated by Viśvāmitra. Vaśiṣṭha consoled Adṛśyanti, the wife of his elder son, when he learned that she was pregnant. Adṛśyanti gave birth to Sage Parāśara. King Ikṣvāku appointed Vaśiṣṭha as the priest of the Solar Dynasty. He composed the *Vaśiṣṭha Saṁhitā*, and he is among the sages who composed the hymns of the *Ṛg Veda*. (*New Bengali Dictionary*, by Āśutoṣa Deva)

The 13th Chapter of the 9th Canto of *Śrīmad Bhāgavatam* describes the dynasty of the king of Videha, Mahārāja Nimi, who was the son of Ikṣvāku. His dealings with Vaśiṣṭha are related as follows:

King Nimi appointed Vaśiṣṭha as head priest for a great *yajña*. Vaśiṣṭha Muni told King Nimi that the king of the demigods, Indra, had already appointed him as *ṛtvija* (head priest); therefore he would complete Indra's *yajña* first, and he requested Nimi to wait. After Sage Vaśiṣṭha had gone to Indra, King Nimi started to think that, because life is uncertain and mortal, it would not be advisable to wait for the arrival of Guru Vaśiṣṭha. Therefore, he arranged for another head priest and inaugurated the *yajña*. After completing Indra's *yajña*, Vaśiṣṭha Muni returned and saw that Nimi had already begun the *yajña* with another head priest. Displeased by such an arrogant action, Vaśiṣṭha cursed his disciple Nimi that his proud body would be destroyed.

When cursed by Sage Vaśiṣṭha, Nimi felt hurt and said, "You cursed me in anticipation of charity. I therefore curse you that your body may also be destroyed." After this, the spiritually learned Nimi left his body. Vaśiṣṭha also departed from his body and took another birth from the union of Urvaśī with Mitra and Varuṇa. As Nimi had left his body while performing the *yajña*, the priests performing the *yajña* preserved his body using preservative essences and concluded the ceremony. Upon completion, when the demigods arrived, the sages said, "If you possess divine powers and are satisfied with us, then please bring our King Nimi back to life." The demigods gave their blessings but the king of Videha, Nimi, refused to accept another material birth. The sagacious Nimi said, "Dear devotees and sages, those who leave this awful body do not crave for bodily pleasures; they desire only to serve the lotus feet of God. I do not wish for another dreadful body. In water, fish and similar creatures fear other large fish. Similarly, those having a human or any other body will always fear death." When King Nimi refused to accept a fresh bodily life, the sages became confused. Thus, the demigods made arrangements such that the conditions of both parties were met. They said, "King Nimi of Videha may live with a transcendental body, without any material body, and may reside as per his own wish on the eyelids of living beings as a cause of the closing and opening of eyelids." The sages foresaw that people would live in fear due to the anarchy that would prevail without a king. Thus they churned the body of Nimi and, as a result, a prince appeared from the body. As he was born in an unusual fashion, the prince was named Janaka. Since he was born from a lifeless body he became known as Videha. Since he was born of churning he was also known as Mithilā. The city established by him is known as Mithilā. In the *Uttara-kaṇḍa* of Vālmīki's *Rāmāyaṇa*, this topic is described where the details of Nṛga, Nimi, Urvaśī, Purūravā and Vaśiṣṭha are mentioned.

Sage Vaśiṣṭha is one of the sons of Brahmā. This is mentioned in the 3rd Canto of *Śrīmad Bhāgavatam*, where the incident regarding Maitreya and Vidura is given:

athābhidhyāyataḥ sargaṁ daśa putrāḥ prajajñire
bhagavac-chakti-yuktasya loka-santāna-hetavaḥ
marīcir atry-aṅgirasau pulastyaḥ pulahaḥ kratuḥ
bhṛgur vasiṣṭho dakṣaś ca daśamas tatra nāradaḥ
(*Śrīmad Bhāgavatam* 3.12.21-22)

"Brahmā, who was empowered by the Supreme Personality of Godhead, thought of generating living entities and begot ten sons for the extension of the generations. Marīci, Atri, Aṅgirā, Pulastya, Pulaha, Kratu, Bhṛgu, Vaśiṣṭha, Dakṣa and the tenth son, Nārada, were thus born."

Nārada appeared from the lap of Lord Brahmā, Dakṣa appeared from the toe of Lord Brahmā, Vaśiṣṭha from the life breath of Lord Brahmā, Pulastya from his navel, Aṅgirā from his mouth, Atri from his eyes, and from the mind of Śrī Brahmā, Marīci was born.

ūrjāyāṁ jajñire putrā Vaśiṣṭhasya parantapa
citraketu-pradhānās te sapta brahmārṣayo 'malāḥ
(*Śrīmad Bhāgavatam* 4.1.40)

"O great Vidura, the great sage Vaśiṣṭha begot in his wife, Ūrjā, sometimes called Arundhatī, seven spotlessly great sages, headed by the sage Citraketu. They became famous as the Saptarṣis."

vaśiṣṭha-tanayāḥ sapta ṛṣayaḥ pramadādayaḥ
satyā vedaśrutā bhadrā devā indras tu satyajit
(*Śrīmad Bhāgavatam* 8.1.2)

"During the reign of the third Manu, Pramada and other sons of Vaśiṣṭha became the Seven Sages. The Satyas, Vedaśrutas and Bhadras became demigods, and Satyajit was selected to be Indra, the king of heaven."

In Chapter 16 of the 11th Canto of *Śrīmad Bhāgavatam*, Śrī Uddhava asks Śrī Kṛṣṇa about his opulences and potencies, as similarly asked by Arjuna in *Bhagavad-gītā*. Kṛṣṇa replied that, of pilgrimages and rivers, He is the sacred Gaṅgā; among water bodies, the ocean; among weapons, the bow; of archers, Lord Śiva; of places of residence, Sumeru; among places difficult to visit He is the Himālayas; among trees, the Pipala; of medicines, barley; among priests He is Vaśiṣṭha; among experts of the *Vedas*, Bṛhaspati; of all military chieftains He is Kārtikeya and of all spiritual preachers He is Brahmā. In Chapter 11 of the 12th Canto of *Śrīmad Bhāgavatam*, where the conversation between Śrī Sūta and Sage Śaunaka and others is narrated, Sage Vaśiṣṭha is mentioned as the presiding sage of the month of Śuci (Āṣāḍha).

It is known from the 9th Chapter of the 1st Canto of *Śrīmad Bhāgavatam* that Sage Vaśiṣṭha was present with Nārada, Parvata, Dhaumya, Vyāsadeva, Bhāradvāja, Paraśurāma, Gautama, Atri and other sages and saintly kings that came for an audience with Bhīṣma at Kurukṣetra. The 19th Chapter of the same canto recounts that when King Parīkṣit was fasting unto death on the banks of the Gaṅgā after being cursed by a *brāhmaṇa*, Sage Vaśiṣṭha was also present along with Atri, Cyavana, Śaradvān, Bhṛgu, Aṅgirā, Parāśara, Dvaipāyana, Agastya, Nārada, Viśvāmitra, Paraśurāma, Gautama and other sages.

It is learned from the *Ādi-parva* of *Mahābhārata* that, in the Kuru Dynasty, the mighty Saṁvaraṇa (son of Śrī Ṛkṣa) married the extremely beautiful Tapti, the daughter of the demigod Sūrya, with the help of Sage Vaśiṣṭha. King Saṁvaraṇa performed severe penance to please Sūrya and was able to win Sūrya's daughter as his wife when assisted by the mystical powers of Sage Vaśiṣṭha. Since then, the Kuru Dynasty is also known as Tapteya. Sage Vaśiṣṭha was the priest of the Ikṣvāku Dynasty. As Bṛhaspati used to perform *yajña*, etc., for the demigods, similarly Vaśiṣṭha used to perform the same for the kings.

In the province of Kanyā-kubjā (part of Uttar Pradesh) there was a famous king by the name of Gādhi, the son of Kuśika. Gādhi had a son named Viśvāmitra. Once, Viśvāmitra went hunting accompanied by his friends. He felt thirsty while roaming in the forest, and reached the *āśrama* of Sage Vaśiṣṭha, who welcomed him. Sage Vaśiṣṭha had a *kāma-dhenu* (wish-fulfilling cow) called Nandinī and he welcomed Viśvāmitra by offering him four types of delicious food, precious diamonds and clothes, which were provided by the *kāma-dhenu*. King Viśvāmitra, his companions and all the members of his army were satisfied by Sage Vaśiṣṭha's offerings. They were all wondering how a resident of an *āśrama* could arrange such delicacies that are rare even for kings. When they learned that everything was obtained from the *kāma-dhenu*, Viśvāmitra became greedy to get her and offered millions of ordinary cows to Vaśiṣṭha in exchange for Nandinī.

Sage Vaśiṣṭha replied that the *kāma-dhenu*, Nandinī, the daughter of Pāyasvinī (*surabhī* cow), was there to satisfy demigods, guests and ancestors as well as being used for *yajñas*. Therefore, he wouldn't be able to exchange Nandinī even for Viśvāmitra's kingdom, to which Viśvāmitra said, "I am a warrior, and you are a *brāhmaṇa*, endowed with the qualities of austerity and Vedic study. If you will not give me the *kāma-dhenu* in exchange for millions of other cows, I will forcibly take her." Vaśiṣṭha then replied, "You are a powerful warrior king and are strong; therefore you may do whatever you wish. You need not ask me for anything."

When Śrī Viśvāmitra tried to take Nandinī away forcibly, she made a noise like humba-humba and ran to Sage Vaśiṣṭha. She did not come out of the *āśrama*, even though the soldiers that had come with Viśvāmitra kept beating her. Vaśiṣṭha expressed his helplessness to the *kāma-dhenu* and said, "Viśvāmitra wishes to take you forcibly; what can I do in this matter?" Nandinī was crying like an orphan as the soldiers of Viśvāmitra were beating her. Observing her miserable state, Sage Vaśiṣṭha neither became upset nor lost his patience. He consoled Nandinī and said, "The strength of a warrior is brilliance, and that of a *brāhmaṇa* is forgiveness. You may do whatever you desire." Nandinī replied, "O *brāhmaṇa*! As long as you do not abandon me, Viśvāmitra will not be powerful enough to take me away." Sage Vaśiṣṭha said, "I have not abandoned you. If you can stay here you may do so." Upon hearing these words of Sage Vaśiṣṭha, the *kāma-*

dhenu took a furious form and raised her head and neck. Her eyes turned red with fury. She began chasing the army of Viśvāmitra while repeatedly sounding humba–humba. Burning sparks showered from her tail, and from each of her organs different types of soldiers emerged. Pallavas appeared from her tail; Draviḍas and Śakas from her udders; Kancigana from her dung; soldiers of the Śabara caste from her back; Pauṇḍra, Kirāta, Yavana, Sinhala, Barbara, Cibuka, Pulinda, Cīna, Hūna, Kerala and other *mlecchas* appeared from the foam of her mouth.

A war broke out between the soldiers of Viśvāmitra and the soldiers that emerged from the *kāma-dhenu*. Nandinī's army defeated the army of Viśvāmitra. Having been badly beaten, Viśvāmitra's army ran away. The army that was fighting for Sage Vaśiṣṭha was angry, but did not kill any of Viśvāmitra soldiers. Viśvāmitra was astonished upon observing the Brahman-like spiritual brilliance (*brahmatejaḥ*) of Sage Vaśiṣṭha, and he felt disgraced in his duty as a warrior. He developed a feeling of detachment, thinking that *brahmatejaḥ* is the real strength, and that superior power can only be obtained by penance. After this incident, Viśvāmitra abandoned his wealth and kingdom and, discarding all royal comforts, engaged in severe penance.

He became perfect and effulgent after performing severe penance. With his new power he shook all the worlds and attained the position of *brāhmaṇattva* (knower of Brahman). Viśvāmitra, the son of Kuśika, drank *soma-rasa* with Indra, the king of the demigods.

It is known from the 9th Chapter of the 9th Canto of *Śrīmad Bhāgavatam* that:

tataḥ sudāsas tat-putro damayantī-patir nṛpaḥ
āhur mitrasahaṁ yaṁ vai kalmāṣāṅghrim uta kvacit
vaśiṣṭha-śāpād rakṣo 'bhūd anapatyaḥ sva-karmaṇā
(*Śrīmad Bhāgavatam* 9.9.18)

"Sarvakāma had a son named Sudāsa, whose son, known as Saudāsa, was the husband of Damayantī. Saudāsa is sometimes known as Mitrasaha or Kalmāṣapāda. Because of his own misdeed, Mitrasaha was sonless and was cursed by Vaśiṣṭha to become a man-eater (*rākṣasa*)."

Once, Saudāsa killed a demon while hunting, but did not harm the demon's brother. To take revenge, the demon's brother began to live at the palace of Saudāsa disguised as a cook. One day, Sage Vaśiṣṭha came to the royal house and was served cooked human flesh by the demon cook. Sage Vaśiṣṭha could judge with his mystical power that he was being served an inedible item, so he became angry and cursed the king that he would become a demon. Later, Sage Vaśiṣṭha learned that it was not the king's doing but that of his cook. Since Sage Vaśiṣṭha had cursed an innocent king, he undertook a fast for twelve years in order to repent and free himself of the accumulated reactions to this wrongful doing. Aggrieved and angered due to being cursed by the *guru* without any reason, King Saudāsa rose to curse Vaśiṣṭha in return using empowered water, but his wife Madayanti stopped him. When his wife stopped him, the king observed that the ten directions, sky, earth, and all places were full of living beings. He then dropped the empowered water on his own feet. As he accepted the advice of his wife, he became known as Mitrasaha. Since that water was dropped on his feet, his feet turned black and he developed a demoniac mentality. Due to his black feet he came to be known as Kalmāṣapāda.

Once, while roaming in the forest, Kalmāṣapāda saw a *brāhmaṇa* couple. Having demonic feelings, Saudāsa was about to eat the male *brāhmaṇa*, when the *brāhmaṇa's* wife very humbly prayed and said, "Saudāsa! You are not actually a demon. You are a brave man of the Ikṣvāku Dynasty and the husband of Damayanti. Please release my husband." In spite of logical pleas and appeals, the demon ate the *brāhmaṇa*. The wife of the *brāhmaṇa* became enraged and cursed the king that he would die while copulating. Saudāsa was relieved of Vaśiṣṭha's curse after twelve years, but because of the curse of the *brāhmaṇa's* wife he did not engage in physical union with his wife. Thus, because of his own actions, he was childless. As desired by the king, Vaśiṣṭha arranged a son from Damayanti's womb. Damayanti was not able to give birth to the child in her womb even after seven years, so Sage Vaśiṣṭha hit her abdomen with a stone, and the child was born. The son born from Damayanti was called Aśmaka (child born of a stone). Bālika was born from Aśmaka, and later escaped the wrath of Paraśurāma because of being surrounded by women. Thus, Bālika is also known as Nārīkavaca (one who is protected by women). When Paraśurāma vanquished all the *kṣatriyas*, Bālika became the progenitor of more *kṣatriyas*. Therefore, he was known as Mūlaka, the root of the dynasty of *kṣatriyas*.

There are some differences between the descriptions of *Kalmāṣapāda* in *Śrīmad Bhāgavatam* and *Mahābhārata*. According to *Mahābhārata* (*Ādi-parva*) there was a brilliant warrior king by the name of Kalmāṣapāda. Sage Viśvāmitra expressed a wish to have Kalmāṣapāda as his host. One day, Kalmāṣapāda went deep into the forest to hunt. He was tired after killing many bears and deer and became restless because of thirst and hunger. He was walking on a very narrow path that was only wide enough for one person to pass, when he met Sage Śakti (son of Sage Vaśiṣṭha), who was also walking on that path. King Kalmāṣapāda asked Śakti Muni to give way to him, but Sage Śakti admonished the king and said, "O King! This is my way. A king should give way to a *brāhmaṇa*. This is the message of *sanātana-*

dharma." A discussion ensued between them. In the end, the king became angry and, due to the spell of ignorance, thrashed the *muni* with his whip. Sage Śakti became angry and cursed the king, "O lowest of mankind, I am a sage and you have thrashed me while behaving as though you were a *rākṣasa*. Therefore, you will become a *rākṣasa*. You will wander about on the earth looking for human flesh." Having spoken in this way, the sage then gave passage to the king.

Previously, there had been a conflict between Sage Vaśiṣṭha and Sage Viśvāmitra regarding the fire-offering rites of King Kalmāṣapāda. When the dispute between the king and Vaśiṣṭha's son Śakti erupted, Sage Viśvāmitra also arrived, but made himself invisible in the hope of gaining some advantage. After being cursed by Śakti, Kalmāṣapāda realized a moment later that he was the son of Sage Vaśiṣṭha, and begged for mercy. Viśvāmitra, understanding the king's feelings, ordered a *rākṣasa* by the name of Kinkara to enter the king's body. Due to the curse of Śakti, the demon was easily able to enter the body of the king. The king became possessed and suffered greatly because of the demon. At that time, while away from his city, he met a hungry *brāhmaṇa* who asked him to give him meat. The king, who was known to take care of others, promised him that he would send him food as per his desire and asked him to wait. The king returned to his palace but forgot his promise and went to sleep. In the middle of the night he woke up and recalled his promise. He immediately sent for his cook to go to the forest to give meat to the *brāhmaṇa*. When the servant informed him that no meat was available, the king asked him to send human meat left by demons. The chef obtained the human flesh, cooked and decorated the preparations, and sent it to the hungry *brāhmaṇa* in the forest. Due to his mystical powers, the *brāhmaṇa* could understand that the meat was unfit to eat, so he also cursed the king in the way that Sage Śakti cursed him: "This king fascinated with human flesh will trouble the living beings and roam the world." In this way, being cursed twice, and combined with the effect of the demon in his body, the king lost his senses. He developed a demonic mentality and when he met Śakti after some days said, "You have cursed me, but I shall eat you first." The king killed him and ate him like a lion. When Viśvāmitra saw that Śakti was dead, he instigated the king to eat the other sons of Vaśiṣṭha, by ordering the *rākṣasa* possessing his body. As a lion eats deer, so the king ate all the hundred sons of Vaśiṣṭha one by one.

Deeply upset by the death of his one hundred sons, Vaśiṣṭha resolved to commit suicide. He jumped from Sumeru Mountain, but did not die, as the rocks felt as soft as cotton to him. After this, he lit a fire in the forest and entered into it. But the fire did not burn him, as the flames became cool and refreshing. He also tried to drown himself in the sea by tying stones to his neck, but the waves of the ocean deposited him safely on the shore. As he could not take his own life by any means, Vaśiṣṭha Muni returned to his *āśrama* in a depressed mood. However, upon seeing his *āśrama* without his sons, and unable to tolerate the grief of separation from them, he again deserted the *āśrama*. Desiring to destroy his body, he tied himself tightly with rope and entered a river swollen from heavy rains. But the river freed him by cutting through the rope. Thus, that river was known as Vipāśā, 'unfettered'. Now Vaśiṣṭha Muni became distraught and began to wander among the hills, rivers, sea and forests. One day, he saw the violent river Hemavati, which was full of crocodiles and, again trying to give up his life, he jumped into the river. The river felt the sage as fire and became afraid and divided herself into hundreds of streams. Realizing that he had not died in spite of so many attempts, Vaśiṣṭha Muni concluded that death would not come according to his own wish, and again returned to his *āśrama*. It is also described in some scriptures that Viśvāmitra's one hundred sons also died when Sage Vaśiṣṭha took a deep, cold breath while in a state of grief (*niśvāsa*). As he approached his *āśrama*, Vaśiṣṭha's daughter-in-law Adṛśyanti walked behind him. When Sage Vaśiṣṭha asked who was following him, Adṛśyanti introduced herself. Sage Vaśiṣṭha previously used to hear his eldest son Śakti chanting Vedic hymns, and now similar sounds were coming from the womb of his daughter-in-law. Sage Vaśiṣṭha was amazed and asked her who was chanting. She replied, "O sage, I have a child by your son Śakti, and he has remained in my womb for twelve years learning the *Vedas*. You have just heard him." The sage was delighted to learn this, so, realizing that his dynasty was still alive, he abandoned the thought of suicide. As he continued walking with Adṛśyanti in the forest, he saw Kalmāṣapāda running toward them, intending to eat him. This frightened Adṛśyanti, but Sage Vaśiṣṭha explained to her that the man was not a demon; he was instead the famous and brave king Kalmāṣapāda. Sage Vaśiṣṭha brought the king's demonic feelings under control with a powerful *mantra* and then sprinkled sacred water on him. The king became liberated from the curse and now appeared as brilliant as the sun. King Kalmāṣapāda bowed before Sage Vaśiṣṭha and said, "O sage! I am the son of King Sudāsa. I am your host. I shall fulfill whatever you desire." Sage Vaśiṣṭha ordered him to go back to his capital to rule, and to never again disobey any *brāhmaṇa*. King Kalmāṣapāda accepted his command and requested Vaśiṣṭha to arrange to beget him a son who would help spread the Ikṣvāku Dynasty. Sage Vaśiṣṭha promised to give him a son. When the great king reached Ayodhyā City with Sage Vaśiṣṭha, the public welcomed them with great pleasure. To fulfill the desire of the king, Sage Vaśiṣṭha took the royal queen with him and went to his *āśrama*. The queen became pregnant but could not deliver the baby for a long time, and so she struck her abdomen with a stone (*aśma*) to induce labor. After staying in the womb for twelve years, a great saintly king was born, named Aśmaka. Adṛśyanti also finally gave birth to Vaśiṣṭha's grandson, who grew similar to his father, Śakti. Sage Vaśiṣṭha performed all the *saṁskāras* of his grandson. Since Vaśiṣṭha Muni had wished to die while his grandson was in the womb, his grandson became known as Parāśara. Parāśara had considered Sage Vaśiṣṭha his father from birth, but later on his mother explained to him that Vaśiṣṭha Muni was his grandfather, not his father.

Parāśara became very sad and angry when he learned that a demon had eaten his father. He decided to destroy all the worlds, but Sage Vaśiṣṭha prevented him from doing so by relating to him the story of Aurva. However, he later engaged in a sacrifice to kill all the *rākṣasas* (demons). The brilliant Sage Parāśara began burning all the demons, including the young and old. Sage Vaśiṣṭha did not prevent him from doing this. This episode has been discussed in detail in the biography of Sage Parāśara.

Supreme Lord Śrī Rāmacandra performed the pastime of accepting Vaśiṣṭha Muni as His spiritual master:

jaṭā nirmucya vidhivat kula-vṛddhaiḥ samaṁ guruḥ
abhyaṣiñcad yathaivendraṁ catuḥ-sindhu-jalādibhiḥ
(*Śrīmad Bhāgavatam* 9.10.48)

"Afterward, the spiritual master, Vaśiṣṭha, had Lord Rāmacandra cleanly shaved, freeing Him from His matted locks of hair. Then, with the cooperation of the elderly members of the family, he performed the bathing ceremony (*abhiṣeka*) for Lord Rāmacandra using the water of the four seas and other substances, just as it was performed for King Indra."

From the description in the scripture called *Aitareya Brāhmaṇa*, one can learn about the relationship between Vaśiṣṭha and Viśvāmitra. When Viśvāmitra took everything from King Hariścandra and caused him trouble, at that time, Vaśiṣṭha and Viśvāmitra fought for a very long time in the guise of birds. Brahmā mediated between them, calmed them down and gave them back their original forms.

Sage Vaśiṣṭha was among the many saints present for an audience with Śrī Kṛṣṇa at the time of the solar eclipse at Kurukṣetra, (*Śrīmad Bhāgavatam* 10.84.4). Sage Vaśiṣṭha was also present at the *rājasūya-yajña* of King Yudhiṣṭhira (*Śrīmad Bhāgavatam* 10.74.7). Vaśiṣṭha Muni was also among the sages who came to the Piṇḍāraka region (on the border of the state of Gujarat, and one *krośa* away from the coast). The young boys of the Yadu Dynasty teased the sages gathered there, which resulted in a curse on the Yādavas that eventually destroyed them (*Śrīmad Bhāgavatam* 11.1.11-16).

The area twenty kilometers southeast of Assam's main city, Guwahati (Prāgjyotiṣapura), is the famous site of Vaśiṣṭha Muni's penance. It is a beautiful pilgrimage place, surrounded by hills on all sides. There is a temple dedicated to Vaśiṣṭha Muni, and according to the local tribal people a temple of his wife Arundhatī is also situated there. A waterfall has also added beauty to the place. At one location the water springs out like a fountain and many people say that the Gaṅgā has appeared there as desired by Sage Vaśiṣṭha. Every year many people visit this site.

Bālakhilya Sages

krator api kriyā bhāryā vālakhilyān asūyata
ṛṣīn ṣaṣṭi-sahasrāṇi jvalato brahmā-tejasā
(*Śrīmad Bhāgavatam* 4.1.39)

"Kratu's wife, Kriyā, gave birth to 60,000 great sages, named the Bālakhilyas. All these sages were greatly advanced in spiritual knowledge, and their bodies were illuminated by such knowledge." Kratu Ṛṣi is one of the seven sons of Brahmā who are celebrated as the Saptarṣis.

In the 29th Chapter of the 4th Canto of *Śrīmad Bhāgavatam*, Sage Kratu is mentioned as one of the stalwart *brāhmaṇas* who can speak authoritatively on the Vedic literature. Also, in the 13th Chapter of the same canto it is mentioned that he was one of the six excellent sons of Ulmuka Ṛṣi and his wife Puṣkariṇī.

kretoshca santatibhāryā bālakhilyansuyata
pashtiryani sahastrani ṛṣīṇām ūrdhvaretāsama
(*Mārkaṇḍeya Purāṇa* 52.24)

"Kratu's wife Santati gave birth to 60,000 Bālakhilyas. All of them were sages, greatly advanced in spiritual knowledge."

vidhinā nirmita pūrvaṁ vedi parampāvanī
agne veshyadi munayo bālakhilyadayah smṛtaḥ
(*Viṣṇu Purāṇa*, Arimsa 1, Chapter 10.2)

"Each one of them was only the size of a thumb, but they were as bright as the blazing sun and had attained control over their senses."

"They appeared from the pores of the skin of Brahmā and were the size of a thumb. The number of these sages is 60,000." (Bharata, *Viṣṇu Purāṇa*).

"One of their names is Bālakhilya. They were all greatly advanced in spiritual knowledge due to severe penance." (*Viśvakoṣa*)

In the *Ādi-parva* of *Mahābhārata*, there is a detailed description of the Bālakhilya sages and their *yajña*, which resulted in the birth of the greatest among birds, Garuḍa. A brief description follows:

Sage Śaunaka asked Ugraśravā Sūta Gosvāmī, "O son of Sūta! What offense and negligence did Indra commit; how did Garuḍa take birth by the power of penance of the Bālakhilya sages, and how did he become *durdharṣaḥ* (unconquerable) and immortal? If this is described in the *Purāṇas*, then I wish to hear it from you."

Ugraśravā Sūta Gosvāmī replied, "When Prajāpati Kaśyapa began a *yajña* with the desire to get a son, at that time, Indra and all the demigods, sages and Gandharvas helped him. Kaśyapa Ṛṣi appointed Indra and the other demigods along with the Bālakhilya sages to collect wood for the *yajña*. By his extreme power, Indra brought heaps of wood along with a mountain, without any effort. On the way, Indra saw that some sages, the size of a thumb, were bringing a twig of *palāśa* (a fruit) with great difficulty. The sages had performed severe penance, remaining hungry for a long time and thus were weak. They were so fragile that they nearly drowned in water filled in the depression made by the hoof of a cow, and were suffering. The demigod King Indra made fun of them and passed by them proudly. This annoyed the Bālakhilya sages and they began to make offerings in the sacrificial fire to produce another frightening Indra, possessing a hundred times more power than the original Indra. When Indra learned this he was stunned and frightened, and took refuge of Kaśyapa Ṛṣi. When the sage learned this from Indra, he went to the Bālakhilya sages and asked, "O sages! Have you accomplished your task?"

The Bālakhilya sages replied, "Yes, it is done." Kaśyapa Ṛṣi consoled them and said, "Indra attained the post of the king of the demigods by means of the instructions of Brahmā. You are trying to create another Indra. It is not proper for you to falsify the words of Brahmā, but I do not desire that your wish should remain unfulfilled. The mighty and powerful person you have resolved to make "Indra" should become an Indra of birds. The king of the demigods Indra is pleading for forgiveness. Now please forgive him." Upon hearing the words of Kaśyapa Ṛṣi, the Bālakhilya sages were pacified and agreed to his desire.

At the same time, the virtuous well-wishing and credit-worthy performer of penances—Vinatā—approached her husband, Kaśyapa Ṛṣi, with the desire for a son. Kaśyapa Ṛṣi said, "O Devī! May your wish be fulfilled! By my resolve and the power of penance of the Bālakhilya sages, you will give birth to two most fortunate kings who will be worshiped by all the denizens of the three worlds." Prajāpati Kaśyapa Ṛṣi said with delight to Indra, "Two brothers will take birth, who will assist you. No harm will come to you from them. However, you should not ignore the greatly learned sages due to the influence of pride." Vinatā's wish was fulfilled and, at the appropriate time, she gave birth to two sons, named Aruṇa and Garuḍa. Aruṇa, who was physically disabled, became the charioteer of the sun, while Garuḍa became the king of birds.

In the *Ādi-parva* of *Mahābhārata* some details about the Bālakhilya sages are given wherein the transcendental bravery of Garuḍa is narrated. Here is a brief synopsis:

Garuḍa went to bring nectar to free his mother, Vinatā, from servitude, as advised by the snakes. Before leaving, he asked his mother what he should eat on the way. His mother told him to eat only Niṣādas[29] in the middle of the secluded ocean. However, she warned Garuḍa not to kill any *brāhmaṇa* out of anger. She told him that *brāhmaṇas* are always worshipable, because they are the spiritual masters of all. The mighty Garuḍa spread his wings and flew off. While flying over the middle of the sea, he became impatient due to hunger and began to eat Niṣādas. While he was eating Niṣādas, a *brāhmaṇa* and his wife got stuck in Garuḍa's throat, and began to burn it like flaming coals. Garuḍa spewed out from his throat the man and woman burning like fire, understanding them to be a *brāhmaṇa* and his wife. The *brāhmaṇa* and his Niṣāda wife then departed to their home. Garuḍa told everything to his father Kaśyapa when he met him.

Vibhāvasu and Supratīka were born as an elephant and tortoise respectively, because of a curse inflicted upon each other. The elephant was about 48 miles (1 *yojana* = approx. 8 miles, therefore approx. 6 *yojanas*) high and twice as long, and the tortoise was about 24 miles high and 80 miles in circumference. The incident of their long-lasting rivalry has been narrated in *Mahābhārata*. Garuḍa caught both of them to eat as instructed by his father, and flew away, clutching them in his talons. On the way, Garuḍa saw many tall trees along the coast of the sea. He attempted to sit on one of the large branches of a banyan tree, which had spread over 800 miles, but the branch snapped by his mere touch. Garuḍa saw that the Bālakhilya sages were hanging upside down on that large branch. Worried that the *brāhmaṇas* engaged in penance would die if the branch fell, Garuḍa lifted the branch with his beak while strongly grasping the elephant and tortoise in his talons. The sages were amazed to see such an impossible task performed by this huge bird, so they named him "Garuḍa." Garuḍa began to fly to different places with the elephant, the tortoise and the branch, to save the Bālakhilya sages. Upon reaching Gandhamādana Mountain, Garuḍa saw his father, Sage Kaśyapa. When Sage Kaśyapa saw the strange, giant bird capable of razing the three worlds looking afraid, he understood the reason and said, "O son! Act cautiously! Please ensure that the Bālakhilya sages and Marīci do not get angry and destroy you." To please the Bālakhilya sages, Sage Kaśyapa said, "Please cooperate with this bird, Garuḍa, who is engaged in the welfare of the world." Due to the appeal of Kaśyapa Ṛṣi, the Bālakhilya sages left the branch of the tree and went to the Himālayas to perform their penance.

After this, Garuḍa asked where to discard the branch and Sage Kaśyapa told him about a desolate, unreachable great mountain. The branch that Garuḍa was carrying was so enormous that it could not be tied even with a rope made of the hide of a hundred cows. However, Garuḍa carried that branch along with the elephant and tortoise in one instant, to a distance of 100,000 *yojanas* and threw it away with a great roar, at the place indicated by his father.

According to *Śrī Rāmāyaṇa*, the 88,000 sages who were born of the semen of Brahmā are the Bālakhilya sages.

Sage Bhṛgu

marīcir atry-aṅgirasau pulastyaḥ pulahaḥ kratuḥ
bhṛgur vasiṣṭho dakṣaś ca daśamas tatra nāradaḥ
(*Śrīmad Bhāgavatam* 3.12.22)

29 Niṣādas are wild and degraded tribes that live by harassing and plundering innocent people.

"Marīci, Atri, Aṅgirā, Pulastya, Pulaha, Kratu, Bhṛgu, Vaśiṣṭha, Dakṣa and Nārada took birth as ten sons of Brahmā."

"Bhṛgu Muni appeared from the touch of Brahmā." (*Śrīmad Bhāgavatam* 3.12.23)

According to the 85th Chapter of the *Anuśāsana-parva* of *Mahābhārata*, it is learned that Bhṛgu, Aṅgirā and Kavi were born from the semen of Brahmā. As he was born from the flames of fire he was therefore known as "Bhṛgu." One of the meanings of *bhṛgu* is "fire."

Aṅgirā was born from the flames (*aṅgare*) with smoke and Kavi was born from the flames without smoke that came from the fire produced by the offering of Brahmā's semen in a fire by the demigod of the sun. Bhṛgu was born from the semen of Brahmā, but a dispute arose when the demigods Mahādeva, Agni and Brahmā each claimed to be the father of Bhṛgu, Aṅgirā and Kavi. The other gods mediated and gave one son to each of them so that the brilliant Bhṛgu became the son of Mahādeva, Aṅgirā Ṛṣi the son of Agnideva, and Kavi the son of Brahmā.

In the 1st Chapter of the 4th Canto of *Śrīmad Bhāgavatam*, a description of the dynasty of Śrī Bhṛgu has been given. From the womb of Bhṛgu's wife, Khyāti, two sons, Dhātā and Vidhātā, as well as a devotee daughter, Śrī, were born. Dhātā and Vidhātā were married to Āyati and Niyati, daughters of Sage Meru respectively. Āyati gave birth to Mṛkaṇḍa and Niyati gave birth to Prāṇa. Sage Mārkaṇḍeya was the son of Mṛkaṇḍa, and Vedaśirā was the son of Prāṇa. Sage Bhṛgu had one more son, Kavi, whose son was the opulent sage Uṣna.

Śrī Mahādeva taught Prācīnabarhi's sons, the Prācetas, a *stotra* (eulogy meant to be sung) glorifying Śrī Hari, and told them that Śrī Brahmā had previously recited the prayer to Bhṛgu and others when desiring to expand the material creation. (*Śrīmad Bhāgavatam* 4.24.72)

In the 11th Canto of *Śrīmad Bhāgavatam* where the discussion between Śrī Kṛṣṇa and Śrī Uddhava is described, Śrī Kṛṣṇa said that among *brahmārṣis* He is Bhṛgu; among *rajarṣis* He is Manu; among *devarṣis* He is Nārada; and among cows, Kāma-dhenu. (*Śrīmad Bhāgavatam* 11.16.14)

In *Śrīmad Bhagavad-gītā*, Śrī Kṛṣṇa says:

maharṣīṇāṁ bhṛgur ahaṁ girām asmy ekam akṣaram
yajñānāṁ japa-yajño 'smi sthāvarāṇāṁ himālayaḥ
(*Bhagavad-gītā* 10.25)

"Of great sages I am Bhṛgu; of utterances I am the single syllabled *oṁ*; of sacrifices I am *japa*; and of that which is immovable I am the Himālayas."

In Verse 38 of the 11th Chapter of the 12th Canto of *Śrīmad Bhāgavatam*, Sage Bhṛgu is mentioned as the guardian of the month of Nābhasya (Bhādra). This means that Sage Bhṛgu associates with Vivasvān, who is the sun-god of the month of Bhādra.

Once a debate arose among the sages about which of the three main gods is superior. At that time, Sage Bhṛgu proved the superiority of Supreme Lord Viṣṇu by means of a test. This incident is recounted in the 89th Chapter of the 10th Canto of *Śrīmad Bhāgavatam* and is summarized as follows:

Long ago, sages were organizing a sacrificial fire on the banks of River Sarasvatī. At that time, a controversy arose among them as to who is supreme among Brahmā, Viṣṇu and Mahādeva. To decide the matter, they sent Sage Bhṛgu, the son of Śrī Brahmā, to Brahmā, Viṣṇu and Mahedeva, for investigation.

Sage Bhṛgu went first to Śrī Brahmā, his father. On arriving there, he neither bowed before Brahmā nor did he glorify him. This angered Śrī Brahmā, but he was able to subdue his anger because Bhṛgu was his son. Just as water is born of fire (in the primeval creation) and fire is pacified with water only, similarly, Śrī Brahmā's anger at his son was pacified by his own expansion, his son.

Sage Bhṛgu then went to Kailāsa-dhāma. Mahādeva, his brother, was pleased to see him and tried to embrace him, but Bhṛgu said with disrespect, "You are a transgressor of the path of religion; hence I cannot embrace you." Śrī Mahādeva became furious and took his trident in his hand ready to kill Bhṛgu. At that time, Pārvatī knelt at his feet and calmed him down with many humble words.

Finally, Sage Bhṛgu went to Śrī Hari in Vaikuṇṭha-dhāma. He approached the Lord, who was lying in the lap of Śrī Lakṣmī-devī, and kicked Him on the chest. Lord Śrī Hari, who is the ultimate shelter of sages and devotees, immediately got up with Lakṣmī-devī, bowed his head to offer obeisances and prayed for forgiveness by saying, "O master! Pardon me by your virtues for the mistake I committed, as I was unaware of your arrival. The water that washes your feet purifies the holy places. Please purify Me, My realm and the realms of the universal rulers devoted to Me, by giving us the water that has washed your feet. This holy water is indeed what makes all places of pilgrimage sacred. Today, my lord, I have become the exclusive shelter of the goddess of fortune, Lakṣmī; she will consent to reside on My chest because your foot has rid it of sins."

Sage Bhṛgu could not offer the Lord any words of praise because his throat was choking with tears of ecstasy. He stood there for some time and then returned to the site of the *yajña*, where he narrated his experiences to the sages.

The sages were amazed and their doubts totally removed after listening to Sage Bhṛgu:

tan niśamyātha munayo vismitā mukta-saṁśayāḥ
bhūyāṁsaṁ śraddadhur viṣṇuṁ
yataḥ śāntir yato 'bhayam
dharmaḥ sākṣād yato jñānaṁ
vairāgyaṁ ca tad-anvitam
aiśvaryaṁ cāṣṭadhā yasmād yaśaś cātma-malāpaham
munīnāṁ nyasta-daṇḍānāṁ śāntānāṁ sama-cetasām
akiñcanānāṁ sādhūnāṁ yam āhuḥ paramāṁ gatim
sattvaṁ yasya priyā mūrtir brāhmaṇās tv iṣṭa-devatāḥ
bhajanty anāśiṣaḥ śāntā yaṁ vā nipuṇa-buddhayaḥ
(*Śrīmad Bhāgavatam* 10.89.14-17)

"Amazed upon hearing Bhṛgu's account, the sages were freed from all doubts and became convinced that Viṣṇu is the greatest Lord. From Him come peace, fearlessness, the essential principles of religion, detachment with knowledge, the eightfold powers of mystic *yoga* and His glorification, which cleanses the mind of all impurities. He is known as the supreme destination for those who are peaceful and equipoised, i.e., the selfless, wise saints who have given up all violence. His most dear form is that of pure goodness, and the *brāhmaṇas* are His worshipable deities. Persons of keen intellect who have attained spiritual peace worship Him without selfish motives."

Lord Paraśurāma appeared in the Bhṛgu Dynasty and is known as Bhṛgupati. Śrī Jayadeva Gosvāmī has glorified Paraśurāma as Bhṛgupati in his *Daśāvatāra-stotra*:

kṣatriya-rudhira-maye jagad-apagata-pāpaṁ
snapayasi payasi śamita-bhava-tāpam

keśava dhṛta-bhṛgupati-rūpa jaya jagadīśa hare
(*Daśāvatāra-stotra*, 6th verse)

"O Keśava! O Lord of the universe! O Lord Hari, who have assumed the form of Bhṛgupati! All glories unto You! At Kurukṣetra You bathe the earth in rivers of blood from the bodies of the demonic *kṣatriyas* that You have slain. The sins of the world are washed away by You and, because of You, people are relieved from the blazing fire of material existence."

In the dynasty of Sage Bhṛgu (the mind-born son of Brahmā), Sage Ṛcīka was born as a son of Urva. Ṛcīka's son was Jamadagni and Paraśurāma appeared as the son of Jamadagni. He is also known as Bhārgava. Bhṛgu's son was Kavi, and Kavi's son was Uśanā, who is also known as Śukrācārya.

It is written in the *Viṣṇu Purāṇa* that Sage Bhṛgu is the founder of the art of archery. In the *Rāmāyaṇa* it is described that when the demons took refuge of Bhṛgu's wife, the *cakra* sent by Lord Viṣṇu to destroy the demons sliced off the head of Bhṛgu's wife. Therefore, Bhṛgu cursed the Lord and that is why Lord Viṣṇu exhibited pastimes of pain of separation from His wife Sītā in His manifestation as Rāma-avatāra. Also, once, he elevated a warrior, Bithavya, to the position of a *brāhmaṇa*.

Sage Bhṛgu is one of the Saptarṣis. An offering is to be made to Bhṛgu as a part of daily oblations. King Sagara became blessed with sons due to the blessings of Sage Bhṛgu. (*Viśvakoṣa*)

In the biography section of the *New Bengali Dictionary* by Āśutoṣa Deva, Bhṛgu is mentioned as follows:

"One day, Sage Bhṛgu went to Śrī Brahmā and Śrī Śiva and intentionally insulted them. When they were annoyed, he calmed them down by glorifying them. When he went to Śrī Viṣṇu, he found Him sleeping; thus he kicked Him on His chest. Viṣṇu began to massage his foot, wondering if the kick on His hard chest might have injured Bhṛgu's soft foot. Lord Viṣṇu always adores the symbol of the kick on His chest, so Bhṛgu declared Viṣṇu to be the Supreme Lord."

According to *Mahābhārata*, Pulomā was the wife of Sage Bhṛgu and his son was Sage Cyavana. One day, when Sage Bhṛgu was absent, a demon kidnapped Pulomā. Observing the miserable situation of his mother, the newborn child Cyavana immolated the demon by his transcendental powers.

According to the 2nd Chapter of the 4th Canto of *Śrīmad Bhāgavatam*, Bhṛgu Ṛṣi was among the sages who were present along with Brahmā, Śiva and other demigods on the occasion of a *yajña* performed by the Prajāpatis (universal progenitors). Dakṣa Prajāpati gave his younger daughter Satī to Śrī Mahādeva in marriage as instructed by his father, Śrī Brahmā. All those present in the assembly stood up and welcomed Dakṣa Prajāpati upon his arrival. Only Śrī Brahmā and Śrī Śiva did not get up. Dakṣa Prajāpati criticized Śrī Śiva because despite being his son-in-law, he did not offer respect. Nandi, one of Lord Śiva's principal associates, became greatly angry. He could not tolerate the criticism and cursed Dakṣa and his *brāhmaṇa* supporters that the critics of Śiva would become attached to the superficial, worldly meanings of the *Vedas*, would become attached to the material body and would wander on earth as beggars. He further cursed that, since Dakṣa had accepted knowledge of *karma* as supreme, he would soon become passionate like the animals and would have a head like a goat. Hearing such a harsh curse aimed at the hereditary *brāhmaṇas*, Sage Bhṛgu, as a reaction, condemned the followers of Lord Śiva with this curse laden with the power of a *brāhmaṇa*:

"One who observes a fast to please Śiva, or follows a follower of Śiva, will certainly become an atheist and be diverted from transcendental scriptural injunctions. Those who vow to worship Lord Śiva will be so foolish that they will imitate him by keeping unclean, not bathing daily, adopting an ignorant mentality and keeping long hair on their heads. When initiated into worship of Lord Śiva, they will prefer to use wine made from *gaudi*, *paiṣṭhi* and *mādhavi*, and alcohol made from a palm tree, as the worshipable items."

It is written in the 4th Canto of *Śrīmad Bhāgavatam* that Satī left her body because she could not tolerate the criticism of Śiva. When Śiva learned of this, he became greatly angry and took a hair from his head and threw it to the ground, from which Vīrabhadra, a fearful demon garlanded with men's heads, was born. He ruined Dakṣa's *yajña* and then killed Dakṣa by the *paśūmaraṇa-yantra*[30], and put out the eyes of Bhaga. He broke the teeth of Puśadeva, and plucked and threw away the beard and moustache of Sage Bhṛgu. Later, by the grace of Lord Śiva, a goat's head was fixed on Dakṣa's body and a goat's beard and moustache were attached to the face of Sage Bhṛgu.

Once, King Aṅga left his kingdom after being troubled by the atrocities of his son Veṇa. Bhṛgu Ṛṣi was among the sages who successfully corrected the conduct of Veṇa by preaching. He then enthroned him in the kingdom to protect the succession of rulers.

The 8th Canto of *Śrīmad Bhāgavatam* reveals the power of the *brāhmaṇas* belonging to the Bhṛgu Dynasty. The king of the demons, Bali, who was killed by Indra in a war, was brought back to life by Śukrācārya, Bhṛgu's descendant. Due to this, Bali Mahārāja accepted Śukrācārya as his spiritual master and began to serve him with great faith. Pleased by the service of Bali Mahārāja, the *brāhmaṇa* descendants of Bhṛgu performed a *viśvajita-yajña* for him. A chariot, horse, flag, bow, quiver with unlimited arrows and a shield appeared from the *yajña*.

Bali's grandfather, Prahlāda, gave him an ever-fresh garland, and his guru Śukrācārya gave him a conch. Bali Mahārāja offered obeisances to his grandfather, guru and the *brāhmaṇas*. He then boarded the divine chariot given by Śukrācārya and reached Indra's residence. After blocking passage with the help of his army, he blew the conch. The king of the demigods was afraid of Bali's power and went to his *guru* Bṛhaspati to ask him the reason for Bali's renewed strength. Bṛhaspati told him that Bali had become powerful due to the grace of the *brāhmaṇas* of the Bhṛgu Dynasty. He told Indra that neither he nor his men would be able to conquer Bali, and that no one but Śrī Hari could defeat Bali. Thus, Bṛhaspati advised the demigods to abandon heaven and live in space.

After His sacred thread ceremony (*upanayana-saṁskāra*), Lord Vāmanadeva came to the Bhṛgukaccha region, on the banks of the Narmada, to beg for alms. The *brāhmaṇas* of the Bhṛgu Dynasty had been performing *yajñas* at that place, but were pleased by an audience with Lord Vāmana and offered prayers to Him. Lord Vāmanadeva accepted the three worlds from Bali and returned the land taken from Devarāja Indra. After this, Dakṣa, Brahmā, all the demigods, sages, forefathers, Manu-gaṇa, Bhṛgu, Aṅgirā and others, along with Kārtikeya and Mahādeva, accepted Vāmanadeva as guardian of all the *lokas* (planets). They did this for the welfare of all living beings and for the satisfaction of Sage Kaśyapa and Mother Aditi.

It is learned from the 11th Canto of *Śrīmad Bhāgavatam* that the Yādavas were destroyed due to a curse from an assembly of *brāhmaṇas*

30 A wooden device in a sacrificial arena by which animals are to be sacrificed.

when the young boys of the Yadu Dynasty made fun of them. The assembly included sages like Bhṛgu who had gathered at the holy Piṇḍāraka region near Dvārakā.

Sage Astika

The details of the birth of Sage Astika are described in the 13th through 15th Chapters of the *Ādi-parva* of *Mahābhārata*. A summary is as follows:

Jaratkaru was the father of Astika. Jaratkaru was equal in splendor to Brahmā. He was celibate, strictly controlled his senses, performed severe penance, was a composer of Vedic hymns, an eminent religious scholar, unflinching in his vows and was an honorable descendant of the community of Yāyāvaras.[31] He would continually wander around the earth on pilgrimage, resting at the place where the setting of the sun occurred and bathing at pilgrimage sites. He was very powerful due to the power of his penance. He would eat decayed leaves, sometimes survive on air, sometimes not eat anything and would roam while taking very little rest, thereby straining his body. One day, Jaratkaru came to a place where his forefathers were hanging upside down in a large pit, holding the end of a tuft of grass. He inquired the reason from them and his forefathers replied, "We are the Yāyāvaras, sages strict in our vows. Due to possibly having reached the end of our family line, we are on the verge of destruction. We are most unfortunate. Our last living descendant is known as Jaratkaru, but we are so unlucky that our foolish descendant cares only for the ascetic life. Therefore, we are hanging upside down due to the possibility of losing our family line. However, who are you and why do you worry about us as if you were our own kin?"

Jaratkaru replied, "My name happens to be Jaratkaru, so please tell me what I should do for you." His forefathers were pleased and said, "For the sake of your own duty and for ours as well, strive with great effort, dear boy, to preserve our family line. In this world, O son, neither by the fruits of virtue nor by heaps of austerities can one attain the high place earned by the parents of good children. Dear child, by our order, put all your effort into finding a wife and make up your mind to continue our family. That for us is the highest benefit." Then Sage Jaratkaru said, "I will not marry with the intention of enjoying sense pleasures. I will not earn money. I will marry only for your welfare. However, I shall only marry a girl having the same name as my own. The parents of the girl should give her to me in charity because it is their own desire. Then I shall accept that girl as charity and marry her with proper rites. I am poor, so who will give me a girl? Yet, if somebody bestows upon me a girl, then I will be able to liberate you by producing a son."

The celibate sage Jaratkaru began to wander across the earth, but could not find a suitable wife for himself anywhere. One day, he went to a forest and prayed thrice very slowly while remembering the words of his forefathers. Immediately, the king of snakes, Vāsuki, came and offered his sister to him. However, Sage Jaratkaru thought that if the name of the girl was not the same as his, and if her brothers would not offer her willingly, then he would not be able to accept her. He asked Vāsuki the name of the girl, to which Vāsuki replied, "The name of my younger sister is Jaratkaru; I am offering her to you in charity. Please accept her as your

31 Yāyāvara: A particular section of *brāhmaṇas*. Their special feature is that they wander about here and there, following the way of life of sages.

wife. I have been keeping her for you only." So Sage Jaratkaru married the girl according to the appropriate Vedic rites. Their mother had cursed the snakes earlier by saying, "The sacred fire at Janamejaya's sacrifice will burn you all." To appease that curse, the greatest of serpents, Vāsuki, presented his sister to the ascetic sage, who faithfully kept his vows. A son named Astika was henceforth born. That child, a great soul, was to become both an ascetic and a great master of the Vedic scriptures. Fair-minded and equal to all, he drove away his parents' fear.

Long after that, Sage Astika relieved his maternal uncles and many other related snakes from the curse of their mother when Janamejaya, the son of Parīkṣit (grandson of Pāṇḍu's son Arjuna) performed a great offering known as the Sacrifice of Snakes (*sarpa-satra-yajña*).

jareti kṣayamāhurvai dāruṇaṁ kārusañjitam,
śarīraṁ kāru tasyāsīt tat sa dhīmācchanaiḥ śanaiḥ
kṣapayāṁas tīvreṇa tapasetyata ucyate
jaratkāruriti brahman vāsukerbhaginī tathā
(*Mahābhārata*, 1.40.3-4)

"The word *jara* means decay, and the word *karu* means strong. This means that originally the physique of the sage was very strong. Later on he ruined or decayed it by his austerities. He was therefore named Jaratkaru." (*Viśvakoṣa*)

Astika was born from the union of Vāsuki's sister and Jaratkaru Muni. Mother Kadru had cursed the kinfolk of Vāsuki, so Vāsuki donated his sister to the sage Jaratkaru in the hope that they would produce a child that would give relief from the curse. However, before accepting her, Jaratkaru said, "You may give her to me, but I shall not carry the responsibility of maintaining her, and if ever your sister displeases me or does not follow my instructions, I shall abandon her." Vāsuki accepted these conditions and his sister was duly married. After that, she became pregnant by union with the sage. One day, Jaratkaru was sleeping. At that time, his wife, the sister of the snakes, observed that the sun was about to set. She realized that the time of the sage's evening worship was going to pass, and thought: "*What shall I do? The sage has a furious nature and if I awaken him now, he will leave me and go away.*" At last she decided that, no matter what would happen, she should wake him up, as this would be a lesser offense compared to his not performing evening prayers. So, she woke him up.

The sage arose and said, "O lady! You have acted against my wishes; therefore I shall not stay with you any longer at any cost. Please do not grieve, and ask your brother not to grieve either." Then the sister of the snakes enquired, "O sage! You are leaving, but what will become of the purpose for which my brother donated me to you?" The sage replied, "*Asti*," and left. By this he meant that his semen had impregnated her. After some time, the sister of the snakes, also named Jaratkaru, delivered a son. He was brought up in a house of snakes,

by snakes. By virtue of his wisdom, he learned all the scriptures from Bhṛgu's son, Cyavana. When he was in the womb, his father had said "Asti," and therefore he became known as Astika. He saved the snakes at the time of the great offering known as the Sacrifice of Snakes performed by Janamejaya. (*Viśvakoṣa*)

"King Janamejaya performed a *sarpa-yajña* as a reprisal for his father's death, which was due to a bite from the serpent Takṣaka. Astika went to the site of the *yajña* and prayed for the final offering of the *yajña*, thereby saving the dynasty of snakes. Because of this, the fear of snakes vanishes as soon as his name is pronounced." (*Brahmāvaivarta Purāṇa*, *Mahābhārata*, Āśutoṣa Deva's *New Bengali Dictionary*)

Sage Kardama

chāyāyāḥ kardamo jajñe devahūtyāḥ patiḥ prabhuḥ
manaso dehataś cedaṁ jajñe viśva-kṛto jagat
(*Śrīmad Bhāgavatam* 3.12.27)

"Sage Kardama, husband of the great Devahūti, was manifested from the shadow of Brahmā's body. Thus, all became manifested from either the body or mind of Brahmā, the creator of the world."

Śrīla Bhakti Siddhānta Sarasvatī Gosvāmī Ṭhākura, in his *Gaudiya-bhāṣya* of verse 42 of the 14th Chapter of the *Madhya-khaṇḍa* of *Śrī Caitanya-bhāgavata*, writes that Sage Kardama is a *prajāpati* (progenitor) of the Svāyambhuva *manvantara* and is the son of Śrī Brahmā. He performed penance for 10,000 years at Bindusara-tīrtha, on the banks of River Sarasvatī, for the purpose of creation, as instructed by Śrī Brahmā. Afterward, he married the daughter of Svāyambhuvā Manu and had nine daughters, including Kāla. Later, Lord Kapiladeva appeared as the son of Sage Kardama. It is mentioned in Āśutoṣa Deva's Bengali Dictionary that Sage Kardama is one of the *prajāpatis*.

His father's name is Kīrtimān and his son's name is Anaṅgasādhu. Śrī Brahmā created man and woman from his own body for the creation of the world as instructed by Śrī Garbhodakśayi Viṣṇu. That man is known as Svāyambhuva Manu and the woman as Śatarūpā. Svāyambhuva Manu and Śatarūpā married as instructed by Śrī Brahmā. They had two sons, named Priyavrata and Uttānapāda, and three daughters, named Ākūti, Devahūti and Prasūti. Svāyambhuva Manu gave his middle daughter, Devahūti to Sage Kardama.

The details about Sage Kardama are given in Chapters 21 through 24 of the 3rd Canto of *Śrīmad Bhāgavatam*. During Satya-yuga Sage Kardama performed severe penance for ten thousand years on the banks of River Sarasvatī after he was instructed by Śrī Brahmā to expand the creation. Pleased by Kardama's intense penance, Lord Śrī Hari appeared before him. While he was sitting in penance, Sage Kardama looked up and saw that Lord Viṣṇu was shining like a sun in the sky. He was wearing a garland of white lotuses around His neck, and His face was most attractive due to His blackish-blue locks of hair. He was wearing clean bright yellow clothes. He had a crown on His head, earrings on His ears and was holding a conch, disc, mace and white lotus in His four hands. He had a faint sweet smile and pleasing look, beautiful feet, the Kaustubha-maṇi (famous gem) on His neck, and the beautiful symbol of Śrīvatsa (mark of Śrī, or Lakṣmī) on his chest. At that time, He was riding His carrier Garuḍa. Sage Kardama was overjoyed to have an audience with the Lord, so, having fulfilled his desire, he paid his obeisances unto the Lord and glorified Him. In his glorification, he said, "O Lord! Though asking You for the fulfilment of desires deserves condemnation, nonetheless you are the root of all endeavours (*dharma*, *artha*, *kāma* and *mokṣa*). Your desireless devotees do not fear anything. They surrender unto You and disregard people embroiled in behavior caused by passion. They continuously glorify You, Lord Hari. Even the wheel of time cannot cut down their life-span." The Lord was pleased with the prayers sung by Sage Kardama, and told him that He had already understood his purpose. The Lord said, "You will get married to Devahūti, the daughter of Svāyambhuva Manu. You will have nine daughters and after that you will have Lord Kapiladeva as your son. By simply following My instructions, and offering all the fruits of your actions to Me, you will become further purīfied and will ultimately attain Me. I will appear as Kapila and expound the Sāṅkhya philosophy." After this, the Lord disappeared and Sage Kardama began residing at Bindusara-tīrtha on the banks of River Sarasvatī, waiting for Svāyambhuva Manu as instructed by the Lord. When Svāyambhuva Manu arrived on his golden airplane accompanied by his wife Śatarūpā and daughter Devahūti, Sage

Kardama offered respects and praised his actions and qualities. Mahārāja Manu was embarrassed by his praise and humbly said, "The Lord has created from His mouth pure-hearted *brāhmaṇas* like you, who are engaged in penance to preach the *Vedas*, while to protect the *brāhmaṇas* in the observance of their duties, the Lord has created us, the warriors, by His own arm. Therefore, *brāhmaṇas* are the heart of the Lord and the warriors are His hands."

Svāyambhuva Manu continued, "*Brāhmaṇas* take care of the warriors by the strength of their penance and the warriors protect the *brāhmaṇas* by means of their physical strength, though the actual guardian is the Lord. My attachment to the world has vanished by a mere glimpse of you. I am fortunate that I am able to have your audience and that you have bestowed your mercy upon me. A sinful person is unable to have your audience. Please listen to my humble prayer, for I am worried about my daughter, the sister of Priyavrata and Uttānapāda. O superior among *brāhmaṇas*! Please accept her as your wife as a gift from me. This girl is worthy of you. She is expert in all household duties. It is improper even for a person fully detached from the objects of desire to refuse a naturally bestowed self-desired object. Anyone who does so is ruined. I have heard that you wish to get married. Therefore, I request you to marry this girl. Since you wish to begin household life after having lead a life of celibacy, please accept from me this girl as your wife."

Sage Kardama replied, "I accept your good proposal. Her marriage ceremony may be performed according to the marriage rituals delineated in the *Vedas*. The radiance of your daughter outshines the brilliance of her own ornaments. When the Gandharva Viśvāvasu saw your daughter, her beauty captivated him. Your daughter is the very ornament of womanhood. However, I shall live as a householder only until she becomes pregnant, after which I shall accept a life of devotional service. Lord Anantadeva, from whom this world is born, in whom this world is situated, and in whom this world is dissolved, is my ultimate shelter."

Sage Kardama thus married Devahūti. Svāyambhuva Manu felt satisfied by having offered his daughter to an eligible candidate, and he boarded his plane with his wife and returned to his own city, Barhiṣmati, in the Brahmāvarta area.

Devahūti began to serve Sage Kardama with full devotion with the desire to obtain a son. Satisfied by his wife's service, and seeing that her body had become weak due to penance, Sage Kardama bestowed upon her divine sight and exhibited to her his opulence. He sent her to bathe in Lake Bindu-sarovara so as to revive her former beauty. According to the wish of his wife, Sage Kardama created an airplane capable of going to all places as desired, and then expanded himself into nine forms and engaged himself in satisfying his wife and her desires for many years. Devahūti gave birth to nine extremely beautiful girls. Then Sage Kardama considered renouncing the world. Devahūti became anxious as she wondered about the future of her daughters, so she sorrowfully requested her husband, "O lord! So far, I have wasted my time in sense enjoyment only. I did not perform devotion to the Lord. I could not recognise that you understand the Lord and are not attached to anything. Please liberate me from the world. Please arrange for my audience with the Lord.

saṅgo yaḥ saṁsṛter hetur asatsu vihito 'dhiyā
sa eva sādhuṣu kṛto niḥsaṅgatvāya kalpate
neha yat karma dharmāya na virāgāya kalpate
na tīrtha-pada-sevāyai jīvann api mṛto hi saḥ
(*Śrīmad Bhāgavatam* 3.23.55-56)

"Association for sense gratification is certainly the path of bondage. But the same type of association, performed with a saintly person, leads to the path of liberation, even if performed without knowledge. Anyone whose work is not meant to elevate him to religious life, anyone whose religious ritualistic performances do not raise him to renunciation, and anyone situated in renunciation that does not lead to devotional service to the Supreme Personality of Godhead, must be considered dead, although he is breathing."

Sage Kardama felt compassion for his wife after listening to her words, which were full of worldly detachment; thus he said, "O princess! Why are you referring to yourself as unfortunate and why are feeling sorry for yourself? There is no reason for you to worry. The Lord will shortly enter into your womb. You must worship the Lord faithfully by controlling your senses, abiding by your duty, performing penance and giving in charity. Satisfied by your devotion, Lord Śrī Hari will appear as your son, thereby spreading my glory. He will preach to you the supreme knowledge and will demolish your false ego." With full faith, Devahūti did as requested by Sage Kardama. After a long time, the Supreme Personality of Godhead, Madhusūdana, the killer of the demon Madhu, having entered the semen of Kardama, appeared as the son of Devahūti. Happiness and goodness manifested everywhere due to the advent of the Lord. Śrī Brahmā, accompanied by Marīci and others, arrived at the *āśrama* of Kardama Ṛṣi on the banks of River Sarasvatī. The Lord appeared to preach knowledge of Sāṅkhya. Śrī Brahmā pleasantly glorified the Lord and told Sage Kardama, "You have followed my instructions without duplicity. I am pleased. All your daughters will increase this creation by their own descendants in various ways. Marīci and other sages have also come with me. You may please hand over your daughters to them according to their nature and interest. I know that the original Supreme Personality of Godhead has now appeared as an *avatāra* by His internal energy. He is the bestower of everything desired by the living entities, and He has now assumed the body of Kapila Muni." Having glorified Lord Kapila, Śrī Brahmā along with the Four Kumāras and Nārada boarded his swan carrier and departed to Satyaloka. Kardama Muni, having been ordered by Brahmā, handed over his nine daughters, as instructed, to the nine great sages who created the population of the world. Kardama Muni handed over his nine daughters as follows: Kalā to Marīci, Anasūyā to Atri, Śraddhā to Aṅgirā and Havirbhū to Pulastya. He delivered Gati to Pulaha, the chaste Kriyā to Kratu, Khyāti to Bhṛgu and Arundhatī to Vaśiṣṭha. He gave Śānti to Atharvā. Due to Śānti, sacrificial ceremonies are well performed.

The girls happily went to their respective *āśramas* as instructed by their father. After that, Sage Kardama stood before Lord Kapila in solitude, offered Him respects and said, "The renounced reside in secluded places and follow devotional processes to see the lotus feet of the Supreme Personality of Godhead. Today that very same Lord has appeared in my house though I am negligible and unimportant. O Lord! You are very loving to Your devotees and will do anything to fulfill their wishes. You have appeared in my house to preach Sāṅkhya-yoga. You do not have a material body and yet You appear in Your transcendental form, sometimes four-armed, for the pleasure of Your devotees. You are complete in opulence, renunciation, transcendental fame, knowledge, strength and beauty, and therefore, O Lord Kapila, I surrender myself unto Your lotus feet."

Satisfied with the praises of Sage Kardama, the Lord said:

mayā proktaṁ hi lokasya pramāṇaṁ satya-laukike
athājani mayā tubhyaṁ yad avocam ṛtaṁ mune
(*Śrīmad Bhāgavatam* 3.24.35)

"Whatever I speak, whether directly or in the scriptures, is authoritative in all respects for the people of the world. O *muni*, because I told you before that I would become your son, I have descended to fulfill this promise."

Lord Kapila continued, "Now you are asking permission to take *sannyāsa*. I therefore permit this; go as you desire. If you have the desire to conquer insurmountable death, surrender all your activities to Me; worship Me for eternal life. I shall also describe to My mother this sublime knowledge that is the door to spiritual life so that she can also attain perfection and self-realization, ending all reactions to fruitive activities. Thus, she will also be freed from all material fear."

Then, Sage Kardama circumambulated Lord Kapila and went joyfully to the forest, where he achieved the desired objective by following the devotional processes properly and surrendering unto the Lord.

Sage Ṛṣyaśṛṅga

The details about Śrī Ṛṣyaśṛṅga are briefly described in the following four verses of *Śrīmad Bhāgavatam*:

suto dharmaratho yasya jajñe citraratho 'prajāḥ
romapāda iti khyātas tasmai daśarathaḥ sakhā
śāntāṁ sva-kanyāṁ prāyacchad ṛṣyaśṛṅga uvāha yām
deve 'varṣati yaṁ rāmā āninyur hariṇī-sūtam
nāṭya-saṅgīta-vāditrair vibhramāliṅganārhaṇaiḥ
sa tu rājño 'napatyasya nirūpyeṣṭiṁ marutvate
prajām adād daśaratho yena lebhe 'prajāḥ prajāḥ
caturaṅgo romapādāt pṛthulākṣas tu tat-sūtaḥ

(*Śrīmad Bhāgavatam* 9.23.7-10)

"From Diviratha came a son named Dharmaratha, and his son was Citraratha, who was celebrated as Romapāda. Romapāda, however, had no son, and therefore his friend Mahārāja Daśaratha gave him his own daughter named Śāntā. Romapāda accepted her as his daughter, and thereafter she married Ṛṣyaśṛṅga. When the demigods from the heavenly planets failed to shower rain, the *brāhmaṇas* discussed the matter and told King Romapāda, also known as Lomapāda, that if he could somehow manage to bring Ṛṣyaśṛṅga to his kingdom, it would start raining again. After many deliberations it was decided that the prostitutes of the kingdom would go to Sage Ṛṣyaśṛṅga and fetch the sage by virtue of their skills. And so it happened that the prostitutes set out on their mission according to the king's orders, and lured the sage by their acting, music, musical instruments and gifts, thereby bringing him to the kingdom. After Ṛṣyaśṛṅga arrived there, the rain started falling again. Thereafter, Ṛṣyaśṛṅga performed a sacrifice to beget a son on behalf of Mahārāja Daśaratha, who had no son, and then Mahārāja Daśaratha was blessed with four sons.

Later from Romapāda, Caturaṅga was also born, and from Caturaṅga came Pṛthulākṣa."

ṛṣyasya mṛgasya śṛṅgamiva śṛṅgamasya
(*Bahu*)

The details of Sage Ṛṣyaśṛṅga are given in the *Rāmāyaṇa* and *Mahābhārata*, which are also narrated in brief in *Viśvakoṣa*. The following is a summary of those narrations:

Once, there was an extremely brilliant sage named Vibhaṇḍaka of the Kaśyapa Dynasty. One day when Sage Vibhaṇḍaka was taking a dip in the river, he discharged semen in the water upon seeing the celestial dancer Urvaśī. A thirsty doe then drank that semen and became pregnant. That doe was a demigoddess in her previous life. However, Śrī Brahmā had cursed her to become a doe and told her that when she would give birth to the son of a sage, she would be liberated from the curse. This was destined to occur, and thus Ṛṣyaśṛṅga, the son of Sage Vibhaṇḍaka, was born from a doe. Śrīnga had a pair of horns on his head due to being born from that doe. That is why he became known as Ṛṣyaśṛṅga.

Since birth he had never seen or met anyone other than his father, and therefore he was a natural celibate who knew nothing about lust for any object. However, at this time, King Lomapāda of Aṅga, a friend of Daśaratha, was deserted by the *brāhmaṇas* because of an offense. The ongoing process of *yajña* was therefore disrupted, which dissatisfied Indra, who stopped the rain from falling on Lomapāda's kingdom. King Lomapāda was very worried about this turn of events, but he somehow managed to please the *brāhmaṇas* enough to ask them for a way to rescue his kingdom from the drought. The *brāhmaṇas* told him that if he managed to bring Sage Ṛṣyaśṛṅga to the kingdom, it would certainly start raining again.

Thus instructed, King Lomapāda arranged for some prostitutes to accomplish this difficult task. With the intention of bringing Ṛṣyaśṛṅga Muni via water, the prostitutes stopped their boat at some distance from the *āśrama* of Vibhaṇḍaka Muni, and then went to meet Sage Ṛṣyaśṛṅga. Upon reaching there, they gave him a variety of palatable things to eat and tried to lure him by dint of their feminine skills. They charmed him with offerings and seductive wiles. The prostitutes then returned to their boat. When Vibhaṇḍaka Muni returned, he was surprised by a sudden change in his son. He thus counseled his son, preached to him and pacified him in many ways and then went to the forest to perform penance.

After the departure of Vibhaṇḍaka Muni, the prostitutes returned and managed to lure Sage Ṛṣyaśṛṅga into their boat, which they quickly started rowing to bring him to the country of Aṅga, the realm of King Lomapāda. King Lomapāda was pleased to see Ṛṣyaśṛṅga in his kingdom; therefore, with much satisfaction, he arranged for him to stay in his palace. When the sage arrived, it began to rain all over the kingdom as foretold by the *brāhmaṇas*. Everyone in Lomapāda's kingdom became much obliged. To save themselves from the curse of Vibhaṇḍaka Muni, they offered Śāntā (the girl given by King Daśaratha) to Ṛṣyaśṛṅga Muni.

In the meantime, Vibhaṇḍaka Muni was anxious when he did not see his son anywhere upon his return to his *āśrama*, so he started meditating in order to locate his son. He found out that his son had been seduced and lured to the kingdom of Lomapāda. When he learned that his son had been lured away by dubious means, Vibhaṇḍaka Muni became angry and stormed into the kingdom of Lomapāda. The people of the kingdom were frightened by Vibhaṇḍaka Muni's arrival, so King Lomapāda advised them that, in order to calm the sage, they should tell him that the kingdom now belonged to Ṛṣyaśṛṅga Muni. Thus, they told him that Ṛṣyaśṛṅga was the ruler of the kingdom and that Śāntā was his queen.

When Vibhaṇḍaka Muni saw his sinless and simple-hearted son sitting on the throne, he calmed down and showered love on his son and daughter-in-law. He then returned to his *āśrama*. After these events, Ṛṣyaśṛṅga lived in that kingdom together with his wife. This Ṛṣyaśṛṅga performed the *putreṣṭī-yajña* for King Daśaratha. As a consequence of this *yajña*, King Daśaratha was blessed by getting the Supreme Lord in the form of His expansions Rāma, Lakṣmaṇa, Bharata and Śatrughna as his sons, as mentioned in *Śrīmad Bhāgavatam*:

tasyāpi bhagavān eṣa
sākṣād brahmāmayo hariḥ
aṁśāṁśena caturdhāgāt
putratvaṁ prārthitaḥ suraiḥ
rāma-lakṣmaṇa-bharata-
śatrughnā iti saṁjñayā
(*Śrīmad Bhāgavatam* 9.10.2)

"Being prayed for by the demigods, the Supreme Personality of Godhead, the Absolute Truth Himself, directly appeared with His expansion and expansions of His expansion. Their holy names were Rāma, Lakṣmaṇa, Bharata and Śatrughna, who appeared in these four forms as the sons of Mahārāja Daśaratha."

Ṛṣyaśṛṅga was famous for being powerful and a performer of righteous *yajña*. This incident about Ṛṣyaśṛṅga Muni has also been mentioned in the *Vana-parva* of *Mahābhārata*, which has not been described in the above narration. Therefore, for the convenience of readers, this incident of *Mahābhārata* is described now:

Ṛṣyaśṛṅga Muni was born from the daughter of a demigod who, because of a curse, had taken the body of a doe. The creator of the material cosmos, Śrī Brahmā, told her that she would be freed of the curse when she would give birth to a sage.

Ṛṣyaśṛṅga Muni was simple by heart, was born in the forest and lived there. He was completely oblivious to the existence of women. Acting upon the advice of his ministers and *brāhmaṇa* advisors, Lomapāda, the king of Aṅga, decided to bring Ṛṣyaśṛṅga Muni to his kingdom. He deputed prostitutes to carry out the task.

The prostitutes were worried that if they did not obey the king, he would certainly punish them, whereas on the other hand if they did obey the king, then Vibhaṇḍaka Muni would certainly curse them. By thus contemplating the inevitable fearful consequences of either choice, their faces turned pale. Somehow they expressed the difficulty of their situation to the king. However, at that time, an old prostitute told the king that she could do the job if the king would fulfill her desire. Upon further enquiry, the prostitute demanded enormous wealth, and the king immediately fulfilled her demand. So, putting her plan into motion, she took some beautiful young girls as well as some men with her and started for the forest where Vibhaṇḍaka Muni lived with his son.

They reached the vicinity of Vibhaṇḍaka Muni's *āśrama* by boat. The prostitute first started gathering information about Vibhaṇḍaka Muni's daily activities by sending out her male spies. After determining a time when he would be away from his *aśrama*, that intelligent woman sent one of her wise girls to Ṛṣyaśṛṅga Muni in the *aśrama*. The girl praised him, his father and their *aśrama*. Ṛṣyaśṛṅga Muni was pleased to hear himself, his father and his *aśrama* being praised, so he gave her fruits to eat and a seat to sit down on. Ṛṣyaśṛṅga did not see her as a woman as he was unaware of the difference between men and women, so he addressed her as he would a male, and asked her about the location of her *aśrama* and what devotional processes she followed. The prostitute replied that her beautiful *aśrama* was behind a 24-mile-long mountain range that she pointed out to him, and that she would not accept anything given to her as a token of respect, nor would she touch *aghrya* (scented water and foodstuff) or *pādya* (foot-washing water) given by anyone. So, she told the sage, "Please do not greet me, but let me greet you and embrace you instead."

Therefore, the prostitute did not eat the fruits given by Ṛṣyaśṛṅga Muni, but instead she began to feed him the delicious food items that she had brought with her as well as passing flattering remarks about him. She also embraced him firmly a few times while joking with him. When they parted company after some time, the sage began to feel lonely and gloomy in her absence. He was unable to comprehend what had happened to him.

When Vibhaṇḍaka Muni returned to the *āśrama*, he found his son sitting alone and feeling sad, taking long, heavy breaths. Observing the state of his son, he asked him lovingly, "My dear son, why haven't you collected the requested items for the *yajña* yet, and why haven't you performed the fire sacrifice? Why haven't you milked the cow for the *yajña*?"

Ṛṣyaśṛṅga Muni replied, "O father! An intelligent celibate with long hair similar to a demigod came here. He was neither tall nor short. His color was like gold. His eyes were like lotuses. His waist was lean and he had some strange sound-producing objects on his ankles. His clothes were both beautiful and strange. My clothes are not that beautiful. I have developed love for that apparent demigod. He embraced me, held my locks of hair and made some peculiar sound by touching mouth to mouth. I felt delighted by this. O father! I wish to go to him quickly and I feel that he should always live with me. Father, what kind of fast is he observing? I wish to observe the same fast."

After listening to his innocent words, Sage Vibhaṇḍaka understood that somebody had cheated his son. He said to his son, "Dear son! Strange demons take on various forms to disrupt our penance. They disgrace the sages with various allurements and cause them to fall from their righteous path. Sages never accept anything from them."

Thus reassuring his son, Vibhaṇḍaka Muni began looking for that wicked person, but he could not find him even though he searched for three days, and so he came back to the *āśrama*. Then Vibhaṇḍaka Muni left to collect fruits according to the Vedic method. At that time, the prostitute came back to Ṛṣyaśṛṅga Muni, who was overjoyed to see her again. The excited Ṛṣyaśṛṅga Muni approached her and said, "Until my father returns I shall go and see your *āśrama*." Thus, Ṛṣyaśṛṅga Muni and the prostitute boarded the boat and, by rowing it very fast, they soon reached the kingdom of King Lomapāda. Immediately upon Ṛṣyaśṛṅga Muni's arrival in the kingdom, it started raining. King Lomapāda was very pleased and offered his daughter Śāntā to Ṛṣyaśṛṅga. They were then married in an excellent manner.

The following incident is described in the *Rāmāyaṇa*:

King Daśaratha could not get a son despite doing severe penance. Later, he resolved to perform an *aśvamedha-yajña*, with the desire to get a son. As instructed by Daśaratha Mahārāja, his chief minister, Sumanta, gathered together Vaśiṣṭha, Jabali, Vāmdeva and other *brāhmaṇas*, who vouched their support for the performance of the *yajña* when they learned of the king's desire. The *brāhmaṇas* directed the king to collect all the necessary materials for the *yajña*, to make a *yajña* site on the banks of River Śarayu and to dispatch the horse intended for the *yajña*.

In a hushed voice Sumanta secretly told the king, "The son of Vibhaṇḍaka Muni is famous as Ṛṣyaśṛṅga. Once, the kingdom of Aṅga suffered from a terrible drought, so with the help of his ministers, King Lomapāda tricked Ṛṣyaśṛṅga, brought him to his kingdom and married his daughter Śāntā to him. Heavy rains began to fall upon the arrival of Ṛṣyaśṛṅga. This very same Ṛṣyaśṛṅga will fulfill your desire."

King Daśaratha was a friend of King Lomapāda of Aṅga. He narrated the incident with Ṛṣyaśṛṅga as told by Sumanta to Sage Vaśiṣṭha. When Vaśiṣṭha gave his consent, King Daśaratha, accompanied by his minister, traveled to Aṅga. After staying there for a week Daśaratha told Lomapāda, "Dear King, I have decided to perform a *yajña* with the desire to obtain a son. To make this *yajña* successful, your son-in-law Ṛṣyaśṛṅga and daughter Śāntā will have to come to Ayodhyā." As instructed by King Lomapāda, Ṛṣyaśṛṅga and his wife prepared to go to Ayodhyā.

King Daśaratha dispatched messengers with the instruction to properly decorate Ayodhyā-purī for the welcoming of Ṛṣyaśṛṅga. At an appropriate time, Daśaratha Mahārāja entered Ayodhyā-purī, keeping Ṛṣyaśṛṅga ahead of him. The people of Ayodhyā were overjoyed by the arrival of Ṛṣyaśṛṅga Muni. When the spring season came, Daśaratha Mahārāja adopted Ṛṣyaśṛṅga Muni as his chief priest and told him about the purpose of this *yajña* through the performing *brāhmaṇas* such as Vaśiṣṭha, Vāmdeva and others.

Then the *yajña* horse, which was released a year earlier, returned. Vaśiṣṭha and other *brāhmaṇas* began the rituals of *yajña* according to the appropriate scriptural injunctions, with Ṛṣyaśṛṅga in charge. After that, Ṛṣyaśṛṅga Muni performed the *putreṣṭī-yajña* (fire sacrifice for obtaining a son) by reciting the hymns of the *Atharva Veda*. By dint of the *yajña* performed by Ṛṣyaśṛṅga Muni, after twelve months and at the auspicious time of Punarvasu-nakṣatra in the 4th zodiacal sign of Cancer, in the month of Caitra on the 9th day of the waxing moon, Lord Śrī Rāmacandra appeared with the support of Mother Kauśalyā. Bharata appeared from the womb of Kaikeyī during the Puṣyā-nakṣatra-Mīna-lagna and Lakṣmaṇa and Śatrughna appeared from the womb of Sumitrā during the Aśleṣa-nakṣatra-Karkaṭa-lagna, as the sons of King Daśaratha.

Śrī Kṛṣṇa-dvaipāyana Vedavyāsa Muni

The pious character of Śrī Kṛṣṇa-dvaipāyana Vedavyāsa Muni is described in *Śrīmad Bhāgavatam*, *Viṣṇu Purāṇa*, *Mahābhārata* and other scriptures.

tataḥ saptadaśe jātaḥ satyavatyāṁ parāśarāt
cakre veda-taroḥ śākhā dṛṣṭvā puṁso 'lpa-medhasaḥ
(*Śrīmad Bhāgavatam* 1.3.21)

"Thereafter, as the seventeenth *avatāra* of Godhead, Śrī Vyāsadeva appeared in the womb of Satyavatī through Parāśara Muni, and he divided the one *Veda* into several branches and sub-branches, seeing that the people in general were less intelligent."

Śrī Śukadeva Gosvāmī has also stated in *Śrīmad Bhāgavatam*:

vicitravīryaś cāvarajo nāmnā citrāṅgado hataḥ
yasyāṁ parāśarāt sākṣād avatīrṇo hareḥ kalā
(*Śrīmad Bhāgavatam* 9.22.21)

"Vicitravīrya, the younger brother of Citraṅgada, was killed by a Gandharva who was also named Citrāṅgada. Satyavatī, the daughter of a boatman, gave birth to the master authority of the *Vedas*, Vyāsadeva, known as Kṛṣṇa-dvaipāyana Vedavyāsa, by union with Parāśara Muni."

In the article titled "Caritavali" of the *New Bengali Dictionary,* by Āśutoṣa Deva, a brief history of the character of Śrī Kṛṣṇa-dvaipāyana Vedavyāsa Muni, as originally described in *Mahābhārata*, is given as follows:

Vyāsadeva is the composer of *Mahābhārata* and the eighteen *Purāṇas*, and he also divided the *Vedas*. He was born at Kṛṣṇa-dvīpa, coming from the union of the daughter of a boatman, Matsyagandha[32] (Satyavati), with Sage Parāśara. As he was born at Kṛṣṇa-dvīpa he was called Kṛṣṇa-dvaipāyana, and because he divided the *Vedas* he is known as Vedavyāsa. He begot three sons: two by the two wives of Vicitravīrya and the third by Vicitravīrya's maidservant. These sons were Dhṛtarāṣṭra, Pāṇḍu and Vidura. By the blessings of Śrī Vedavyāsa, Sañjaya was bestowed with divine sight that enabled him to narrate to Dhṛtarāṣṭra the happenings of the war of the *Mahābhārata*. By Vedavyāsa's mystical power, the women of the Kaurava Dynasty were able to have an audience with their dead relatives after the battle. He invited Śrī Ganeśa to do the actual writing of *Mahābhārata*, but Śrī Ganeśa told Śrī Vyāsadeva that if his pen were to stop even once, he would not write any further. To this, Śrī Vyāsadeva retorted that Ganeśa should not write without first understanding the subject matter. Therefore, in many parts of *Mahābhārata*, Śrī Vyāsadeva[33] has written difficult verses, which are known as Vyāsakūṭa.

It is said in *Viṣṇu Purāṇa*:

vedmekam caturbhedam kṛtvā shakha shatai vibhur
karoti bahulam bhūyo vyāsadeva svarūpa dhrīka
dvaparetu yuge viṣṇurvyasa roopi mahāmune
vedmekam sa bahudha kurute jagato hitāḥ
yaya ca kurute tanva vedamekam prīthaka prabhuḥ
vyāsadeva abhidana tu sa sa matirmadhudviṣaḥ

He who segmented the one *Veda* into four parts with one hundred subparts is known as Vyāsadeva.

According to *Viśvakoṣa*:

---

32 "Matsyagandha" is one of the names of Satyavati, who smelled like a fish.

33 The meaning of Vedavyāsa in Sanskrit is *veda vyāsati pṛthak-karoti vi-asa-aṇ*, which means that he is a special sage who divided the *Vedas* and is famous as Kṛṣṇa-dvaipāyana.

"He is generally known as Mathara, Dvaipāyana, Parāśarya, Kānīna, Bādarāyaṇa, Vyāsa, Kṛṣṇa-dvaipāyana, Satyabhārata, Parāśara, Satyavrata, Satyavatī-suta and Satyarata."

In the *Mahābhārata*, *Ādi-parva*, details regarding the appearance of Sage Vyāsadeva (and by his blessings the birth of Dhṛtarāṣṭra, Pāṇḍu and Vidura) are given. These are described in short as follows:

In the past, Paraśurāma, the son of Jamadagni, angered by the murder of his father, destroyed Kārtavīryārjuna, the ruler of the Haiheya country, by means of his axe (*paraśum*). However, Paraśurāma was not satisfied even after cutting off the thousand arms of Kārtavīryārjuna; thus he again boarded his chariot and wiped the whole warrior class from the face of the earth twenty-one times. Then, the wives of the warriors produced children by means of union with *brāhmaṇas* who were expert in the *Vedas*. In the *Vedas* it is mentioned that if a woman marries a person from one caste, and after marriage begets a child from a person belonging to another caste, then the child is said to belong to the caste of the person to whom the woman was originally married. The wives of the warriors produced children from *brāhmaṇas* only after having contemplated this aspect of the scriptures; hence the warrior class was reborn. In the past, Sage Utathya had a dear wife named Mamatā. Bṛhaspati, the younger brother of Utathya, was the priest of the demigods. At that time, the son of Utathya studied the *Vedas* while in the womb of Mamatā. Then, Bṛhaspati desired to produce a son from the womb of Mamatā, who did not support this, as she was already carrying a son in her womb and thus it was not possible for her to beget another. This annoyed Bṛhaspati and so he cursed the unborn son of Utathya to become blind. Mamatā then gave birth to that boy, who was as bright as Bṛhaspati, and since he was blind he became known as Dīrghatamā. Learned in the *Vedas* but blind since birth, Dīrghatamā took a *brāhmaṇa* girl named Pradveśi as his wife, by the power of his knowledge. Sage Dīrghatamā produced Gautama and some other sons. However, Gautama and the other sons were captivated by greed and illusion. Therefore, Dīrghatamā desired to produce a son from Kāmadhenu. However, the other resident sages of the *āśrama* did not support his unnatural proposal and expelled him from the *āśrama*. Dīrghatamā's wife was also not happy with her blind husband in terms of begetting a son, so one day Dīrghatamā inquired from his wife about the cause of her dissatisfaction and rude behavior. She replied, "The husband always takes care of his wife; therefore he is known as the caretaker. Along with this, he brings her up and maintains her and so he is called *pati* (husband). Since you are blind, I have been taking care of you and your sons instead. Now I am tired and not in a position to take care of you any further." This annoyed Dīrghatamā and he cursed his wife. "Following the virtues established by ethical society, the wife will always be under the shelter of the husband. Even if the husband dies, she shall not take shelter of any other husband." Hearing this, his wife got angry and threw her old and blind husband in the Gaṅgā with the help of her sons. The *brāhmaṇa* did not drown however, and he reached the kingdom of the religious King Bali by letting himself drift along with the flow of River Gaṅgā. Bali brought him to his palace and sought his blessings for a son. When Dīrghatamā gave his consent, the king asked his queen to go to the sage, but instead the queen sent a maidservant to him. From the womb of that maidservant, Kakśivata and other sons were born. Upon finding them to be studious, the king claimed them as his own sons.

The sage said to the king, "These sons are not yours. They are born from the womb of a maidservant. Your queen has insulted me, finding me to be old and blind." When he heard this, King Bali was aggrieved, and to appease the sage he sent his wife Sudeśna to him. With the blessings of the sage, Sudeśna gave birth to five sons as brilliant as the sun. They were Aṅga, Baṅga, Kaliṅga, Punda, and Sūkṣma. The separate regions of earth became known as Aṅgadeśa, Baṅgadeśa, Pundadeśa and Sūkṣmadeśa. Besides the previously mentioned personalities, many brave and religious archers and other kinds of warriors were born by the association of *brāhmaṇas*.

Great-grandfather Bhīṣma once said, "I shall take a lifelong vow of celibacy," just for the fulfillment of his father's desires. Therefore, he brought Satyavatī, the daughter of Daśarāja, and offered her to his father. Śāntanu and Satyavatī had two sons, Citraṅgada and Vicitravīrya. After the departure of Śāntanu, Citraṅgada became the next king. When a Gandharva killed him, Bhīṣma performed Citraṅgada's last rites and carried out the coronation of Vicitravīrya. However, Vicitravīrya was still just a child at the time, so Bhīṣma took care of the people as per the desire of Mother Satyavatī. Bhīṣma was the topmost of all warriors of that time. He abducted and brought the three girls Ambā, Ambikā and Ambālikā from the *svayaṁvara* ceremony of the king of Kāśī to his kingdom. Ambā loved Śālva, so Bhīṣma allowed her to go but brought Ambikā and Ambālikā and married them to Vicitravīrya. However, Vicitravīrya died before physically associating with his wives. Satyavatī was shocked by the death of her son. She wondered how to save the dynasty and requested Bhīṣma to rescue it, but Bhīṣma reminded her of his vow of celibacy and refused.

Bhīṣma said to his mother, "Mother! To save the dynasty, may I suggest that you please call upon some virtuous *brāhmaṇa* who will produce children from the wives of Vicitravīrya."

Satyavatī told Bhīṣma, "You have advised correctly. However, due to my faith in you, please do not refuse to do whatever I ask of you for the propagation of our lineage, because you alone are the righteous, truthful and ultimate savior of our dynasty. My father was a religious man. He possessed a boat. One day during my youth I went to row that boat. At that very time, the great sage Parāśara boarded my boat to cross the river. Out of his love, Sage Parāśara gifted me with unique blessings. My body smelled like fish and he converted it to a pleasant fragrance. I was impressed with him after this incident. Subsequently, during my younger days, I associated with Sage Parāśara and gave birth to a great sage known as Dvaipāyana. That same sage, by virtue of his power of penance, divided the *Vedas* and became famous as Vyāsa, i.e., 'divider of the *Vedas*,' and is further known as Kṛṣṇa because of his dark complexion. He is truthful, peaceful and sinless. That sage went away with his father soon after his birth. Only the brilliant Vyāsa can produce noble sons from your brothers' wives. Before leaving he told me that when in need, I could call upon him. O Bhīṣma! If you so desire, I can call him now."

After hearing this, Bhīṣma paid his respects to Sage Śrī Kṛṣṇa-dvaipāyana internally and then gave his consent to his mother with folded hands. At that time, Vedavyāsa Muni was explaining the *Vedas*. He was aware that his mother was meditating upon him, so he immediately appeared before her. Satyavatī, the daughter of a boatman, greeted him properly and said, "As destined, you are my eldest son and Vicitravīrya was my youngest son. Since Vicitravīrya and Bhīṣma are brothers by virtue of being born of the same father, in the same way, according to me, Vicitravīrya and you are also brothers by virtue of being born from the same mother. Maintaining a vow of celibacy, Śāntanu's son Bhīṣma has not agreed to rule or produce a son. Your younger brother had two beautiful wives; therefore, you should produce worthy offspring from those queens for the propagation of our dynasty." After agreeing to his mother's instructions, Sage Vedavyāsa told her that if a son were to be produced untimely,[34] his ugliness would have to be tolerated. The sage first went to Ambikā. Ambikā was scared and she closed her eyes when she saw the yellowish matted hair, large beard, long moustache and shining eyes of the dark-complexioned man. Śrī Vyāsa told his mother, "The offspring in Ambikā's womb will be as strong as ten thousand elephants, will be wise, superior among kings, and extremely intelligent. Furthermore, he will have a hundred sons in the future, but will be blind due to his mother's fault." After that, when Vedavyāsa Muni went to Ambālikā, she became frightened, morose and turned pale. Her son became famous as Pāṇḍu (pale). When Satyavatī requested her eldest daughter-in-law to again go to the sage, Ambikā decorated one of her maidservants with her own ornaments and sent her to Kṛṣṇa-dvaipāyana. The maidservant offered obeisances to the sage and acted according to the wishes of the sage. This pleased the sage, and he told her that she would remain a maidservant no longer, and that the offspring in her womb would be religious, fortunate and superior among the wise. With the blessings of Śrī Kṛṣṇa-dvaipāyana, the two wives of Vicitravīrya, Ambikā and Ambālikā, along with the maidservant, begot Dhṛtarāṣṭra, Pāṇḍu and Vidura respectively.

A description in *Devī Bhāgavatam* regarding the appearance of Vedavyāsa Muni is similar to the above-mentioned narration, and will now be given in brief as follows:

Sage Parāśara reached the banks of River Yamunā while on pilgrimage. He sought the help of a boatman to cross the river. The boatman was busy, so he asked his daughter Matsyagandha to take him across the Yamunā instead. She did as instructed by her father but as per destiny, when they reached the middle of the Yamunā, Sage Parāśara suddenly started to feel emotionally attracted to her. Matsyagandha's body carried a strong fish stench, but by the blessings of the sage, she turned into a maiden with a beautiful face and body, and her bodily odor changed to an enchanting fragrance. By the request of Matsyagandha, Parāśara Muni then used his own powers to surround the boat with a dense layer of mist. He further blessed Matsyagandha that she would not lose her virginity and that the son born from her womb would be as brilliant and virtuous as his father. Additionally, she would continue to have the same sweet bodily fragrance forever. The meeting of Matsyagandha with Parāśara Ṛṣi occurred by providence. From the womb of Matsyagandha and with the support of Sage Parāśara, a partial expansion of Lord Viṣṇu, the world-famous Śrī Kṛṣṇa-dvaipāyana Vedavyāsa Muni appeared at Kṛṣṇa-dvīpa at an auspicious time. Immediately after birth, Vedavyāsa Muni requested his mother to return home and told her that whenever she would remember him, he would appear before her, irrespective of

34 When Satyavatī requested Śrī Vedavyāsa to produce sons, he told her that for this to happen, the wives of Vicitravīrya would have to fast for one year as prescribed by him. Then only would they be eligible to approach him. However, Satyavatī told him that she could not wait. That is why when a waiting period of one year was not agreed upon, it was considered as untimely.

where he might be. Vedavyāsa Muni engaged in penance immediately after his birth.

The following is from an excerpt of *Mahābhārata*, 63rd Chapter, *Ādi-parva*:

'Dvaipāyana was thus born from the union of Parāśara and Satyavatī. He became known as Dvaipāyana because he was born at Dvīpa. The wise Dvaipāyana observed that, with the passing of each age, one pillar of religion was being removed, and that the lifespan of human beings was greatly reducing as well. Consequently, he then performed the division of the *Vedas* (*vyāsa* of the *Vedas*) for the purpose of protecting them, thereby favoring the *brāhmaṇas*. Due to this, he became known as Vedavyāsa. Superior among the bestowers of blessings, Lord Vedavyāsa taught *Mahābhārata* and the four *Vedas* to his disciples Sumanta, Jaimini, Paila, Vaiśampāyana and his son Śukadeva. These same disciples published a separate Saṁhita of *Mahābhārata*.'

Kṛṣṇa-dvaipāyana Vedavyāsa Muni composed the conclusion of the *Vedas* known as *Vedānta-sūtras*, and also wrote their commentary, which is known as *Śrīmad Bhāgavatam*:

artho'yaṁ brahma-sūtrāṇāṁ bhāratārtha-vinirṇayaḥ
gāyatrī-bhāṣya-rūpo'sau vedārtha-paribṛṁhitaḥ
(*Garuḍa Purāṇa*)

"*Śrīmad Bhāgavatam* is the authorized explanation of the *Brahma-sūtras*, and it is a further explanation of *Mahābhārata*. It is the explanation of the Gāyatrī-mantra and the essence of all Vedic knowledge."

prabhu kahe, vedānta-sūtra īśvara-vacana
vyāsa-rūpe kaila yāhā śrī-nārāyaṇa
bhrama, pramāda, vipralipsā, karaṇāpāṭava
īśvarera vākye nāhi doṣa ei saba
(*Śrī Caitanya-caritāmṛta, Ādi* 7.106-107)

Śrīla Bhakti Siddhānta Sarasvatī Gosvāmī Ṭhākura has written in his commentary: 'According to the great dictionary compiler Hemacandra, also known as Koṣakāra, the word *vedānta* refers to the purport of the *Upaniṣads* and the *Brāhmaṇa* portion of the *Vedas*. The supplement of the *Vedas* is called *Vedānta-sūtra*. *Veda* means "knowledge," and *anta* means "the end." In other words, proper understanding of the ultimate purpose of the *Vedas* is called *vedānta*, or knowledge. The *Upaniṣads* must support such knowledge given in the aphorisms of *Vedānta-sūtra*. There are three different sources of knowledge—*śruti-prasthāna*, *smṛti-prasthāna* and *nyāya-prasthāna* that, together, are called *prasthāna-traya* (three proofs). *Vedānta-sūtra* is known as *nyāya-prasthāna* (Vedic knowledge based on logic and sound arguments), while the *Upaniṣads* are known as *śruti-prasthāna* (Vedic knowledge based on hearing), and the *Gītā*, *Mahābhārata* and *Purāṇas* are known as *smṛti-prasthāna* (Vedic knowledge based on remembering).'

It is said that both the Vedic knowledge and the supplement of the *Vedas* called *Sātvata-pañcarātra* emanated from the breathing of Nārāyaṇa, the Supreme Personality of Godhead. The *Vedānta-sūtra* aphorisms were compiled by Śrīla Vyāsadeva, a powerful manifestation of Śrī Nārāyaṇa, although it is sometimes said that they were compiled by a great sage named Apāntaratamā, which is Vedavyāsa's name in one of his births. (*Śrīmad Bhāgavatam* 6.15.12)

Pañcarātra and *Vedānta-sūtra*, however, express the same opinions. Śrī Caitanya Mahāprabhu has confirmed this. He further declares that because *Śrīmad Bhāgavatam* was compiled by Śrīla Vyāsadeva, it should be understood to be the direct words of Śrī Nārāyaṇa. While Vyāsadeva was compiling *Vedānta-sūtra*, he also commented on the perspectives of *vedānta* by seven of his great saintly contemporaries. *Śrīmad Bhāgavatam* is the transcendental commentary on *vedānta* by Śrī Vedavyāsa. Besides *Śrīmad Bhāgavatam*, there are commentaries on *Vedānta-sūtra* composed by all the four Vaiṣṇava *ācāryas* and their spiritual descendants, and in each of them devotional service to the Lord is described very explicitly. Even those who follow the impersonal path, without reference to Viṣṇu-bhakti, or devotional service to Lord Viṣṇu, respect this commentary on *Vedānta-sutra*. All the impersonal descriptions of *Vedānta-sūtra*, all the commentaries that are devoid of devotional service to Lord Viṣṇu, must be considered to differ in purpose from the original *Vedānta-sūtra*.

What Śrīla Bhakti Siddhānta Sarasvatī Ṭhākura has written in his Sindhu-vaibhava commentaries of *Śrīmad Bhāgavatam*, 1st Canto, 1st Chapter, deserves special attention:

"*Śrīmad Bhāgavatam* is the crown of all Vedic scriptures. There are three branches of Vedic scriptures. One deals with lowly, limited and momentary fruits of action. The second branch deals with the superior, eternal knowledge of knowing the impersonal Brahman while renouncing all the fruits of one's actions, which is exactly opposite to the first. However, the third branch is the unique branch that is superior to even enjoyment or renunciation; it is that of eternal service with devotion in the eternal abode (Vaikuṇṭha) of the Supreme Lord."

There once was a time when the people were being greatly deceived due to the preaching of scriptures that only established the first two branches of the Vedic scriptures, which deal with the importance of *karma* (action) and *jñana* (knowledge). Consequently, the public was developing an attitude of distaste regarding the conception of the eternal nature of the soul. At that time, the Supreme Lord appeared in the form of the essence of the third branch of the *Vedas*, namely the *Śrīmad Bhāgavatam*, and by appearing so He dispelled all such disgust and established the truth about our eternal nature. Therefore, *Śrīmad Bhāgavatam* alone is the ripened fruit of the wish-fulfilling tree of Vedic knowledge.

Śrīmad Bhāgavatam is dear to the Vaiṣṇavas because its only subject matter is the transcendental knowledge of pure devotees. This establishes the ultimate conceptions of eternal knowledge, detachment and devotion. *Śrīmad Bhāgavatam* demolishes the tenet of enjoying the fruits gained by good actions. Those who hear *Śrīmad Bhāgavatam*, who study it properly under the guidance of pure devotees and dwell upon it, are relieved of the fruits of their actions by the influence of devotion.

Vedic knowledge describes three categories: *sambandha*, *abhidheya* and *prayojana*[35] in relation to Kṛṣṇa. *Śrīmad Bhāgavatam* is the fruit of love of Kṛṣṇa and, as such, it belongs to the category of *prayojana*.

Śrīmad Bhāgavatam is the transcendental commentary on *Vedānta-sūtra*. The *Vedānta-sūtras*, or *Brahma-sūtras*, were compiled by Vyāsadeva, an empowered manifestation of the Lord, with a view to presenting only the cream of Vedic knowledge. Observing that people were unable to understand the real meaning of the *Vedānta-sūtras*, Vyāsadeva wrote *Śrīmad Bhāgavatam* as a commentary to enable them to understand the true meaning of these *sūtras*. After obscuring the actual meaning of the Vedanta-sūtras, some writers tried to establish *vivartavāda*[36] and others tried to establish

35 These three categories are respectively: Attainment of the realization of one's relationship with the Lord, actions according to that final relationship, and realization of the final goal.

36 The Vedantic theory that propounds the unreality of the world and opines that it is mere illusion.

ārambhavāda.[37] In order to override those commentaries, which were against the *Vedas*, the original creator of the *sūtras* wrote *Śrīmad Bhāgavatam* to explain in simple words that *śakti-pariṇāmavāda* is the true meaning of the *Vedas*.

Śrīmad Bhāgavatam is the light of knowledge. It is like a sun among the *Purāṇas*. It is the ripened fruit. The Lord Himself narrated the complete *Bhāgavatam* to Brahmā and, later, Brahmā preached this *Śrīmad Bhāgavatam* to Nārada. After that, Vyāsadeva received it from Śrī Nārada. Therefore, this became a tradition among *ācaryas* of the Brahmā Sampradāya. *Śrīmad Bhāgavatam* is among the eighteen *Purāṇas* and is written by Śrī Kṛṣṇa-dvaipāyana Vedavyāsa. Before the appearance of Śrīdhara Svāmī (original commentator on *Śrīmad Bhāgavatam*), there was an effort to file *Devī Bhāgavatam*, written by a non-devotee, under the eighteen *Purāṇas*, but other bonafide *Purāṇas* never accorded purāṇic status to such an imaginary, passionate and new composition.

37 The theory that propounds a beginning to this world.

Śrīmad Bhāgavatam, the *Mahā-purāṇa* in which the glories of the *gāyatrī-mantra* are described in the beginning, is the divine commentary on the Brahmā-sūtras. In this *Purāṇa*, Śukadeva narrates the episode of the killing of Vṛtrāsura, the acquisition of transcendental knowledge by Hayagrīva, and other pertinent histories. *Padma Purāṇa*, *Matsya Purāṇa* and other pure *Purāṇas* have accepted this very *Śrīmad Bhāgavatam* as the main scripture.

Some modern arrogant, illogical non-devotees enviously consider *Śrīmad Bhāgavatam* to be a scripture written by Bopadeva or some other medieval poet. Bopadeva has independently written a commentary and treatise in support of *Śrīmad Bhāgavatam*. However, it should be noted here that unfortunate, illogical nonbelievers of Lord Hari will never become successful in maligning *Śrīmad Bhāgavatam*. Śrī Mahāprabhu has described *Śrīmad Bhāgavatam* as being non-different from Śri Kṛṣṇa, and He portrayed this scripture as the ultimate among all authentic scriptures. Śrīman Mahāprabhu has described *Śrīmad Bhāgavatam* as the scripture explaining the path to attain love of Godhead (*abhidheya*). Some devotees say that there is a difference between the followers of *Pañcarātra* and *Bhāgavatam*, but Lord Mahāprabhu said that the real message of *Pañcarātra* and *Bhāgavatam* is one and the same. The *abhideya-tattva* delineated in *Pañcarātra* is mentioned in *Śrīmad Bhāgavatam* as well.

After expanding the Vedic scriptures into four sections, Śrī Vedavyāsa composed the Vedic history and other works, for the welfare of the souls of this world and all other worlds. Scriptures like *Mahābhārata* describe the paths of *dharma*, *artha*, *kāma* and *mokṣa*. However,

Śrī Vyāsa was not pleased with any of these compositions. He began meditating on his accomplishments, and then his spiritual master, Śrī Nārada, appeared before him. Śrī Vyāsa asked him why he (Vyāsa) was still unsatisfied and Śrī Nārada answered, "For the welfare of the people you have composed scriptures, but these compositions do not fall under the category of devotional service unto Lord Hari. Now you should describe the pastimes of Lord Hari, and thereby serve Him. By doing this you will develop love of Godhead and this will be the process to satiate your soul." Thus, for the pleasure of the soul, *Śrīmad Bhāgavatam* came into existence.

So, for the welfare of the people, Śrī Vedavyāsa manifested this eternal scripture, *Śrīmad Bhāgavatam*, which was not available earlier in this world. By listening to *Śrīmad Bhāgavatam*, even a conditioned soul will develop a service attitude (which is the destroyer of sorrow, fear, etc.) toward the Supreme Personality of Godhead, Śrī Kṛṣṇa.

Śrī Vyāsa taught this scripture to his son Śrī Śukadeva. Later, Śrī Śukadeva narrated this to Parīkṣit and others such as Lomaharṣaṇa Sūta. After that, Śrī Sūta narrated this to Sage Śaunaka and others at Naimiṣāraṇya. Then again, in the beginning of the age of Kali, Śrī Vyāsa composed *Śrīmad Bhāgavatam* in the form of a book.

namas tasmai bhagavate vāsudevāya vedhase
papur jñānam ayaṁ saumyā yan-
mukhāmburuhāsavam
(*Śrīmad Bhāgavatam* 2.4.24)

"I offer my respectful obeisances unto Śrīla Vyāsadeva, the *avatāra* of Vāsudeva who compiled the Vedic scriptures. The pure devotees drink up the nectar of transcendental knowledge dropping from the lotus-like mouth of the Lord."

nāradaḥ prāha munaye sarasvatyās taṭe nṛpa
dhyāyate brahmā paramaṁ vyāsāyāmita-tejase
(*Śrīmad Bhāgavatam* 2.9.45)

"O King! The unlimitedly brilliant Sage Vyāsadeva, sitting on the bank of River Sarasvatī, was meditating upon Lord Kṛṣṇa, and there he learned this *Śrīmad Bhāgavatam* from Śrī Nārada, through the disciplic succession."

yaṁ pravrajantam anupetam apeta-kṛtyaṁ
dvaipāyano viraha-kātara ājuhāva
putreti tan-mayatayā taravo 'bhinedus
taṁ sarva-bhūta-hṛdayaṁ munim ānato 'smi
(*Śrīmad Bhāgavatam* 1.2.2)

In this verse Śrī Sūta Gosvāmī offers his obeisances unto his spiritual master, Śrī Śukadeva Gosvāmī, and the temperament of those obeisances reflects that Śrī Śukadeva was detached from material sense enjoyment since childhood, and that he was a liberated, exalted devotee. Although in *Devī Bhāgavatam* the birth and marriage of Śrī Śukadeva Gosvāmī is mentioned, it has been proven incorrect by the above text of *Śrīmad Bhāgavatam*. That is why Śrīla Bhakti Siddhānta Sarasvatī Ṭhākura never accepted *Devī Bhāgavatam* as an authentic scripture.

Śrī Viśvanātha Cakravartī comments on this verse as follows:

"When Śrī Vyāsadeva saw that Śukadeva had left for the forest on his own, even though his sacred thread ceremony (*yajñopavita-saṁskāra*) had yet to take place, he felt sudden pangs of separation and began calling out for him, "Son! Son!" When he called out to him, not only did he enchant his son by the sound of his voice, but the trees as well. *Padma Purāṇa* says that a person who prays to Lord Hari satisfies the whole world. The trees all around took on the mood of Śrī Vyāsa and also began calling out, 'Son! O son!' Attraction to any object is known as *tanmayata* (trance). Especially, Śrī Śukadeva resides in the hearts of all beings. That is why the attachment that Śrī Vyāsa displayed for Śrī Śukadeva (similar to attachment to the *vigraha* of Lord) could not be termed as material."

Śrīla Bhakti Siddhānta Sarasvatī Gosvāmī Ṭhākura has explained this verse thus:

"Śrīla Vyāsa called after Śrī Śukadeva, 'Son! Son!' Conditioned souls might misconstrue him as suffering from mundane pains of separation between a material son and father. But one might remember that the service of Śrīla Vyāsadeva unto the Lord never promoted extreme attachment for anyone's son, or any emotions of pain of separation from one's son. Śrī Vedavyāsa is the foremost master of the Brahmā Sampradāya. Thus, we cannot consider him or his actions in the context of mundane thoughts. *Na prākṛtatvam iha bhakta janasya paśyet*: as per this injunction, in the *sampradāya* of Śrī Vyāsa, Śrīla Gurudeva is not considered to be a conditioned soul suffering from the threefold material miseries. Neglecting meditation on Lord Hari, a conditioned soul would instead be inclined to meditate on his son, regardless of whether he was good or bad. Conditioned souls live under the spell of illusion, but Śrīla Vyāsa is not subject to illusion. He merely exhibited these pastimes to attract the conditioned souls. It is also true that Śrīla Śukadeva is a pure devotee and is beyond the state of desiring enjoyment of the fruits of *karma*. It would not be beneficial for devotees, or even masters like Śrī Vyāsa, to be devoid of the association of such a great personality as Śrī Śukadeva, as he is a great personality and an example for all—indeed, he is the master of all."

In the *Padma Purāṇa*, Sage Śrī Kṛṣṇa-dvaipāyana Vedavyāsa has stated the glories of listening to *Śrīmad Bhāgavatam*, which is among the eighteen *mahā-purāṇas*. Sanaka, Sanandana, Sanātana and Sanat Kumāra once discussed the method of performing a week-long *yajña* (*saptaḥ-yajña*) with Sage Nārada Gosvāmī. Śaunaka and other sages inquired about this topic from Śrī Sūta Gosvāmī. There, the story of Gokarṇa and Dhundhukārī came up. When Sage Śrī Nārada inquired about the topmost liberation of the sinful beings of Kali-yuga, all the fools, birds and animals, as well as the associates of Vaikuṇṭha such as Śrī Sanaka and other Kumāras answered, "If sinners of all kinds such as the envious, the angry, cheaters, the lustful, liars, those who speak disrespectful words to their parents, those who don't follow *varṇāśrama-dharma*, egoists, the cruel, drunkards, the killers of *brāhmaṇas*, thieves, molesters of a *guru's* wife, bigamists and all other kinds of most sinful persons perform a week-long *yajña*, then they will attain liberation and go to the abode of the Lord." In this connection, the ancient details of Ātmadeva, Gokarṇa and Dhundhukārī were discussed. The sinner Dhundhukārī performed all sorts of misdeeds, so he became a ghost and had to endure much suffering as a result. Even the performance of oblations (*piṇḍa*) at Gāya could not liberate him, but he was liberated of his sins and attained Vaikuṇṭha by listening to *Śrīmad Bhāgavatam* with single–pointed devotion from the pure devotee named Gokarṇa. However, the other listeners present, who were not as sinful as Dhundhukārī and had performed a fair amount of good deeds (*puṇya-phala*), still did not attain Vaikuṇṭha. *Śrīmad Bhāgavatam Māhātmya* ("Glories of *Śrīmad Bhāgavatam*") explains that those others were not as attentive as Dhundhukārī in hearing *Śrīmad Bhāgavatam*. That is why the others who were hearing *Śrīmad Bhāgavatam* from Śrī Gokarṇa were unable to attain liberation or Vaikuṇṭha, whereas Dhundhukārī did, due to attentively hearing *Śrīmad Bhāgavatam* from him.

Thousands of pious listeners heard *Śrīmad Bhāgavatam* from none other than the great devotee Gokarṇa. King Parīkṣit attained perfection when he listened attentively to *Śrīmad Bhāgavatam* from the pure devotee Śukadeva Gosvāmī. The actual fruit of *Bhāgavatam* cannot be attained even if the speaker is eligible but the listener is not a pure devotee of the Lord, is not trustworthy or does not have one-pointed concentration. When the speaker is a professional speaker and an audience has all sorts of material aspirations, such week-long programs of *Śrīmad Bhāgavatam* do not deliver actual results. A week-long *yajña* of *Śrīmad Bhāgavatam* is meant to focus on the complete *Bhāgavatam*, not only partial chapters for the purpose of satisfying the audience. Devotion under the guidance of a pure devotee is true devotion. Any act without the guidance of a devotee is not *bhakti*:

mahat-kṛpā vinā kona karme 'bhakti' naya
kṛṣṇa-bhakti dūre rahu, saṁsāra nahe kṣaya
(*Śrī Caitanya-caritāmṛta, Madhya Līlā* 22.51)

In his commentary on this verse, Śrīla Bhakti Siddhānta Sarasvatī Gosvāmī Ṭhākura has written that those who desire their own welfare should read *Śrīmad Bhāgavatam*. Any furtively performed pious material deed is unhelpful in transcendental devotion to Śrī Kṛṣṇa. Without the mercy of a pure devotee of the Lord, one can never attain divine devotion to Kṛṣṇa. One will not be able to get rid of his or her material attachments without the mercy of a pure devotee, what to speak of attaining devotion to Kṛṣṇa. No one can attain greatness without being a devotee of Śrī Kṛṣṇa. Only a devotee of Śrī Kṛṣṇa is divine. With material eyes, one may see a pure devotee of the Lord as a denizen of this material world. However, the pure devotee of Kṛṣṇa who has given up all attachments to the material world is incomparable and the only real well-wisher of all the conditioned souls. One should beg for mercy only from such devotees. By doing so, we may overcome our lust for material sense pleasures and get a chance to serve Śrī Kṛṣṇa.

Śrīla Bhakti Siddhānta Sarasvatī Ṭhākura Gosvāmī and our worshipable Gurudeva did not support any *Bhāgavatam* weeklies, nor any 24-hour *kīrtana* for the purpose of fulfilling material objectives. If one does not follow a pure devotee (who is actually a physician for conditioned souls), one will not be able to overcome the material desires for wealth, illicit sex and prestige, which are considered to be diseases.

"There is nobody as pure as me." Such foolish thinking and egoism will close the door to all sorts of welfare. Followers of *sanātana-dharma* organize Vyāsa-pūjā on Āṣād-pūrṇimā to celebrate the appearance of Sage Śrī Kṛṣṇa-dvaipāyana Vedavyāsa. He is the foremost guru, the instructor of all. However, the manner in which pure devotees take themselves to be eternally related to him and worship him with great love and affection is not seen anywhere else. In the 5th Chapter of the *Madhya-khaṇḍa* of *Śrī Caitanya Bhāgavata*, Śrīla Bhakti Siddhānta Sarasvatī Gosvāmī Ṭhākura relates four points while describing Śrī Vyāsa-pūjā. They are as follows:

The introductory knowledge of the Absolute Truth, Śrī Kṛṣṇa, who is the predominating deity of the *samvit* potency, is called *Veda*.

The marginal potency, one of the three primary potencies of the Supreme Lord, has spiritual characteristics. *Advaya-jñāna* Śrī Kṛṣṇa is situated within the conceptions of knower, knowledge, and the object of knowledge. The Lord, who is the personification of knowledge, takes the form of sound and manifests Himself as the Vedic literatures. When the Vedic literatures, consisting of knowledge related to *sambandha*, *abhideya* and *prayojana*, fail to check the impersonal concept, then the *advaya-jñana*, or Absolute Truth, gives up its variegated characteristics. In the perfected stage of their impersonal conceptions, those who give importance to material variety while negating spiritual variety lose their individuality. Śrī Kṛṣṇa-dvaipāyana Vedavyāsa divided the *Vedas* into three parts. The *Ṛg*, *Sāma* and *Yājur Vedas* entangle materialistic persons in *karma-kanda* and create an illusory understanding of the actual purport of the *Vedas*. Due to their perplexed thinking, believers of the impersonal think that the devotee, devotional practice and the Lord are all perishable. They do not accept the eternality of distinctions such as great and small, and they are unable to accept Śri Vyāsadeva as the spiritual master. Therefore, they forcibly consider him to be the propounder of their ignorance.

Being unable to understand the actual intention of Śrīmad Vyāsa, those covert Buddhists (crypto-Buddhists) who claim that the Supreme Lord is a product of matter and are thus bereft of His service falsely consider themselves to be Brāhmaṇ, devoid of distinctions such as individuality, devotion, aversion, etc. Śrīmad Ānanda Tirtha remained a true servant of his spiritual master and became renowned as the topmost follower of Śri Vyāsa by establishing a difference of opinion with such persons. In the disciplic succession from Madhva we hear topics of great personalities like Śrīman Lakṣmīpati Tīrtha and Śrī Mādhavendra Purīpāda. Although the tradition of Guru-puja, or Vyāsa-pūjā, is current among the Māyāvādīs (impersonalist followers of the doctrine of *māyā*) and the Pañcopāsakas (followers of five gods), such Vyāsa-pūjā bears a prominence of false ego. Due to the absence of pure devotional service, they can never conduct Śrī Vyāsa-pūjā. In the Māyāvāda Sampradāya the pretense of observing Vyāsa-pūjā is seen on Guru-pūrṇimā day in the month of Āśādha (June-July).

The *Vedas* state that the very moment one develops detachment, one will retire from material enjoyment and achieve a taste for the service of the Lord. In this regard there is no consideration of proper or improper time. As soon as the living entity's material enjoyment is vanquished, he or she approaches an *ācārya* and takes shelter of the lotus feet of such a divine personality. Taking shelter of the lotus feet of an *ācārya* is the real meaning of the term Vyāsa-pūjā. Śrī Vyāsa-pūjā is a prescribed function for all the four *āśramas*, but, particularly, *sannyāsīs* should observe this function. The members of those *sampradāyas* in Āryavarta who accept the teachings of Śrī Vyāsadeva are famous as Vedanugas, or followers of the *Vedas*. Every year they all worship their spiritual master on his or her appearance day. The most suitable day for accepting *sannyāsa* is Pūrṇimā, the full-moon day. Whether impersonalist or personalist, all renouncers worship their spiritual masters. That is why Vyāsa-pūjā is generally celebrated on the full moon day of Āśādha, which is considered to be the appearance day of the spiritual master. As a sign of respect, the servants of Śrī Gaudiya Matha observe Śrī Vyāsa-pūjā every year on the fifth day of the waning moon in the month of Māgha (January-February).

The observance of Śrī Vyāsa-pūjā differs in various branches. Since *brāhmaṇas* of all the four *āśramas*, who have undergone the prescribed purification rites, are under the shelter of a spiritual master who represents Śrī Vyāsa, they more or less regularly worship Śrī Vyāsadeva as a prescribed duty; but the annual observance of Vyāsa-pūjā marks the beginning of worshiping the spiritual master throughout the year. Another name for Śrī Vyāsa-pūjā is Śrī Guru-pāda-padme Padyārpana, meaning "bathing the lotus feet of the spiritual master with five ingredients," the process by which it is made known that the inner desire of the spiritual master is to properly serve the Lord. This is the real purpose of Vyāsa-pūjā.

Śrīla Bhakti Siddhānta Sarasvatī Gosvāmī Ṭhākura delivered the following lecture to his disciples on his fiftieth appearance day:

"Divine knowledge appeared in the heart of Śrī Brahmā. That same divine knowledge appeared to Śrī Nārada and was later attained by Vaiṣṇava Guru Śrī Vedavyāsa-jī. That same knowledge is now being distributed through our *guru-paramparā* by his mercy. Actually, this is the right path (*praśastā*) and is known as *śrauta-panthā*. Those persons who are not keen to accept the teachings of Śrī Vyāsa become engulfed by material knowledge and leaves *śrauta-panthā*.

"They instead abide by the techniques of argument and have no praise for scriptures. They thereby form their own cults. If one accepts these cults as *śrauta-panthā*, one gets cheated. To confirm the beauty and sanctity of the preaching of Śrī Vedavyāsa, Śrī Gaurasundara illumnated the path followed by great *ācāryas*. That is the only means and end for all devotees. The devotees who are dependent on Śrī Gaurasundara possess knowledge of the service attitude and how to attain the ultimate goal by its means. With the passage of time, bogus devotees calling themselves believers, which resulted in the transformation of those practices from devotional to non-devotional, accepted a part of that. However, the path prescribed by Śrī Kṛṣṇa, Śrī Brahmā, Śrī Nārada and Śrī Vyāsa is celebrated as *bhāgavata-dharma* or *pañcarātra-dharma*. This *bhāgavata-dharma* will dispel the darkness of nescience and is the actual truth. But because of the desire for material titles, this path has also adopted various forms and these bogus offshoots are trying to eliminate the pure path, either on a small or large scale. Due to their efforts to attain titles, men are following the path of imitation instead of *anuśaraṇa* (following with understanding)."

Many writers from western countries have written about Śrī Vyāsadeva, though their writings are short and incomplete:

"Vyāsa: Sanskrit arranger or compiler of the *Vedas*, also called Kṛṣṇa-dvaipāyana or Vyāsadeva: a legendary Indian sage, who is traditionally credited with composing or compiling the *Mahābhārata*, a collection of legendary and didactic poetry worked around a central heroic narrative."

"According to legend, Vyāsa was the son of the ascetic Parāśara and the Dasa princess Satyavatī, and he grew up in the forests living with hermits who taught him the *Vedas*. Thereafter, he lived in the forests near the banks of River Sarasvatī, where he became a teacher and priest, the father of a son and disciple, Śuka, and gathered a large group of followers. Later in life, while living in the caves of the Himālayas, he is said to have divided the *Vedas*, composed the *Purāṇas* and, in a period of two and a half years, composed his great poetic epic, *Mahābhārata*, allegedly dictating it to his scribe Ganeśa, the elephant god." (*The New Encyclopaedia Britannica*, Volume 12, Page 440, Column 3)

Badrika-āśrama/Śamyāprāsa-āśrama: The cave of a mountain on the banks of River Sarasvatī, situated at almost 1000 feet of height from the Badrinārāyaṇa temple, is known as Śamyāprāsa-āśrama. Here, Śrī Vyāsadeva composed *Śrīmad Bhāgavatam* while meditating on the pastimes of Lord Kṛṣṇa. The mountain where this cave is situated is shaped like a large book. The mountain cave is quite spacious, and is big enough to accommodate six or seven people.

Sage Cyavana

cyavate māturudarāt cyu-karttari lyu
cyavaner pitā bhṛgu ṛṣi jananī pulomā
(Purāṇa)

Cyavana Ṛṣi's father was Bhṛgu Ṛṣi and his mother was Pulomā. Details of the birth of Cyavana Ṛṣi have been described in *Mahābhārata*, *Ādi-parva*, Chapters 5-6 . When Śaunaka and the other ṛṣis expressed their desire to learn how Bhṛgu Ṛṣi's son became known as Cyavana, Ugraśravā Sūta started describing Cyavana Ṛṣi. He said that Bhṛgu had a wife named Pulomā, who was as religious and famous as her husband. Once, at the time when Pulomā was pregnant and Bhṛgu Ṛṣi had gone for a bath, a demon entered the *āśrama* in disguise. He saw the sage's beautiful wife and felt attracted to her. Bhṛgu's wife offered the demon some fruits and flowers from the forest and welcomed him as a guest, but the demon was overcome with lusty desires and decided to kidnap Bhṛgu's wife. This demon had sought Pulomā as his wife earlier as well, but at that time he had been rejected because Pulomā's father had decided to marry his daughter to Bhṛgu according to the appropriate scriptural injunctions. To confirm that this was the very same Pulomā, the demon inquired from the blazing fire in which Agnideva resided, "Please confirm that this woman in this lonely place is the wife of Bhṛgu, whom I chose as my wife initially and who was later unjustly taken by Bhṛgu. O Agnideva! You reside in all the living being as a witness to both good and bad actions. May you therefore speak the truth about this action; did Bhṛgu take her by force or not?"

However, Agnideva was reluctant to answer the demon's question. It was improper to lie and there was the fear of being cursed by Bhṛgu, so Agnideva said, "O son of a demon! It is indeed true that you first chose Pulomā to be your wife, but you did not marry her according to the scriptural rules and rituals. Pulomā's father, desiring to obtain a decent candidate, thus dedicated his daughter to Bhṛgu instead. Bhṛgu has married her according to the Vedic rituals, using me as witness. I know that she is the same Pulomā whom you desired to marry and I do not lie because nobody respects lies." Upon hearing the words of Agnideva, the demon at once transformed himself into a large boar and kidnapped Pulomā with the speed of wind. By the demon's despicable action, the child in Pulomā's womb became annoyed and came out to protect his mother. That is why the son of Bhṛgu and Pulomā was called Cyavana (fallen from the womb). As soon as he suffered the angry vision of this bright and lustrous child, the demon turned to ashes and fell to the floor. Shocked and aggrieved by this incident, the wife of Bhṛgu left for the *āśrama* carrying her child in her hands. Then Grandfather Brahmā consoled his daughter-in-law. The tears from Pulomā's eyes became a river and, consequently, Brahmā named that river Vasundhara, as it was flowing from the *āśrama* due to the tears of his daughter-in-law. Thus, that river came to be known as Vasundhara and Bhṛgu's son came to be known as Cyavana.

Bhṛgu Ṛṣi was angry and asked Pulomā, "The demon did not know that you were my wife, so who introduced you? Tell me the truth. I am very angry and I shall curse him." Pulomā replied, "It was Agni who introduced me to the demon. Although I was weeping like a *kurāri* bird, the demon still took me away from here. However, the demon was turned to ashes by the overwhelming effulgence of my son and I was thus saved from that evil spirit." When he heard this from Pulomā, a terrible wrath took hold of Bhṛgu Muni, and he cursed Agnideva, the god of fire, declaring, "You, Fire, shall eat all things!"

Chapters 121-123 of the *Vana-parva* of *Mahābhārata* detail the divine influence of Cyavana Ṛṣi. The story will now be summarized as described in *Viśvakoṣa*:

Once upon a time, Cyavana Ṛṣi was performing penance on the banks of a river somewhere in a forest. His body gradually became riddled with holes created by earthworms. After some time, only his two brilliant eyes were still visible. As such, when Sukanyā, the daughter of King Śaryāti, chanced upon the unrecognizable body of Cyavana Ṛṣi, she could only see those shining eyes and, thinking them merely to be two bright objects, she ignorantly pierced them with a thorn. After she pierced them, blood began to ooze from them. Angered by this action, the sage stopped the discharge of urine and stool of all the soldiers in Śaryāti's army. The king came to know of this incident after much enquiry, and sought forgiveness from Cyavana. Cyavana agreed to forgive him, but expressed his desire to marry Princess Sukanyā. Feeling compromised, the king felt obliged to Cyavana Ṛṣi due to the awkwardness of the situation, so he accepted his proposal. For reasons unknown, the princess did not object to marrying the old sage, Cyavana, whose face looked wrinkled and worn. After some time, the Aśvinī Kumāras (twin physicians of the demigods) came to the *āśrama* of Cyavana Ṛṣi and requested the beautiful and graceful young Princess Sukanyā to leave her old husband and accept them as her new husbands, but she did not agree to the indecent request. The Aśvinī Kumāras became pleased by this behavior and transformed Cyavana Ṛṣi into a young man. Gratified by this, Cyavana Ṛṣi took an oath in a *yajña* of King Śaryāti and offered the Aśvinī Kumāras *soma-rasa* to drink. Indra objected to this, but the sage paid him no heed.

Being thus ignored by the sage, Indra became angry and, with the intention to kill, he began to strike Sage Cyavana with his powerful Vajra (thunderbolt) weapon. However, by the power of his chants, Cyavana Ṛṣi immobilized Indra's arms. Then, by dint of his mystical power, Cyavana Ṛṣi brought forth a large demon in order to kill Indra. The frightened Indra then took Cyavana's refuge. The sage gave the right to drink *soma-rasa* to both of the Aśvinī Kumāras and thereafter released Indra. Simultaneously, he divided the demon he had summoned into women, drinking, gambling and hunting, among other things. According to Āyurveda, the medicine that gives lasting youth is called Cyavanaprāśa.

The details of Cyavana Ṛṣi are also described in *Śrīmad Bhāgavatam*, Chapter 3, Canto 9. As per evidence given in *Mahābhārata*, whatever has been written in *Viśvakoṣa* and the narration of *Śrīmad Bhāgavatam* regarding Cyavana Ṛṣi are similar. It is known from the description in *Śrīmad Bhāgavatam* that, as providence would have it, when the daughter of Śaryāti pierced the two shining objects, blood oozed out from them:

sā sakhībhiḥ parivṛtā vicinvanty aṅghripān vane
valmīka-randhre dadṛśe khadyote iva jyotiṣī
te daiva-coditā bālā jyotiṣī kaṇṭakena vai
avidhyan mugdha-bhāvena susrāvāsṛk tato bahiḥ
(*Śrīmad Bhāgavatam* 9.3.3-4)

"While Sukanyā, surrounded by her friends, was collecting various types of fruits from the trees in the forest, she saw within the hole of an earthworm two things glowing like luminaries. As if induced by providence, the girl, filled with child-like tendencies, pierced those two objects with a thorn and, when they were pierced, blood began to ooze out of them."

According to the description in *Śrīmad Bhāgavatam*, it is known that Cyavana Muni was very old. When one day the two eminent physicians known as the Aśvinī Kumāras came to his *āśrama*, the sage prayed to them for youth and in return offered them the right to drink *soma-rasa* obtained from a *yajña*.

Due to the request of Cyavana Ṛṣi, both Aśvinī Kumāras entered a large lake along with the sage, and as they emerged from the lake, they had all gained the appearance of fresh youths similar to each other in appearance. Śaryāti's daughter, Sukanyā, however, was able to recognize her husband and took refuge of the two Aśvinī Kumāras. Both Aśvinī Kumāras were satisfied by her devotion to her husband and reacquainted her with her now youthful husband.

When a *brāhmaṇa* boy cursed Parīkṣit Mahārāja, he handed over the reins of his kingdom to his son Janamejaya and came to Sukartala on the banks of River Gaṅgā, taking an oath to fast until death. At that time and place, Śrīla Śukadeva Gosvāmī narrated *Śrīmad Bhāgavatam* non-stop for seven days and seven nights. The great Cyavana Ṛṣi was among the sages who were present in the great assembly of Parīkṣit Mahārāja and heard the narration.

Sage Pulastya

"He is one of the Saptarṣis (Seven Sages). He is the *mānasa-putra* (son born from the mind) of Śrī Brahmā." (*Manu Saṁhitā* 1.35)

"Sage Pulastya is also counted among the Prajāpatis (early progenitors of the living entities). According to *Viṣṇu Purāṇa*, he preached in this world the *Ādi Purāṇa*, narrated by Brahmā. He received the *Viṣṇu Purāṇa* from Brahmā and passed it on to Sage Parāśara. That same Pulastya was the father of Viśrava and the great-grandfather of Kuvera and Rāvaṇa. The demon community appeared from Sage Pulastya." (*Viśvakoṣa*)

There is also a scripture written by Pulastya Muni. The statements from Pulastya's scripture have been quoted in Kamalakara's book *Śūdradharmā-tattva*. A short description of the ancestors and descendants of Pulastya Muni is given in *Śrīmad Bhāgavatam* (4.1.34-36). It is known from *Śrīmad Bhāgavatam* that, in the Svārociṣa *manvantara*, Sage Aṅgirā had two sons, of which one was known as Utathya, who was an *avatāra* of Godhead, and the second was known as Bṛhaspati. Havirbhū was the wife of Maharṣi Pulastya. Agastya Ṛṣi (according to evidence in the *Vedas*, Agastya Ṛṣi was reborn as the son of Mitra and Varuṇa) was born by the union of Pulastya Ṛṣi and Havirbhū. In one of his births, that same Agastya Ṛṣi appeared as Jaṭharāgni (fire of digestion). Pulastya Ṛṣi had another son, named Viśravā, who performed severe penance. Viśravā had two wives. One was Iḍaviḍā, from whom Kuvera, the master of all Yakṣas, was born, and the other, Keśinī, from whom three sons were born, named Rāvaṇa, Kumbhakarṇa and Vibhīṣaṇa respectively.

"To disturb him, celestial dancers used to come to the area of Sumeru Mountain where Pulastya Ṛṣi was performing penance. He therefore cursed them that any woman that would come before him would become pregnant. He was staying near the *āśrama* of Tṛṇabindu Ṛṣi, and one day the daughter of Tṛṇabindu, Havirbhū, appeared before him and thus became pregnant. Pulastya Ṛṣi then married Havirbhū to fulfill the request of Sage Tṛṇabindu. Havirbhū gave birth to a son named Viśravā. This Viśravā was the father of Rāvaṇa." (Āśutoṣa Deva's *New Bengali Dictionary*)

While describing the appearance of Śrī Govardhana, Śrī Gargācārya mentioned Pulastya Ṛṣi in his *Garga Saṁhitā*. A summary goes as follows:

At the time when Śrī Kṛṣṇa thought of appearing on the earth to relieve the earth of its burden, He sent His whole abode, 84 *krośas* of land, Govardhana and the Yamunā to earth. Govardhana appeared as the son of Droṇa Parvata on the Shalmali Island in the west of Bhārata (India). Pleased by the arrival of Govardhana, the demigods showered flowers from above. The kings of all mountains (Himālayas, Sumeru, etc.) performed *pūjā* of Govardhana. In their glorification of Govardhana, these mountains mentioned that Govardhana is the site of Lord Śrī Kṛṣṇa's playful escapades in Goloka-dhāma. Govardhana, the king of all mountains and the crown of Goloka, appeared in the form of Lord Śrī Kṛṣṇa's umbrella. Having been glorified by the kings of mountains, Govardhana became famous as Girirāja.

One day, Pulastya Muni, the son of Brahmā and one of the famous Seven Sages, went to Shalmali Island. There he became wonderstruck when he beheld the son of Droṇāncala, the very beautiful mountain called Girirāja, who was full of flowers, fruit trees, water springs and other natural beauties. Droṇāncala offered his prayers to Pulastya Muni when he approached him. Pulastya Muni then addressed Droṇāncala Parvata, "I am Sage Pulastya and I reside in Kāśī (Vārāṇasī). Kāśī is situated on the banks of the Gaṅgā. Viśveśvara Mahādeva also resides there. If any sinful person goes there, he will very quickly attain liberation. I perform penance at Kāśī and it is my desire that I might install your son Girirāja in Kāśī; therefore please give your son to me in charity."

Grieved by the prospect of becoming separated from his son, but fearing the possibility of being cursed by the sage, Droṇāncala reluctantly instructed his son to go to Bhārata with the *muni*.

Girirāja, or Govardhana Parvata, was 8 *yojanas* (approx. equal to 64 miles) long, 5 *yojanas* (approx. equal to 40 miles) wide and 2 *yojanas* (approx. equal to 16 miles) high. When asked how he planned to take such a large mountain with him, the sage replied, "Do not worry about it. I will take Girirāja with me by carrying him on the palm of my hand." Govardhana thereafter agreed to go with the *muni* on one condition: if Pulastya Muni would put him down anywhere along the way, he would stay there and would not move from that place again.

Thereupon, Sage Pulastya vowed to take Girirāja Govardhana to Kāśī without putting him down anywhere along the way. The powerful Govardhana offered his obeisances to his father and placed himself on the palm of the sage. The sage began to walk slowly with Govardhana resting on the palm of his right hand. In this way, the sage eventually reached the Vraja region, slowly but steadily. However, upon observing the natural beauty of Vraja, Govardhana recalled the sweet pastimes of Lord Kṛṣṇa such as His childhood pastimes and later pastimes with Śrīmatī Rādhikā, the *gopīs* and others. He also remembered all the associates of Śrī Kṛṣṇa. After that, Girirāja Govardhana was reluctant to go anywhere except Vraja, so he started to increase his weight. He increased his weight so much that, troubled by his sudden increasing weariness of carrying Girirāja, Pulastya forgot his oath and put Govardhana down in Vraja-bhūmi and began to relax, chant and meditate there.

After going through the daily needs of the body and after performing his various duties, the sage returned and asked Govardhana to climb on his hand again. To his surprise, however, Giri Govardhana refused to do so. As Govardhana did not accede to the repeated requests of the angry Pulastya Muni, he cursed him, saying, "You could not fulfill my desire; may you therefore daily sink into the earth by the measure of one sesame seed." Ever since then Giri Govardhana has been steadily reducing in height by the size of one sesame seed on a daily basis. As long as Bhāgīrathī Gaṅgā and Govardhana Hill remain on this earth, it will not be possible for the effects of Kali-yuga to dominate anywhere.

It is known from the 8th Chapter of the 5th Canto of *Śrīmad Bhāgavatam* that the eldest son of Ṛṣabhadeva attained the birth of a deer while meditating on a young deer at the time of his death. However, due to his *bhakti* for the Supreme Lord, he was granted remembrance of his previous life, despite being born as a deer. As a result of his remembrance, he would stay near sages instead of other deer.

He left his deer mother in a place known as Kālañjara Mountain, where he was born. He then went to the *āśrama* of Pulastya, the favorite place of the sages. It is known from the 11th Chapter of the 12th Canto of *Śrīmad Bhāgavatam* that the Supreme Personality of Godhead, manifesting His potency of time as the sun-god, travels about with a different set of six associates in each of the twelve months. Pulastya Ṛṣi is his associate as a sage for the month of Chaitra.

Pulastya Muni was among the sages accompanying Nārada when he came to have an audience with Śrī Kṛṣṇa at the time when His wives (residents of Dvārakā) met Nārada on the occasion of a solar eclipse. This is mentioned at the end of the 10th Canto of *Śrīmad Bhāgavatam*. It is known from the discussions between Maitreya and Vidura in the 3rd Canto of *Śrīmad Bhāgavatam* that Lord Saṅkarṣaṇa narrated the *Bhāgavatam* to Sanat Kumāra. Saṅkhyāna Muni learned of those same discussions from Sanat Kumāra, and Parāśara Muni and Bṛhaspati in turn learned of them from Sāṅkhyāyana Muni. Later, the extremely merciful Parāśara Ṛṣi, due to the request of Pulastya Muni, recited this *Bhāgavata Purāṇa* to Maitreya Ṛṣi.

Sage Śaradvān

By virtue of a curse from a *brāhmaṇa* boy, Parīkṣit Mahārāja, having taken a vow to fast from food and water until death, arrived on the banks of the Gaṅgā after handing over his kingdom to his son. At that time, all the great minds and thinkers, accompanied by their disciples, as well as sages who could verily sanctify a place of pilgrimage merely by their presence, gathered at that place.

The spot where Mahārāja Parīkṣit sat down is famous as Śukartāla. At present, that place is situated about twenty kilometers away from Muzaffarnagar. There is a bus route going to Śukartāla from Muzaffarnagar. Even today this place is secluded and beautiful. Some of the pious sages who came there at that time are mentioned in the 19th Chapter of the 1st Canto of *Śrīmad Bhāgavatam*:

atrir vaśiṣṭhaś cyavanaḥ śaradvān
ariṣṭanemir bhṛgur aṅgirāś ca
parāśaro gādhi-suto 'tha rāma utathya
indrapramadedhmavāhau
(*Śrīmad Bhāgavatam* 1.19.9)

"Atri, Vaśiṣṭha, Cyavana, Śaradvān, Ariṣṭanemi, Bhṛgu, Aṅgirā, Parāśara, Viśvāmitra, Paraśurāma (son of Gādhi), Utathya, Indrapramada, Idhmavāhu and others arrived at that place."

Kṛṣṇa-dvaipāyana Vedavyāsa has mentioned the name of Śaradvān Muni among the pious saints. However, scant details of Śaradvān Ṛṣi are to be found in any of the scriptures.

gautama gotrasya śaradvātoapatyam gautam-āna
(*Viśvakoṣa*)

"The name of the father of Śaradvān Muni was Gautama. He had one son, named Kṛpa, and a daughter, named Kṛpī. By virtue of being in the lineage of Gautama, Śaradvān's son Kṛpa was also known by the name Gautama. Sage Gautama is the one of the composers of the hymns of the *Ṛg Veda.*" (Āśutoṣa Deva's *New Bengali Dictionary*)

Sage Kaśyapa, Atri, Vaśiṣṭha, Viśvāmitra, Gautama, Jamadagni, and Bhāradvāja were the Saptarṣis during the Vaivasvata *manvantara*. The *Mahābhārata* describes the significance of the name Gautama as follows:

"All darkness was dispelled by the effulgence emanating from his body. He is therefore called Gautama. It is mentioned in *Vāyu Purāṇa* that he takes birth from the meditation of Brahmā during the age of Śveta-vārāha." (as quoted in *Viśvakoṣa*)

The written description of Śaradvān's son Kṛpa as mentioned in the *New Bengali Dictionary* by Āśutoṣa Deva is as follows:

Śaradvān was exceptionally expert in archery. Upon discovering his expertise in the field of archery, Indra sent a damsel named Janapadī to Śaradvān in order to disturb his penance. Thereafter, a son and daughter were born from the womb of Janapadī. However, after their birth, their mother and father deserted them. Later, Mahārāja Śāntanu mercifully looked after them. Therefore, they were named Kṛpa and Kṛpī. Kṛpa became an expert in archery just like his father, and later participated in the battle of Kurukṣetra, siding with the Kauravas (he sided with the Pāṇḍavas after the destruction of the Kaurava Dynasty). He taught the art of archery to Mahārāja Parīkṣit.

In *Harivaṁśa Purāṇa*, details of Śaradvān are described differently:

'Śaradvān had a son named Śatānanda; Śatānanda's son was Śatyadhṛti. Once, upon seeing an Apsarā (celestial dancer), Śatyadhṛti discharged semen on the grass known as *śara*, from which twins were born. Later on Śāntanu looked after them.'

The details of the ancestors and dynasty of Śāntanu are described in *Śrīmad Bhāgavatam*:

mithunaṁ mudgalād bhārmyād divodāsaḥ pumān abhūt
ahalyā kanyakā yasyāṁ śatānandas tu gautamāt

tasya satyadhṛtiḥ putro dhanur-veda-viśāradaḥ
śaradvāṁs tat-suto yasmād urvaśī-darśanāt kila
śara-stambe 'patad reto mithunaṁ tad abhūc chubham

tad dṛṣṭvā kṛpayāgṛhṇāc chāntanur mṛgayāṁ caran
kṛpaḥ kumāraḥ kanyā ca droṇa-patny abhavat kṛpī
(*Śrīmad Bhāgavatam* 9.21.34–36)

"Mudgala, the son of Bharmyāśva, had twins, a boy and a girl. The boy was named Divodāsa, and the girl was named Ahalyā. Śatānanda was born by the union of Ahalyā and Gautama. The son of Śatānanda was Satyadhṛti, who was expert in archery, and the son of Satyadhṛti was Śaradvān. One day, when Śaradvān saw Urvaśī, he discharged semen, which fell on a tussock of *śara* grass. From this semen were born two all-auspicious babies, one male and the other female. While Mahārāja Śāntanu was on a hunting excursion, he saw the male and female children lying in the forest and, out of compassion, took them home. Consequently, the male child was known as Kṛpa, and the female child was named Kṛpī. Kṛpī later became the wife of Droṇācārya."

Sage Pulaha

It is learned from a description given in the 3rd Canto of *Śrīmad Bhāgavatam* that, after receiving his powers from the Lord, Brahmā produced ten sons in order to populate the world. Since Brahmā produced these sons while meditating they became known as *mānasa-putra*. One of these ten sons was Pulaha. These ten *ṛṣis* were born from the different bodily parts of Brahmā, and so it came to be that Pulaha was born from the navel of Brahmā. Pulaha is also one of the Saptarṣis.

As instructed by Brahmā, Kardama Ṛṣi gave his nine daughters to the above-mentioned rulers of mankind, or Prajāpatis. Pulaha Ṛṣi was married to Kardama's daughter Gati. Pulaha had three sons, named Karmaśreṣtha, Varīyān and Sahiṣṇu:

pulahasya gatir bhāryā trīn asūta satī sutān
karmaśreṣṭhaṁ varīyāṁsaṁ sahiṣṇuṁ ca mahā-mate
(*Śrīmad Bhāgavatam* 4.1.38)

Discourses given by Nārada Muni to Prācīnabarhi are described in detail in *Śrīmad Bhāgavatam* Canto 4, Chapter 29. There it is described that most powerful Lord Brahmā, the father of all progenitors; Lord Śiva, Manu, Dakṣa and the other rulers of humankind; the great sages Marīci, Atri, Aṅgirā, Pulastya, Pulaha, Kratu, Bhṛgu, Vaśiṣṭha and Nārada Muni are all stalwart *brāhmaṇas* who are very powerful because of austerities, meditation and education. Nonetheless, they do not possess perfect knowledge about the Supreme Personality of Godhead. Thus, it follows that it is extremely difficult to attain the Supreme Lord.

It is known from the 11th Chapter of the 12th Canto of *Śrīmad Bhāgavatam* that the Supreme Personality of Godhead, manifesting His potency of time as the sun-god, travels about with a different set of six associates in each of the twelve months. Pulaha Ṛṣi is his associate as a sage for the month of Vaiśākha.

It is stated in *Viśvakoṣa* that, according to some, Kśama was the wife of Sage Pulaha and that Kardama, Arvarivata, and Sahiṣṇu were his sons.

It is known from *Śrīmad Bhāgavatam*, Canto 10, Chapter 79, that Lord Baladeva killed the demon named Balvala, who was roaming the sky, by hitting him with a mallet. He then took permission from the sages to leave and went to River Kauśika along with *brāhmaṇas* and took a bath there. He also visited the lake that is known as the source of River Sarayū. From there he went to Prayāga-rāja and took a bath there as well. There, he offered oblations to the demigods, and then went to the *āśrama* of Pulaha Muni. This explains why Lord Baladeva cherished the *āśrama* of Pulaha Muni.

Sage Marīci

marīcir manasas tasya jajñe tasyāpi kaśyapaḥ
dākṣāyaṇyāṁ tato 'dityāṁ vivasvān abhavat sūtaḥ
(*Śrīmad Bhāgavatam* 9.1.10)

"From the mind of Brahmā, Marīci took birth. Marīci's son was Kasyapa and from his wife Aditi, the daughter of Dakṣa Mahārāja, Vivasvān (sun), took birth."

From the 10th Canto of *Śrīmad Bhāgavatam*, it is learned from the statements by Lord Śiva to Durvāsā that Marīci is among the all-knowing sages.

It is mentioned in *Śrīmad Bhāgavatam* in the 12th Chapter of Canto 3 that Brahmā begot ten sons for expanding the universal population. Those ten sons were Marīci, Atri, Aṅgirā, Pulastya, Pulaha, Kratu, Bhṛgu, Vaśiṣṭha, Dakṣa and Nārada respectively. In verses 23-24 it is stated that Nārada was born from the lap of Brahmā, Vaśiṣṭha from his breath, Dakṣa from his thumb, Bhṛgu from his touch, Kratu from his hand, Pulastya from his ears, Aṅgirā from his mouth, Atri from his eyes, Marīci from his mind and Pulaha from his navel.

mriyate pāparāśir yasmin iti mṛ
(mṛkanibhyāmīciḥ | uṇa 4.30)
iti īci, tapaḥ-prabhāvādasya tathātvaṁ.

Marīci was born from the mind of Brahmā. His wife was Kalā, the daughter of Kardama Muni, and his sons were Kaśyapa and Pūrṇimās. He was the most famous sage of his time.

"Oblations should be offered to him every day. He is chief among the Saptarṣis." (*Viśvakoṣa*)

It is mentioned in the *Bhāgavatam*:

patnī marīces tu kalā
suṣuve kardamātmajā
kaśyapaṁ pūrṇimānaṁ
ca yayor āpūritaṁ jagat
Śrīmad Bhāgavatam (4.1.13)

As instructed by Brahmā, Sage Kardama gave his nine daughters to Marīci and the other Prajāpatis, following the ritual specified in the scriptures. He gave away his daughter Kalā to Marīci while giving away Anusūyā to Atri, Śraddhā to Aṅgirā, Havirbhū to Pulastya, Gatī to Pulaha, Kriyā to Kratu, Khyātī to Bhṛgu, Arundhatī to Vaśiṣṭha, and Śāntī to Atharva. Kardama Muni's daughter Kalā, who was married to Marīci, gave birth to two children, whose names were Kaśyapa and Pūrṇimās. Their descendants are spread all over the universe. In *Śrīmad Bhāgavatam*, Chapter 7, Canto 4, Prajāpati Marīci is addressed as being a part of a partial expansion of the Supreme Lord. The 12th Chapter of the 8th Canto of *Śrīmad Bhāgavatam* describes how Lord Śiva was captivated upon beholding the beautiful Mohinī-mūrti manifestation of the Supreme Personality of Godhead. While glorifying the Mohinī-mūrti manifestation, Lord Śiva said that the great *ṛṣis*, headed by Marīci, who were born of the mode of goodness, could not understand this world, created by the illusory energy of the Supreme Personality of Godhead, so what to speak of others, such as the demons and mortal human beings?

In the 21st Chapter of the 8th Canto of *Śrīmad Bhāgavatam*, Lord Vāmanadeva covered the length and breadth of the three worlds by taking only two steps, while having agreed with King Bali to accept an amount of land equivalent to three of His steps. At the time when the Lord's lotus foot entered Satyaloka after covering the three worlds with His first two steps, Lord Brahmā and Marīci along with other *ṛṣis* glorified the lotus feet of the Supreme Lord. Accompanied by other sages, Marīci washed and worshiped the lotus feet of the Lord with various paraphernalia.

While expressing the pain in her heart, Devakī told Śrī Kṛṣṇa, "Kaṁsa cruelly killed six of my sons immediately after birth. I could not even feed them, so I am suffering from tremendous grief. If You bring my sons to me, my agony will go away. You are the omnipotent Lord; therefore You can do anything. To fulfill the desire of Your *guru*, Sāndīpani, You brought back the dead sons of Your *guru* from the abode of Yama and presented them as *guru-dakṣiṇā*."[38]

38 *Guru-dakṣiṇā*: A gift to the *guru* after the completion of education.

Śrī Kṛṣṇa smiled when he learned about Mother Devakī's desire. Actually, those six sons were not the sons of Devakī, but of Marīci. Earlier, Marīci's sons were unable to understand the purport, and had criticized Brahmā for lustily chasing after his own daughter. Thus, due to a curse, they were immediately born as sons of Kālanemi, who was under the sway of Hiraṇyakaśipu.

Once, Kālanemi sent his sons to perform penance without taking the permission of Hiraṇyakaśipu. Because they engaged in an act that was against the rules, Hiraṇyakaśipu cursed Kālanemi that he would kill his own sons. As such, due to Hiraṇyakaśipu's curse, the demon Kālanemi took birth as Kaṁsa in Dvāpara-yuga. The sons of the previous birth of Kaṁsa then took birth as the sons of Devakī. Therefore, in his birth as Kaṁsa, Kālanemi killed his own sons.

However, Devakī understood them to be her sons only. By that time, her sons had taken birth in Sutala-purī. To fulfill the desire of His mother, Śrī Kṛṣṇa went to Sutala-purī and he took those sons from Bali Mahārāja and presented them to his mother. Devakī lovingly placed them on her lap and fed them mother's milk. Marīci's sons suckled milk from the same breast that was suckled by Śrī Kṛṣṇa, so as a result they were liberated from the curse. They offered obeisances to Mother Devakī and came back to Marīci after accepting the divine bodies they had before.

In a lecture delivered at Śrī Saccidānanda Maṭh in Cuttack, Odisha, on July 9th, 1929, His Divine Grace Oṁ Viṣṇupāda 108 Śrī Śrīmad Bhakti Siddhānta Sarasvatī Gosvāmī Ṭhākura, founder of the worldwide Śrī Caitanya Maṭh and Śrī Gauḍīya Maṭh, spoke the following words: *adhokṣaja tattva śravaṇaik vedya.*

Sage Atri

Atri is among the Saptarṣis, born from the mind of Lord Brahmā. In the 12th Chapter of the 3rd Canto of *Śrīmad Bhāgavatam*, Maitreya tells Vidura that, while meditating after receiving his powers from the Supreme Personality of Godhead, Lord Brahmā produced ten sons from his mind for the purpose of procreation. Atri, who was one of those ten sons, was born from the eyes of Brahmā. As ordered by Brahmā, Kardama Ṛṣi gave his nine daughters to the procreators of mankind, the Prajāpatis. He gave his second daughter, Anusūyā, to Sage Atri. Details of the three famous sons of Atri Ṛṣi are given in *Śrīmad Bhāgavatam*, Chapter 1, Canto 4.

When Lord Brahmā ordered Atri Muni, best among those who know of Brahman, to produce generations of offspring after marrying Anasūyā, Atri Muni and his wife went to perform severe austerities in the valley of the mountain known as Ṛkṣa. Ṛkṣa Mountain was full of flowers and laden with *palāśa* flowers and *aśoka* trees, and the sweet sound of water flowing from a waterfall of the River Nirvindhyā could always be heard there.

There, the great sage Atri focused his mind by dint of *prāṇāyāma* (*yogic* breathing exercises), thereby controlling his mind. As such, he performed great penance by standing on one foot for a hundred years, while ingesting nothing but air. He was thinking: *"May the Lord of the universe, of whom I have taken shelter, kindly be pleased and offer me a son exactly like Him."* By the virtue of his *prāṇāyāma,* a blazing fire came out of his head and that fire began scorching the three worlds. At that time, the three deities Brahmā, Viṣṇu and Śiva, accompanied by the inhabitants of the heavenly planets such as the Apsarās, Gandharvas, Siddhas, Vidyādharas and Nāgas, appeared at the *āśrama* of the great sage Atri.

Atri Ṛṣi was very pleased by the arrival of Brahmā, Viṣṇu and Śiva, who are worshiped by the three worlds, and the audience of other *devatas* (demigods) gratified him. He saw that Lord Śiva was riding his bull, Lord Brahmā a swan, and Garuḍa carried Lord Viṣṇu. They were holding a trident, water pot and disc respectively. Atri Muni was greatly pleased to see that the three *devas* were gracious to him. He relieved himself from his penance and offered obeisances by falling flat on the earth before them. He then offered them prayers and flowers. As the effulgence of their bodies dazzled his eyes, he glorified them with folded hands.

Glorifying them, he said, "O Lord Brahmā, Lord Viṣṇu and Lord Śiva, you have divided yourself into three bodies, as you do in every millennium for the creation, maintenance and dissolution of the cosmic manifestation. I performed worship of the Supreme Lord. Among the three of you, whom did I worship? I performed worship unto the Supreme Lord, the possessor of six opulences, by various means, but why have all three of you now appeared simultaneously before me? I am very much confused. Please disclose the reason behind this act."

The trio smiled and said, "Dear *brāhmaṇa*, you are perfect in your determination; therefore, as you have decided, so it will happen. We do not have any separate existence from the Supreme Personality of Godhead, on whom you were meditating and whose knowledge is beyond our senses. We are all dependent upon Him. You will have sons who will represent a partial manifestation of our potency and, because we desire all good fortune for you, those sons will glorify your reputation throughout the world."

Thus, they disappeared after bestowing their blessings upon Atri. Thereafter, from the partial representation of Brahmā, Soma (moon-god) was born; from the partial representation of Viṣṇu, the great mystic Dattātreya was born; and from the partial representation of Śaṅkara (Lord Śiva), Durvāsā was born:

atreḥ patny anasūyā trīn jajñe suyaśasaḥ sutān
dattaṁ durvāsasaṁ somamātmeśa-brahma-sambhavān
(*Śrīmad Bhāgavatam* 4.1.15)

"Anasūyā, the wife of Atri Muni, gave birth to three very famous sons—Soma, Dattātreya and Durvāsā—who were partial representations of Lord Brahmā, Lord Viṣṇu and Lord Śiva. Soma was a partial representation of Lord Brahmā, Dattātreya was a partial representation of Lord Viṣṇu, and Durvāsā was a partial representation of Lord Śiva."

The details of Atri Ṛṣi are mentioned in the 19th Chapter of the 4th Canto of *Śrīmad Bhāgavatam*. Once, King Pṛthu commenced an especially potent *yajña*. This disturbed Indra, who went there in disguise and disrupted the *yajña* by stealing the last horse that would otherwise have topped Indra's *yajña*. However, when Pṛthu's son pursued Indra, after being asked to do so by Atri Ṛṣi, he escaped, leaving the horse behind. That is why Pṛthu's son is known as Vijitāśva. Indra did not give up, though, and being the king of heaven, he stole the now chained horse by covering the sacrificial arena in a dense darkness. Then, upon being encouraged by Atri Ṛṣi to kill Indra, the son of Pṛthu shot arrows at Indra, who was fleeing via the sky. As Indra was scared, he dropped his disguise and ran away, leaving the horse behind. Indra adopted several false forms of a *sannyāsī*. Since then these forms have been adopted by naked Jains, red-dressed Buddhists and Kāpālikas. Annoyed by this Indra's devioius behavior, Pṛthu Mahārāja planned to kill him but Brahmā stopped him.

kaśyapo 'trir vaśiṣṭhaś ca viśvāmitro 'tha gautamaḥ
jamadagnir bhāradvāja iti saptarṣayaḥ smṛtāḥ
(*Śrīmad Bhāgavatam* 8.13.5)

"The Saptarṣis in the Vaivasvata-manvantara were Kaśyapa, Atri, Vaśiṣṭha, Viśvāmitra, Gautama, Jamadagni and Bhāradvāja."

sahasra-śirasaḥ puṁso nābhi-hrada-saroruhāt
jātasyāsīt suto dhātur atriḥ pitṛ-samo guṇaiḥ
(*Śrīmad Bhāgavatam* 9.14.2)

"Lord Viṣṇu (Garbhodakaśāyī Viṣṇu) is also known as Sahasra-śīrṣā Puruṣa. From the lake of His navel sprang a lotus, upon which Lord Brahmā was generated. Atri, the son of Lord Brahmā, was as qualified as his father."

tasya dṛgbhyo 'bhavat putraḥ somo 'mṛtamayaḥ kila
viprauṣadhy-uḍu-gaṇānāṁ brahmāṇā kalpitaḥ patiḥ
(*Śrīmad Bhāgavatam* 9.14.3)

"From Atri's tears of jubilation was born a son named Soma, the moon, who was full of soothing rays. Lord Brahmā appointed him the director of the *brāhmaṇas*, drugs and luminaries."

It is known from *Śrīmad Bhāgavatam* 3.7.4 that the great sage Atri prayed for a son, and the Lord, being satisfied with him, told him that He Himself would become his son. Having said this, the Lord accepted the name Dattātreya (*datta* – "donating," *atreya* – "son of Atri").

Although Kārtavīryārjuna and other persons obtained the wealth of yoga from Dattātreya, they yet created obstacles to the penance of Vaśiṣṭha, Jamadagni and other *ṛṣis*. Such behavior was offensive, and thus Paraśurāma killed them.

ṣaṣṭham atrer apatyatvaṁ
vṛtaḥ prāpto 'nasūyayā
ānvīkṣikīm alarkāya
prahlādādibhya ūcivān
(*Śrīmad Bhāgavatam* 1.3.11)

"When Atri's wife requested a son, God appeared as the son of Atri Ṛṣi in His sixth *avatāra* (Dattātreya). During His appearance on earth He preached transcendental knowledge to Prahlāda and Haihaya, along with other kings and a *brāhmaṇa* named Alarka."

Once, Śīlavatī, a chaste wife devoted to her leprous *brāhmaṇa* husband, was carrying her husband to some destination. Along the way, they passed by Sage Ani Māṇḍavya (pierced by a giant stake, or nail, yet still alive), who put a curse on the leprous *brāhmaṇa* that he would die before sunrise, because Ani Māṇḍavya had come to learn about some bad habits of that *brāhmaṇa*. Śīlavatī, who had accrued some *yogic* powers, then prevented the sun from rising by dint of her powers. As a result, the sun would not rise, and being the wife of the leper *brāhmaṇa* she maintained her vow to stop the sun from rising. Thus, the whole creation was headed for destruction and the demigods became fearful about the situation. After pleading their case, the demigods then managed to console and pacify Śīlavatī with the help of Anusūyā, the wife of Atri Ṛṣi, and thus saved the entire creation from annihilation by convincing her to let the sun rise again.

Atri Ṛṣi was among the sages who went along with Yudhiṣṭhira Mahārāja to visit and obtain the blessings of Bhīṣma, who was lying on a bed of arrows at the battlefield of Kurukṣetra. Atri Ṛṣi was among the sages who were present at the time when Śukadeva Gosvāmī recited *Śrīmad Bhāgavatam* to Parīkṣit Mahārāja. Atri Ṛṣi was also among the sages who cursed the Yādavas in the Pindarka region.

In reference to the *Manu Saṁhitā*, *Viśvakoṣa* and *Śānti-parva* of *Mahābhārata*, it is written in the 1st Chapter of *Manu Saṁhitā* that the creator of the world divided his body into two parts. He produced a man from one part of his body and a woman from the other part. That same creator then created Manu after performing severe penance for a long time. Atri was one of the Prajāpatis who appeared from Manu later on:

marīcimatryaṅgirasau
pulastyaṁ pulahaṁ kratum
pracetasaṁ vaśiṣṭhaṁ ca
bhṛguṁ nāradameva ca
(*Manu Saṁhitā* 1.35)

It is mentioned in the *Śānti-parva* of *Mahābhārata* that Atri Muni was one of the Saptarṣis created by Brahmā. It has been said in *Ṛg Veda* that Atri Muni was a *ṛṣi* of *pāñcajātis* (five castes):

ṛṣiṁ narāvaṁhasaḥ pāñcajanyaṁ
ṛbīsādatriṁ muñcatho gaṇena
(*Ṛg Veda* 1.117.03.1)

It cannot be rightly said which people were counted as *pāñcajātis*. However, referring to another mantra of *Ṛg Veda*, it can be assumed that the word *pāñcajāti* refers to a follower of the five dynasties of Yadu, Turvasu, Druhyu, Anu and Pūru respectively. It is assumed that Atri Ṛṣi was performing the duties of priest for all these five dynasties; therefore, he is known as the *ṛṣi* of *pāñcajātis*. Atri Ṛṣi composed many Vedic mantras.

By quoting evidence from the *Rāmāyaṇa*, we find reference to Sage Atri in *Navīn Bangla Śabdakoṣa*, stating that Lord Rāmacandra stayed for some time in the *āśrama* of Atri Ṛṣi during His stay in the forest. Anusūyā, the wife of Atri, presented various kinds of dresses and ornaments to Sitadevī, and Atri Muni came to bless Rāmacandra on his return to Ayodhyā.

Sage Atharvā

Atharvān: '*atha – jha vanip śaka*'. He is a special sage by the name of Atharvā. It is mentioned in the beginning of *Muṇḍaka Upaniṣad* that he was the eldest son of Brahmā:

brahmā devānāṁ prathamaḥ sambabhūva
viśvasya kartā bhuvanasya goptā.
sa brahma-vidyāṁ sarva-vidyā-pratiṣṭhām
atharvāya jyeṣṭha-putrāya prāha.
atharveṇa yaṁ pravadeta brahmātha
vārtāṁ purovācāṅgire brahma-vidyāṁ
sa bhāradvajāya satyavāhāya prāha
bhāradvājo 'ṅgirase parāvaram.
(*Muṇḍaka Upaniṣad* 1.1-2)

"Lord Brahmā, who is the first-born of the demigods and the creator and protector of the worlds, spoke this knowledge of the Supreme Personality of Godhead, the best of all knowledge, to his eldest son, Atharvān. Atharvān then spoke this spiritual knowledge to Aṅgirā Muni, and Aṅgirā Muni spoke it to Satyavāha Muni of the Bhāradvāja Dynasty. Satyavāha taught that same superior knowledge to Aṅgirasa."

As instructed by Brahmā, Sage Kardama married his nine daughters in a proper ceremony to the *prajāpatis*, the creators of mankind. He gave his nine daughters to nine sages. Among them, he gave Śānti to Atharvā Ṛṣi.

This is mentioned in *Śrīmad Bhāgavatam*:

atharvaṇe 'dadāc chāntiṁ yayā yajño vitanyate
viprarṣabhān kṛtodvāhān sadārān samalālayat
(*Śrīmad Bhāgavatam* 3.24.24)

"He delivered Śānti to Sage Atharvā. Because of Śānti, sacrificial ceremonies are well performed. Thus, Kardama Ṛṣi got the foremost *brāhmaṇas* married, and he maintained them along with their wives."

It is mentioned in the *Śatapatha Brāhmaṇa* that a *ṛṣi* named Dadhyañca was the son of Atharvā. *Tamutvā dadhyaṅṛṣiḥ putra īdhe atharvaṇaḥ* means "Atharvā's son Dadhyañca Ṛṣi lit the fire."

cittis tv atharvaṇaḥ patnī lebhe putraṁ dhṛta-vratam
dadhyañcam aśvaśirasaṁ bhṛgor vaṁśaṁ nibodha me
(*Śrīmad Bhāgavatam* 4.1.42)

"Citti, the wife of Sage Atharvā, gave birth to a son named Dadhīci,[39] who performed severe penances. Now you may hear from me about the descendants of Sage Bhṛgu."

It is mentioned in *Mārkaṇḍeya Purāṇa* that the *Atharva Veda* originated from the northern mouth of Brahmā (Lord Brahmā has four faces). The *Atharva Veda* deals with many Vedic rituals and procedures.

It has been mentioned in *Viśvakoṣa* that the actual name of the *Atharva Veda* is *Athavaṅgirāsa*. The word *Athavaṅgirāsa* is thus abbreviated to become *Atharva Veda*. It is necessary to understand the meaning of the word *atharva*. The word *atharva* is mentioned many times in the *Ṛg Veda*. Sayanācārya has generally given the meaning of *atharva* to be *ṛṣi*.

39 "According to the *Vedas*, Dadhīci is the son of Atharvā Ṛṣi, but according to the *Purāṇas* he is the son of either Maharṣi Bhṛgu or Cyavana. He is a great devotee of Lord Śiva. When Dakṣa organized a *yajña* without Śiva, Dadhīci left the site of the *yajña*. Devarāja Indra felt intimidated by observing the effect of Dadhīci's penance, and thus disturbed his penance by sending the celestial dancer named Alambuva. He donated all his bones when requested by Indra to kill Vṛtrāsura. Indra killed Vṛtrāsura with the help of the Vajra weapon made from his bones." (*New Bengali Dictionary* of Āśutoṣa Deva)

According to the Persian scripture *Avesta*, written by Jorstara, the meaning of *atharva* is Agni-purohita (priest of fire). (Reference from *Ig Sahib*)

The word *atharva* also appears in the *Atharva Veda* at many places. For example, we find:

ajījano hi varuṇa svadhāvan atharvāṇaṁ
pitaraṁ devabandhum
(*Atharva Veda* 5.11.11)

"O Svadhavana Varuṇa! You gave birth to Atharvā."

This could very easily be understood to mean that Atharvā is the name of a *ṛṣi* only. There is evidence in the *Atharva Veda* that there was sage called Atharvā, who was the elder son of the original creator, Brahmā. Aṅgirā is also an important *ṛṣi*. The name Āṅgirāsa is mentioned in the *Ṛg Veda* and other *Vedas* also. It appears that the predecessors of Atharvā and Aṅgirā have compiled the Atharvaṅgirāsa Saṁhita, or *Atharva Veda*. According to some, the predecessors of Bhṛgu have written many of the *mantras* of this particular *Veda*.

According to the *New Bengali Dictionary* of Āśutoṣa Deva, Atharvā is a distinctive sage of the Vedic period. He is the eldest son of Śrī Brahmā. He is the one who first ignited fire and commenced *yajñas*, etc., among the Āryans (noble ones). He separated the *Atharva Veda* from the other three *Vedas* and it is thus named after him.

According to page 289, 2nd column, 12th volume of *The New Encyclopedia Britannica*:

"To these three *Vedas*—*Ṛg*, *Yajur* and *Sāma*—known as *trayi-vidyā* (threefold knowledge), is added a fourth, the *Atharva Veda*, a collection of hymns, magic spells and incantations that represents a more folk level of religion and remains partly outside the Vedic sacrifice."

Also, on page 462, 1st column, 2nd volume of *The New Encyclopedia Britannica* we find:

"Finally, the *Atharva Veda* belongs to the comparatively late *Gopatha Brāhmaṇa* relating only secondarily to *Saṁhitās* and *Brāhmaṇas*. It is in part concerned with the role played by the *brāhmaṇa* (prayer) priest who supervised the sacrifice."

In ancient days *brāhmaṇas* used to read the *Ṛg*, *Yajur* and *Sāma Vedas* with devotion and considered that there were only three *Vedas*. Therefore, the *Vedas* were also known as *trayi*. It is found by exploring *Manu Saṁhitā* and other ancient scriptures that they are full of references to the three *Vedas*. It is written in *Viśvakośa*: "For the perfection of *yajña*, the *brāhmaṇas* extracted the *Ṛg Veda* from Agni (fire-god), the *Yajur Veda* from Vāyu (air-god) and the *Sāma Veda* from Sūrya, the sun-god (*Manu Saṁhitā*)."

The Prajāpatis heated the three worlds and extracted the result obtained by that process. More specifically, this implies that they took Agni (fire-god) from earth, Vāyu (air-god) from space and Sūrya (sun-god) from heaven. Later, they proceeded to heat those three demigods. The result of that was also extracted. The result was the *Ṛg Veda* extracted from Agni, the *Yajur Veda* from Vāyu, and the *Sāma Veda* from Sūrya. Then the Prajāpatis proceeded to heat the three *Vedas*. By heating these three *Vedas*, *bhu* from the *Ṛg*, *bhuvaḥ* from the *Yajur* and *svara* (musical tone) from the *Sāma Veda* were obtained. It can thus be concluded that the *brāhmaṇas* of ancient times used to study only the *Ṛg*, *Yajur* and *Sāma Vedas*. The three classifications of *Ṛg*, *Yajur* and *Sāma Veda* were established for the purpose of *yajña*. The *Atharva Veda*, however, is not suitable for *yajña*, as in this *Veda* only topics of peace, health, customs, etc., are discussed.

Offerings to and glorifications of Indra, Sūrya, Agni, the Aśvinī Kumāras and other demigods are given in the *Ṛg Veda*. However, the *Atharva Veda* is an extraordinary scripture in the sense that it glorifies Kāla, Yama, death, demigods, demons and others. The descriptions of not only the things that exist in this world, but also of all the things that one can imagine are given. Nowhere in the *Ṛg Veda* do we find sages who offer obeisances to wicked men. In the *Atharva Veda*, *mantras* to increase diseases are also found. Such things are rarely found in the other *Vedas*. *Mantras* to control one's master, to remove the effects of poison, to kill a foe, to make a barren woman pregnant, etc., can be found in this *Veda*.

The supremacy of *Atharva Veda* has been indicated in the *Vāyu Purāṇa*:

bahvṛco hanti vai rāṣṭraṁ adhvaryur nāśayet sutam
chandogo dhanaṁ nāśayet tasmād atharvaṇo guruḥ

"The *bahvṛca* (priest of the *Ṛg Veda*) ruins the king, the *adhavaryu* (priest of the *Yajur Veda*) ruins children and the *candoga* (priest of the *Sāma Veda*) ruins wealth; therefore the *Atharva Veda* is superior among all."

In this verse of the *Vāyu Purāṇa*, the importance of the *Atharva Veda* has been specially mentioned. The priests of the *Atharva Veda* protect the *yajña*. The person knowledgeable in the *Atharva Veda* pacifies the troubles of heaven, space and earth. It is therefore necessary to maintain Bhṛgu in the south. Only Brahmā, who is a knower of the *Atharva Veda*, can calm such troubles. The *adhvaryu*, *candoga* or *bahavṛca* cannot calm them. Brahmā can also provide protection from demons. Therefore, the learner of the *Atharva Veda* is Brahmā.

It has been mentioned in *Śrīmad Bhāgavatam* 10.74.9 that Yudhiṣṭhira Mahārāja performed a *yajña* and, with the permission of Śrī Kṛṣṇa, selected a number of *brāhmaṇas* who were Vedic experts. It is a essential to select *brāhmaṇas* who are knowledgeable in the *Vedas* for a *yajña* to be successful. Any *yajña* performed without *brāhmaṇas* is fruitless, so, after contemplation, King Yudhiṣṭira appointed a number of eligible *brāhmaṇas* as priests for his *yajña*, and Atharvā Ṛṣi was one of them.

Sage Devala

Devala was an exceptional sage and a speaker of religious scriptures. He was the son of Sage Asita. His body was bent in eight places (*aṣṭāvakra*) due to the curse of Rambhā, a celestial damsel. (*Viśvakoṣa*)

It is written in Āśutoṣa Deva's *New Bengali Dictionary* that Devala Ṛṣi was the son of Asita Ṛṣi. He would practice *yoga* with Jaigīṣavya Ṛṣi[40] in the same *āśrama*. Devala Ṛṣi observed that Jaigīṣavya Ṛṣi attained mystical powers before he did. Thus, he became his disciple (*Ṛg Veda*).

ahaṁ yugānāṁ ca kṛtaṁ dhīrāṇāṁ devalo 'sitaḥ
dvaipāyano 'smi vyāsānāṁ kavīnāṁ kāvya ātmavān
(*Śrīmad Bhāgavatam* 11.16.28)

"Among ages I am Satya-yuga, the age of truth, and among steady sages I am Devala and Asita. Among those who have divided the *Vedas*, I am Kṛṣṇa-dvaipāyana Vedavyāsa, and among learned scholars I am Śukrācārya, the knower of spiritual science."

Devala Ṛṣi is mentioned in the 4th Chapter of the 9th Canto of *Śrīmad Bhāgavatam* where the details of King Ambarīsa are narrated. When Durvāsā Ṛṣi tried to punish Ambarīṣa Mahārāja, Sudarśana-cakra (disc weapon) began to chase and burn him. To save himself Durvāsā Ṛṣi fled in all the ten directions one after the other, for example, under the ocean and in the cave of Sumeru Mountain, but he could not get relief, so he went to Brahmā in Satyaloka. When Brahmā said he could not help, he took refuge of his father, Mahādeva. When Śrī Mahādeva consoled Durvāsā Ṛṣi, he mentioned Devala Ṛṣi among the omniscient sages. Śrī Mahādeva said to Sage Durvāsā, "I, Sanat-kumāra, Nārada, the worshipable Brahmā, Kapila, Apāntaratam (Vyāsadeva), Devala, Yamāsuri, Marīci and other important sages are all mystics and no one is less than the other. Though we are omniscient, being engulfed by the external potency of the Supreme Lord we cannot understand Him, so how can I face the *cakra* of the Supreme Lord?"

The incident of Gajendra Mokṣa is narrated in the 8th Canto of *Śrīmad Bhāgavatam*. The devotee of Lord Viṣṇu named Indradyumna, the king of Pāṇḍudeśa, was born as the elephant king, Gaja, in his next birth due to the curse of Agastya Muni. When Gaja was bathing with his wife and children and other elephants in the Ṛtumata garden of Varuṇa Deva, a powerful crocodile caught him. When he failed to free himself after a struggle of a thousand years, he glorified and took refuge of Lord Nārāyaṇa. The Lord was satisfied and arrived on the scene riding on the back of Garuḍa, His eagle carrier. Lord Nārāyaṇa rescued Gaja after killing the crocodile. The crocodile had been a Gandharva named Hūhū in his previous birth. One day Hūhū was playing water games with his wives in a lake. At that time, Sage Devala came to bathe in the river. In a playful mood, the Gandharva swam under the water and caught

40 Sage Jaigīṣavya went to the *āśrama* of sages Asita and Devala at Āditya Tirtha to perform penance. There he attained mystical powers. He preached to the sages Asita and Devala about the *dharma* of liberation. (*Mahābhārata*)

hold of the sage's legs and pulled. This annoyed the sage and he cursed him that he would take birth as a crocodile. Hūhū panicked and with anxiety offered prayers and praises to the sage while asking him for forgiveness. Then the sage blessed him and said, "At the time of the liberation of Gajendra the elephant, you will be liberated also by the disc of Śrī Hari."

It is described in the last chapter of the 1st Canto of *Śrīmad Bhāgavatam* that when cursed by a *brāhmaṇa*, Parīkṣit Mahārāja came to Sukartāla on the banks of the Gaṅgā River, and many known sages along with their disciples approached the place on the pretext of pilgrimage. Sage Devala was also there:

medhātithir devala ārṣṭiṣeṇo bhāradvājo
gautamaḥ pippalādaḥ
maitreya aurvaḥ kavaṣaḥ kumbhayonir
dvaipāyano bhagavān nāradaś ca
(*Śrīmad Bhāgavatam* 1.19.10)

"Medhātithi, Devala, Ārṣṭiṣeṇa, Bhāradvāja, Gautama, Pippalāda, Maitreya, Aurva, Kavaṣa, Kumbhayoni, Dvaipāyana and the great personality Nārada were present among the saints in the assembly of Parīkṣit Mahārāja-jī."

According to *Śrīmad Bhāgavatam* (10.84.3-5), Devala Ṛṣi was also among the sages who came for an audience with Śrī Kṛṣṇa at Śrī Kurukṣetra, at the time of the solar eclipse when Śrī Kṛṣṇa arrived with His family.

Sage Kratu

Kratu was born from the thought of Brahmā. He married Kriyā, the daughter of Devahūti and Sage Kardama. Sixty thousand Bālakhilya *ṛṣis* were born from them. (*Śrīmad Bhāgavatam*)

In Āśutoṣa Deva's *New Bengali Dictionary*, it is quoted from the *Viṣṇu Purāṇa* that Sannati was the wife of Kratu, and that 60,000 Bālakhilya *ṛṣis* were born from Sannati. It has been also described in the *Rāmāyaṇa* that 88,000 *ṛṣis* were born from Brahmā and that they are the Bālakhilya Ṛṣis.

In the 12th Chapter of the 3rd Canto of *Śrīmad Bhāgavatam* during the discussions between Sage Maitreya and Vidura regarding the creation, it is stated that, for the purpose of expansion, Brahmā produced ten sons, who were famous as the Prajāpatis. Kratu Ṛṣi is one of those Prajāpatis, having appeared from the hands of Brahmā. It is mentioned in the 24th Chapter of the 3rd Canto of *Śrīmad Bhāgavatam* that Sage Kardama, when asked by Brahmā, bestowed his daughters to the Prajāpatis.

kratror api kriyā bhāryā vālakhilyān asūyata
ṛṣīn ṣaṣṭi-sahasrāṇi jvalato brahma-tejasā
(*Śrīmad Bhāgavatam* 4.1.39)

"Kratu's wife, Kriyā, gave birth to 60,000 great sages, named the Vālakhilyas (famous *vānaprasthas*). All these sages were greatly advanced in spiritual knowledge, and their bodies were illuminated by such knowledge."

It is mentioned in the seventeenth verse of Chapter 13 of the 4th Canto of *Śrīmad Bhāgavatam* that Ulmuka and Puṣkariṇī were the mother and father of Kratu. They had six sons, namely: Aṅga, Sumanā, Khyāti, Kratu, Aṅgirā and Gaya.

It is mentioned in the thirty-fourth verse of Chapter 6 of the 6th Canto of *Śrīmad Bhāgavatam* that Vaiśvānara, the son of Manu, had four beautiful daughters. One of those four, who was named Hayaśirā, was married to Kratu Muni.

It is described in the 61st Chapter of the 10th Canto of *Śrīmad Bhāgavatam* that Lord Kṛṣṇa had 16,000 wives and each had ten sons. The name of one of the ten sons of Jāmbavantī was also Kratu.

In the 74th Chapter of the 10th Canto it is mentioned that of the *brāhmaṇas* selected as the priests for the *rājasuya-yajña* performed by Yudhiṣṭhira Mahārāja with authorization from Śrī Kṛṣṇa, one was Sage Kratu.

Sage Gokarṇa

Śrī Kṛṣṇa-dvaipāyana Vedavyāsa composed eighteen *Purāṇas*. Among them, six are *sāttvika Purāṇas*, in the mode of goodness, and one of these is the *Padma Purāṇa*. In the *Uttara-khaṇḍa* (1st part) of *Padma Purāṇa*, in the section glorifying *Śrīmad Bhāgavatam*, the details of Ātmadeva, Gokarṇa and Dhundhukārī are mentioned.

When Śaunaka and other sages expressed their desire to hear the discussions between Sanaka-kumāra, Sanandana-kumāra, Sanātana-kumāra, Sanat-kumāra (Four Kumāras) and Sage Nārada regarding the procedure of *saptāha-yajña*, at that time the episode of Ātmadeva, Gokarṇa and Dhundhukārī was discussed.

Nārada Gosvāmī expressed his desire to learn about the *saptāha-yajña* for the supreme salvation of sinful living beings, conditioned souls, and even birds and animals. In reply, Śrī Sanaka and the other Kumāras, residents of Vaikuṇṭha, said, "Even a sinner, a person with poor conduct, one who is angry, who is crooked or passionate, who is a liar, who does not respect one's mother and father, who does not follow *varṇāśrama-dharma*, who is a boaster, a drunkard, a slayer of *brāhmaṇas*, a gold thief or cheater, one who is cruel, and other types of sinners may become free of sin and attain Vaikuṇṭha by means of a *saptāha-yajña*. Please listen to an ancient story in this connection. Merely by listening to this episode one will be relieved from all sins:

In bygone times, there was a beautiful city on the banks of River Tungabhadra. *Padma Purāṇa* says that the name of the city was Kohala. The residents of that city were righteous followers of *varṇāśrama*. Ātmadeva, a rich *brāhmaṇa* who was an expert in Vedic knowledge, also lived there. His wife, Dhundhulī, was a beautiful woman from an aristocratic family who was skilled in household affairs, but she had a rigid and compelling nature. She was also cruel, pitiless, miserly, insensitive to the feelings of others and rebellious by nature. The *brāhmaṇa* was rich, so there was no shortage and they possessed all the things necessary for a happy household such as a beautiful home and furnishings for comfort, but they were still unhappy because they did not have any children. They did not get any child in spite of freely donating cows, land, gold, etc. Ātmadeva was desperate, as he could not beget a child even after fifty years. He remained distressed. One day he left home in such a condition and, after walking for some time, entered a dense forest. He felt thirsty during the afternoon and became restless, so he began to search for water. Then he saw a pond. He went to the pond, drank some water and sat under the shade of a tree on a bank of that pond. Fortunately for him, at that time a sage arrived at the pond and began to drink water. After the sage had satiated his thirst, he also sat down under the tree. Ātmadeva was attracted to him and approached him. He offered obeisances but continued to take deep breaths. The sage asked with compassion, "O best among *brāhmaṇas*! What is troubling you? Please do not worry; you may express your grief without any hesitation."

The *brāhmaṇa* replied, "How might I describe my grief? I am so unfortunate that neither demigods nor *brāhmaṇas* accept with pleasure anything offered by me. I see everything as void in the absence of a child of my own. I have come here only to give up my life. Everything I own—my house, wealth, dynasty and even my life—is useless without a son. I am unaware of the wrongs I committed in my previous life. However, I have observed that I am staying childless, and the cows that I take care of do not reproduce. The trees that I plant do not give fruits and flowers. Therefore, it will be better if this cursed life should not continue." The *brāhmaṇa* then began to weep loudly. The sage consoled him by saying, "O *brāhmaṇa*! You will not get a son in this life because of your previous deeds, and I see that you may not get a son in your next seven births as well. O *brāhmaṇa*! Please remember the story of Mahārāja Citraketu, and what happened in his life. One whose efforts are not appreciated by destiny may never get happiness from a son. If destiny is unfavorable and one forcibly strives for that, then he or she will attain only grief instead of happiness.

"Think calmly about the terrible pains suffered by King Bhagīratha and King Sagara for want of a son. You should therefore abandon the desire for a son." The *brāhmaṇa* replied, "I cannot live without a son. Therefore, O great performer of penance, please bless me with a son by your mystical powers, even though I am not supposed to have a son." When he heard such statements from the *brāhmaṇa*, that great sage gave him a fruit and said, "O *brāhmaṇa*! Please give this fruit to your wife to eat. If your wife observes truth and cleanliness for one year, she will certainly get a child." Then the sage left. The *brāhmaṇa* returned to his house and told everything to his wife and asked her to eat the fruit. But Dhundhulī did not want to eat the fruit. After her husband had left, the cruel and rude Dhundhulī went to her friend and began to weep, saying, "My dear friend, I am in great trouble. My husband has given me this fruit that he received from a sage in order to get a son, and sages do not lie. Therefore, I will surely become pregnant. Then I will not be able to eat properly. I will not be able to perform household work. There is much wealth in my house, so if the dacoits come to loot it, how will I be able to run away? Also, if the child does not come out of the womb, like Śukadeva, the son of Vyāsadeva, how will I possibly take it out? If the child should bend at the time of delivery, I will die. Besides that, I have heard that the time of delivery is very painful. Dear friend, please tell me how I can possibly bear that pain? I will become weak. At that time, my husband's sister will come and take away all my wealth. As far as I am concerned, it is beyond me to follow the path of truth and cleanliness. I have observed that mothers endure much hardship bringing up their children. According to me, a woman can only be happy if she is childless and widowed."

Not willing to fulfill the desire of her husband, she did not eat the fruit. However, when her husband asked her, she replied that she had eaten it. Fortunately, her sister came to stay at her place. She discussed the pains of pregnancy with her. Her sister told her that she was pregnant and that she would gladly give her child to Dhundhulī at birth and that in the meantime she should act like a pregnant woman. Furthermore, she told her that her husband was poor and needed money, so he wouldn't say anything or interfere if he was given some money. Her sister promised to help her and asked her that, in order to check the truth of the sage's words, they should feed the fruit to a cow. Acting upon female instinct, Ātmadeva's wife did as advised by her sister.

Dhundhulī's sister gave birth to a child at the appropriate time and her husband secretly took the child to Dhundhulī. The sober Ātmadeva believed his wife when she proclaimed that she had given birth to a son. The villagers were pleased to hear of the birth of a son after such a long time. Ātmadeva performed the *jāta-karma-saṁskāra* rituals and gave wealth to *brāhmaṇas* in charity. One day, Dhundhulī informed her husband that for no reason she could discern, there was no milk in her breasts for the child. She therefore wanted her sister, whose child had died, to come and stay with them for a few days. In the interest of his son's life, Ātmadeva agreed. Mother Dhundhulī named the boy Dhundhukārī. Three months after the birth of Dhundhukārī, the household cow of Ātmadeva also gave birth to a human-like calf. That child was very beautiful and possessed a golden brilliance. All the people were astonished at the birth of the human calf and praised the luck of Ātmadeva. No one could understand how the human calf was born to a cow. Observing the child's cow-like ears, Ātmadeva affectionately named him Gokarṇa.

Both the children grew under the love and care of Ātmadeva. Gokarṇa grew to become graceful, wise, obedient, intelligent and virtuous with a pleasing personality, whereas Dhundhukārī grew to become a great rogue, who engaged in many foul activities. He did not have any schedule for bathing and eating. He became non-vegetarian and even used to take away and eat things touched by the dead. He possessed a very angry disposition and engaged in heinous activities such as stealing, violence, arson, and throwing other children in wells, along with harassing the blind and destitute. He continually associated with dog-eaters and always carried a trap to hunt and kill animals and birds. Gradually, he became involved with prostitutes and began to drain his father's wealth. When his parents tried to stop him from such activities, he would beat them and take away their property. In this way, when he became penniless, Ātmadeva began to cry and said, "It would have been much better if my wife had remained childless, but what should I do now? Where should I go? Who will console me in my grief? It would better if I were to die." Observing his father crying, Gokarṇa preached to him by saying, "O father! This world is temporary and full of sorrows. Who is a father here and who is a son? All this is but the illusion of false identification. The living being enchanted by *māyā* suffers day and night from the countless troubles of this world. Indra, the king of the demigods, is not happy in heaven despite experiencing enormous amounts of sense pleasure. The opulent and glorious great kings of this world are also unhappy. Only sages who are detached from material sense objects are happy. Therefore, please abandon the affection for your son and leave for the forest. Today or tomorrow this body will surely be destroyed. It is better to strive for one's eternal benefit before this body is destroyed." Listening to the virtuous and religious Gokarṇa, Ātmadeva resolved to go to the forest, but first he enquired how he would be able to free himself from his attachment to wife and son.

Gokarṇa replied, "O father! Stop identifying yourself with this body made of bone and flesh. Stop considering the relatives of this human body as your own. Do not get attached to any object of this world, by falsely taking that object as eternal. Engage yourself with full concentration in devotion for the ever-blissful Lord. There is no duty superior to devotion to the Lord. May you discard all worldly duties and take refuge of the Supreme Lord. Serve His pure devotees and make such efforts that the mind is not diverted by sense pleasures.

Therefore, dispense with blaming others and resolve to perform devotion to the Lord. This is the only duty of all humans."

Impressed by the sweet and powerful words of his son, Ātmadeva left for the forest while meditating upon the pastimes of Lord Kṛṣṇa, with the aim of discarding the sorrows of the world. He took the 10th Canto of *Śrīmad Bhāgavatam* with him and, in the forest, would recite it every day. By performing *kīrtana* of the Name, Form, Qualities and Pastimes of Śrī Kṛṣṇa he eventually became free from the sorrows of the world and attained Śrī Kṛṣṇa.

Dhundhukārī began to wreak more harm by his destructive activities after his father had gone to the forest. Due to his lust for prostitutes, he demanded money from his mother, but when his mother did not want to give him any, he became furious and beat her, saying, "Give me money now or else I shall burn you to death." Grieved and panicked, his mother jumped into a well and died. Meanwhile, the detached and learned Gokarṇa left for pilgrimage.

Dhundhukārī became utterly negligent in the absence of his parents. He brought five prostitutes to his house and committed heinous actions for their pleasure. He was out of his mind. Those wicked women demanded many ornaments, so, blinded by passion for them, Dhundhukārī stole jewelry, money and clothes from many places and gave that loot to the prostitutes. Once, the prostitutes discussed among themselves at night. "Now Dhundhukārī does not have any money, so he gets money by stealing. One day he will be caught, and the king may punish him by putting him to death. We could live in comfort with the wealth we have now. It is therefore better to escape quietly after murdering him." The sinful prostitutes tried to kill the sleeping Dhundhukārī by tying a noose around his neck, but when this did not kill him they threw burning charcoal on his body. The burned Dhundhukārī suffered greatly before dying, after which the prostitutes buried him. No one found out about this heinous act. For as long as the prostitutes lived there, when someone asked about Dhundhukārī they would reply, "Dear Dhundhukārī has gone somewhere to earn money, but we do not know where."

Wise persons, who seek their own welfare, should never rely on wicked women. Passionate people find the love of prostitutes like nectar, but the results of this are very frightening, as the feelings of wicked women are like a sharp knife. The prostitutes ran away, taking the Dhundhukārī's money with them. Due to his sins, Dhundhukārī became a ghost. He began to roam here and there like a cyclone, because of sufferings resulting from heat, cold, thirst and hunger. He began to repent for his sins. When the wise Gokarṇa learned about the death of his brother, he immediately sensed his pitiable situation and performed oblations (*piṇḍa-dāna*) at Gaya for him. He also performed *śrāddha* (oblation ceremony) wherever he went on pilgrimage. While on pilgrimage he reached his birth town, Kohala, and went to his father's house to sleep, without asking anyone. The ghost Dhundhukārī observed his brother sleeping and began to scare him at midnight by assuming forms such as a sheep, an elephant, an anaconda, a camel, an ox, Indra, a human and fire. The great sage Gokarṇa understood that this was an act of some ghost. Fearlessly, he asked the the ghost to identify himself but Dhundhukārī could not speak even though he wanted to. He could merely weep and cry loudly. Gokarṇa sprinkled pure water (empowered by *mantra*) on the ghost, thereby enabling the ghost to speak. Then the ghost Dhundhukārī pitifully requested Gokarṇa, "O brother! I am Dhundhukārī. I lost my *brāhmaṇa* virtues due to my bad actions. I performed uncountable foul deeds and committed immeasurable violence to so many persons. Those prostitutes for whom I gave up all my possessions ended up killing me in a merciless fashion. I am greatly suffering after becoming a ghost and am surviving only on air. You are a well-wishing sage; you are an ocean of mercy, so please liberate me from all this." Gokarṇa said to his brother, "I knew earlier about your bad state, and therefore I performed oblations for you, but you did not get salvation; this is quite amazing. I am unaware of any means to liberate you, other than performing *śrāddha* at Gaya."

The ghost Dhundhukārī once again prayed humbly, "For a wretched soul like me, it will not be possible to attain liberation, even after performing oblations one hundred times at Gaya. I am suffering intensely. Could you please arrange for some other means to liberate me?" Gokarṇa was surprised to hear such words from the ghost Dhundhukārī. He consoled Dhundhukārī and wondered about other means to liberate him, but he could not decide on anything, even after thinking about it all night.

The residents of Kohala and the surrounding area recognized Gokarṇa as a devotee and had great faith in him. When they saw him in the morning they came and sat around him. Gokarṇa narrated the whole incident of the previous night. There were many intelligent and learned persons as well as Vedic experts among those present. However, even they could not advise anything. Thus, they suggested that Gokarna should seek the help of the sun-god in this matter.

By his yogic powers, Gokarṇa stopped the movement of the sun, offered obeisances to him and sought the means of liberation for Dhundhukārī. The sun-god instructed Gokarṇa, "Dhundhukārī will be liberated by a *saptāha-yajña* (seven-day narration) of *Śrīmad Bhāgavatam*."

It is mentioned in *Padma Purāṇa* that when Gokarṇa failed to find a way to liberate Dhundhukārī, the *brāhmaṇas* of that place glorified the sun-god for a very long time. Pleased by this, the sun-god announced that, as a consequence of the good deeds of Ātmadeva, the son of Dhundhulī would be liberated after hearing *Śrīmad Bhāgavatam* for a week from Gokarṇa.

The news of the narration of *Śrīmad Bhāgavatam* spread everywhere. The lame, blind, elderly, sinful, and all types of people from many places arrived there to listen to *Śrīmad Bhāgavatam*. The demigods were astonished to see such a large gathering of people. After this, Gokarṇa sat on a *vyāsāsana* (seat of Vyāsā) and began reciting *Śrīmad Bhāgavatam* as if to an audience of Vaiṣṇavas and *brāhmaṇas*. The ghost Dhundhukārī also came and, looking for an appropriate place to sit, found a bamboo stick with seven knots. He entered that bamboo in the form of air and began listening to the *Bhāgavatam* intently. Every day, Gokarṇa would take rest after the recitation of *Śrīmad Bhāgavatam* and a strange incident would occur: a knot of bamboo would burst with a great sound in the presence of the audience. In this way, Dhundhukārī became liberated and attained Vaikuṇṭha after all the seven knots of bamboo burst one by one.

Gokarṇa was surprised and pleased to see the divine body of his brother. At that time, he had a dark complexion similar to clouds; he was dressed in yellow and around his neck he wore *tulasī* beads; he had a crown on his head and *kuṇḍalas* (ornaments worn on the ear) on his ear lobes. After liberation from the ghost species, Dundhukārī paid obeisances to his brother and said, "O giver of salvation, my brother! I am released from being a ghost because of you. It is glorious to hear and speak of *Śrīmad Bhāgavatam*. Glorious is the weeklong recitation of *Śrīmad Bhāgavatam*. As fire burns wood, similarly all sins turn to ashes upon listening to *Śrīmad Bhāgavatam*. The births of those who do not listen to or speak about *Śrīmad Bhāgavatam*, even though they are born in Bhārata, are in vain." While Dhundhukārī was glorifying the hearing and recitation of *Śrīmad Bhāgavatam*, denizens of Vaikuṇṭha appeared with a celestial plane to take him to Śrī Hari. Gokarṇa promptly asked those associates of Śrī Hari why they had brought only one plane to take Dhundhukārī to Vaikuṇṭha. He asked, "Why did you not bring many planes for this pure-hearted audience? Why are you partial?"

The associates of Lord Viṣṇu replied, "It is correct that everyone did hear *Śrīmad Bhāgavatam*, but they did not meditate upon what they heard. Thus, the result is different. The ghost Dhundhukārī concentrated on listening while observing a fast, and simultaneously he meditated upon what he was hearing. Unsteady knowledge is useless. The real fruit is achieved by listening humbly and intently with faith to the words of a spiritual master." Thereafter, the residents of Kohala attained Vaikuṇṭha after intently listening to Gokarṇa reciting *Śrīmad Bhāgavatam* in the month of Śrāvaṇa. Śāṇḍilya, who was a great sage among sages, meditated upon this pious incident at Citrakūṭa Mountain. If one merely listens to this narration, all one's sins are destroyed. One's ancestors become satisfied if one performs recitation of *Śrīmad Bhāgavatam* at the time of *śrāddha*.

Sage Maitreya

The details of Maitreya Ṛṣi are described by Śrī Kṛṣṇa-dvaipāyana Vyāsadeva Ṛṣi in *Śrīmad Bhāgavatam*, which is the essence of all scriptures. According to *Śrīmad Bhāgavatam*, the father of Sage Maitreya was Sage Kuśāru. He is addressed as Kauśārava in the 26th Verse, 4th Chapter of the 3rd Canto of *Śrīmad Bhāgavatam*. From this it is confirmed that Maitreya Ṛṣi was the son of Kuśāru Ṛṣi. Maitreya Ṛṣi was the disciple of Parāśara Ṛṣi, the father of Śrī Kṛṣṇa-dvaipāyana Vyāsadeva Ṛṣi: *maitreya parāśarasya śiṣyah*. The relationship between Maitreya and Vyāsadeva is described in Śrī Viśvanātha Cakravartī's *Śrīmad Bhāgavatam* commentary 3.4.9, where Uddhava describes Sage Maitreya as a friend of Śrī Kṛṣṇa-dvaipāyana Vyāsadeva as well as a *mahā-bhāgavata*, a great devotee and knower of *Śrīmad Bhāgavatam*.

It is written in *Śrīmad Bhāgavatam*:

tasmin mahā-bhāgavato dvaipāyana-suhṛt-sakhā
lokān anucaran siddha āsasāda yadṛcchayā
(*Śrīmad Bhāgavatam* 3.4.9)

"O Vidura! At that time, after traveling in many parts of the world, Maitreya, a great devotee of the Lord and a friend and well-wisher of the great sage Kṛṣṇa-dvaipāyana Vyāsa reached that spot out of his own perfect accord."

Parīkṣit Mahārāja requested Śrī Śukadeva Gosvāmī to narrate the discussions between Sage Maitreya and Śrī Vidura, and Śrī Sūta Gosvāmī narrated the same to Śaunaka and the other sages. Dhṛtarāṣṭra, instead of halting his son Duryodhana from perpetrating heinous actions, supported his actions, so much so that he ignored the advice of Śrī Kṛṣṇa, but Vidura tried to prevent him by advising Duryodhana and others. Consequently, Duryodhana became angry and, following the advice of Karṇa, Duḥśāsana and Śakuni, snubbed Vidura with harsh words, which hurt Śrī Vidura greatly.

Therefore, he deserted Hastināpura and all his relatives.

He then visited the various pilgrim centers in the manner of an *avadhūta* (person beyond worldly concerns), reaching Prabhāsa-kṣetra after visiting Viṣṇu-tīrtha. Vidura felt sad to learn the news of the annihilation of the Yādavas and, with a grieving heart, began to roam in the Matsya, Kuru and Jāṅgala countries. While thus roaming, he met the greatest devotee, Uddhava, on the banks of the Yamunā.

Uddhava was an intimate associate of Śrī Kṛṣṇa and one of the early disciples of Bṛhaspati. He was calm and expert in morality. Vidura was happy to see Uddhava and embraced him with affection. He enquired with curiosity about Śrī Kṛṣṇa and his dependents, but, being overwhelmed, Uddhava could not reply. When asked repeatedly by Śrī Vidura, Uddhava replied in a choked voice, "O Vidura! Śrī Kṛṣṇa has left. The great snake in the form of *kāla* (time) has swallowed all our homes. What can I say about Śrī Kṛṣṇa and other brothers and relatives of Śrī Kṛṣṇa under these circumstances?" After this, Uddhava narrated in detail, one by one, all of Śrī Kṛṣṇa's exhibited pastimes, such as going to Mathurā from Vraja-dhāma, the killing of Kaṁsa, and His activities at Dvārakā. Filled with the grief of hearing about the annihilation of the family members and the disappearance of Śrī Kṛṣṇa, Vidura wanted to get free of the anguish of separation and thus he expressed to Uddhava his desire to hear the most secret knowledge that enlightens the soul. Śrī Uddhava then asked him to approach Sage Maitreya. Accordingly, Vidura, meditating upon the mercy of Śrī Kṛṣṇa and overwhelmed with intense love, approached Maitreya. Śrī Vidura inquired from the learned Sage Maitreya while at Haridvara:

vidura uvāca
sukhāya karmāṇi karoti loko
na taiḥ sukhaṁ vānyad-upāramaṁ vā
vindeta bhūyas tata eva duḥkhaṁ
yad atra yuktaṁ bhagavān vaden naḥ
(*Śrīmad Bhāgavatam* 3.5.2)

"Vidura said: O great sage, everyone in this world engages in fruitive activities to attain happiness, but finds neither satiation nor the mitigation of distress. On the contrary, one is only aggravated by such activities. You are omniscient. Therefore, please give us directions on how one should live for real happiness."

Besides this, Vidura expressed his desire to learn about the all-blissful Lord and His pastimes of various manifestations of Godhead, as well as the Lord's activities connected with creation, the Lord as the non-doer, and the social system of *varṇāśrama-dharma,* etc. In reply, Sage Maitreya praised him, "O *sādhu*! You have raised good questions. Śrī Kṛṣṇa is your life. You have raised these questions only for the welfare of people. You are the son of Lord Vyāsadeva. In your previous birth you were Yamarāja, who punishes the sinners. You were born from the union of Satyavatī's son Vyāsadeva and the maid who was adopted by Vicitravīrya as his wife. You are an eternal associate of Śrī Hari:

bhavān bhagavato nityaṁ sammataḥ sānugasya ha
yasya jñānopadeśāya mādiśad bhagavān vrajan
(*Śrīmad Bhāgavatam* 3.5.21)

"Your good self is one of the eternal associates of the Supreme Personality of Godhead for whose sake the Lord, while going back to His abode, left instructions with me."

In His form as the transcendental Pūruṣa, the *adhokṣaja* Lord, who is beyond the reach of the senses, is always being served in His eternally blissful abode. His partial expansion Kāraṇodakaśāyī Mahaviṣṇu, who impregnates *māyā* by His glance, creates the *mahat-tattva* and provides the false impression of eternity in the material nature. *Mahat-tattva*, or the great causal principle (total material energy), distorted by *māyā*, transforms into false ego. The false ego is represented by three different modes—goodness (*sāttvika*), passion (*rājasika*) and ignorance (*tāmasika*). In this world the interaction of false ego with the mode of goodness produces mind and *devatas*; its interaction with the mode of passion produces philosophical speculative knowledge and fruitive activities; and its interaction with the mode of ignorance produces sound. The sky (ethereal element) is a product of sound. The sky develops the touch sensation, from which the air in the sky is produced. Thereafter, the extremely powerful air, interacting with the sky, generates the light (fire) to see the world (form sensation). Fire mixed with air causes the creation of water and taste. Thereafter, the water produced from fire is glanced over by the Supreme Personality of Godhead and mixed with eternal time and external energy. Thus it is transformed into earth, which is qualified primarily by smell:

The property of space is sound.

The property of air is touch and sound.

The property of fire is form, touch and sound.

The property of water is taste, form, touch and sound.

The property of earth is smell, taste, form, touch and sound.

viṣṇostu trīṇi rūpāṇi pūruṣākhyānyatho viduḥ
ekastu mahataḥ sraṣṭṛ dvitīyaṁ tvaṇḍasaṁsthitam
tṛtīyaṁ sarvabhutasthaṁ tāni jñātvā vimucyate
(*Laghu-Bhāgavatāmṛta*, *Pūrva-khaṇḍa* 5)

"Viṣṇu has three forms called *pūruṣas*. The first, Kāraṇodakaśāyī Mahāviṣṇu, is the creator of the total material energy (*mahat-tattva*). The second omniscient, Garbhodakaśāyī Viṣṇu, is within every universe, and the third omniscient, Kṣīrodakaśāyī Viṣṇu, who resides in the Kṣīra Ocean, lives in the heart of every living being as the Supersoul. One who recognizes these three as the Personality of Godhead becomes liberated from the bondage of material illusion."

In the very beginning of the 3rd Canto of *Śrīmad Bhāgavatam*, Śrī Śukadeva Gosvāmī told Parīkṣit Mahārāja that the question he had raised was the same as the one that was raised by Vidura to Maitreya. Śrī Parīkṣit Mahārāja expressed his desire to hear those discussions in detail. Śrī Śukadeva Gosvāmī repeated the essential knowledge which is mentioned in the 3rd Canto of *Śrīmad Bhāgavatam*. During the discussions of Śrī Vidura and Śrī Maitreya, the discussions between Kapila and Devahūti are also described. While going through the first to the last chapter of the 3rd Canto of *Śrīmad Bhāgavatam* as well as while studying the 4th Canto, by their mercy one may gain knowledge of the deep meanings of the topics discussed by Śrī Vidura and Śrī Maitreya:

codito vidureṇaivaṁ vāsudeva-kathāṁ prati
praśasya taṁ prīta-manā maitreyaḥ pratyabhāṣata
(*Śrīmad Bhāgavatam* 4.17.8)

"When Vidura became inspired to hear of the activities of Lord Kṛṣṇa in His various *avatāras*, Maitreya, also being inspired and being very pleased with Vidura, began to praise him. Then Maitreya narrated the pastimes of Śrī Vāsudeva."

Sage Maitreya was among those *brāhmaṇas*, expert in the *Vedas* who were selected as priests by Yudhiṣthira Mahārāja for his *rājasuya-yajña*.

In the Videha kingdom of Mithilā, there lived Śrutadeva, a peaceful, detached *brāhmaṇa* who lived on whatever was available without causing harm to anyone. He was surrendered unto Śrī Kṛṣṇa only. The king of Videha, Bahulāśva, who was born in the dynasty of Janaka, was also devoid of any ego, like Śrutadeva. Both of them were devotees of Śrī Kṛṣṇa. Being pleased, Śrī Kṛṣṇa went to meet them, and Sage Maitreya was among those sages who accompanied Him.

In the 12th Chapter of the 12th Canto of *Śrīmad Bhāgavatam*, hearing and singing the glories of Śrī Hari are mentioned as being the topmost devotional processes. *Śrīmad Bhāgavatam* concludes with the glorification of *nāma-saṅkīrtana*:

nāma-saṅkīrtanaṁ yasya sarva-pāpa praṇāśanam
praṇāmo duḥkha-śamanas taṁ namāmi hariṁ param
(*Śrīmad Bhāgavatam* 12.13.23)

"I offer my respectful obeisances unto Supreme Lord Hari, the congregational chanting of whose holy names destroys all sinful reactions, and the offering of obeisances unto whom relieves all material suffering."

Only those words by which the Lord is glorified are true and, for the welfare of others, all others are false. Of all the topics in *Śrīmad Bhāgavatam*, the discussions between Śrī Vidura and Śrī Maitreya are of special importance.

Akrūra

Akrūra was a gentleman born in the Yadu Dynasty. His father was Śvaphalka and his mother was Gāndhinī. He was Śrī Kṛṣṇa's uncle and since Vasudeva was the son of King Śūrasena, it is therefore assumed that Śvaphalka was one of the brothers of King Śūrasena. According to the 10th Canto of *Śrīmad Bhāgavatam*, he was born in the Madhu Dynasty and was therefore known as Mādhava. Madhu was one of the kings of the Yadu Dynasty and because of this his successors are called Mādhavas:

yaduputrasya madhorpatyam pumana iti madhu-an
(*Viśvakoṣa*)

śrī-śuka uvāca
pṛṣṭo bhagavatā sarvaṁ varṇayām āsa mādhavaḥ
vairānubandhaṁ yaduṣu vasudeva-vadhodyamam
(*Śrīmad Bhāgavatam* 10.39.8)

Śukadeva Gosvāmī said, "In response to the Supreme Lord's request, Akrūra, the descendant of Madhu, described the whole situation, including King Kaṁsa's enmity toward the Yadus and his attempt to murder Vasudeva."

When Akrūra, as ordered by Kaṁsa, went to Nandagaon to bring Śrī Kṛṣṇa and Balarāma back to Mathurā, Śrī Kṛṣṇa enquired about his well-being and asked the reason of his arrival. In reply, Akrūra described in detail the antagonistic conduct of Kaṁsa and related an incident where the wicked king tried to kill Vasudeva. King Kaṁsa relied only upon Akrūra among the Yādavas, as Akrūra was brought up in the house of Kaṁsa for a long time.

Akrūra's father, Śvaphalka, was a pious person and his glories are described in the *Purāṇas*. A short description from *Viśvakoṣa* is as follows:

"Shortage of food, untimely death, disease and sorrow did not appear at the place where Śvaphalka resided. Once, it did not rain in the kingdom of Kāśīrāja and there was a drought. All unpleasantness vanished once Śvaphalka went there. The king of Kāśī married his daughter Gandhini to Śvaphalka. Sometime later, Akrūra was born. In his early years, Akrūra used to stay at Kaṁsa's house. While residing there, he went to Vṛndāvana to bring Kṛṣṇa and Balarāma for Kaṁsa's bow sacrifice (*dhanur-yajña*). When Śatadhanvā went against

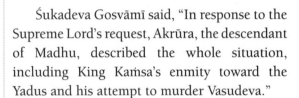

Śrī Kṛṣṇa, he handed the Syamantaka jewel over to Akrūra. After the death of Śatadhanvā, Akrūra kept the precious stone hidden inside his clothes. It is said that a large amount of gold was produced from the Syamantaka jewel and that Akrūra used to perform many *yajñas* with the help of that wealth. There was one more virtue of the Syamantaka jewel. The place wherever that jewel remained would never suffer from drought, flood, untimely death and other such bad occurrences. Once, some descendants of the Bhoja Dynasty, on Akrūra's side, killed Śatrughna, the great grandson of Satvata. Akrūra fled Dvārakā out of fear. Then drought, flood, untimely death and other natural calamities began to occur at Dvārakā. The inhabitants thought that the calamities were happening due to Akrūra leaving Dvārakā, so they contrived to bring him back. However, Śrī Kṛṣṇa did not believe that previously calamities were absent in Dvārakā due to Akrūra's presence, but that they were due to Akrūra possessing the Syamantaka jewel. Therefore, in the presence of the Yādavas, Śrī Kṛṣṇa said to Akrūra, "King Śatadhanvā has given you the Syamantaka jewel. Show that jewel to Me at once." Akrūra could not deny it and revealed the jewel wrapped in his clothes. Śrī Kṛṣṇa did not keep the jewel but gave it back to him to wear. Thereafter, Akrūra wore the jewel without any hesitation."

Śrī Kṛṣṇa-dvaipāyana Vedavyāsa has written a short description about Akrūra in the 10th Canto of *Śrīmad Bhāgavatam*:

Once Ariṣṭāsura, disguised as a frightening bull, entered Vraja to kill Śrī Rāma-Kṛṣṇa. He began to make frightening sounds and spread the dust by digging the earth with his hoofs and horns. All the residents of Vraja were scared by the demon but Śrī Kṛṣṇa pacified everyone and, after a brief struggle, killed Ariṣṭāsura. The residents of Vraja were relieved by the demon's death and even the demigods glorified Śrī Kṛṣṇa and showered flowers. After this incident, Sage Nārada Ṛṣi visited Kaṁsa and they had a long and secret meeting.

Sage Nārada said to Kaṁsa, "The girl child that is considered to have been born from the eighth pregnancy of Devakī is in reality the daughter of Yaśoda and He who is known as the son of Yaśoda is in reality the son of Devakī. The son of Rohiṇī known as Balarāma is in fact the seventh son of Devakī. Vasudeva, being afraid of you, has kept Śrī Kṛṣṇa and Śrī Balarāma in the care of his brother Nanda Mahārāja. Kṛṣṇa and Balarāma killed all the servants that you sent." Kaṁsa was enraged upon hearing this and pulled out his sword to kill Vasudeva. Then Sage Nārada warned him, "Kṛṣṇa and Balarāma will run away out of fear if you kill Vasudeva. By this your purpose will not be served." Nonetheless, the furious Kaṁsa ordered shackles to be put on Vasudeva and his wife Devakī. After Sage Nārada had gone, Kaṁsa sent the demon Keśi to Vraja to kill Rāma-Kṛṣṇa, but instead Kṛṣṇa killed the demon. After this, Kaṁsa called upon Cāṇūra, Muṣṭika, Śala, Tośala and his other ministers, telling them, "O brave Cāṇūra! O brave Muṣṭika! Listen to me with full attention. Śrī Vasudeva's sons Rāma-Kṛṣṇa are staying in the house of Nanda. My death is destined from their hands. You must trick them and kill them after they arrive at the wrestling match. Arrange to construct an arena large enough so that all the residents of the city and nearby villages can watch the wrestling." Kaṁsa instructed the elephant keeper to position the elephant Kuvalayāpīḍa at the entrance of the wrestling arena. The *dhanur-yajña* (bow sacrifice) was to begin on the fourteenth day. Kaṁsa arranged for an animal sacrifice for the pleasure of Mahādeva. After explaining this to his associates, the expert politician Kaṁsa held the hand of Akrūra and said, "O Akrūra!

You will have to do something in line with our friendship, because only you are my reliable well-wisher in the Bhoja Dynasty as well as the Vṛṣṇi Dynasty. As Indra destroys demons and gets his kingdom due to the help of Viṣṇu, in the same way I am relying on you in a time of dire need. You may go to Nandagaon by chariot. Both the sons of Vasudeva—Kṛṣṇa and Balarāma—are there. Bring them here without any delay. Upon their arrival, I shall annihilate them with the help of an elephant as powerful as Yamarāja. If they survive the elephant, I shall annihilate them with the help of wrestlers as powerful as the Vajra (Indra's thunderbolt weapon). After this, I will kill Vasudeva and other senior members of the Vṛṣṇi Dynasty as well as all the grieving relatives of the Bhoja and Daśāhra dynasties. Then, one by one, I shall kill my kingdom-greedy father Ugrasena, his brother Devaka and all my enemies. Jarāsandha is my *guru*, Dvivida is my dear friend, and Śambarāsura, Narakāsura, Bāṇāsura and other kings are my well-wishers. I therefore need not fear. You must go to Vraja and bring Kṛṣṇa-Balarāma here by giving them the excuse of showing them the glory of the Yadu Dynasty."

Akrūra replied, "O King! The method you have prepared to save yourself from death is all right, but please be equipoised about the outcome of your desired task, as destiny only gives the result of an action. The end result granted by destiny is sometimes good and sometimes bad. Nonetheless, I shall obey your order."

As instructed by Kaṁsa, Akrūra boarded a chariot the next day and left for Nandagaon to fetch Kṛṣṇa-Balarāma. While on the way to Nandagaon, he wondered: "Am I fortunate enough to have an audience with Śrī Kṛṣṇa, who is worshiped by Brahmā and Rudra? Have I performed any pious deeds or have I performed some penance such that I might be able to have an audience with Śrī Kṛṣṇa?

"Since I am very lowly, I may not get an audience with Śrī Kṛṣṇa, but this also is not proper to say. As a straw may flow in a river from one bank to the other, similarly some people flowing in time may cross the ocean of material miseries. From today, all of my sorrows are over. Today my birth has become meaningful, because today I will have an audience of the lotus feet of Śrī Kṛṣṇa, which are always meditated upon by *yogīs*. It is a matter of surprise that Kaṁsa, in spite of being crooked, has done me a great favor that I shall be able to have an audience of the lotus feet of Śrī Kṛṣṇa, who has descended to this earth. Only His devotees have the good fortune to have the audience of His lotus feet. *Yogīs* meditate upon those lotus feet in their hearts to attain true transcendental knowledge. I will surely offer obeisances unto those lotus feet as well as all the cowherd boys. At that time, Śrī Kṛṣṇa will place His merciful lotus hand on my head, which will be bowed unto His lotus feet. Surely today I will also have the opportunity of having the audience of the lotus face of Śrī Kṛṣṇa. Indra and Bali Mahārāja have achieved their kingdoms by offering prayers and worship unto Śrī Hari. Though I have been deputed by Kaṁsa and am a messenger of Kaṁsa, Śrī Kṛṣṇa would not consider me to be a foe. Śrī Kṛṣṇa is omnipresent and omnipotent; hence He clearly sees everything. I will be liberated of my sins by Śrī Kṛṣṇa's merciful glance, which will drown me in an ocean of bliss. Śrī Kṛṣṇa will embrace me, taking me as His servant and relative, and then my body will become purified. When I offer Him prayers with folded hands, Śrī Kṛṣṇa will address me thus: 'O Akrūra! O Uncle!' My life will become meaningful. Though there is no one loved or hated by Śrī Kṛṣṇa, yet as a wish-fulfilling tree grants the fruits as per one's desire, in the same way, Kṛṣṇa reciprocates the same feelings with which one offers Him prayers and devotion."

Thinking like this while riding the chariot, Śrī Akrūra reached Nandagaon. At that time, the sun was about to set. Śrī Akrūra entered the village and saw footprints with the symbols of lotus, barley, *aṅkuśa*,[41] etc, which were like ornaments of the earth. He was so pleased to be in the presence of those footprints that he began to roll in the dust, uttering, "Oh! This is the dust that was touched by the lotus feet of Śrī Kṛṣṇa." Then he saw Śrī Kṛṣṇa-Balarāma where cows are milked. Śrī Kṛṣṇa was dressed in yellow and Śrī Balarāma in blue. Their eyes were bright like the open lotus of the winter season. He saw that Śrī Kṛṣṇa and Śrī Balarāma were adolescent, had dark and white complexions respectively, long arms touching the knees, cheerful faces, and both were extremely happy, beautiful, as strong as elephants, and having feet with symbols of flag, mace, *aṅkuśa* and lotus, thus adding to the beauty of Vraja. Being decorated with diamond necklaces and garlands of forest flowers, They had appeared to remove the burden of the earth. Overwhelmed with love, Akrūra jumped down from the chariot and fell at the feet of Śrī Kṛṣṇa. Tears of joy were flowing from his eyes, his hairs stood on end and his body was in a trance. In an emotional voice, he said to Śrī Kṛṣṇa, "I, Akrūra, offer my obeisances unto You." As soon as Śrī Kṛṣṇa saw him, He pulled him up and embraced him. Baladeva also embraced Akrūra and, while holding both his hands, entered the house along with Śrī Kṛṣṇa. They entertained Akrūra with sweet words, offered him a comfortable place to sit, washed his feet, and then offered him various delicacies, after which They offered *betel* nut, cardamom and a fragrant garland.

All the weariness of the journey vanished and Akrūra engaged in a lengthy discussion with Nanda Mahārāja. Welcomed by Rāma-Kṛṣṇa and settled comfortably on the seat, Akrūra found that all of the desires which he had thought of during his journey to Vraja were fulfilled. There is nothing that cannot be achieved if the husband of Goddess Lakṣmī is satisfied. However, surrendered devotees of Kṛṣṇa seek only love for Kṛṣṇa, nothing else. Then, after supper, Kṛṣṇa-Balarāma inquired from Akrūra about his journey, welfare, the conduct of Kaṁsa, the welfare of Their mother and father, the death of Their brothers and, finally, the reason for his visit to Vraja.

Akrūra narrated to Śrī Kṛṣṇa in detail about the conduct of Kaṁsa based on rivalry, the Yādavas, the discussion between Kaṁsa and Śrī Nārada, the torture of Śrī Vasudeva, the desire of Kaṁsa to bring Kṛṣṇa and Balarāma to Mathurā on the pretext of a sacrifice and his plan to murder them by means of the elephant Kuvalayāpīḍa, the discussions with Cāṇūra and Muṣṭika, etc., and the sending of Akrūra as an envoy. After jovially hearing all this, Śrī Kṛṣṇa and Balarāma narrated the orders of Kaṁsa to Their father. The king of cowherds, Śrī Nanda, proclaimed Kaṁsa's order to the residents of Gokula. He asked them to go to Kaṁsa's sacrifice with a variety of gifts for him. As ordered by Śrī Nanda Mahārāja, Śrī Kṛṣṇa and Śrī Balarāma rode the chariot and proceeded to Mathurā. The gopis were grieved with the pain of separation and were distraught when they failed to prevent the departure of Kṛṣṇa and Balarāma for Mathurā, as instructed by Śrī Nanda Mahārāja. The pinnacle of love of the cowherd damsels of Vraja for Kṛṣṇa is the element of focus in this pastime, when Kṛṣṇa leaves for Mathurā. The *gopīs* lost their worldly discrimination and ran behind Śrī Kṛṣṇa. Overwhelmed by the pain of separation from Śrī Kṛṣṇa, they criticised

41 *Aṅkuśa*: a rod for driving elephants

the creator and said, "O Creator! You have no mercy. You make a mutual love relationship and break the companionship before the desire is fulfilled. You are very cruel. Coming here in the guise of Akrūra, you are taking away the same eyes that you yourself gave us. We left everything for Kṛṣṇa, our bodies, relatives, sons and husband—everything. But alas, that same son of Nanda is not looking at us with the same cheerful face as before.

"Tonight is the auspicious night for the women of Mathurā. The next morning will be auspicious for them too. Blessings granted to them by *brāhmaṇas* have today borne fruit because soon they will be able to taste the sweet nectar of the lotus face of sweet-smiling Śrī Kṛṣṇa. He will be captivated by the soft and sweet voices of the women of Mathurā. Will He ever return to village women like us? The name 'Akrūra' (one who is not cruel) seems inappropriate. Akrūra is taking away our dear Kṛṣṇa to a place inaccessible to us without giving us any promise. Oh! Hard-hearted Kṛṣṇa is riding the chariot of cruel-hearted Akrūra. Even the elders are not stopping them. Surely destiny is hostile to us. We ourselves will go and prevent Kṛṣṇa from leaving. What can the elders and other relatives do to us? For us, separation from Kṛṣṇa for even half a second is torturous. We are not afraid of dying. How will we be able to forget Kṛṣṇa's sweet smile, gestures and attractive glance and how will we overcome this limitless pain of separation? How will we stay alive without His audience?"

Suffering from the intense pain of separation, and with their minds constantly thinking of Śrī Kṛṣṇa, the cowherd damsels abandoned their so-called shame and began to shout, "O Govinda! O Damodāra! Hey Mādhava!" They began to cry loudly. At sunrise, Akrūra completed his morning prayers (*sandhyā-vandana*) and other duties and drove the chariot away without looking at or consoling the wailing *gopīs*. Nanda Mahārāja and other *gopas* (cowherd men) placed many pots full of cow's ghee on bullock carts and followed Śrī Kṛṣṇa. Kṛṣṇa saw the extremely grieved *gopīs* and consoled them by sending a messenger with the heartfelt message, "I will return soon." The *gopīs* stood motionless until the flag of the chariot withdrew from sight.

Soon, Śrī Kṛṣṇa-Balarāma, along with Akrūra, reached the banks of the Yamunā, the annihilator of sins. Śrī Kṛṣṇa drank the water of the Yamunā after reciting prayers using the Yamunā's sacred water and again sat on the chariot with Baladeva. Akrūra saw Rāma-Kṛṣṇa were sitting safely on the chariot, and then went for a quick bath in the Yamunā. He began to recite Vedic *mantras* while standing in the holy waters of the Yamunā. While he was reciting he suddenly saw Śrī Kṛṣṇa and Śrī Balarāma in the water. Akrūra was wonder-struck to see Them in the water. He wondered how They could be there since he had left Them sitting on the chariot. He came out of the water but saw that Śrī Balarāma and Śrī Kṛṣṇa were still sitting on the chariot. He then wondered whether the Kṛṣṇa-Balarāma he had seen in the water were false. Thus, he went back to the river again and this time inside the water he saw Lord Anantadeva as large as Mount Kailāsa, and he saw that Siddhas, Cāraṇas, Gandharvas and Asuras were glorifying Anantadeva, who had thousands of heads. There were crowns on the heads of Lord Anantadeva; He was wearing blue clothes on his body and the four-handed Nārāyaṇa was reclined on His lap. The brilliance of the four-armed Puruṣa was like a newly made cloud, He was wearing yellow clothes and His eyes were like lotus petals. He was of an exceedingly benevolent nature with a beautiful and cheerful lotus face, glancing with a sweet smile and having a beautiful body. He was holding the conch, disc, club and lotus; His chest was decorated with the Kaustubha Maṇi and He was wearing a *vanamālā*.[42] Along with this, he saw that Sunanda-Nanda and other main associates, four-faced Brahmā, Rudra and other demigods, Marīci and other sages, Prahlāda, Nārada, Vasu and other superior devotees were all glorifying Him with their various expressions and superior words. Śrī, Puṣṭi, Sarasvatī and other goddesses were serving Him. Akrūra became overwhelmed with emotion upon seeing the Lord. He was choked with love and, with folded hands, began to glorify the four-armed Supreme Lord with the following words: "The creator of the material worlds, Brahmā, has materialized from the lotus that emerged from Your navel. The five gross material elements (*pañca-mahābhūta*), the five sense objects (*pañca-tanmātra*), the ten senses, the mind (*manas*), the false ego (*ahaṅkāra*), the *mahat-tattva*, material nature (*prakṛti*) and the demigods have all materialized from Your body:

naite svarūpaṁ vidur ātmanas te hy
ajādayo 'nātmatayā gṛhītaḥ
ajo 'nubaddhaḥ sa guṇair ajāyā guṇāt
paraṁ veda na te svarūpam
(*Śrīmad Bhāgavatam* 10.40.3)

"The total material nature and these other elements of creation certainly cannot know You as You are, for they are manifested in the realm of dull matter. Since You are beyond the modes of nature, even Lord Brahmā, who is bound up in these modes, does not know Your true identity."

The *karmī*, or fruitive laborer, worships the Lord by means of elaborate fire sacrifices (*yajñas*); the *jñānī*, or learned philosopher, worships by means of renouncing all material activities to perform philosophic investigation; the *yogī* worships by means of meditation; and others worship the Lord by the system of worshiping the deity form. All other types of worship finally merge into the worship of Viṣṇu:

ye 'py anya-devatā-bhaktā yajante śraddhayānvitāḥ
te 'pi mām eva kaunteya yajanty avidhi-pūrvakam
(*Bhagavad-gītā* 9.23)

"Those who are devotees of other gods and who worship them with faith actually worship only Me, O son of Kuntī, but they do so in a wrong way."

In *Śrīmad Bhāgavatam*, Vyāsadeva has explained the meaning of *avidhi-pūrvakam* by means of an example. Just as by watering the roots of a tree, all of its parts—the trunk, the large and small branches, leaves, etc.—are nourished, and as all the senses are nourished by giving food to the stomach, similarly by service to Supreme Lord Śrī Hari all the demigods are served. By giving water to the branches of a tree, neither the tree nor the branches are nourished.

Therefore, those who worship demigods, considering them to be independent of Śrī Kṛṣṇa, Who is the enjoyer of all sacrifices, are ignorant of Absolute Knowledge. They meditate upon worldly thoughts and stay away from reality. Enchanted by Viṣṇu's *māyā*, the conditioned souls roam on the path of fruitive actions, immersed in the ignorance of body, family, home, "me and mine," etc., while being averse to Śrī Kṛṣṇa. People working for sense gratification cannot take absolute shelter of the lotus feet of the Absolute:

so 'haṁ tavāṅghry-upagato 'smy asatāṁ durāpaṁ
tac cāpy ahaṁ bhavad-anugraha īśa manye
puṁso bhaved yarhi saṁsaraṇāpavargas
tvayy abja-nābha sad-upāsanayā matiḥ syāt
(*Śrīmad Bhāgavatam* 10.40.28)

42 Vanamālā: a garland of forest flowers.

"Being thus fallen, I am approaching Your feet for shelter, O Lord, because although the impure can never attain Your feet, I think it is nevertheless possible by Your mercy. Only when one's material life has ceased, O lotus-naveled Lord, can one develop consciousness of You by serving Your pure devotees."

After the Supreme Lord withdrew His four-armed form, Akrūra returned to the chariot, whereupon Kṛṣṇa asked, "Did you see anything wonderful while taking a dip in the Yamunā?" Akrūra replied, "O Kṛṣṇa! Whatever wonder exists is all situated in You. Nothing is left to see after seeing You."

Continuing their journey, Akrūra reached Mathurā during the afternoon with Rāma-Kṛṣṇa on his chariot. Meanwhile, Nanda and the other cowherds had already arrived and were waiting for the Supreme Lord, Śrī Kṛṣṇa. Akrūra wanted to take Śrī Kṛṣṇa to his house, but Kṛṣṇa said that He would go there only after killing Kaṁsa. Then, with a sad heart, Akrūra went home and informed Kaṁsa about the arrival of Śrī Kṛṣṇa and Śrī Balarāma. Later, Rāma-Kṛṣṇa went to the arena for the wrestling match, and eventually killed the elephant Kuvalayāpīḍa, Cāṇūra, Muṣṭika and, finally, Kaṁsa.

After the death of Kaṁsa, Śrī Kṛṣṇa went to the house of Kubjā, a hunchbacked maidservant, and blessed her by giving her an opportunity to serve Him. Kubjā had not performed any pious deeds but she achieved the association of Śrī Kṛṣṇa due to decorating Him with sandalwood paste.

After bestowing mercy on Kubjā, Śrī Kṛṣṇa with Balarāma and Uddhava went to the house of Akrūra. Akrūra got up and offered respect when he saw the three of them and arranged comfortable seats for them. Akrūra then washed the feet of Śrī Kṛṣṇa and Balarāma while offering prayers. He took the water from Their feet on his head and glorified Śrī Kṛṣṇa as follows: "O Kṛṣṇa! You are affectionate to Your devotees. You give Your everything to the devotee who demonstrates even a meager effort of devotion to You. So much so, that being controlled by the love of Your devotee, You dedicate Yourself unto him."

Pleased by his glorification, Śrī Kṛṣṇa told him, "You are our uncle, so according to this relationship We are junior to you. We seek your mercy. You are an absolute gentleman; therefore, you are obliging others. Saints purify living beings merely by their audience."

Thus praising Akrūra, Śrī Kṛṣṇa requested him to go to Hastināpura to enquire about the welfare of the fatherless Pāṇḍavas.

As instructed by Śrī Kṛṣṇa, Akrūra went to Hastināpura and met the Kauravas and Pāṇḍavas. To observe how Dhṛtarāṣṭra was treating the Pāṇḍavas, Akrūra stayed there for a few months. Kuntīdevi and Śrī Vidura related to Akrūra all the tortures that the Kauravas inflicted upon the Pāṇḍavas due to the Kauravas being envious of the fame and glory of the Pāṇḍavas. They wanted to harass and disgrace the Pāṇḍavas. Kuntīdevi, with her eyes filled with tears, asked Akrūra whether or not her mother, father, Kṛṣṇa-Balarāma and other relatives remembered her and her sons. Would Śrī Kṛṣṇa console them, the grief-stricken people? At this, Akrūra reminded Kuntī that her sons were born from Dharma, Vāyu, Indra and other demigods. Therefore, there was no possibility of any untoward incident happening to them. On the contrary, there was the likelihood of their utmost well-being. Akrūra also went to the partial Dhṛtarāṣṭra to convey the message of Rāma-Kṛṣṇa and said, "After the death of Pāṇḍu, you attained this royal throne. According to the rules of politics your glory will spread if you take care of the public and your relatives without any partiality, and you will get all-round benefit. If your conduct is partial, you will be defamed not only in this world, but after death also you will go to hell. You must be well aware that the living being takes birth alone, leaves the body alone and he alone has to pay for all his sins by suffering alone. In the absence of knowledge of the self and due to ignorance, you consider your sons your own, have blind love for them, and take care of them by non-religious methods. This is against your duty. These sons and your wealth are all mortal. Children and wealth leave us before we are able to satisfy the desires that we aimed to satisfy through them. Persons with unfulfilled desires who have deviated from the path of righteousness go to hell after death. Therefore, it is appropriate to consider the world to be a dream, to lead a regulated life, to become peaceful and to see all with equality."

Dhṛtarāṣṭra replied, "You have given me much good advice for the sake of my better interests, but as a dying person does not become satisfied even if he gets nectar, I am not satisfied by your recommendations. These teachings are not acceptable to my mind, which is drowning in the love for my sons. No one has the power to disobey destiny as defined by the Lord. The purpose of the Lord's appearance in the Yadu Dynasty will surely be served."

After learning Dhṛtarāṣṭra's opinion, Akrūra took permission from his friends and relatives and returned to Mathurā. He narrated everything he had heard to Śrī Kṛṣṇa and Śrī Balarāma.

Satrājita, the father of Satyabhāmā, obtained the Syamantaka Jewel from the demigod of the sun. It used to release eight *bharas*[43] of gold every day and ensured the well-being of the place where it was kept. However, in practice, it was noticed that anyone who possessed this jewel died. Śrī Kṛṣṇa demanded that jewel from Satrājita, but he refused due to his material lust for the jewel. One day, Satrājita's brother Prasena went to the forest, taking the precious jewel with him. A lion killed him and took away the jewel. The lion was about to enter a cave in the mountain when Jāmbavān, the king of bears, killed the lion and took the jewel. Satrājita became suspicious of Śrī Kṛṣṇa, as Prasena had not returned for a long time. To reveal the truth to the residents of Dvārakā, Śrī Kṛṣṇa took them to the forest in search of Prasena. While searching they located the dead lion and the dead Prasena. After this, Śrī Kṛṣṇa asked all the people to sit outside the cave and He alone went inside the cave of Jāmbavān. He saw the jewel in the hands of Jāmbavān's son. Jāmbavān fought with Śrī Kṛṣṇa for twenty-eight days. The residents of Dvārakā returned when Śrī Kṛṣṇa did not come out of the cave even after so many days. Afterwards, when Jāmbavān learned that Śrī Kṛṣṇa was none other than his worshipable deity, he offered his prayers and glorified the Lord. He offered

43 Four rice grains are called a *guñjā*; five *guñjās* make a *paṇa*; eight *paṇas* make a *karṣa*; four *karṣas* make a *pala*; and one hundred *palas* make a *tulā*. Twenty *tulās* make a *bhāra*. Since there are approximately 3,700 grains of rice in an ounce, the Syamantaka Jewel was producing approximately 170 pounds of gold every day.

his daughter Jāmbavatī as well as the jewel to the Lord. After His return to Dvārakā, Śrī Kṛṣṇa narrated the whole incident to the residents of Dvārakā and returned the jewel to Satrājita. Satrājita was ashamed and offered his daughter Satyabhāmā and the jewel to the Lord. Śrī Kṛṣṇa accepted Satyabhāmā but returned the jewel.

When Lord Śrī Kṛṣṇa heard that the Pāṇḍavas had supposedly been burned to death in the palace of lac, He went to Hastināpura with Lord Balarāma to maintain the principles of worldly protocol, even though, being omniscient, He knew the report was false. With Kṛṣṇa away from Dvārakā, Akrūra and Kṛtavarmā incited Śatadhanvā to steal the Syamantaka Jewel from Satrājita. Bewildered by their words, the sinful Śatadhanvā murdered King Satrājita in his sleep and ran away with the gem. Queen Satyabhāmā was overcome with grief at the death of her father, and she rushed to Hastināpura to report the sorrowful news to Śrī Kṛṣṇa. Together with Lord Baladeva, Kṛṣṇa then returned to Dvārakā to kill Śatadhanvā. Śatadhanvā left the jewel with Akrūra and fled for his life. Kṛṣṇa and Balarāma pursued him and killed him but could not find the Syamantaka jewel on him. Lord Kṛṣṇa returned to Dvārakā and had the funeral rites performed for Satrājita. When Akrūra and Kṛtavarmā heard how Śatadhanvā had met his death, they fled Dvārakā. Soon many kinds of disturbances—mental, physical and so on—began to afflict Dvārakā, and the citizens concluded that the cause of these troubles must be Akrūra's exile.

The city elders explained, "Once there was a drought in Kāśī, and the king of Kāśī gave his daughter in marriage to Akrūra's father, who was visiting Kāśī at the time. As a result of this gift, the drought ended." The elders, thinking Akrūra had the same power as his father, declared that Akrūra should be brought back. Lord Kṛṣṇa knew that Akrūra's exile was not the main cause of the disturbances. Still, He had Akrūra brought back to Dvārakā, and after properly honoring him with worship and greeting him with sweet words, Kṛṣṇa told him, "I know Śatadhanvā left the jewel in your care. Since Satrājita had no sons, his daughter's offspring are the just claimants to whatever property he has left behind. Nonetheless, it would be best for you to keep the jewel in your care. Just let Me show it once to My relatives." Akrūra presented Kṛṣṇa with the jewel, which shone as brilliantly as the sun, and after the Lord had shown it to His family members He returned it to Akrūra.

It is described in the 12th Chapter of the 1st Canto of *Śrīmad Bhāgavatam* that when Śrī Kṛṣṇa installed Yudhiṣṭhira on the throne of Hastināpura and left for Dvārakā, Vasudeva and the residents of Dvārakā, upon learning that Śrī Kṛṣṇa was coming, suddenly stopped all their daily activities, including eating and sleeping. All the residents of Dvārakā began waiting for the arrival of Śrī Kṛṣṇa. They made arrangements to have a large elephant, flowers and other sacred objects ready for His welcome. They were chanting Vedic hymns and other verses to greet Him. At that time, Akrūra was also present.

Lord Paraśurāma eliminated the warrior class from the earth. He formed a large pond with the blood of the warriors at Kurukṣetra-dhāma. To observe the proper worldly principles, He performed a *yajña* there to relieve Himself of the sin of all such killings. At that pious Kurukṣetra-dhāma, the Yādava clan gathered on the occasion of the solar eclipse to rid themselves of sins and, at that time, Akrūra was among them. It is known from the 16th, 17th, and 18th Verses of the 24th Chapter of the 9th Canto of *Śrīmad Bhāgavatam* that Akrūra had two sons, Devavana and Upadeva.

Lord Śrī Kṛṣṇa Caitanya Mahāprabhu exhibited transcendental symptoms of divine love while visiting Akrūra-ghāṭa:

prātaḥ-kāle akrūre āsi' randhana kariyā
prabhure bhikṣā dena śālagrāme samarpiyā
eka-dina sei akrūra-ghāṭera upare
vasi' mahāprabhu kichu karena vicāre
ei ghāṭe akrūra vaikuṇṭha dekhila
vrajavāsī loka 'goloka' darśana kaila
eta bali' jhāṅpa dilā jalera upare
ḍubiyā rahilā prabhu jalera bhitare
(*Śrī Caitanya-caritāmṛta, Madhya Līlā* 18.134-137)

"Mahāprabhu would reach Akrūra-tīrtha early in the morning. There, the *brāhmaṇas* would cook food and offer it to the *śālagrāma-śilā*. One day, Śrī Caitanya Mahāprabhu was sitting at Akrūra-tīrtha and thought: '*At this bathing place, Akrūra saw Vaikuṇṭha, the spiritual world, and all the inhabitants of Vraja saw Goloka Vṛndāvana.*' While considering how Akrūra remained within the water, Śrī Caitanya Mahāprabhu immediately jumped in and stayed under the water for some time."

teṅtula-tale vasi' kare nāma-saṅkīrtana
madhyāhna kari' āsi' kare 'akrūre' bhojana
(*Śrī Caitanya-caritāmṛta, Madhya Līlā* 18.78)

"Śrī Caitanya Mahāprabhu used to sit beneath the old tamarind tree and chant the holy names of the Lord. At noon He would return to Akrūra-tīrtha to take lunch."

Glorification of Akrūra-tirtha:

dekha 'śrī akrūra-tīrtha'—tīrtha-śreṣta haya
sarvatra vidita kṛṣṇa-priya atiśaya
kahiba ki phala—snāna kaile pūrṇimāte
mukta haya saṁsāre viśeṣa kārtikete
sarva-tīrthe snāna kaile ye phala milaya
akrūra tīrther snāne tāhā prāpta haya
sūrya-grahaṇete ae tīrthe ye snāna kare
rājasūya aśvamedha phala mile tāre
(*Bhakti-ratnākara* 5.1857-1860)

"O Śrīnivāsa, see the best of all holy places, Śrī Akrūra-tīrtha. This well-known place is very dear to Kṛṣṇa. By bathing here on Pūrṇimū, especially during Kārtika, one is liberated from this material world. Whatever result can be achieved by bathing in all the holy places can be attained by bathing here."

In the *Saura Purāṇa* it is said:

ananta-vasati-śreṣṭhaṁ sarva-papa-vinaśanam
akrura-tīrtham aty-artham asti priyataraṁ hareḥ
purnimayaṁ tu yaḥ snayat tatra tīrtha-vare naraḥ
sa mukta eva saṁsarat karttikyaṁ tu viśeṣataḥ

"The best of the Lord's innumerable abodes and the destroyer of all sins, Akrūra-tīrtha is very dear to Lord Hari. A person who, on the full-moon day of the month of Kārtika, bathes at that very holy place becomes freed from the cycle of repeated birth and death."

In the *Ādi-varāha Purāṇa* it is said:

tīrtha-rajaṁ hi cakruraṁ guhyanaṁ guhyam uttamam
tat-phalaṁ samavapnoti sarva-tīrthavagahanat
akrure ca punaḥ snatva rahu-graste divakare
rājasūyaśvamedhabhyaṁ phalaṁ prapnoti niścitam

"Akrūra-tīrtha is the king of holy places, the most confidential of confidential abodes. There, one attains the result of bathing in all other holy places. A person who, during a solar eclipse, bathes in Akrūra-tīrtha certainly attains the result of performing a *rājasūya-yajña* and an *aśvamedha-yajña*."

Sage Dadhīci

Dadhīci Muni is described in the *Purāṇas*. He is known as Dadhyañca in the *Vedas*, and in *Mahābhārata* as Dadhica and Dadhīci as well. According to *Nirukta*[44] by Yaska, he is the son of Atharvā. Therefore, he is recognized as Atharvana in the *Ṛg* and other *Vedas* (*Nirukta* 12.33).

According to the *Brahmānda Purāṇa*, Dadhīci is the son of Śukrācārya. A son, Sarasvata, was born to Dadhīci and Sarasvatī (*Brahmānda Purāṇa*, Ch.1). According to some *Purāṇas* he was born from the union of Atharvā and Śāntī, Kardama Ṛṣi's daughter.

Two hymns of the *Ṛg Veda* mention Dadhīci:

dadhyaṁ ha yan madhvātharvaṇo
vāmaśvasya śīrṣṇā pra yadīmuvāca
(*Ṛg* 1.116.12)

"This son of Atharvā, Dadhīci, taught *madhu-vidyā* (the science of intoxicating drinks) to you (both the Aśvinī-kumāras) by accepting the head of a horse."

ātharvaṇāyāśvinā dadhīce.aśvyaṁ
śiraḥ pratyairayatam
sa vāṁ madhu pra vocad ṛtāyan tvāṣṭraṁ
yad dasrāvapikakṣyaṁ vām
(*Ṛg* 1.117.22)

"O Aśvinī-kumāras! You both implanted a horse's head on the body of Atharvana Dadhīci. Adhering to the truth, he taught you *madhu-vidyā* learned from Tvaṣṭā Ṛṣi, that you still possess today in the form of *apikaksya*."(*Viśvakośa*)

It is described in *Śrīmad Bhāgavatam* 4.1.42 also:

cittis tv atharvaṇaḥ patnī
lebhe putraṁ dhṛta-vratam
dadhyañcam aśvaśirasaṁ
bhṛgor vaṁśaṁ nibodha me

"Citti, the wife of Sage Atharvā, gave birth to a son named Aśvaśirā by accepting a great vow called Dadhyañca. Now you may hear from me about the descendants of Sage Bhṛgu."

Bali Mahārāja expressed his inability to obey the instruction of his own *guru*, Śukrācārya, when his *guru* asked him not to give land equivalent to three steps as desired by Lord Vāmana. He said:

śreyaḥ kurvanti bhūtānāṁ
sādhavo dustyajāsubhiḥ
dadhyaṅ-śibi-prabhṛtayaḥ
ko vikalpo dharādiṣu
(*Śrīmad Bhāgavatam* 8.20.7)

"Dadhīci, Śibi and many other great personalities were willing to sacrifice even their lives for the benefit of the people in general. This is the evidence of history. So what is the need to ponder so much upon giving up this insignificant land?"

The following is found in the 9th Chapter of the 6th Canto of *Śrīmad Bhāgavatam*:

Tvaṣṭā Ṛṣi was outraged when Indra killed his son Viśvarūpa. He performed a *yajña*, and from that *yajña* the frightening demon Vṛtrāsura appeared. His personal effulgence even diminished the power of the demigods. Finding no other means of protection, the demigods took refuge at the lotus feet of the Lord and requested Śrī Hari to advise them about the means to overcome this trouble that had befallen them. The Lord told them, "You should approach the exalted saint Dadhyañca (Dadhīci). He has become very accomplished in knowledge, vows and austerities, and his body is very strong. Go ask him for his body without delay. Dadhīci personally assimilated the spiritual knowledge of the *brāhmaṇas* and then delivered it to the Aśvinī-kumāras. It is said that Dadhyañca gave them the spiritual

44 *Nirukta* is Vedic lexicography which explains the meaning and etymology of less familiar words.

knowledge through the head of a horse. Therefore, this knowledge is called Aśvaśira. After obtaining the knowledge of spiritual science from Dadhīci, the Aśvinī-kumāras became *jīvan-mukta*, liberated even in this life. Dadhīci, who received the invincible protective covering known as the Nārāyaṇa-kavaca from Me, gave it to Tvaṣṭā, who delivered it to his son Viśvarūpa, from whom you have received it. Because of this Nārāyaṇa-kavaca, Dadhīci's body is now very strong. You should therefore beg him for his body. When the Aśvinī-kumāras beg for Dadhīci's body on your behalf, he will surely give it out of affection. When Dadhyañca awards you his body, Viśvakarmā will prepare a thunderbolt from his bones. This thunderbolt will certainly kill Vṛtrāsura, because it will be imbued with My power."

Following the Lord's instructions, the demigods approached Dadhīci, the son of Atharvā. He was very liberal, and when they begged him to give them his body, he was very satisfied. However, just to hear religious instructions from them, he smiled and jokingly spoke as follows. "O elevated demigods, are you unaware of how much unbearable pain a living being suffers at the time of death? In this material world, every living entity is very much addicted to his material body. Thus, for those who desire to live, it is appropriate for them to protect their bodies by all means. Therefore, who would be prepared to deliver his body to anyone, even if it were demanded by Lord Viṣṇu personally?"

The demigods replied, "O exalted *brāhmaṇa*, pious persons like you, whose activities are praiseworthy, are very kind and affectionate to people in general. What can such pious souls not give for the benefit of others? Those who are too self-interested beg something from others, not knowing of others' pain. But if the beggar knew, he would not ask for anything. Similarly, he who is able to give charity, if he knows the beggar's difficulty, will not refuse to give charity."

The great sage Dadhīci said, "Only so I could hear from you about religious principles did I refuse to offer my body as per your request. Now, although my body is extremely dear to me, I know that it will leave me today or tomorrow. I must give it up for your better purposes. One who has no compassion for humanity in its suffering and does not sacrifice his impermanent body for the higher causes of religious principles or eternal glory is certainly pitied even by the immovable beings. If one is unhappy to see the distress of other living beings and happy to see their happiness, his religious principles are appreciated as imperishable by exalted persons who are considered pious and benevolent. This body, which is to be eaten by jackals and dogs after death, does not actually do any good for me, the spirit soul. It is usable only for a short time and may perish at any moment. The body and its possessions, riches and relatives must all be engaged for the benefit of others, or else they will be sources of tribulation and misery." Dadhīci Muni, the son of Atharvā, thus resolved to give his body to the service of the demigods. He placed himself, the spirit soul, at the lotus feet of the Supreme Personality of Godhead and in this way gave up his gross material body constituted of five elements.

It is known from *Viśvakoṣa* that Sayana Ṛṣi wrote a commentary on *Ṛg Veda*. In one of his texts, he states that Indra cautioned Dadhīci, while imparting *madhu-vidyā* and *pravarga-vidyā* to him, that if he imparted this knowledge to anyone else his head would be cut off. To attain this knowledge, the Aśvinī-kumāras sliced off the head of Dadhīci Ṛṣi and kept it in a safe place. Then they attached the head of a horse to his torso. The Aśvinī-kumāras studied

Ṛg Veda, *Sāma Veda*, *Yajur Veda*, *pravarga-vidyā*, *madhu-vidyā* and *pratipadaka-brahma-vidyā* from Dadhīci while having the head of a horse. When Indra learned that Dadhīci Ṛṣi had taught *brahma-vidyā* and other knowledge to the Aśvinī-kumāras, he became angry and beheaded Dadhīci. The Aśvinī-kumāras then re-attached the original human head to the torso of Dadhīci Ṛṣi.

We can find some additional history regarding this topic in *Viśvakoṣa*:

"The demons had lost to the demigods in war, but then saw Atharvā's son Dadhīci alive again. Later, when Dadhīci left for the heavenly planets, the earth became full of demons. Their strength increased in all respects. Unable to fight them, the demigods began looking for Dadhīci. Being unable to find him, they even went to heaven. When they enquired about his remaining body parts, he said that it would be impossible to find all of them but, of course, the head of the horse could be located, as that was used to impart the Vedic knowledge to the Aśvinī-kumāras. Thus, Indra ordered a search for the horse head. After a long search, the horse head was finally located at Kurukṣetra. Indra killed the demons with the bones of that head."

Details of Dadhīci are described in *Mahābhārata* as well:

"Dadhīci Muni had counseled Dakṣa at the time of his *yajña* at Haridvara when he did not call upon Lord Śiva, but Dakṣa Prajāpati had not paid any attention to him. Dissatisfied by this, Dadhīci, being a devotee of Rudra, left the assembly. Nandi took initiation into the Śiva *mantra* from him and was recognized as an associate of Śiva."

Once, Sage Dadhīci began performing severe penance. Devarāja Indra was scared of his penance so he sent a celestial dancer, Alambuṣā, to entice him. When Alambuṣā reached Dadhīci Muni he was performing oblations at Sarasvatī-tīrtha. Alambuṣā succeeded in distracting him. He became passionate and had seminal flow. The sperm fell into the river. The river became pregnant and in due course delivered a child named Sarasvata. When the demigods became troubled by fear of Vṛtrāsura, they learned that the Vajra (thunderbolt weapon) made from the bones of Dadhīci Muni would kill Vṛtrāsura. That same Indra, who felt strong rivalry for Dadhīci, then approached Dadhīci Muni to ask him for his bones. Dadhīci, this time for Indra's and the other demigods' welfare, gave away his own body. *Agni Purāṇa* states that many other weapons besides Vajra were made from his bones.

Śrī Madhvācārya

Place of Appearance

Śrī Madhvācārya's place of birth is Pājakākṣetra in the village of Uḍupī, which is north of Mangalore, one of the major cities in South Karnataka. Karnataka district is on the western side of the Sahyādri mountain range in South India. (Śrīla Prabhupāda)[45]

Śrīpāda Madhvācārya took his birth near Uḍupī, which is situated in the South Kanara district of South India, just west of Sahyādri. This is the chief city of the South Kanara province and is near the city of Mangalore, which is situated to the south of Uḍupī. Near the city of Uḍupī is a place called Pājakākṣetra, where Madhvācārya appeared in a Śivāllī *brāhmaṇa* dynasty as the son of Madhyageha

45 "Śrīla Prabhupāda" refers to Śrīla Bhakti Siddhānta Sarasvatī Gosvāmī Ṭhākura.

Bhaṭṭa, in the year 1040 Śakābda (A.D. 1118). According to some, he was born in the year 1160 Śakābda (A.D. 1238). (Śrīla Prabhupāda)

Uḍupī City is located about 36 miles north of Mangalore in the South Karnataka district and about 3 miles away from the shore of the Arabian Ocean toward the east. About 8 miles toward the southeast corner of Uḍupī, a mountain named Vimānagiri is situated on the banks of River Pāpanāśinī. The birthplace of Śrī Madhvācārya, Pājakākṣetra, is situated about a mile to the east of Vimānagiri Mountain. River Pāpanāśinī is combined with River Udyavara. (*The History and Significance of Gauḍīya Darśana*)

Uḍupī, which is situated on the banks of River Pāpanāśinī, is about 37 miles away from Mangalore of Trivankore kingdom in South India. (*Gauḍīya Vaiṣṇava Abhidhāna*)

He is the son of Śrī Madhijī Bhaṭṭa, who hailed from Tuluva in South India. (*Encyclopedia*)

His birthplace is Tuluva in South India. (*New Bengali Dictionary*, by Āśutoṣadeva)

Year of Appearance and Family

1040 Śakābda or as per others 1160 Śakābda (Śrīla Prabhupāda)

1160 Śakābda - 1238 A. D. (*Gauḍīya Darśana*)

1121 Śakābda (*Encyclopedia*)

Śrī Madhvācārya appeared on the *tithi* of Śrī Rāmacandra's Vijaya-utsava in a Śivāllī *brāhmaṇa* family. His father was Śrī Madhvageha Bhaṭṭa and his mother was Śrī Vedavidyā. His father named him Śrī Vāsudeva. (Śrīla Prabhupāda)

His father's name was Śrī Madhvageha Nārāyaṇa Bhaṭṭa and his mother's was Śrī Vedavatī. (*Gauḍīya Vaiṣṇava Darśana*)

His father's name was Śrī Madhijī Bhaṭṭa. His father named him Śrī Vasudevācārya. (*Encyclopedia*)

His father's name was Śrī Madhijī Bhaṭṭa. (*New Bengali Dictionary* by Āśutoṣadeva)

Praṇāma Mantra

Regarding the most prevalent *praṇāma-mantra* in the lineage of Śrīman Madhvācārya, Most Revered Śrīmad Bhakti Promode Pūri Gosvāmi Maharāja, who was the chief editor of the monthly magazine *Śree Chaitanya Vāṇī*, wrote the following:

śrīmad-hanumad-bhīma-madhvāntargata-rāma-
kṛṣṇa-vedavyāsātmaka-lakṣmī-hayagrīvāya-namaḥ.

Śrī Madhvācārya is an *avatāra* of Śrī Hanumān of Tretā-yuga and Śrī Bhīma of Dvāpara-yuga. The *viśaya-vigrahas* (worshipable forms of God), Śrī Rāma and

Śrī Kṛṣṇa, are included in the *āśraya-vigrahas* (worshiper forms of God), Śrī Hanumān and Śrī Bhīma, respectively. Lord Vyāsadeva (an *avatāra* of the Supreme Lord) is the *viśaya-vigraha* of Śrī Madhva. Hence, offerings are made to Śrī Lakṣmi-Hayagrīva, who is the protector of the *Vedas* and non-different from Śrī Rāma, Śrī Kṛṣṇa and Śrī Vedavyāsa.

Childhood Pastimes

Śrīla Bhakti Siddhānta Sarasvati Gosvāmī Ṭhākura has narrated the following divine events that occurred during the childhood and adolescence of Śrī Madhvācārya:

Śrī Madhvācārya was known as Vāsudeva in his childhood. Many supernatural incidents took place during that time. On one occasion, as a young child, he returned alone from Uḍupī to Pājakākṣetra. In another instance, when his mother was not present at home, he ate a large tank of husk, which is feed for cattle, in front of his elder sister. Another time he was found swinging at the back of a wild bull, after tying himself to the bull's tail. In yet another incident, when a moneylender obstinately demanded an immediate payment from his father, he transformed a tamarind seed into a coin and cleared his father's debt. In his adolescence he went missing during a festival in the village Mediyuḍu and was later found in the Ananteśvara temple in Uḍupī. He also baffled a *brāhmana* named Śiva in a village called Niyampalli.

Śrī Vāsudeva underwent the sacred thread ceremony (*upanayana-saṁskāra*) at the age of five. A demon named Maṇimān (mentioned in *Mahābhārata*) was residing as a snake at the place of the ceremony. With the big toe of his left foot, Vāsudeva, soon after his thread ceremony, killed the snake. Seeing his mother perturbed, he leapt before her. At such a young age, he exhibited great competency in learning and education. He accepted *sannyāsa* (renounced order of life) from Śrī Acyutaprekṣa at the age of twelve despite his father's total disapproval, and became known as Śrī Pūrṇaprajña Tīrtha. After touring various places in South India, he had a debate with Śrī Vidyāśankara, the leader of Śringi Matha at that time. Śrī Vidyāśankara's exalted position was humbled by Śrī Madhva.

In the *Encyclopedia*, the events of Śrī Madhva's life are described further. In *Madhvācārya-vijaya* and other literatures of that lineage written by Śrī Nārāyaṇa Paṇḍita, it is mentioned:

Being ordered by Śrī Nārāyaṇa to establish *dharma*, the wind-god, Vāyu, appeared as the famous Madhvācārya. As a child he studied at Ananteśvara Maṭha. At the age of nine, he took *dīkṣā* (initiation) from Śrī Acyutāprekṣa Ācārya, also known as Śrī Śuddhānanda, who belonged to the Sanat family lineage. His given *dīkṣā* name was Śrī Pūrṇaprajña. His renunciation rose to new heights after taking *dīkṣā*. After leaving family life, he became known by names such as Ānandatīrtha, Ānandajñāna, Jñānānanda, Ānandagiri, etc.

At the age of twelve, he took *sannyāsa* from Śrī Acyutaprekṣa without the knowledge of his parents. His *sannyāsa* name was Śrī Pūrṇaprajña Tīrtha. After his investiture ceremony, he was known as Ānanda Tīrtha, and after he exhibited the pastime of an *ācārya* he became known as Śrī Madhvācārya. (*The History and Significance of Gauḍīya Darśana*)

Vyāsadeva Blesses Madhva

It can be seen in the literatures of the Madhva lineage that Śrī Madhvācārya had a divine vision (*darśana*) and received the blessings of Śrīla Vyāsadeva at Śrī Badarīkāśrama. Later, by his order, Madhvācārya wrote the *Brahma-sūtra-bhāṣyam* (commentary on the *Brahma-sūtras*). He wrote three commentaries on *Vedānta*:

1. *Śrīmad Brahma-sūtra-bhāṣyam*, or *Sūtra-bhāṣyam*: A vast commentary in which other philosophical opinions are not refuted but, by means of the evidence of *śruti* and *smṛti*, the *siddhānta* (scriptural conclusions) and *saṁgati* (reconciliation) are demonstrated.

2. *Anu-vyākhyānam*, or *Anu-bhāṣyam*: A compilation in the form of verses refuting other philosophical conclusions and establishing his own.

3. *Anu-bhāṣyam*: A brief commentary on each *adhikaraṇa* (sub-section or specific topic) of *Vedānta* is presented in the form of verses.

In *Śrī Caitanya-caritāmṛta*, *Madhya-līlā*, Śrīla Bhakti Siddhānta Sarasvati Gosvāmī Ṭhākura has written in his *Anu-bhāṣya* (purport):

Śrī Madhva went to Badarika along with a *sannyāsī* named Śrī Satyatīrtha, where he took the approval of Śrī Vyāsadeva after the latter listened to the commentary on *Gītā* (*Gīta-bhāṣyam*) from him. In a very short period, he learned a variety of subjects from Śrī Vyāsadeva. While returning from Badarikāśrama to Ānanda Maṭha, he completed *Sūtra-bhāṣyam* and Satyatīrtha transcribed it. From Badarikāśrama, Madhvācārya went to Godāvari in Ganjām district, where he met the two scholars Śrī Śobhan Bhaṭṭa and Śrī Svāmī Śāstrī. Later, they became Śrī Padmanābha Tīrtha and Śrī Narahari Tīrtha respectively, of the Madhva lineage.

The Bāla-Kṛṣṇa Deity

One day, after reaching Uḍupi while on his way to the sea to bathe, he compiled five chapters of *stotrams* (prayers to the Lord). While sitting on the sand, deeply immersed in remembrance of Śrī Kṛṣṇa, he saw a ship sinking in the sea, which was loaded with saleable paraphernalia en route from Dvāraka. As soon as he displayed some *mudrās* (signs or gestures) in order to make it float, the ship reached the shore safely. When the passengers of the boat requested him to accept something in return, he only agreed to accept some *gopīcandana* lying on the boat. He took a huge portion of *gopīcandana* but, while returning from the ocean, it broke at a place called Baḍabandeśvara and a beautiful deity of Bāla-Kṛṣṇa (little Kṛṣṇa) was found inside. In one hand, Bāla-Kṛṣṇa holds a churning rod for curd and, in the other, a rope used for churning. As soon as he obtained the Kṛṣṇa deity he completed the remaining seven chapters of *Dvādaśa-stotram* (twelve prayers to Lord Kṛṣṇa).

The Kṛṣṇa deity was so heavy that thirty powerful men could not lift it , but Madhvācārya, the *avatāra* of Vāyu, Hanumān and Bhīma, picked it up single-handedly and brought it to the *maṭha* in Uḍupi. His eight prominent *sannyāsī* disciples were the in-charges of the eight maṭhas there. In Vṛndāvana, the eight principle *gopīs* serve Śrī Kṛṣṇa, so in a like manner the service of Bāla-Kṛṣṇa was performed by Madhvācārya himself, and later his followers who were in-charges of the North Rāḍhī Maṭha performed the service with the help of those eight principle *sannyāsīs*. Even today this tradition is followed.

It can be known from the description of the *Encyclopedia*:

"In *Madhva-vijaya* it is written that Śrī Madhvācārya compiled *Gīta-bhāṣyam* and gifted that book to Śrī Vedavyāsa in Śrī Badarikāśrama. Being pleased, Vyāsadeva gave him three *śālagrāma-śilās* (manifestation of the Supreme Lord in the form of sacred stones). Madhvācārya later installed Them in the Subrahmanya, Uḍupi and Madhyatala *maṭhas*. Apart from the *śālagrāmas*, he also installed a deity of Kṛṣṇa in Uḍupi. There is a also the narration with respect to the establishment of the Kṛṣṇa deity in Uḍupi.

"A merchant's boat suddenly sank in the sea at Tuluva while on its way to Malabār from Dvāraka. In that boat there was a deity of Kṛṣṇa covered by *gopīcandana*. When Madhvācārya came to know this by his divine vision, he lifted the deity and installed Him in Uḍupi. Since that time, Uḍupi has become the main place of pilgrimage for the followers of Madhvācārya. He stayed in Uḍupi for some time and compiled thirty-seven primary literatures and many commentaries (*Bhāṣyams*)."

The Refuter of Māyāvāda Philosophy

Śrī Madhvācārya refuted the Māyāvāda (doctrine of the impersonal existence of Absolute Reality) school of thought and established Tattvavāda (devotional doctrine of Transcendental Reality); hence his lineage became very renowned by that name. Śrī Madhvācārya is the third *avatāra* of the wind-god, Vāyu, after Śrī Hanumān and Śrī Bhīma. For this reason, Śrī Madhvācārya is a very mighty person with inconceivable power. In a book describing his holy life, many incidents that prove his supra-mundane power are described. Several such instances have already been presented in previous portions of this work. One more such transcendental incident heard from the most revered Vaiṣṇavas is related as follows:

One time, Śrī Madhvācārya told his father, Madhyageha Śrī Nārāyaṇa Bhaṭṭa, that he would refute the Māyāvāda philosophy of Śrī Śaṅkarācārya. Listening to his insolent statement, his father was skeptical and told him, "Śrī Śaṅkarācārya's philosophy is widely spread and respected throughout India. I do not think that there is any capable person who can refute his philosophy. I consider your achieving this task as impossible as the staff in my hand becoming a tree and bearing fruits." After listening to his father's words, Śrī Madhvācārya addressed him, "My dear father! If I transform your staff into a tree and make it bear fruits, then will you believe?" After saying this, the powerful Madhvācārya took the stick from his father's hands, implanted it in the ground with great force and said, "O stick! If I can refute the Māyāvāda philosophy, then immediately transform into a tree and produce fruits." That very moment the stick became a tree and produced very sweet fruits. Śrī Madhvācārya gave the fruits to his father and others. Seeing such an uncommon incident, his father could understand that his son was not an ordinary child and that he would become a greatly elevated soul gifted with transcendental power. He now believed that, through him, the Māyāvāda philosophy would be refuted. It did, in fact, come to pass that Madhvācārya wrote *Māyāvāda-śata-dūṣaṇi*, in which he exposed hundreds of defects in the Māyāvāda philosophy.

Śrī Madhvācārya, like Śrī Hanumān, could become heavier and lighter at will. One time, a mighty person named Karañjaya, who possessed strength equal to that of thirty persons put together, could not lift the big toe of Madhva's foot, which was pressed firmly to the ground. In another instance, he assumed a light body and sat on the shoulders of a child without the child feeling his weight. Also, in his childhood, he transformed the seeds of a tamarind into gold coins and cleared his father's debt.

Literary Works of Śrī Madhva

Most Revered Śrīla Bhakti Promode Pūri Gosvāmī Mahārāja mentioned the reason for Śrīla Madhvācārya's father's name becoming Madhyageha Nārāyaṇa Bhaṭṭa: "Out of the 120 *brāhmanas* brought by King Rāmabhoja, those who constructed their houses in the center of the village in Pājakākṣetra and resided there were known as Madhyageha. Madhyageha Nārāyaṇa Bhaṭṭa came to know through a celestial voice that his son was *asudeva* (*avatāra* of the wind god) and that he was a great devotee of Lord Vāsudeva. Hence, he named his son Vāsudeva.

Śrī Madhvācārya compiled thirty-eight main scriptures including many commentaries (*Bhāṣyas*). The main scriptures compiled by him are: (1) *Gīta-bhāṣya*, (2) *Brahma-sūtra-bhāṣya*, (3) *Anu-bhāṣya*, (4) *Anu-vyākhyāna*, (5) *Pramāṇa-lakṣaṇa*, (6) *Kathā-lakṣaṇa*, (7) *Upādhi-khaṇḍana*, (8) *Māyāvāda-khaṇḍana*, (9) *Prapañca-mithyātvānumāna-khaṇḍana*, (10) *Tattva-saṁkhyāna*, (11) *Tattva-viveka*, (12) *Tattvodyota*, (13) *Karma-nirṇaya*, (14) *Śrīmad Viṣṇu-tattva-vinirṇaya*, (15) *Ṛg-bhāṣya*, (16) *Aitreya-bhāṣya*, (17) *Bṛhadāraṇyaka-bhāṣya*, (18) *Cāndogya-bhāṣya*, (19) *Taittirīya Upaniṣad-bhāṣya*, (20) *Īśāvāsya Upaniṣad-bhāṣya*, (21) *Kaṭhopaniṣad-bhāṣya*, (22) *Atharvana Upanisad-bhāṣya*, (23) *Māṇḍūkya Upanisad-bhāṣya*, (24) *Ṣaṭ-Praśnopaniṣad-bhāṣya*, (25) *Talavakāra Upaniṣad-bhāṣya*, (26) *Śrīmad Bhagavad-Gīta-tātparya-nirṇaya*, (27) *Śrīman nyāya-vivaraṇa*, (28) *Narasiṁha-nakha-stotra*, (29) *Yamaka-bhārata*, (30) *Dvādaśa-stotra*, (31) *Śrī Kṛṣṇāmṛta-mahārṇava*, (32) *Tantra-sāra-saṁgraha*, (33) *Sadācara-smṛti*, (34) *Śrīmad Bhāgavat-tātparya*, (35) *Śrīman Mahābhārata-tātparya-nirṇaya*, (36) *Yati-praṇava-kalpa*, (37) *Jayantī-nirṇaya*, (38) *Śrī Kṛṣṇa-stuti*.

The *ācāryas* of the Śrī Madhva Tattvavāda Sampradāya term their main *maṭha* in Uḍupi as Uttarāḍhī Maṭha. The names of the eight *maṭhas* and their respective in-charges in Uḍupi are (1) Śode Maṭha - Viṣṇu Tīrtha, (2) Kṛṣṇapura Maṭha - Janārdana Tīrtha, (3) Kaniyur Maṭha - Vāmana Tīrtha, (4) Admar Maṭha - Narasiṁha Tīrtha, (5) Puttige Maṭha - Upendra Tīrtha, (6) Śirur Maṭha - Rāma Tīrtha, (7) Palimar Maṭha - Hṛṣīkeśa Tīrtha, (8) Pejavara Maṭha - Akṣobhya Tīrtha.

The *guru-paramparā* of the Śrī Madhva lineage is: (1) Haṁsa Paramātmā, (2) Chaturmukha Brahmā, (3) Catuḥsana, (4) Durvāsā, (5) Jñānanidhi, (6) Garuḍavāhana, (7) Kaivalya Tīrtha, (8) Jñāneśa Tīrtha, (9) Para Tīrtha, (10) Satyapragña Tīrtha, (11) Prāgña Tīrtha, (12) Acyuta Prekṣācārya Tīrtha, (13) Śrī Madhvāchārya - 1040 Śakābda.

Śrīla Prabhupāda on Śrī Madhva

On the appearance day of Śrī Madhvācārya, Śrīla Bhakti Siddhānta Sarasvati Gosvāmī Ṭhākura offered prayers to him as follows:

ānanda tīrtha nāmā sukhamaya dhāmā yatirjīyāt
saṁsāra-arṇava-taraṇīṁ yamiha janaḥ kīrtayanti budhāḥ

"I bow down to that Ānandatīrtha named Śrī Madhvamuni with great respect; all victory to him! The learned glorify him as being like a boat to cross over the ocean of material existence. That *yatirāja* (chief among those in the renounced order) is an abode of bliss."

"All the Gauḍīya Vaiṣṇavas of Bengal who are followers of Śrīman Mahāprabhu are also followers of Śrī Madhvācārya, or Madhvamuni. Śrī Caitanya Mahāprabhu is the eighteenth and Śrī Advaita Prabhu and Śrī Nityānanda Prabhu are the seventeenth in the preceptorial channel after Śrī Ānandatīrtha, or Śrī Pūrṇaprajña. The three Lords have accepted Śrī Madhvamuni in their preceptorial channel. Śrī Madhvamuni was born in north Kerala (present-day Karnataka). He reformed Pañcopāsanā (worship of five gods: Sūrya, Gaṇeṣa, Durgā, Śiva and Viṣṇu) in India and propagated the worship of Śrī Viṣṇu as the sole duty of everyone. Before his appearance, Śrī Śaṅkarācārya, the *ācārya* of the Māyāvāda philosophy and the son of Śrī Śivaguru, had established the *ārya* (Vedic) *dharma* with much effort. Later, Śrī Madhvamuni reestablished fidelity and service to Lord Viṣṇu as the essence of *ārya-dharma*. By a certain gesture of his fingers, Śrī Madhvamuni demonstrated to the living entities that the basis of theism is eternal servitorship to the Supreme Lord. There is no separate resort for the living entities other than devotion to the Supreme Lord.

"The followers of Śrī Madhvācārya consider the demigods to be devotees of Śrī Viṣṇu. They worship Viṣṇu as supreme, and with the *prasāda* of Viṣṇu the demigods are worshiped. In the northern part of Uḍupi, a Viṣṇu-śilā kept above Lord Śiva is worshiped. There is also a deity of Lord Śiva under the hand of Śrī Ananta Padmanābha. Though the worship of demigods and forefathers is not completely rejected in the lineage of Śrī Madhva, they are not in favor of propagating material reconciliation in the name of Pañcopāsanā." (Śrīla Prabhupāda's *Vaktṛtāvali*, Part 1)

Śrī Madhvācārya manifested his disappearance pastime at the age of 79 on Māghī-śukla-navamī (ninth day of the bright fortnight in the month of Māgha / Jan-Feb) while explaining the purport of *Aitareya Upaniṣad* to his disciples.

Śrīman Madhvācārya's School of Thought

The *ācāryas* of the Tattvavādi Sampradāya have described the doctrines of Śrīman Madhvācārya in the following *śloka*:

śrīman-madhva-mate hariḥ paratamaḥ
satyaṁ jagat-tattvato,
bhedo jīvagaṇā harer-anucarā
nīca-ucca-bhāvaṁ gatāḥ
muktir-naija-sukha-anubhūtir-
amalā bhaktiś ca tat-sādhana
mokṣādi-tritayaṁ pramāṇam-akhila-
āmnāyeika-vedyo hariḥ

"As per Śrī Madhvācārya: Śrī Hari or Śrī Viṣṇu is the Ultimate Reality; this world is real; the difference between the Lord, living entities and matter is eternal; the living entities are the servants of Śrī Hari; the higher and lower states of consciousness of living entities exist eternally as per the difference in their competency; *mokśa*, or salvation, is the realization of one's true nature, which is the permanent state of being blissful; pure devotion is the only means to attain salvation; *pratyakṣa* (direct sense perception), *anumāna* (inference from observation) and *śabda* (knowledge via revealed scriptures)—these three are the principal means of testimony; Śrī Hari is the only truth to be known in all the *Vedas* and other sacred literatures."

Dr. Nāgarāja Sharma, in his treatise *The Philosophy of Madhva Dvaita Vedānta*, indicated that the above *śloka* was written by Śrī Vyāsarāja, the compiler of *Nyāyāmṛta*.

Śrī Gauḍīya Vedāntācārya Śrī Baladeva Vidyābhūṣaṇa Prabhu wrote a similar verse in his *Prameya Ratnāvali* describing the doctrines of Śrī Madhva briefly:

śrīmadhvaḥ prāha viṣṇuṁ paratamam-
akhilāmnāya-vedyañca viśvaṁ
satyaṁ bhedañca jīvān hari-caraṇa-
juṣas-tāratamyañca-teṣām

mokṣaṁ viṣṇvanghri-lābhaṁ tad-amala-
bhajanaṁ tasya hetuṁ pramāṇaṁ
pratyakṣa-ādi-trayancetyupa-diśati
hariḥ kṛṣṇa-caitanya-candraḥ

"Śrī Madhvācārya said: Śrī Viṣṇu is the Ultimate Truth; He is to be known through the *Vedas* and revealed scriptures; the world is real; the living entities are separate from Viṣṇu; the living entities are the servants of Lord Hari's lotus feet; there is distinction among living beings; salvation is the attainment of the lotus feet of Śrī Viṣṇu; pure devotion to Śrī Viṣṇu is the only way to attain salvation; *pratyakṣa*, *anumāna* and *śabda* are the principal means of evidence. Lord Śrī Kṛṣṇa Caitanya-candra, who is non-different from Lord Śrī Hari, presented the same teachings."

Śrī Caitanya-caritāmṛta, *Madhya Līlā* 9, presents an account of Śrīman Mahāprabhu's philosophical discussion with the followers of Śrī Madhvācārya, revealing that, as per the Tattvavādi Sampradāya, "The worship of Śrī Kṛṣṇa by dedicating the fruits of *varṇāśrama-dharma* to Him is the best devotional practice. By doing so one attains one's highest objective, i.e., the five types of liberation (living on the same planet as Lord Viṣṇu, having the same opulence as Lord Viṣṇu, being a personal associate of Lord Viṣṇu, having the same bodily features as Lord Viṣṇu, as well as oneness with Lord Viṣṇu) and attains Vaikuṇṭha-dhāma." In reply Śrīman Mahāprabhu said, "As per the scriptures, *śravaṇa* and *kīrtana* (hearing and chanting the glories of Śrī Kṛṣṇa) are the highest devotional practices and by performing them one attains one's highest object of worship—loving devotional service to Śrī Kṛṣṇa."

In his *Amṛta-pravāha-bhāṣya* commentary Śrīla Bhaktivinoda Ṭhākura wrote: "By dedication of the results of fruitive actions (*karma*), one's consciousness is purified. By purified consciousness combined with the strength of *sādhu-saṅga* (saintly association) one attains firm faith in one-pointed devotion to Śrī Kṛṣṇa. After the manifestation of firm faith, *sādhana-bhakti* (devotional practice) in the form of *śravaṇa*, *kīrtana*, etc., begins. After this, *prema* (loving devotion) will manifest to the extent the *anarthās* (unwanted obstructions) are destroyed. The purport is that, by following *karma* and dedication of the fruits of *karma*, there is no guarantee that *kṛṣṇa-bhakti* will manifest, as it is dependent on the manifestation of *śraddhā* (firm faith), one of the symptoms of *śaraṇāgati* (surrender), which develops in the association of devotees.

prabhu kahe karmī, jñāni dui bhakti-hīna
tomār sampradāye dekhi sei dui cihna
sabe, eka-guṇa dekhi tomāra sampradāye
'satya-vigraha īsvare' karaha niścaya
(*Śrī Caitanya-caritāmṛta*, *Madhya-lilā*, 9.276-277)

"Śrīman Mahāprabhu said, 'O Tattvavādi *ācāryas*, the doctrines of your *sampradāya* are almost against pure devotion. Nevertheless, one great virtue that can be appreciated is that you accept the Lord and His deity form as Eternal Truth. My *parama-gurudeva*, Śrī Mādhavendra Pūrī, accepted the Śrī Madhva Sampradāya upon observation of this principal doctrine.'" (Śrīla Ṭhākura Bhaktivinoda)

From this, it can be understood that although Śrī Mādhavendra Pūrī took *dīkṣā* from a *sannyāsī* of the Pūrī order at first, upon seeing that in the Śrī Madhva Sampradāya, the eternal, cognizant *sat-cid-ānanda* form of the Lord endowed with spiritual qualities and transcendental variegatedness is accepted, he took shelter of Śrī Lakṣmīpati Tīrthapāda and accepted the Sri Madhva lineage. That is why our *sampradāya* is known as the Śrī Brahma-Madhva-Gauḍīya Vaiṣṇava Sampradāya. (Śrīla Bhakti Promode Pūrī Gosvāmī Maharāja)

Śrī Madhva's school of thought is known as *Dvaitavāda* (doctrine of dualism). This school is also known by other names such as Svatantra-asvatantravāda, Svābhāvika-bhedavāda, Kevala-bhedavāda and Tattvavāda. *Svatantra* and *asvatantra* indicate that there is an eternal distinction between the fully independent Lord and the dependent living entities (*jīvas*). There are five categories of distinction: (1) Between the living entity and the Lord, (2) Between a living entity and another living entity, (3) Between the Lord and matter, (4) Between the living entity and matter, (5) Between matter and matter. These distinctions are eternally existent from time immemorial.

Differences Between the Śrī Śaṅkarācārya and Śrī Madhvācārya Schools of Thought

1. Śrī Śaṅkara did not accept the concept of duality. According to him, *Nirguṇa Brahman* (Absolute Spirit without attributes) is the eternal truth and *Saguṇa Brahman* (Absolute Spirit with attributes) is false.

Śrī Madhva accepted duality on the basis of the *svatantra* (independent) and *paratantra* (dependent) principles. The difference between the *svatantra* Lord and the *paratantra* entities is real, eternal and beginningless.

2. According to Śrī Śaṅkara, the *jīva* is a false identification due to ignorance and deluded Brahman. In reality, there is no separate existence of the *jīvas* except for their misidentification due to bewilderment.

According to Śrī Madhva, the *jīva* is a conscious dependent entity, a separate potency of Brahman and eternally different from Brahman. The *jīvas* are real, everlasting and atomic.

3. According to Śrī Śaṅkara, the world is an illusion and its existence is not factual but imaginary.

According to Śrī Madhva, the world is ontologically different from Brahman, real, a conscious creation of the Lord, under the control of Viṣṇu and perpetual.

4. According to Śrī Śaṅkara, *tattvamasi*–comprising the words *tat* (that) and *tvam* (thou), which have a common receptacle—indicate the complete oneness of Brahman and *jīva*.

Madhvamuni did not accept *tattvamasi* as the principal Vedic aphorism. According to him, *sa ātmātattvamasi* = *sa ātma* + *atattvamasi*, the *jīva* and the Lord are different. He said that in the *Cāndogya Upaniṣad* the *atattvamasi* term is repeated nine times to Śvetaketu (son of a *muni*) along with examples indicating the distinction between *jīvātma* and *paramātma*. *Atattvamasi* can also be found in the *Sāma-saṁhita*. A detailed commentary on '*sa ātmātattvamasi*' can be seen in *Nyāyāmṛta*. Śrī Gauḍa Pūrṇānanda, the compiler of *Tattva-muktāvali* and a disciple of Śrī Nārāyaṇa Bhaṭṭa, who in turn is a follower of Śrī Madhva's school of thought, explained that *tasya tvamasi* means "you are of Him," i.e., "you are the servant of Paramātma or that you are for Him." (*The History and Significance of Gauḍīya Darśana*)

"Madhva, also called Ānandatīrtha or Pūrṇaprajña (b.c. 1199, Kalyānpura, near Uḍupi, Karnataka, India - d.c. 1278 Uḍupi). Hindu philosopher, exponent of Dvaita (qv. dualism or belief in a basic difference in kind between God and the individual souls). His followers are called Madhvas.

"Born into a *brāhmana* family, his life in many respects parallels the life of Jesus Christ. Miracles attributed to Christ in the New Testament were also attributed to Madhva.

"Madhva set out to refute the non-dualistic Advaita philosophy of Śaṅkara, who believed the individual self to be a phenomenon and the absolute spirit (*Brahman*) the only reality." (*Encyclopedia Britannica*, Vol. 7, page 654)

Śrī Rāmānujācārya

Śrī Rāmānujācārya appeared in a village called Śrī Perambadur in the district Chengalpet in South India in 1017 A.D. His father, Śrī Keśava Tripāṭhī, belonged to the Hārita *gotra* and was a follower of the Āpastamba branch of the *Yajurveda*. As per *Śrī Prapannāmṛta*, his father was Śrī Nṛsiṁhācārya of Kuśika *gotra*.

Śrī Rāmānujācārya's father, who resided in the town of Bhūtapuri in the Toṇḍira region, was an unmatched scholar. Śrī Rāmānuja studied the *Vedas* from his father until he was fifteen. Later, he went to Śrīrangam and studied the *Vedas*, *Vedānga*, *Vedanta* and other scriptures after becoming a disciple of Śrī Mahāpūrṇācārya. His power of remembrance was so sharp that, while in Śrīrangam, he learned all the scriptures in a very short time." (*Viśvakoṣa*)

"Śrī Lakshmaṇa Deśika, who became renowned as Śrī Rāmānujācārya, appeared in the village Śrī Perambadur, which is about 13 *krośas* (1 *krośa* = 2 miles) from Madras (present day Chennai) on the western side, on the fifth day of the bright fortnight of the month of Caitra (Caitra-śukla-pancami-tithī) in 938 Śakābda (1016 A.D.). Others say 937 Śakābda (1017 A.D.) and yet others, 940 Śakābda (1018 A.D.). His father's name was Āsuri Keśavācārya Dikṣita and his mother's name was Śrī Kāntimatī, the younger sister of Śrī Śailapūrṇa. Śrī Śailapūrṇa was a prominent disciple of the renowned Śrī Yāmuna Muni of the Śrī Sampradāya." (*The History and Significance of Gauḍīya Darśana*)

"Śrī Rāmānujācārya took birth in the village of Śrī Perambadur in the Chola province in South India in the eleventh century." (Caritāvali section of Śrī Āśutoṣadeva's *New Bengali Dictionary*)

"With a desire to compile *Śrī Bhāṣyam*, Śrī Rāmānuja went to Śāradāpīṭha in Kashmir along with his disciple Kureśa to bring the *Bodhāyana-vṛtti* (Bodhāyana's explanation of the Purva Mimamsa school of thought). Though the followers of Kevalādvaita (absolute non-duality) in the Śāradāpīṭha were reluctant to give the *Bodhāyana-vṛtti*, by the grace of Śrī Śāradādevi Śrī Rāmānuja gained possession of it and escaped from there. The followers of Kevalādvaita swiftly chased after Śrī Rāmānuja and his disciple for a month and eventually caught up with them and snatched

the book from them. However, Kureśa, who had a remarkably retentive memory, had gone through that book every night for a month and had memorized it in its entirety. Based on that, Śrī Rāmānujācārya compiled *Śrī Bhaṣya* and Kureśa wrote it down.

"Kulottunga I (1098 A.D.), the king of the Chola province at that time, who was a follower of Lord Śiva and hostile toward the Vaiṣṇavas, had resolved to pluck out the eyes of Śrī Rāmānuja. Knowing this, Kureśa, whose life was dedicated to the service of his guru, came to the assembly of the king in the garb of Śrī Rāmānujācārya. As a result, he lost his eyes. Later, however, by the grace of Lord Śrī Varadarāja (Lord Nārāyaṇa) he was blessed with divine eyes. Meanwhile, the king died in a state of intense suffering from a bruise in his throat.

"Between 1118-1120 A.D. the king Ballalrao, who was a follower of Jainism, and many other followers of Buddhism became disciples of Śrī Rāmānujācārya. Śrī Rāmānujācārya spent his last sixty years in Śrīrangam and propagated the teachings of Śrī Vaisṇavism. While he was present in this world, his *śrī mūrti* (deity) was installed in Śrīrangam. The followers of the Śrī Rāmānuja lineage worship him as an *avatāra* of Śrī Lakṣmaṇa. In 1059 Śakābda (1137 A.D.) on Saturday, the tenth day of the bright fortnight of the month of Māgha (Māghī-śukla-daśamī-tithi), he entered the Vaikuṇṭha abode." (*The History and Significance of Gauḍīya Darśana*)

"Śrī Rāmānujācārya was inclined toward the worship of Śrī Viṣṇu right from his childhood. He came to Kāncipura along with his *gurudeva* and preached the doctrine of Viśiṣṭādvaita (non-duality with particular attributes) while staying in the temple of Śrī Varadarāja Svāmī. Many persons came to take shelter of his feet during his long stay there. During the same period, he compiled *Śrī Bhāṣyam* of *Vedānta-sūtra* and wrote a commentary on the *Gītā*, thereby refuting the doctrine of Kevalādvaita (pure non-duality) of Śrī Śaṅkarācārya and establishing the principles of Viśiṣṭādvaita. He performed penances on Venkaṭādri (Venkaṭa Mountain) in Tirupati for some days and also established the mode of worship of Lord Venkaṭeśa. Later, when he came to Śrīrangam and preached the tenets of Vaiṣṇavism, thousands of people were won over. Observing that countless people were joining the fold of the Vaiṣṇava school of thought, the governor of Triśirāpalli (present day Trichy), Kṛmikānta Cola, developed hostility toward Śrī Rāmānujācārya to such an extent that he employed some persons to kill him. Śrī Rāmānujācārya left Śrīrangam for Yādavapuri (Melkote) in the province of Mahisura.

"The king of Melkote, Ballālrāja, was a follower of Jainism but was broad-minded. When Śrī Rāmānujācārya freed the daughter of King Ballālrāja from a *brahma-daitya* (evil spirit) by the power of *mantra*, he gave up Jainism and accepted Śrī Rāmānujācārya as his *guru*. He became Śrī Viṣṇuvardhana. Due to this, the teachers of Jainism were enraged and subsequently engaged in a scriptural altercation and debate with Śrī Rāmānujācārya. When the great scholars of Jainism could not uphold their position in the debate and dropped out, many persons accepted the shelter of Śrī Rāmānujācārya and became Vaiṣṇavas. Since then Melkote has become a prime place of pilgrimage for the Vaiṣṇavas.

"Twelve years later when Kṛmikānta Cola died, Śrī Rāmānujācārya returned to Śrīrangam. Later, he went to various parts of India to preach *Vaiṣṇava-dharma*. He preached the doctrine of Viśiṣṭādvaita profoundly in many places of pilgrimage such as Tirupati, Maharāṣṭra, Girnar (prime pilgrimage center for Jainas), Dvāraka, Prayāg, Mathurā, Vāraṇāsī, Haridvāra, etc.

Due to his authoritative preaching, many followers of Jainism and Śaṅkara's school of thought became Vaiṣṇavas. After his pilgrimage he went to Śāradāpīṭha in Kashmir via Śrī Badarīkāśrama. The in-charges of Śāradāpīṭha were not accustomed to keeping scriptures contrary to their ideology, but later they were obliged to preserve the literature because of being defeated by Śrī Rāmānujācārya in a scriptural debate. There is hearsay that Goddess Sarasvatī had personally come to Śāradāpīṭha and posed puzzling questions from *Vedānta* to Śrī Rāmānuja. Satisfied with his replies, the goddess gave him the title Bhāṣyakāra and also presented him with a deity of Śrī Hayagrīva.

"Śrī Rāmānujācārya also converted many Bauddhas (followers of Lord Buddha) to *Vaiṣṇava-dharma*, in Gaya. After visiting the holy places Padmanābha, Siṁhācal, Kāncipurām, etc., he reached his favorite, Ṣrīrangam. At the age of 120, in 4238 Kaliyugābda he disappeared at Śrīrangam. Among his *jñānī* and *bhakta* disciples, seventy-four became *ācāryas* and *pīṭhādhipatīs* (in-charges of sacred institutions)." (*Viśvakoṣa*)

The *ācāryas* of all four Vaiṣṇava *sampradāyas* hold the same opinion that the object of worship, the worshiper and worship are eternal. According to them, if the object of worship and the worshiper are not accepted as eternal then the worship or devotion also becomes non-eternal. Such thoughts are not in favor of pure devotion. Śrīla Bhaktivinoda Ṭhākura has instructed, "The tendency to enjoy and renounce exists in this world. Harmony in this world means to keep these propensities intact. The material enjoyers desire to get rid of miseries and gain pleasures in this world and in the upper worlds by obtaining the objects of their enjoyment from the five treasurers (Viṣṇu, Śiva, Śakti, Ganeśa and Sūrya)."

Distressed by the end results of the path of enjoyment, Śākyasiṁha (prince who propagated Buddhism) took a stand against the process of *karma-kāṇḍa* (path of fruitive activities) and propagated the ideology of renunciation and austerities. According to him, the highest accomplishment is to become free from one's own independent identity and consciousness by performing austerities, sacrifices or other severe practices. That state is identified as *nirvāṇa* or *mukti*. Such consideration of liberation in which the living entity loses his or her identity results from the concept of an attempt to synthesize matter and spirit. Śrīpād Śaṅkarācārya also established most of the principles of Śākyasiṁha in a concealed way. This unifying concept, i.e., the *jiva* loses his or her identity after liberation, emerges from a combination of *nirviśeṣa* (impersonalism) and *pañcopāsanā* (worship of five deities: Viṣṇu, Śiva, Śakti, Gaṇeśa and Sūrya). In the name of universality and liberalism, unifying the imaginary (*kalpanika*) atheistic ideas that are truly deceptive and transient with the undisputed eternally existing Truth is meant only for the gross pleasure of those who are devoid of devotion and who are averse to the Supreme Lord. These so-called non-sectarian classes are the creators of the imagined cult of averseness to the Supreme Lord. Such unifying attempts, which are an indication of aversion to Śrī Viṣṇu, are not new; they were also prevalent in the past. By observing such a state of affairs, two magnanimous great personalities (Śrī Rāmānujācārya and Śrī Madhvācārya) mercifully appeared in this world, having been sent by the Lord. In order to differentiate the so-called non-sectarian worldly-minded people from the true followers of the Supreme Lord, they distinctly designated the false temporary lineage and the eternal lineage. Lakṣmaṇa Deśika became the leader in this regard.

The bona fide preceptorial channel is not a fabricated path; its followers do not give shelter to atheism in the name of non-sectarianism, which is highly deceptive. The Supreme Lord is the only eternal Truth and eternal Supreme Entity. His inconceivable potency is also eternal. The followers of the eternal path eternally worship the Supreme Entity, who has incomprehensible potencies; therefore they are the most magnanimous. No one except the worshipers of Lord Adhokṣaja can be more benevolent in this world. Material generosity is not true generosity; it is only sense gratification pretending to be generosity or, in other words, duplicity. The Samanvyavādis (followers of the unifying conception) initiated the worship of any one of Viṣṇu, Śiva, Śakti, Gaṇeśa and Sūrya in the name of magnanimity. However, factually, they have broken and destroyed with swords, figuratively speaking, the deities they have worshiped for such a long time. To illustrate using an analogy, first you whitewash and then apply plaster, but then after some time, you end up blatantly discarding the plaster!

In this way, when the Supreme Lord's eternal form and eternal worship were not being accepted, by His desire a very powerful spiritual personality, Śrī Lakṣmaṇa Deśika, later known as Śrī Rāmānujācārya, appeared in the town Mahābhūtapurī in Andhra Pradesh. After him, Śrīman Madhvācārya Pūrṇaprajña appeared. Wherever and whenever, in this world, there occurs propagation of the eternal religion of devotion to the Supreme Lord, those who are averse to Him and even the demigods, will become inimical to such propagators.

The scriptural conclusions of Śrī Rāmānujācārya are mentioned briefly in *The History and Significance of Gauḍīya Darśana* as follows:

"The conclusions of *Vedānta* of Śrī Rāmānujācārya are prevalent as Viśiṣṭādvaitavāda (non-duality with particular attributes). *Cid-acid-viśiṣṭa-advaitaṁ-tattvam*: the principles that deal with *sthūla-cid* (gross consciousness) and *acid* (that which is inanimate), *sukṣma-cid* (subtle consciousness) and *acid* (devoid of animation), the oneness and diversity (living entities) of the Supreme Brahman with principal attributes, and the prime non-dual Brahman. The name of his commentary is *Śrī Bhāṣyam*.

"**Brahman** (primordial substance): The principle meaning of 'Brahman' is 'supremely vast and unlimited by nature and qualities.' He is the supreme controller and, by virtue of being devoid of defects, the ultimate destination (*avadhi*), equal to all, infinitely auspicious—the Supreme Personality. At other places the word 'Brahman' signifies a figurative or secondary aspect only due to a partial understanding or realization of the above qualities.

"**Jīva** (living entity): The partial attribute of the substantive Paramātma (Supersoul). Since *jīva* is the body of Brahman, at particular places there is an indication of non-difference between the two. The *jīva* is eternal, without beginning, infinite, the product of Brahman, knowledgeable and the knower, the doer and the enjoyer or sufferer, finite in size, infinite in number, by state conditioned or liberated, and among the liberated either eternally liberated or liberated from the conditioned state.

"**Jagat** (material world): The gross body of personified Brahman—a partial manifestation. Like Brahman, this world endowed with attributes or qualities is also real and not false like a rope mistaken for a snake due to illusion. Brahman is the Highest Truth. Though the *jīva* and *jagat* are also real like Brahman, they are controlled by the latter, and form a hierarchy from higher to lower in the order of Brahman, *jīva* and *jagat*. The world of matter is the lowest because the other two can enjoy it. The *jīvas* are higher than *jagat* as they are conscious enjoyers, but Brahman is the highest due to being capable of mastering and controlling everything. Brahman is the ultimate and instrumental cause of the material world.

"**Māyā** (illusory potency): The potency of Parabrahman, i.e., the material nature comprised of the three modes or qualities (goodness, passion and ignorance), the creator of variegatedness. Māyā is not unreal; she enamors the *jīvas*, but the Supreme Lord, who is the controller of Māyā, creates the material world through her. Māyā is not synonymous with inexplicability or false existence—she is the energy of the Supreme Lord."

According to the Māyāvādis, there are two types of Brahman: Saguṇa-Brahman (Brahman with material attributes) and Nirguṇa-Brahman (Brahman without material attributes). They say that those who are deficient in experience and knowledge, who are incapable of worshiping the Supreme Brahman devoid of material attributes, material potency and material qualities, worship the temporary, illusioned, imaginary Brahman with material attributes.

Sādhakānāṁ hitārthāya brahmaṇarūpa kalpanaṁ: the Supreme Lord assumes form by accepting the mode of goodness of *māyā*. According to them, when the three veils of object of worship, worshiper and worship—or object of service, servitor and service or object of meditation, meditator and meditation—are broken, one attains the ultimate attainment of oneness with Nirguṇa-Brahman (formless Brahman without attributes). Vaiṣṇavas do not use the term Saguṇa-Brahman. However, if Saguṇa-Brahman does not signify the meaning given by the Māyāvādis but instead indicates the all-auspicious non-material attributes of Nirguṇa-Brahman, then the Vaiṣṇavas have no objection to such an interpretation. Māyāvādis do not understand that Nirguṇa-Brahman can have transcendental attributes of the highest auspiciousness.

Śrī Rāmānujācārya's literary contribution: (1) *Śrī Bhāṣya* (commentary on the *Brahma-sūtras*), (2) *Vedāntadīpa* (*Vedānta Brahma-sūtra-vṛtti*), (3) *Vedāntasāra* (purports to the *Brahma-sūtras*), (4) *Śrīmad Bhagavad-gītā Bhāṣya*, (5) *Vedārthasāra Saṁgraha*, (6) Prose on Vaikuṇṭha, Śaraṇāgati, Śrīrangam, (7) *Nitya-grantha* (worship of Śrī Nārāyaṇa). Other writings include: Vedānta-tattva-sāra; a commentary on Viṣṇu-sahasra-nāma (thousand names of Śrī Viṣṇu); prayers of glorification of the deity form of Śrī Viṣṇu; commentaries on Śrī Īśopaniṣad, Praśnopaniṣad, *Muṇḍaka Upaniṣad*, Śvetasvatāra Upaniṣad, Kūṭa-saṁdoha, Divyasūri-prabhāva-dīpika, etc. (Ref: *The History and Significance of Gauḍīya Darśana*)

Apart from the above, there are many more literatures compiled by Śrī Rāmānujācārya as per *Viśvakoṣa*: *Aṣṭādaṣa-rahasyam, Kaṇṭakoddhāra, Cakrollās, Devatāpāramya, Nyāya-ratnamāla-ṭīka, Nārāyaṇa-mantrārtham, Nityārādhanam-vidhi, Nyāya-pariśuddhi, Nyāya-siddhānjanam, Pancapaṭala, Pancarātra-rakṣā, Maṇidarpaṇam, Matimānuṣa, Yoga-sūtra Bhāṣya, Ratnapradīpa, Rāmapaṭala, Rāmapaddhati, Rāma-pūja-paddhati, Rāma-mantra-paddhati, Rāma-rahasya, Rāmāyaṇa-vyākhyā, Rāmārcā-paddhati, Vārttā-mālā, Viśiṣṭādvaita Bhāṣya, Śatadūṣaṇī, Sankalpa-sūryodaya-ṭīkā, Saccaritra-rakṣā, Saccaritra-rakṣā-sāra-dīpikā* and *Sarvārtha-siddhi*.

Parampūjyapāda Parivrājakācārya Tridaṇḍiyati Śrīmad Bhakti Pramode Pūri Gosvāmī Mahārāja wrote about Śrī Rāmānujācārya in his article entitled "Ācārya Śrī Rāmānuja and Śrī Yādava Prakāśa" published in the monthly magazine *Śree Chaitanya Vāṇī*, 22nd Year, Issue No. 5, page 88:

Śrī Yāmunācārya, the most prominent *ācārya* of the Śrī Rāmānuja Sampradāya, appeared in a *brāhmaṇa* family in 916 A. D. in Madurai City. His father's name was Śrī Īśvara Muni. At the time of his appearance, his grandfather Śrīnātha Muni was still living. Sri Īśvara Bhatta was the father of Śrīnātha Muni. These three personalities—Śrī Śrīnātha Muni, Śrī Īśvara Muni and Śrī Yāmunācārya—were residents of Vīrnārāyaṇpūra, which is located fifteen miles away from Cidambaram (Citrakūṭam). Śrīnātha Muni's full name was Śrī Ranganātha Muni. In Vīrnārāyaṇpūra, the temple of his family deity Mannār Koil or Mannāvāra—Śrī Kṛṣṇa or Śrī Rājagopāla Jiu—is situated. His father died when Śrī Yāmunācārya was only ten years old, and his grandfather Śrīnātha Muni entered the *sannyāsa* order. Therefore, Yāmuna Muni was brought up with great difficulty by his elderly grandmother and widowed mother. From an early age, he displayed uncommon intelligence. When he was only twelve years old he defeated the Viddvajjana Kolāhal, the court *paṇḍita* (scholar) of the king of Pāṇdya, in a scriptural debate and obtained half of the Pāṇdya kingdom as a result. Later, by the unlimited mercy of Śrī Ranganātha Muni, he accepted *sannyāsa* from Śrī Rāma Miśra, became popular as Śrī Yāmunācārya or Ālbandāra and a coronation was performed to fill the seat of *sārvabhauma-ācārya* (sovereign leader) of the Śrī Sampradāya. His four Sanskrit literary works—*Stotra-ratna*, *Siddhi-traya*, *Āgama prāmnāya* and *Gītārtha Saṁgrāha*—are held in the highest esteem in the Śrī Sampradāya.

Śrī Nambi, or Mahāpūrṇa, the disciple of Śrī Yāmunācārya, had two sisters: Bhūmipa Pirāṭṭi, or Bhūdevi, and Periya Pirāṭṭi, or Śrīdevi. The elder sister, Bhūdevi, was married to Āsuri Keśava Perumāl, or Āsuri Keśavācārya (he who performed many sacrifices), a resident of Śrī Perambudur near Cennai (Madras). Bhūdevi and Śrīdevi were also known as Kāntimatī and Dyutimatī. Śrīdevi was married to Śrī Kamalanayana Bhaṭṭa, who was born in the family of Bhaṭṭamaṇi in a village named Majhlai Mangalam. From the womb of Śrī Bhūdevi, Śrī Rāmānuja, the *ācārya* of the Śrī Sampradāya and founder of the Viśiṣṭādvaita school of thought, appeared in 938 Śakābda (1016 A.D.) Others say 939 or 940 Śakābda. As soon as Śrī Nambi, the disciple of Śrī Yāmunācārya, got news of Rāmānuja'ṣ birth, he quickly rushed to Śrī Perambudur, which is ten miles away from Tiruvallur Station on the Madras railway line. After reaching there, he embraced Śrī Keśavācārya with great pleasure and congratulated him for being blessed with the birth of a wonderful divine jewel-like son. Seeing many uncommon symptoms in the child, he repeatedly said that in the future the child would become a great spiritual personality. During the name-giving ceremony he was named Lakṣmaṇa Deśika, as it seemed that Lord Rāma's younger brother Lakṣmaṇa Himself had appeared in the form of that boy. Later, he became known worldwide as Śrī Rāmānuja.

By the order of his father, Śrī Āsuri Keśavācārya, Śrī Rāmānuja entered into family life at the age of sixteen. He studied *Vedānta* under Śrī Yādavaprakāśa, a resident of Tirupuṭkujhi near Kāncīpuram, or Kāncībharam. Śrī Yādavaprakāśa was a scholar in the Śaṅkara school of thought. Though Rāmānuja was performing the activities of studying, he was not an ordinary person. Śrī Rāmānuja was an *avatāra* of Śrī Lakṣmaṇa, the younger brother of Lord Rāmacandra. Hence he possessed transcendental powers. While he was studying under Śrī Yādavaprakāśa, transcendental activities and illumination of the highest knowledge were manifest in him.

As an illustration, the following two incidents are worthy of mention:

(1) One time, Śrī Yādavaprakāśa, while commentating on the statement *satyaṁ jñānaṁ anantaṁ brahma* in the *Taittirīya Upaniṣad*, said to his disciple Rāmānuja, "Brahman cannot simultaneously be eternal, cognizant and unlimited. Just as a cow cannot simultaneously have an unbroken horn, a broken horn and no horn, Brahman cannot have a variety of attributes simultaneously. Therefore, it is illogical to say that Brahman has qualities, as it is devoid of qualities." After listening to this commentary, the dissatisfied Rāmānujācārya said, "If Brahman is said to be eternal without qualities, then it is ascertained that Brahman is unreal. If Brahman is to be accepted as real, then one has to accept that it (He) is endowed with attributes, especially those of being eternal, cognizant and unlimited. Such a state is neither contradictory nor impossible. As per the words of *śruti*, Brahman is real. By saying that Brahman is cognizant, His eternal consciousness is to be accepted. Otherwise, Brahman will be nothing more than dull matter. Cognizance is an inseparable feature of Brahman. Brahman is unlimited and cannot be fathomed by the limited knowledge perceived by the material senses of a human. Brahman is beyond material perception, limitless and beyond all material considerations or anxieties. Therefore, Brahman's qualities of being eternal, cognizant and unlimited are interrelated and perfectly coherent. *Nirguṇa* indicates Brahman's lack of material qualities but He is the embodiment of unlimited transcendental qualities." Upon hearing this, Śrī Yādavaprakāśa was astounded by the logical statements of Śrī Rāmānuja.

(2) One time, Śrī Rāmānujācārya was massaging oil on the body of his teacher Śrī Yādavaprakāśa, who was commenting on two *ślokas* from the *Chāndogya Upaniṣad*:

atha yadevaitadādityasya śuklaṁ bhāḥ saiva
sā'tha yannīlaṁ paraḥ kṛṣṇaṁ tadamastat
sāmātha ya eṣo'ntarāditye hiraṇmayaḥ
puruṣo dṛśyate hiraṇyaśmaśṛrhiraṇyakeśa
āprāṇathāt sarva eva suvarṇaḥ (1.6.6)
tasya yathā kapyāsaṁ puṇḍarīkamevam-
akṣiṇī tasyoditi nāma sa eṣa sarvebhyaḥ
pāpmabhya udita udeti ha vai
sarvebhyaḥpāpmabhyo ya evaṁ veda (1.6.7)

The following is the essence of the treatise given by Śrī Yādavaprakāśa based upon the commentaries of Śrī Śaṅkarācārya: "Although all the limbs of the effulgent Supreme Lord are of a golden-colored complexion, His eyes possess a special significance. As the organ of evacuation of a monkey is brighter than its other organs, similarly, the Lord's eyes resemble that brilliance. Through those brilliant eyes He sees everything." Listening to the comparison between the most beautiful eyes of the Supreme Lord and the excretory organ of a monkey, the extremely agonized Śrī Rāmānujācārya shed tears incessantly. A few drops of tears fell on the body of Śrī Yādavaprakāśa. He was astounded to see that Rāmānuja was crying with a heavy heart. When the *ācārya* asked the reason for Rāmānuja's disturbed state, he replied that he was deeply hurt by listening to such a perverted meaning of the word *kapyāsaṁ*. He explained, "The word *ka* means water. As per *kaṁ pibati iti kapiḥ*, which means 'that which absorbs or dries water', the word *kapi* indicates the sun. As per *asa dhātu vikasane, na tu upaveśane* the word *āsa* means fully opened or blossomed. *Puṇḍarīka* means lotus. The two eyes of the radiant face of the Supreme Lord are thus as beautiful as the lotus that is blossomed by the sun." Even though Śrī Yādavaprakāśa was astonished by listening to the narration of his disciple Rāmānuja, he became angry and censured him.

Initially, though Śrī Yādavaprakāśa was a *guru* of the Śaṅkara lineage of Kevalādvaita (pure non-duality) and had aversion to Rāmānuja, he later became his disciple. This is an indication of Śrī Rāmānujācārya's supernatural power.

According to Śrī Śaṅkarācārya, Pūrva-mīmāṁsā by Śrī Jaimini Muni and Uttara-mīmāṁsā (Vedānta) by Śrī Vedavyāsa Muni are two independent scriptures. However, according to Śrī Rāmānujācārya both these together comprise a single scripture. The only one *Mīmāṁsā* (investigation) started by the Pūrva-mīmāṁsā (prior inquiry) of Jaimini Muni was complete with the Uttara-mīmāṁsā (posterior inquiry) of Vedavyāsa Muni. After careful contemplation of Pūrva-mīmāṁsā, when one understands *karma* and its fleeting results, then inquiry about Brahman arises. The great commentators such as Bodhāyana and others presented explanations of both the Mīmāṁsās, considering them to be a single scripture. After the death of Kuluttunga, Śrī Rāmānujācārya came to Śrīrangam along with his disciple Kureśa, and completed the commentary on *Vedānta* named *Śrī Bhāṣya* there.

In the lineage of Śrī Rāmānuja many incidents are heard that illustrate the glory of serving the Lord's own associates, or the Vaiṣṇavas. The Founder/Acārya of Śree Chaitanya Gauḍīya Maṭh, our Most Revered Gurudeva Nitya-līla-praviṣṭa Om 108 Śrī Śrīmad Bhakti Dayita Mādhava Gosvāmi Mahārāja, often used to narrate one such incident during *hari-katha* discourses: One time, during his preaching engagements along with his *sannyāsa* and *brahmacāri* disciples, Śrī Rāmānujācārya arrived at a place where he had both a wealthy *brāhmaṇa* disciple and an extremely poor *brāhmaṇa* disciple. The name of the poverty-stricken disciple was Śrī Varadārya. Upon the arrival of Śrī Rāmānujācārya along with his other disciples at the house of the wealthy devotee, initially, seeing his indifference toward serving the Vaiṣṇavas, Śrī Rāmānujācārya set his holy footprints along with his other associates in the house of the devout Varadārya. When he said the name of Varadārya at the door, he did not get any reply from inside, but instead heard the sound of three claps. He saw a threadbare woman's dress drying outside in the sun. Understanding what the claps indicated, the all-knowing Śrī Rāmānuja threw his *uttarīya* (shawl) inside the house. The wife of Varadārya wrapped herself in that cloth and came in front of her *gurudeva*, offering obeisances while crying in ecstasy. Even in her wildest dreams she never thought that her *gurudeva* would come to their house. She started weeping in an extremely distressed state, as no proper seat was available to offer to her *gurudeva*. Seeing this, Śrī Rāmānujācārya consoled her by saying, "What could be a better seating place than the natural God-given beautiful grass under the shade of a tree?" Being ordered by Śrī Rāmānujācārya, all the devotees sat under the trees where he sat on a torn *āsana* (seat) provided by the devout lady.

Śrī Rāmānujācārya had earlier told his disciples that Varadārya was extremely poor and that he could not make arrangements for their food. Rather, they had come there only to take rest for a few minutes in the house of that devotee. Varadārya's wife was extremely worried about how she would make arrangements for the midday meals of her *gurudeva* and her god-brothers.

Varadārya's wife was extremely beautiful. Attracted by her beauty, a rich merchant had earlier tried to allure her several times to get her company. However, due to her strict chastity and devoutness to her husband, the merchant could not get even the sight of her. *My husband is not home and the Vaiṣṇavas will leave without eating.* Contemplating her misfortune thus, she made up her mind to sell her body, made only of blood and flesh. She arrived at the house of the rich merchant in order to collect ingredients for the service of the Vaiṣṇavas. Seeing her all of a sudden, the astonished merchant enquired as to the cause of her arrival. She replied that she needed the necessary ingredients for the service of her *gurudeva* and other Vaiṣṇavas who had come to her house, and that in return she would offer her body to him. She promised that she would come again after dusk to fulfill his desires. On hearing this, the greatly pleased merchant sent twice the amount of the ingredients she had requested.

In the house of the *brāhmaṇa* Varadārya, a Nārāyaṇa Śālagrama was worshiped daily. Varadārya's wife offered many delicacies to the Lord, pleased her *gurudeva* and the Vaiṣṇavas by serving them the *prasāda* remnants of the Lord and waited fasting until the arrival of her husband. After taking *prasāda*, Śrī Rāmānuja and the other Vaiṣṇavas rested under the trees in the afternoon. Varadārya returned with the bag he carried for begging alms and was astonished to see them. He offered prostrated obeisances to his *guru* and cried incessantly in an overjoyed state. For a long time he had been extremely eager for the *darśana* of his *gurudeva* but never thought even in a dream that *gurudeva* himself would come along with his other disciples to the house of such a poverty-stricken person like him. He had only a few grains of rice in his bag that he had collected by begging alms. The grieved Varadārya entered the house and was astonished to see various types of delicacies and remaining ingredients. He enquired from his wife how she could have collected so much. When she requested him to honor *prasāda* first, he said that his mind had become restless and that he could not take even a morsel of food until he knew from where she had acquired the necessary items. Upon his repeated questioning, she fell at his feet and started crying. She revealed her guilt and begged for his forgiveness. Varadārya was dumbstruck listening to such impossible words from his chaste wife and honored the *prasāda* with much gravity. After he had finished his meal she took his remnants. Before leaving that place, the all-knowing Śrī Rāmānuja told Varadārya and his wife to give the remaining Nārāyaṇa *prasāda* to the person who had supplied the ingredients for the offering.

In order to keep her promise, Varadārya's wife fell at his feet and requested his permission to leave. Both of them cried in separation from each other. After some time, Varadārya became composed and boldly said, "I am extremely poor. I cannot even sumptuously feed you two times a day, cannot give you clothes to wear, what to speak of giving you ornaments. I know how many enticements the merchant, to whom you sold your body, used earlier to gain your grace on him. However, he could not even get a glimpse of you. That very person has sold her body for the service of *guru* and the Vaiṣṇavas. I don't believe that any person in this universe has the capacity to touch even the tip of your hair. You please go fearlessly."

When Varadārya's wife reached the merchant's place he was extremely pleased and astonished. She told him that she would fulfill his desire but requested him to first honor the *prasāda* that was prepared using the items sent by him for the service of Lord Nārāyaṇa, guru and the Vaiṣṇavas. When the merchant agreed, she offered him the remnant *prasāda* of her *gurudeva*. Such is the wonderful nature of *prasāda* that as soon as the merchant honored it, his consciousness was transformed and his mind's pollution was expelled. The merchant, who was burning in the flames of repentance, started crying loudly while falling at the feet of Varadārya's wife. With an aggrieved heart he said, "You are not an ordinary but a celestial woman. I am not even destined for hell. I desired to enjoy a chaste and saintly woman like you. In spite of my countless attempts and allurements I could not even get the sight of you, what to speak of your physical association. Yet today that very person has come to sell her own body in lieu of some small quantity of rice, pulses and vegetables. Please tell me who visited your house."

When the merchant heard about the arrival of Śrī Rāmānujācārya, he immediately left in search of him. The merchant fell at the feet of Varadārya and his wife and begged forgiveness for his offenses. He took *dīkṣā* from Śrī Rāmānujācārya and served Varadārya and his wife throughout their lives.

Extracts from the *New Encyclopaedia Britannica*, Volume 9: "Rāmānuja, also called Rāmānujācārya or Ilaiya Perumal (Tamil: Ageless Perumal, i.e. God) [b.c. 1017, Sriperumbudur, India-d. 1137, Srirangam], South Indian *brāhmaṇa* theologian and philosopher, the single most influential thinker of devotional Hinduism. After a long pilgrimage, Rāmānuja settled in Sri Rangam, where he organized temple worship and founded centers to disseminate his doctrine of devotion to the God Viṣṇu and His consort Śrī. He provided an intellectual basis for the practice of *bhakti* (devotional worship) in three major commentaries: the Vedārtha-sangraha (on the *Veda*), the Śrī Bhāṣya (on the *Brahma-sūtras*) and the *Bhagavad-gīta-bhāṣya* (on the *Bhagavad-gītā*).

"Information on the life of Rāmānuja consists only of the accounts given in the legendary biographies about him, in which a pious imagination has embroidered historical details. According to tradition, he was born in South India, in Tamil Nadu state. He showed early signs of theological acumen and was sent to Kanci (Kancipuram) for schooling under the teacher Yādavaprakāśa, who was a follower of the monistic system of Vedānta of Śaṅkara, the famous 8th century philosopher. Rāmānuja's profoundly religious nature was soon at odds with a doctrine that offered no room for a personal God. After falling out with his teacher, he had a vision of God Viṣṇu and His consort 'Śrī' or 'Lakṣmi' and instituted a daily worship ritual at the place where he beheld Them.

"He became a temple priest at the Varadarāja temple at Kanci, where he began to expound the doctrine that the goal of those who aspire to final release from transmigration is not impersonal Brahman but rather Brahman as identified with the personal God, Viṣṇu. In Kanci as well as Śrīrangam, where he was to become associated with the Ranganātha temple, he developed the teaching that the worship of a personal God and the soul's union with Him is an essential part of the doctrines of the *Upaniṣads* upon which the system of *Vedānta* is built. Therefore, the teachings of the Vaiṣṇavas and Bhāgavatas (worshipers and ardent devotees of Viṣṇu) are not heterodox. In this way he continued the teachings of Yāmuna (Yāmunācārya, 10th century), his predecessor at Śrīrangam, to whom he was related on his mother's side. He set forth this doctrine in his three major commentaries.

"Although Rāmānuja's contribution to *Vedānta* thought is highly significant, his influence on the course of Hinduism as a religion has been even greater. By integrating the urge for devotional worship (*bhakti*) into his doctrine of salvation, he aligned popular religion with the pursuits of philosophy and gave *bhakti* an intellectual basis. Ever since, *bhakti* has remained the major force in the systems of religion under the umbrella of the term 'Hinduism'. His emphasis on the necessity of religious worship as a means of salvation, framed in a more systematic context, was a continuation of the devotional effusions of the Alvars, the 7th-10th century poet-mystics of Southern India, whose verses became incorporated into temple worship. This devotional sentiment or mood (*bhakti*), guided by Rāmānuja, made its way into Northern India, where its influence on religious thought and practice has been profound.

"Rāmānuja's doctrine, which was passed on and augmented by later generations, still identifies a caste of *brāhmaṇas* in Southern India, the Śrī Vaiṣṇavas. They became divided into two sub-castes, the northern, or 'Vaḍakalai' and the southern, or 'Tenkalai'. At issue between the two schools is the question of God's grace. According to the Vaḍakalai, who seem to align with Rāmānuja's intention more closely, God's grace is certainly active in man's quest for Him but does not supplant the necessity of man's extending effort toward God. The Tenkalai, on the other hand, hold that God's grace is paramount and that the only gesture needed from man is his total submission to God (*prapatti*).

"A temple and an active Viśiṣṭādvaita school now commemorate the site of Rāmānuja's birthplace in Śrī Perembudur. The doctrines he promulgated still inspire a lively intellectual tradition, and the religious practices he emphasized are still carried on in the two most important Vaiṣṇava centers in Southern India, the Ranganātha temple in Śrīrangam and the Venkaṭeśvara temple in Tirupati, both in Tamil Nadu." (The *New Encyclopaedia Britannica*, Volume 9, Page 918-Extracts)

Footnotes:

Vaḍakalai: like a monkey; the offspring of a monkey holds firmly to its mother, signifying the importance of practice or endeavor of the practitioner (devotee).

Tenkalai: like a cat; the offspring of a cat completely surrenders fearlessly to its mother, signifying the importance of surrender of the practitioner to God.

Śrī Viṣṇusvāmī

Śrī Viṣṇusvāmī is the founder of Śrī Rudra Sampradāya, which is one of the four Vaiṣṇava lineages and which has originated from Śrī Rudra. The Rudra Sampradāya is also famous as the Viśṇusvāmī Sampradāya, having taken his name. Different scriptures describe Viṣṇusvāmī in various ways. *The History and Significance of Gauḍīya Darśana* mentions these different opinions.

Śrī Viṣṇusvāmī is the founder of the doctrine of Śuddhādvaita (purified monism). Śrī Vallabhācārya propagated this doctrine widely. Śrī Yadunāthajī, the grandson of Śrī Vallabhācārya, established Śrī Vallabhācārya to be the successor *ācārya* in the lineage of Śrī Viṣṇusvāmī, in his Sanskrit compilation *Śrī Vallabha-digvijaya*. That scripture describes the history of Śrī Viṣṇusvāmī serially.

The Vaiṣṇava *ācāryas* appeared in the Draviḍa region of South India. However, the place of appearance of Śrī Viṣṇusvāmī has not been ascertained clearly. The original Viṣṇusvāmī is indicated to be the son of Śrī Devasvāmī, the priest of the Pāndya king Pāndyavijaya. In the disciplic succession of Śrī Viṣṇusvāmī, which is known as Śrī Rāja Viṣṇusvāmī, appeared 700 *ācāryas* after the original Śrī Viṣṇusvāmī. He installed the Dvārakādhīśa deity in Dvāraka. Later, he went to Kānchī and coronated Śrī Bilvamaṅgala, chief among the renunciates in the Draviḍa region, as his successor. Sri Bilvamaṅgala further appointed Śrī Devamaṅgala as his successor *ācārya* and left for Vṛndāvana. It is said that, by his yogic powers, Śrī Bilvamaṅgala lived for 700 years under a tree on a bank of the Brahma-kuṇḍa by the order of Śrī Kṛṣṇa. Meanwhile, the third Vīṣṇusvāmī, named Śrī

Prabhu Viṣṇusvāmī, appeared. He engaged a few renunciates—Śrī Saptabodhi Paṇḍita, Śrī Somagiri Yati and others—in the worship of Śrī Nṛsiṁhadeva. Śrī Lakṣmaṇa Bhaṭṭa, the father of Śrī Vallabha Bhaṭṭa, or Śrī Vallabhācārya, is among the household disciples of this third Vīṣṇusvāmī.

In the scripture *Rāmpaṭala* a brief history of the Viṣṇusvāmī lineage is mentioned. The *pañca-saṁskāra* (five purificatory processes for *sannyāsa*) of Vaiṣṇavas is also mentioned there.

Bhaviṣya Purāṇa tells us that Śrī Viṣṇusvāmī appeared as the son of Śrī Śiva Datta in the town Kalinjar on the full-moon day of the month of Bhādra. He exclusively worshiped Śrī Viṣṇu as the Supreme Godhead, as the cause of the entire universe, as an eternal, cognizant and blissful form, and propagated the same. Hence, he became famous as Viṣṇusvāmī.

Dr. Farkuhar states that Śrī Viṣṇusvāmī appeared somewhere in South India. Like Śrī Madhvācārya, he also worshiped Śrī Kṛṣṇa, considering the living entities' identity to be separate from the Lord. Śri Madhvamuni was not a worshiper of Śrī Rādhā, whereas Śrī Viṣṇusvāmī was a worshiper of Śrī Kṛṣṇa along with Śrī Rādhika—this was the difference between them. It is said that Śrī Viṣṇusvāmī penned the literatures *Vedānta-sūtra-bhāṣyam* (commentary on *Vedānta-sūtra*), *Śrī Gītā-bhāṣya* (commentary on *Śrī Gītā*), *Śrīmad Bhāgavata-bhāṣya* (commentary on *Śrīmad Bhāgavatam*), *Viṣṇu-rahasya* and *Tattva-traya*.

In an assembly of *puṣṭi-marga* Vaiṣṇavas on Clive Street in Kolkata, the invitee Śrīla Bhakti Siddānta Sarasvati Gosvāmī Ṭhākura Prabhupāda spoke about the loving relationship and exchange between the Gauḍīya Vaiṣṇavas and Śrī Vallabhācārya. He said that Śrī Rūpa Gosvāmī had given the eligibility to Śrī Viṭṭhalanātha, the son of Śrī Vallabha, for worshiping the Bālagopāla and Kiśoragopāla deities. Śrī Vallabha Bhaṭṭa appeared in the lineage of Śrī Viṣṇusvāmī. In the institution of Viṣṇusvāmī near Mārkaṇḍeya Sarovara in Śrī Puruṣottama-dhāma, a deity of Śrī Mahāvīra or Śrī Bajrāṅgajī is seated. There are two places of Vaiṣṇava assembly situated toward the south on the way to the Guṇḍicā temple that belong to the Śrī Viṣṇusvāmī Sampradāya. As per some others, the *maṭha* in Śrī Jagannātha Vallabha Udyān was the original sacred sanctum of the Viṣṇusvāmī Sampradāya. The family religious guide of Śrī Rāi Rāmānanda was in the lineage of Śrī Viṣṇusvāmī. That is the reason Śrī Rāi Rāmānanda used to stay in Śrī Jagannātha Udyān many times.

In the second division of the *Śrī Vallabha-digvijaya* scripture, where a description of Śrī Viṣṇusvāmī and his lineage is found, the following is mentioned:

Śrī Devasvāmī, who was an ardent devotee, was a priest of the king of the Pāṇḍya province that belonged to ancient Draviḍa. Śrī Viṣṇusvāmī, the son of Devasvāmī, is an *avatāra* of Śrī Viṣṇu. Right from his childhood Śrī Viṣṇusvāmī was a worshiper of Bālagopāla. In spite of worshiping Bālagopāla for a year, when he did not get His direct vision (*darśana*), he was aggrieved at heart but fasted completely and continued the worship. On the seventh day, the Supreme Lord gave the child a divine vision in the form of Bālagopāla and ordered him to preach the *veda-dharma*, *Śrīmad Bhāgavatam*. This had been instructed by Śrī Śukadeva as the natural commentary on *Vedānta* intended by Śrī Vyāsadeva after hearing it directly from Śrī Vyāsadeva himself. Later, Śrī Viṣṇusvāmī received a divine vision and direct instructions from Śrī Vyāsadeva on Gandhamādana Mountain. The divine knowledge obtained through Śrī Nārāyaṇa to Śrī Sankarṣana to Purāri Śrī Rudra to Nārada to Śrī Vyāsa was attained by Śrī Viśṇusvāmī.

In Kāncī Śrī Viṣṇusvāmī instructed *bhāgavata-dharma* to his disciples Devadarśana, Śrīkaṇṭha, Sahasrārci, Śatadhṛti, Kumārapāda, Parābhūti, etc. Śrī Viṣṇusvāmī gave his literature and the deity he worshiped to his disciple Śrī Devadarśana and entered into the eternal pastimes of the Supreme Lord. Seven hundred *ācāryas* appeared in the disciplic succession of Śrī Viṣṇusvāmī. (*Acintya Bhedābhedavāda*, by Śrī Sundarānanda Vidyāvinode)

The Śuddhādvaitavāda of Śrī Viṣṇusvāmī

As per this school of thought, the Supreme Lord, His form and His devotees are pure and eternal. The living entities, material world and *māyā* are the objective aspects of the Supreme Lord, and hence they are non-different from Him. Therefore, Śrī Viṣṇusvāmī's school of thought is famous as Śuddhādvaitavāda (pure non-duality). The living entities are covered by the *māyā* of the Supreme Lord in all respects. Though conscious and self-luminous by nature, they are receptacles of distress. There are two types of living entities: conditioned and liberated. The liberated souls are many in number.

The Lord controls Māyā. She is the oppressor of the living entities and the symbol of nescience. As per the statement of Śrī Śrīdhara Svāmipāda, Śrī Viṣṇusvāmī accepted the existence of the internal potency of the eternal, conscious and blissful Supreme Lord.

In the commentary by Medhātithi on *Manu-saṁhita* there is mention of Śrī Viṣṇusvāmī.

Differences Between the Doctrines of Śrī Śaṅkarācārya and Śrī Viṣṇusvāmī

1) Another description of Śrī Śaṅkara's Kevalādvaita (monism) is oneness with un-variegated Brahman. Brahman is the only eternal and non-dual substance. The living entities and the material world are nothing but a transformation of Brahman.

In the Śuddhādvaita (purified monism) school of thought of Śrī Viṣṇusvāmī, the Supreme Lord is pure. The form of the Lord and the forms of His devotees are also pure and eternal. The non-duality of the Lord with the living entities, material world and *māyā* is due to them being the objective aspects of the Supreme Lord.

2) As per Śrī Śaṅkara, the Ultimate Reality is without form, attributes and qualities. All that has form, attributes and qualities is illusory, temporary, material and false.

As per Śrī Viṣṇusvāmī, the Ultimate Reality is eternal, conscious and transcendental with a completely blissful form. His form is eternally blissful and truly spiritual. This Transcendental

Reality is an eternal personality. He is neither illusioned nor temporary.

3) As per Śrī Śaṅkara, Māyā is indescribable. She is insignificant from the perspective of scripture, indefinable by logic and real only from the worldly perspective.

As per Śrī Viṣṇusvāmī, *māyā* is completely under the control of the Lord. *Māyā* can oppress the living entities but cannot so much as touch the Lord. There is no existence of *māyā* in the Supreme Lord and there is no existence of the internal potency (*svarūpa-śakti*) in the living entities.

4) As per Śrī Śaṅkara, the living entity is the deluded Brahman due to its identification with nescience, but in reality there is no actual existence of the living entity.

As per Śrī Viṣṇusvāmī, the *māyā* of Paramātmā covers the living entities. She censures them. Though they are self-luminous by nature, yet they are receptacles of distress. The liberated beings have eternal spiritual forms by the desire of the Supreme Lord and perform service to His eternal personality. (*The History and Significance of Gauḍīya Darśana*)

Śrī Amṛtalala Cakravarti in his book *Śuddhādvaita-darśana* examined various aspects of the doctrine of Śuddhādvaita in depth. In the preface to this book he remarked, "Therefore, it is understood that the doctrine of Śuddhādvaitavada must be the subject of proper deliberation by philosophers and the intelligent class of people. However, it is a matter of regret that, though this highest and excellent ideology is capable of bringing about the topmost spiritual welfare to the entire universe and is the most profound source of knowledge, even today it is limited to the consideration of a particular lineage only."

"Vallabhācārya himself belonged to the Rudra sect established by Viṣṇusvāmī, and his philosophical system of 'pure non-dualism' (Śuddhādvaita), i.e. the identity of God and the universe, closely follows that of the Viṣṇusvāmī tradition. God is worshiped not by fasting and physical austerities, but by love of Him and the universe. Salvation arises only by virtue of the grace of God. In order to receive divine love, the devotee must surrender himself wholly (*samarpaṇa*) to God's gift of love." (*Encyclopedia Britannica*, Volume 12, page 247)

The well-known commentator Śrī Śrīdhara-Svāmīpāda considered some teachings of Śrī Viṣṇusvāmī as the source of liberation and some others as apothegms of great wisdom.

"When knowledge of the simultaneous difference and non-difference (between the living entity and Supreme Lord) disappears due to misidentification of the self, one commits offenses to the feet of Śrī Śrīdhara-Svāmīpāda, the non-different manifestation of Śrī Viṣṇu-svāmipāda, the protector of devotees. By mistaking the ideology of Śuddhādvaita (purified monism) to be the same as that of Kevalādvaita (monism), we become deprived of the service activities of the dear associates of our dearmost Lord. Further, due to being deprived of following in the footsteps of Śrī Vyāsa, we become divorced from the conclusions of devotion (*bhaktisiddānta*), thereby inviting ignorance. Thus, bewildered by false ego, we become material sense enjoyers and empiric speculators, resulting in the abandonment of the process of descension (*śrota-panthā*)." (Śrīla Prabhupāda's *Vaktṛtāvalī*, Part 1, page 18-19)

śrīnārayaṇera śiṣya 'rudra' kṛpāmaya
tānra śiṣya-praśiṣyera anta nāhi haya
viṣṇusvāmī-śiṣya hailena sei gaṇe
bhakti-rasa-matta haila nija śiṣya-sane
param prabhāv-vidyā sakala śāstrete
viśṇusvāmī-sampradākhyā haila tānha haite

"Rudra (Śiva), the merciful disciple of Śrī Nārāyaṇa, had many disciples and grand-disciples. Among them was Śrī Viṣṇusvāmī, who was intensely absorbed in the devotional mellows along with his disciples. He was extremely powerful and well-versed in all scriptures, and thus the appellation Viṣṇusvāmī Sampradāya." (*Bhaktiratnākara*, Chapter 5, 2124-26)

In *Śrī Navadvīpa-dhāma Māhātmya* Śrīla Bhaktivinoda Ṭhākura, while describing the glories of Rudradvīpa, states that Śrī Viṣṇusvāmī arrived in Śrī Navadvīpa-dhāma and received Śrī Gaurānga Mahāprabhu's mercy:

kadācid viṣṇusvāmī āsi' digvijaye
rudradvīpe rahe rātre śiṣyagaṇa laye
hari hari boli' nṛtya kare śiṣyagaṇa
viṣṇusvāmī śṛti-stuti karena paṭhan
bhakti-ālocanā dekhi' haye harṣita
kṛpā kari' dekhā dila śrīnīla-lohita
vaiṣṇava sabhāya rudra haila upanīta
dekhi' viṣṇusvāmī ati haila camakita
kara judi stava kare viṣṇu tatakṣaṇa
dayārdra haiya rudra balena vacana
"tomarā vaiṣṇavajana mama priya ati
bhakti-ālocanā dekhi' tuṣṭa mama mati
vara māga, diba āmi haiya sadaya
vaiṣṇave adeya mor kichu nāhi haya"
daṇḍavat praṇamiya viṣṇu mahāśaya
kara judi vara māge premānandamaya
'aei vara deha prabhu āmā sabākāre
bhakti-sampradāya-siddhi labhi ataḥpare'
parama ānande rudra vara kari dān
nija sampradāya bali' karila ākhyān
sei haite viṣṇusvāmī svīya-sampradāya
śrī-rudra-nāmete khyāti diyā nāce gāya
rudra-kṛpā-bale viṣṇu ei sthāne rahiyā
bhajila śrī gauracandra premer lāgiyā
svapne āsi śrīgaurānga viṣṇure balila
mama bhakta rudra-kṛpā tomāre haila
dhanya tumi navadvīpe pāile bhakti-dhana
śuddhādvaita mata pracāraha eikṣaṇa
kata dine habe mora prakaṭa samaya
śrī vallabha bhaṭṭa-rūpe haibe udaya'
"madhva haite sāradvaya kariba grahaṇ
ek haya keval-advaita nirasan
kṛṣṇa-mūrti nitya jāni tānhāra sevan
sei ta dvitīya sār jāna mahājan
rāmānuja haite āmi lai dui sār
ananya-bhakati, bhakta-jana-seva ār
viṣṇu haite dui sār kariba svīkār
tadīya sarvasvabhāv, rāgamārga ār
toma (nimbārka) haite laba āmi dui mahāsār
ekanta rādhikāśraya, gopībhāva ār

"One time, Viṣṇusvāmī came here during the course of his tour to defeat opposing philosophies. He stayed the night with his followers in Rudradvīpa. The disciples began dancing and singing 'Haribol!' while Viṣṇusvāmī recited prayers from the *śrutis*. Pleased by their devotional discussions, Nīla-lohita (another name of Śiva) mercifully appeared there. Upon Śiva's arrival in the assembly of Vaiṣṇavas, Viṣṇusvāmī became surprised. With folded hands, he offered prayers and recited appropriate praises. Mercifully, Śiva spoke to him, 'All of you Vaiṣṇavas are very dear to me. Your devotional talks have pleased me. Ask a boon and I will grant it. There is nothing I will not give to the Vaiṣṇavas.'

"The great saint Viṣṇusvāmī offered his *daṇḍavats* and, filled with ecstatic love, he said, 'Give us this one gift that henceforth we will attain success in a lineage that teaches devotional service.'

"In great bliss, Rudra consented and named the *sampradāya* after himself. Thus, Viṣṇusvāmī's *sampradāya* is called the Rudra Sampradāya. With the mercy of Rudra, Viṣṇusvāmī stayed there and worshiped Śrī Gauracandra with a desire to attain love of God.

"Śrī Gaurāṅga appeared to him in a dream and said, 'By Rudra's mercy you have become My devotee. You are fortunate to attain the treasure of *bhakti* in Navadvīpa. Now go out and preach the philosophy of Śuddhādvaita (pure non-duality). The time of My appearance on earth will soon come. At that time, you will appear as Śrī Vallabha Bhaṭṭa. From Madhva I shall receive two essential items: his complete defeat of the Mayāvāda philosophy and his service to the deity of Kṛṣṇa, accepting the deity as an eternal spiritual being. From Rāmānuja I shall receive two great teachings: the concept of one-pointed devotion and service to the devotees. From Viṣṇusvāmī's teachings I shall receive two main elements: the sentiment of exclusive dependence on Kṛṣṇa and the path of *rāga-bhakti*. And from you (Nimbārka) I shall receive two excellent principles: the exclusive shelter of Śrī Rādhika and the high esteem for the *gopīs'* love of Śrī Kṛṣṇa." (*Śrī Navadvīpa-dhāma Māhātmya* - "Glories of Śrī Bilvapakṣa-Belpukur") Note: Among the writings of the Śrī Viṣṇusvāmī lineage the following scriptures are mentioned: *Sākāra-siddhi*, by Śrīkānti Miśra, *Śrī Kṛṣṇa Karṇāmṛta*, by Śrī Bilvamaṅgala Ṭhākura, and *Bhāgavata-laghu-ṭīkā*, by Śrī Varadarāja.

Śrī Nimbārka

Śrī Nimbārka appeared in the family lineage of Trailanga *brāhmaṇas* who belong to a place called Mungerpaṭṭaṇ or Mungipaṭṭaṇ of Telangadeśa. His father's name was Śrī Āruṇi Muni and his mother's was Śrī Jayantī Devī.

Śrī Nimbārka, the manifestation of the Sudarśana-cakra of Śrī Viṣṇu, appeared in this world during dusk on a full-moon day in the month of Kārtik. According to some others, Nimbārkācārya appeared on the third day of the waxing moon in the month of Vaiśākha. It is said that, by the strength of his *yogic* powers, Nimbārkācārya stopped the sunset by inducing the sun-god to wait on a *nīm* (margosa) tree, thus allowing Nimbārkācārya to serve a guest *sannyāsī* before sundown. Due to this pastime, he became famous as Nimbāditya or Nimbārka. (*The History and Significance of Gauḍīya Darśana*)

As per the opinion of the members of the Nimbārka lineage, his father, Āruṇi, was a descendant of Aruṇa Muni, who arrived in the assembly of King Parīkṣit. Aruṇa Muni is mentioned in *Śrīmad Bhāgavatam* 1.19.11:

anye ca devarṣi-maharṣivaryā
rājarṣivaryā aruṇādayaśca
nānārṣeya pravarān sametān
abhyarcya rāja śirasā vavande

"(In Śukratala on the banks of River Gangā) many *devarṣis* (great sages among demigods), *maharṣis* (great sages), *rājarṣis* (saintly kings) and *kāṇḍarṣis* like Aruṇa Muni, etc., had arrived. Seeing the assembled highly exalted sages, King Parīkṣit worshiped them as per the scriptural injunctions and prostrated himself on the ground."

According to the *New Bengali Dictionary* by Āśutoṣadeva, Aruṇa was the elder brother of Garuḍa. His father was the great sage Kaśyapa, and his mother's name was Vinatā. Kadrū was the other wife of Sage Kaśyapa and was the daughter of Dakṣa Prajāpati.She mothered a hundred snakes from a hundred eggs. The jealous Vinatā gave birth to two eggs and broke one of them in an undeveloped state. From this egg, Aruṇa came forth without thighs. He became the chariot driver of the sun-god. His wife's name is Śyenī. Sampāti and Jaṭāyu are his two sons.

Nimbārkācārya's Appearance

The exact time of Nimbārkācārya's appearance is unknown. At Jainath, there is a temple that is approximately six miles southeast of Ādilābād within Hyderabad province. An inscription has been found on a stone there. From this inscription, it can be inferred that Śrī Nimbārkācārya appeared before the eleventh century A.D. The inscription reads:

oṁ namaḥ sūryāya
akāle 'pi raverväre nimba-punyodgamairayam
pratyayaṁ pūrayan bhānunniratyayam upāsyatām

"Worship the sun-god, who fulfills the desires of all, with the sacred leaves and flowers of a *nīm* tree on Sunday—even at an unusual or forbidden time, without fail"

As per this inscription, it can be understood that there was a system of worshiping the sun-god. In *Bhaviṣya Purāṇa* it is written: *nimbañca sūryadevasya vallabhaṁ tathā*—the *nīm* tree with its leaves and flowers are especially dear to the sun. Hence the *nīm* tree is worshiped as a symbol of the sun-god.

It is also stated in *Bhaviṣya Purāṇa* that Nimbārka, or Nimbāditya, is a distinctive name for the sun-god:

udayavyāpinī grāhyā kūle tithirūpoṣaṇaiḥ
nimbārko bhagavāneṣāṁ vāñchitārtha phalapradaḥ

In *Viśvakoṣa*, the well-known Bengali dictionary, it is written:

"Nimbārkācārya is the pioneer of the Nīmat branch of the Vaiṣṇava lineage. He was a famous scholarly and saintly person. He used to reside on Dhruva Mountain near Vṛndāvana. After his disappearance, his disciples constructed a shrine for him there. This is a place of pilgrimage for Vaiṣṇavas. His father, Jagannātha, named him Bhāskarācārya in his childhood. He was believed by people to be a partial manifestation of the sun-god. He was an ardent devotee of Lord Śrī Kṛṣṇa. He was also known as Niyamānanda. In order to preserve the honor of His devotee, Lord Nārāyaṇa appeared as the sun and fulfilled his prayers. In this regard there is hearsay that one time a *daṇḍī* (renunciate) came to him and, seeing the sunset as they were discussing the scriptures, Nimbāditya brought some eatables in order to remove the fatigue of his guest. However, that *daṇḍī* would not eat anything after dusk; therefore he would not accept the hospitality of Nimbāditya. As a remedy, Nimbāditya obstructed the sun from setting. Pleased by his prayers and devotion, the sun-god waited on a nearby *nīm* tree until the guest finished his meals. Since then, he became famous as Nimbārka or Nimbāditya, as the sun-god had obeyed his command."

The Doctrines of Nimbārkācārya

According to Śrī Nimbārka, Brahman has attributes. The *Brahma-sūtra* aphorism *athāto brahma jijñāsa* ascertains Brahman as an object of knowledge and, therefore, that

one should inquire about Him. If Brahman were not an object of knowledge, then the possibility of inquiring about Him would not exist. The form of Brahman is described by Śrīnivāsācārya, a disciple of Śrī Nimbārkācārya, in his commentary to *Brahma-sūtra*, *Vedānta-kaustubha*.

The following passages are taken from the book *Acintya-bhedābhedavāda*:

The doctrine of Nimbārkācārya is described as factual or intrinsic Bhedābhedavāda (dualistic non-dualism). The commentary on *Vedānta* by Nimbārka is called *Vedānta-pārijāta-saurabha*. Oneness and difference eternally coexist and, in all states at all times, oneness and difference exist uniformly. Brahman is the cause; the living entities and the world are effects. Brahman is powerful; the living entities and the world are his two potencies. Brahman is a complete entity, whereas the *jīvas* and the material world are within Brahman and are His minutest particles.

Difference between the cause and effect, the energetic and energy and the Complete Entity and His fragments is factual, innate and eternal. Brahman is the object of meditation, knowledge and attainment. The living entities are the meditators, knowledge seekers and recipients. Brahman is the cause of creation, sustenance and annihilation. He is all-pervasive and completely independent. The living entities are devoid of the power of creation, maintenance and annihilation; they are atomic and controlled.

Both the conditioned souls and liberated souls are different from Brahman. This natural and intrinsic difference between Brahman and the other sentient beings is eternal. Brahman is conscious, non-material, not gross and eternally pure. Contrarily, the world is devoid of consciousness, material, gross and impure. Therefore, the constitutional difference between Brahman and the world exists eternally. Just as the difference between Brahman, the living beings and the world is eternal, the intrinsic similarity between them is also equally true and eternal.

The cause is different from the effect in the context of features and activity, but similar by nature. The cause is different from the effect because the properties and activities of both are not the same, e.g., a clay pot is different from clay because the pot has a specific shape and function/activity—to carry water, a purpose different from that of clay. However, in spite of this, they are non-different because the clay pot is nothing but clay. Therefore, the effect is the result of the causal potency of the cause, and rests in the cause. Hence the cause and effect are non-different. The doctrine of Nimbārkācārya is therefore known as intrinsic oneness and difference.

Characteristic Opinions of Śrī Śaṅkarācārya, Śrī Bhāskarācārya, and Śrī Nimbārkācārya

The following brief summaries were compiled from *The History and Significance of Gauḍīya Darśana*:

Śrī Śaṅkarācārya was a proponent of Kevalādvaitavāda, pure monism. He concluded that the absolute knowledge principle without variety, attributes, activities and transformation is the nature of Brahman.

Śrī Bhāskarācārya was a proponent of temporary or figurative oneness and difference. He advocated the formless to be the cause of everything and accepted its effect, the living entities and the world, as real.

Śrī Nimbārkācārya was a proponent of factual or intrinsic oneness and difference. According to him, Absolute Truth and Ultimate Reality is an infinite, inconceivable, colossal principle possessing intrinsic transcendental potency.

Śrī Bhāskarācārya designated Ultimate Reality to be Brahman, unlike Śrī Nimbārkācārya, who described the Supreme to be Kṛṣṇa and Puruṣottama, and conceived His internal potency to be Śrī Rādhikā. Śrī Bhāskarācārya did not describe the beauty, sweetness, supremacy and Transcendental Personality of Brahman. His ideology is not in line with the Vaiṣṇava philosophy that recognizes transcendental divine qualities in Brahman. It is a variant of Śrī Śaṅkarācārya's undifferentiated monism.

The famous *vedānta-ācāryas* of the Śrī Nimbārka Sampradāya, Śrī Devācārya and Śrī Sundarabhya, refuted the doctrine of Śrī Bhāskarācārya in their respective commentaries on the *Brahma-sūtras* (*brahma-sūtra-vṛtti*).

Śrī Nimbārkācārya's Initiation into the Sanaka Sampradāya

The well-known *guru-paramparā* (spiritual lineage) of Śrī Nimbārkācārya is Śrī Haṁsa to Śrī Catuḥsana to Śrī Nārada to Śrī Nimbārkācārya. Hence, the Nimbārka Sampradāya is known as the Catuḥsana Sampradāya or Haṁsa Sampradāya. The conventional name is Nimāyet or Niyamānandi.

In the book *Śrī Nimbārka and Dvaitādvaita-darśana* (originally from *Vedānta-pārijāta-Saurabha*, by Śrī Nimbārkācārya in his commentary on the *Brahma-sūtras* 1.3.8), the following is cited:

paramācāryaiḥ śrī kumārairasmad-gurave śrīman
nāradāyopadiṣṭo bhūmātveva vijijñāsitavya iti

Śrī Nimbārkācārya himself very clearly said that he is a disciple of Śrī Nārada, who in turn is a disciple of the Four Kumāras. The following verses appear in *Bhakti-ratnākara* 5.2127-2131:

sanaka-sampradā yeiche śuna śrīnivās
nārāyaṇa haite haṁsavigraha-vilās
tāṇra śiṣya sanakādi cāri mahāṣay
tāṇra śiṣya-praśiṣyera lekhā nāhi hay

sei gaṇa madhye nimbāditya śiṣya haila
tāṇha haite nimbāditya-sampradā calila
nimbāditya--prabhāv param camatkār
tāṇra śiṣya-praśiṣyete vyāpila saṁsār

śrī-brahma-rudra-sanaka sampradāyagaṇe
haila sampradā bahu prabhāv-kāraṇe

"Hear now, Śrīnivāsa, about the Sanaka Sampradāya. From Nārāyaṇa, the Haṁsa *avatāra* appeared. His disciples were the Four Kumāras, headed by Sanaka. Their disciples and grand-disciples were innumerable. In this line Nimbāditya became a disciple, thus becoming the initiator of the Nimbāditya Sampradāya. The influence of Nimbāditya is supremely wonderful. His disciples and grand-disciples filled the world. The influence of the Śrī, Brahmā, Rudra and Sanaka lineages expanded further into many branches."

Śrī Nimbārkācārya in Gaura-līlā

In *Śrī Navadvīpa-dhāma Māhātmya* (16.23-31), while describing the glories of Śrī Bilvapakṣa (Belpukhuria), Śrīla Saccidānanda Bhaktivinoda Ṭhākura has written the following:

"In Bilvapakṣa, the five-faced Mahādeva, the lord of Bael (*bilva* tree leaves), graced a group of *brāhmaṇas* after they worshiped Him. Nimbārkācārya was one among those blessed *brāhmaṇas*. By the grace of Mahādeva, Nimbārkācārya attained divine sight (*darśana*) of the Four Kumāras: Sanaka, Sanandana, Sanātana and Sanat Kumāra in Śrī Bilvavana. Addressing Nimbārkācārya, Śrī Sanaka Kumāra said:

kalighor hoibe jāniyā kṛpāmay
bhakti pracārite citte karila niścay
cārijan bhakter śakti kariyā arpaṇ
bhakti pracārite viśwe karilā preraṇ
rāmānuja, madhva, viṣṇu - ei tin jan
tumi ta caturtha hau bhakta mahājan
śrīdevī karila rāmānuje angīkār
brahmā madhvācārye, rudra viṣṇuke svīkār
āmrā tomāke āj jāninu āpan
śiṣya kari dhanya hai, ei prayojan
pūrve morā abhed-cintāy chinu rata
kṛpāyoge sei pāp haila dūragata
ebe śuddha bhakti ati upādeya jāni
saṁhitā racanā kariyāchi aka khāni
sanatkumār-saṁhitā ihār nām hay
ei mate dīkṣā tava haibe niścay
guru anugraha dekhi nimbārka dhīmān
avilambe āilā kari bhāgīrathī snān

"'Knowing that Kali-yuga would be dark, the merciful Lord decided to preach devotion. He empowered four devotees and sent them to preach devotion throughout the world. Śrī Rāmānujācārya, Śrī Madhvācārya and Śrī Viṣṇusvāmī are three of them. You are the fourth of those great devotees. Lakṣmīdevī accepted Rāmānujācārya, Brahmā accepted Madhvācārya, and Lord Śiva accepted Viṣṇusvāmī. Today, we have accepted you as our own.

'We will make you our disciple and thus become fortunate. This is our purpose. Previously, we were absorbed in the meditation of non-duality but, by the grace of the Lord, we were rescued from such sin. We now understand that pure devotion is extremely relishable and we have written a scripture by the name of Sanat *Kumāra-saṁhitā* about it. You will certainly be initiated into its teachings. Seeing the grace of his *guru*, the wise Nimbārka came immediately after bathing in River Gangā.'

"After receiving the Śrī Śrī Rādhā-Kṛṣṇa *yugala-mantra* from the Four Kumāras, he performed worship in that holy place according to the instructions of the *Sanat Kumāra-saṁhitā*. Being pleased with his worship, Śrī Śrī Rādhā-Kṛṣṇa revealed Themselves to him. After that, he achieved the divine *darśana* of Śrī Gaurānga Mahāprabhu, the combined manifestation of Śrī Śrī Rādhā-Kṛṣṇa.

"Seeing this form, Nimbārkācārya was overwhelmed with divine love. Mahāprabhu then mercifully said to him, 'When I appear in this form in the blessed Kali and blissfully engage in the pastimes of learning, at that time you will take birth in Kāśmīra. You will become famous as Keśava Kāśmīrī, earning praises from all corners for your erudite scholarship. While traveling, you will come to the village of Māyāpura, where we will engage in a scholarly debate and I will defeat you. By the grace of Sarasvatī, you (as Keśava Kāśmīrī) will understand My identity and take My shelter.' Mahāprabhu then ordered Nimbārkācārya to keep His (Mahāprabhu's) identity secret and preach the conception of Dvaitādvaita (dualistic non-dualism)."

Nimbārkācārya Visits North India

Dr. Amar Prasād Bhaṭṭācārya wrote a treatise called *Śrī Nimbārka and Śrī Dvaitādvaita-darśana*. Subject matter of special note from that work is presented below:

In various *Purāṇas*, different names of Śrī Nimbārka can be seen, viz. (1) Āruṇi (son of Aruṇa), (2) Jayanteya (son of Jayanti), (3) Haridāsa Haripriya (one dear to Śrī Hari), (4) Sudarśana (*avatāra* of the Śrī Sudarśana disc), (5) Havirdhāna (maintainer and protector of sacrificial items of *yajña*), (6) Niyamānanda (one who is devoted and blissful in the execution of religious prescripts). However, he became famous as Niyamānanda or Nimbārka. In the section *Naimiśa-khaṇḍa* of *Śrī Skanda Purāṇa*, his name is mentioned as Havirdhāna.

Nimbārkācārya appeared in Andhra Pradesh in South India during the era of the Ālvar devotees. Due to the predominance of Buddhism and Jainism in North India during that time, devotional practices were not prevalent there. However, owing to the influence of the Ālvars, the devotional practices were significantly spread throughout South India. Therefore, Nimbārkācārya came to North India to propagate the path of devotion.

The South Indian Ālvars were worshipers of Śrī Kṛṣṇa, with a particular inclination toward service in the conjugal mood. The principal limbs of worship according to Śrī Nimbārka are devotion, surrender and complete self-dedication. In his self-composed ten verses, Śrī Nimbārkācārya has mentioned contemplation of worship of the Divine Couple, of Śrī Radhā being served by thousands of Her female consorts (*sakhīs*), of the characteristics of the topmost loving devotion and of the glory and importance of the Lord's mercy.

Śrī Nimbārkācārya came to North India from the south and stayed in Nimbagrāma near Govardhana in Vraja-maṇḍala in an *āśrama* (place of residence for sādhus) he constructed. There, he was engaged in severe austerities such as drinking only the juice of the *nīm* fruit. He traveled to various localities and visited several places of pilgrimage such as Kurukṣetra, Naimiṣaraṇya, Puṣkara, and Dvāraka, propagating Bhāgavata-dharma.

Śrīnivāsa was the most prominent among the disciples of Śrī Nimbārkācārya and became his successor as *ācārya*.

Dr. Amar Prasād Bhaṭṭāchārya ascertained the Nimbārka Sampradāya to be the most ancient of the Vaiṣṇava lineages. Śrī Nimbārkācārya wrote a commentary on the *Brahma-sūtra* of Śrī Vedavyāsa by the name of *Vedānta-pārijāta-saurabha*. In his writings he neither refuted the opinions of other *ācāryas* nor mentioned the names of their conceptions including: Advaitavāda (monism), Dvaitavāda (dualism), Viśiṣṭādvaitavāda (non-duality with particular attributes) and Śuddhādvaitavāda (purified monism). He simply wrote commentaries on the *Brahma-sūtras*, thereby substantiating his own conception of Dvaitādvaitavāda (dualistic non-dualism). On this basis, it can be proven that this commentary was written before the other conceptions or opinions had originated.

Branches of the Nimbārka Sampradāya

The author of *Bhāratvarṣīya Upāsak Sampradāya*, Śrī Akṣay Kumāra Datta Mahoday, has mentioned a Nimbārka Sampradāya by the name of Nimāt. He also wrote that the neck beads and chanting beads of this *sampradāya* are both made from the Śrī Tulasī tree. Their object of worship is the Divine Couple, Śrī Śrī Rādha-Kṛṣṇa, and their principal scripture is *Śrīmad Bhāgavatam*. It is said that Nimbāditya wrote a commentary on the *Vedas*. Currently there are no scriptures available of this *sampradāya*, as they disappeared from Mathurā during the time of the Mughal Empire.

According to the two disciples of Nimbāditya known as Keśava Bhaṭṭa and Harivyāsa, two branches originated: *virakta* (detached) and *gṛhastha* (householder). Nimbārka's divine shrine is in Dhruva-kṣetra on the banks of River Yamunā in the vicinity of Mathurā. Some say that this place is being taken care by the descendants of Harivyāsa. But the head of the monastery calls himself a descendant of Nimbārkācārya's family. He claims that the shrine in Dhruva-kṣetra was established more than 1,400 years ago.

The Nimāt devotees reside at many places in North India. There is a large community of these devotees, particularly in Mathurā and its surroundings.

Summary

Encyclopedia Britannica (Volume 8, Page 714) states:

"Nimbārka, also called Nimbāditya or Niyamānanda, was a Telugu speaking *brāhmaṇa*, yogi, philosopher and prominent astronomer who founded the devotional sect of Nimbārkas, Nimandi or Nimavats who worshiped the deity Kṛṣṇa and His consort Rādhā.

"Nimbārka has been identified with Bhāskara, the ninth or tenth-century philosopher and celebrated commentator on *Brahma-sūtra* (*Vedānta-sūtra*). Most historians of Hindu mysticism, however, hold that Nimbārka probably lived in the twelfth or thirteenth century because of the similarities between his philosophical and devotional attitudes with those of Rāmānuja, traditionally dated 1017-1137. Both adhered to Dvaitādvaita (dualistic non-dualism), the belief that the creator God and the souls he created were distinct but shared the same substance. Both stressed devotion to Kṛṣṇa as a means of liberation from the cycle of rebirth.

The Nimānanda sect flourished in the thirteenth and fourteenth centuries in eastern India. Its philosophy held that men were trapped in physical bodies constructed by *prakṛti* (matter) and that only by surrender to Rādhā-Kṛṣṇa (not through their own efforts) could they attain the grace necessary for liberation from rebirth; then, at death, the physical body would drop away. Thus, Nimbārka stressed *bhakti-yoga*, the *yoga* of devotion and faith. Many books were written about this once popular cult, but most sources were destroyed by Muslims during the reign of the Mughal Emperor Aurangazeb (1659-1707 A.D.) and little information has survived about Nimbārka and his followers."

Author

Śrīla Bhakti Ballabh Tīrtha Gosvāmī Mahārāja

His Divine Grace Śrīla Bhakti Ballabh Tīrtha Gosvāmī Mahārāja is one of the foremost spiritual leaders of the mission of Śrī Caitanya Mahāprabhu and His associates in the modern world. He is the dearly beloved disciple of His Divine Grace Śrīla Bhakti Dayita Mādhava Gosvāmī Mahārāja, who is in turn the equally beloved disciple of His Divine Grace Śrīla Bhakti Siddhānta Sarasvatī Gosvāmī Prabhupāda.

His Divine Grace Bhakti Ballabh Tīrtha Gosvāmī Mahārāja appeared in 1924 in Assam, India, on Rāma-navamī, the most auspicious appearance day of the Supreme Lord Kṛṣṇa in His form as Rāmacandra. Having been brought up in a pious environment, he developed a strong inclination to search for the ultimate goal of life, which led him to take up the study of philosophy at Calcutta University. While studying at the university he came in contact with his spiritual master, His Divine Grace Śrīla Bhakti Dayita Mādhava Gosvāmī Mahārāja, and immediately became attracted by his transcendentally powerful personality. After completing his Masters Degree in Philosophy in 1947, Śrīla Bhakti Ballabh Tīrtha Mahārāja wholeheartedly and unreservedly dedicated his life to the service of his spiritual master.

His service attitude was so exemplary that soon Śrīla Mādhava Mahārāja established him as the secretary of the devotional institution, known as Sree Chaitanya Gaudiya Math, which has over twenty *āśramas* in India alone. He was awarded *sannyasa*, the order of renunciation, in 1961. Eventually, Śrīla Mādhava Mahārāja, seeing his disciple's degree of dedication and sincerity combined with an astute and practical mind, selected him as his worthy successor. After the disappearance of his beloved spiritual master, Śrīla Mādhava Gosvāmī Mahārāja, in 1979, Śrīla Tīrtha Mahārāja was appointed as president-*ācārya* of the *maṭha*. He received the fortunate blessings and great affection of many of Śrīla Bhakti Siddhānta's prominent followers such as Śrīla Bhakti Rakṣaka Śrīdhar Deva Gosvāmī Mahārāja, Śrīla Bhakti Promode Purī Gosvāmī Mahārāja, Śrīla Bhakti Hridaya Vana Gosvāmī Mahārāja, Śrīla Bhakti Akiñcanā Kṛṣṇa Dāsa Bābājī Mahārāja, Śrīla Bhakti Kumud Santa Gosvāmī Mahārāja and many others.

For the last five decades, Śrīla Tīrtha Mahārāja was engaged in the propagation of the all-embracing doctrine of Transcendental Divine Love of Śrī Caitanya Mahāprabhu to counter the present trend of violence and cruelty, and to bring about unity of hearts among all, irrespective of caste, creed or religion. "Example is better than precept" was his way of preaching. He would always practice what he preached. Śrīla Tīrtha Mahārāja is known for not even deviating one inch outside of the four corners of the prescripts of the holy scriptures. His Divine Grace is a renowned authority on Gauḍīya Vaiṣṇava philosophy and he is beloved by thousands of devotees throughout the world as the very embodiment of humility and spiritual affection.

Even at a very advanced age, inspired by the grace of his Gurudeva, Śrīla Tīrtha Mahārāja was always on the move, going from town to village in India and also abroad, propagating the divine message of *Bhagavad-gītā* and *Śrīmad Bhagavatam*.

At the behest of his beloved *śikṣā-guru* (instructing preceptor), His Divine Grace Śrīla Bhakti Promode Purī Gosvāmī Mahārāja, Śrīla Tīrtha Mahārāja preached the message of Śrī Caitanya Mahāprabhu throughout the world, beginning with a tour of the United States in 1997.

As well as being the president-*ācārya* of the Śree Chaitanya Gaudiya Math devotional institution, he was also the Founder of GOKUL (Global Organisation of Kṛṣṇachaitanya's Universal Love). His Divine Grace Śrīla Bhakti Ballabh Tīrtha Gosvāmī Mahārāja also served as the President of the World Vaiṣṇava Association (WVA).

His Divine Grace was always engaged in writing articles and books of a profoundly spiritual nature in several native languages, as well as English, for the eternal benefit of the conditioned souls of the world. To date, his books in English include *Śuddha Bhakti*, *A Taste of Transcendence*, *Sri Chaitanya & His Associates*, *The Holy Life of Śrīla Bhakti Dayita Mādhava Gosvāmī Mahārāja*, *Guru Tattva*, *Daśāvatāra*, *Path of Pure Devotion*, *Philosophy of Love*, *Teachings of Bhagavad-gitā*, *Hari Katha and Vaiṣṇava Aparādha*, *Affectionately Yours*, this present book (*Sages, Saints & Kings of Ancient India)*, and a number of others still to be published.

On April 21, 2017, on the *navamī* of the second fortnight of the Vaiśākha month, one of the greatest saints of the modern era, His Divine Grace Śrīla Bhakti Ballabh Tīrtha Gosvāmī Mahārāja, left this world and entered into the eternal transcendental pastimes of Śrī Śrī Rādhā-Kṛṣṇa.

Alphabetized Index